THE MILITARISATION OF PEACEKEEPING IN THE TWENTY-FIRST CENTURY

Since the end of the last century, UN peacekeeping has undergone a fundamental and largely unexamined change. Peacekeeping operations, long expected to use force only in self-defence and to act impartially, are now increasingly relied upon by the Security Council as a means to maintain and restore security within a country. Operations are established under Chapter VII of the UN Charter and some are empowered to use 'all necessary measures', language traditionally reserved for enforcement operations.

Through a close examination of these twenty-first century peacekeeping operations – including those in Sierra Leone, the Democratic Republic of the Congo, Liberia, Côte d'Ivoire, Haiti and the Darfur region of Sudan – the book shows that they are, for the most part, fundamentally ill-suited to the enforcement-type tasks being asked of them. The operations, which are under-funded, under-equipped and whose troops are under-trained, frequently lurch from crisis to crisis. There is scant evidence that matters are likely to improve.

The book argues that bestowing enforcement-type functions on a peacekeeping operation is misguided. Such operations are likely to be unsuccessful in their enforcement-type tasks, causing serious damage to the excellent reputation of UN peacekeeping and the UN more broadly. In addition, because operations of this nature are likely to be perceived as partial, their ability to carry out traditional (non-forceful) peacekeeping tasks may be impeded. Finally, the Security Council's practice of charging peacekeeping operations with enforcement functions lessens the pressure on the Council to work to establish genuine enforcement operations – that is, operations that are considerably better suited to restoring peace and security.

Volume 35 in the series Studies in International Law

Studies in International Law

Recent titles in this series

Human Dignity and the Foundations of International Law
Patrick Capps

Sovereignty and the Stateless Nation: Gibraltar in the Modern Legal Context
Keith Azopardi

The International Court of Justice and Self-Defence in International Law
James A Green

State Liability in Investment Treaty Arbitration: Global Constitutional and Administrative Law in the BIT Generation
Santiago Montt

Reappraising the Resort to Force: International Law, Jus ad Bellum and the War on Terror
Lindsay Moir

International Law and Dispute Settlement: New Problems and Techniques
Edited by Duncan French, Matthew Saul and Nigel White

The Democratic Legitimacy of International Law
Steven Wheatley

Reflections on the UN Declaration on the Rights of Indigenous Peoples
Edited by Stephen Allen and Alexandra Xanthaki

Contracting with Sovereignty: State Contracts and International Arbitration
Ivar Alvik

Multi-Sourced Equivalent Norms in International Law
Edited by Yuval Shany and Tomer Broude

The Distinction and Relationship between *Jus ad Bellum* and *Jus in Bello*
Keiichiro Okimoto

International Humanitarian Law and Terrorism
Andrea Bianchi and Yasmin Naqvi

Promises of States under International Law
Christian Eckart

The Militarisation of Peacekeeping in the Twenty-First Century
James Sloan

For the complete list of titles in this series, see 'Studies in International Law' link at www.hartpub.co.uk/books/series.asp

The Militarisation of Peacekeeping in the Twenty-First Century

James Sloan

·HART·
PUBLISHING

OXFORD AND PORTLAND, OREGON
2011

Published in the United Kingdom by Hart Publishing Ltd
16C Worcester Place, Oxford, OX1 2JW
Telephone: +44 (0)1865 517530
Fax: +44 (0)1865 510710
E-mail: mail@hartpub.co.uk
Website: http://www.hartpub.co.uk

Published in North America (US and Canada) by
Hart Publishing
c/o International Specialized Book Services
920 NE 58th Avenue, Suite 300
Portland, OR 97213-3786
USA
Tel: +1 503 287 3093 or toll-free: (1) 800 944 6190
Fax: +1 503 280 8832
E-mail: orders@isbs.com
Website: http://www.isbs.com

British Library Cataloguing in Publication Data
Data Available

ISBN: 978-1-84946-114-6

Typeset by Hope Services, Abingdon
Printed and bound in Great Britain by
Lightning Source UK Ltd

Foreword

When I published my four volumes on *United Nations Peacekeeping* between the years 1969 and 1981, there were 13 UN peacekeeping operations to be covered. Since then there have been countless more, and yet more being established virtually all the while.

It is not just a matter of numbers. In the first fifteen years of peacekeeping, the circumstances in which peacekeeping operations were established fell – even though they each differed – into a recognisable grouping. And certain 'givens' had been developed as to their establishment and conduct. All that has changed, and Dr Sloan is able to show, in knowledgeable detail, not only what has changed over the years, but also what has brought these changes about.

His analysis leads him to offer not only well-informed insights, but critical observations, too. These are the more interesting, because he has been able clearly to demonstrate that the changes over the years have not been linear. Some of them, especially related to the concept of what he terms 'militarised peacekeeping', have entailed distinct changes of direction, and sometimes reversals. In short, a confusing 'to-ing and fro-ing'.

The Hammarskjold 'Fundamental Principles', which rapidly followed on the establishment of UNEF I, have turned out to be not so fundamental after all. Dr Sloan tracks each one of the elements contained in those Principles, showing how they have fared over time and where the accumulation of practice leaves them today.

Dr Sloan has a thesis to advance. But even had he not, this book would be invaluable to scholars and those who ply their work within the UN – as officials or as members of Government Missions. This is because he has managed to tell the tale of what has happened, from 1956 to the present day, in UN peacekeeping, not by reference to generalities but by tracing identified specifics through the various peacekeeping operations. His organisational skills are very impressive. The chapter headings are quite unusual. But they provide the vehicle for showing what has happened to peacekeeping, as a genre, over the years – with every single one of the numerous operations playing its part in the story. It goes without saying that this could not have been done without a very deep knowledge and understanding of the subject matter.

The reader will not find the story of each operation deployed *seriatim*. But he/she will find that the important decisions and trends, through time, are identified and subjected to scrutiny by reference to each and all of these operations. The careful reader will emerge feeling that he/she knows, to take an example, all about the issue of consent over the years – but equally knows about the key legal and political issues concerning MONUC, UNOCI, UNAMSIL – and the now very large number of other operations that have occurred and often still are occurring.

The author's knowledge of his subject matter is impressive. The political events that formed the background of each operation (never quite the same in any two cases) is clearly fully understood and deployed to the extent necessary to illustrate both the characteristics and the changes through time in peacekeeping. Dr Sloan clearly knows his way around the internal world of the UN, and he efficaciously draws upon the role played by particular UN personalities, as well as upon the literature on the particular point under examination. And if the politics of each operation is well explained, so also is the background, changing through the years, of the UN's own attempt to get to grips with the very real difficulties of providing successful peacekeeping. The stream of concern by the UN is fully described, and well analysed: the original Fundamental Principles, the Agenda for Peace, the relationship to the concept of Responsibility to Protect (and the circumstances in which that concept came about). Such examples, along with the Brahimi Report, the Capstone Doctrine, the various Lessons Learned reports of operations, and much else, are all subjected to careful analysis.

Contemporary events make the chapter devoted to peacekeeping in relation to powers of the Security Council and their limitations (Chapter 3) of particular interest. Dr Sloan systematically takes the reader through the various issues of law and of politics, always by reference to the literature, particular operations, and UN debates. The reader will find a first rate survey of Article 40, which is indeed the most frequently invoked basis for peacekeeping operations. Throughout this book, Dr Sloan is interested in the move (to, fro and to again) to 'militarised peacekeeping'; and of course there is an interesting question as to whether this form of peacekeeping can indeed find its constitutional basis in Article 40.

This book is a pleasing combination of detailed scrutiny of topics already familiar (provisional measures, consent, so-called 'Chapter VI½' action, implied powers) and a rigorous questioning as to their place in – or indeed, relevance at all to – militarised peacekeeping. The reader will find much new terrain traversed, and plenty of out-of-the-box thinking. The issue of consent, to give but one example, becomes fresh and intellectually challenging thus treated. There is also a very useful section on what is termed 'sanctions-related enforcement', and the UN resolutions and modalities, from *Joanna V* onwards, directed towards this.

A further useful offering within the book is the study of the relations between particular UN forces and other forces in the field of operation, for example, UNOSOM II and UNITAF. The impressive marshalling of his raw materials, and the intellectual use he makes of them, is only part of the story. For Dr Sloan has another purpose in mind in this scholarly and well written book.

My remarks thus far have been directed to showing – even if there were no underlying theme – why it is that I have found this an original and informative volume. But there is, of course, a 'theme', and indeed that theme is central to everything else in this book. Dr Sloan shows that the UN Security Council has in recent years adopted a practice of routinely bestowing enforcement-type tasks, such as maintaining security and providing civilian protection, on its peacekeeping operations. Of course, even in the era of classical peacekeeping, it was not unusual for there to be mission creep. Protecting civilian authority, ensuring that road communications would be safe, allowing crops to be grown, were activities found necessary from the outset. But, Dr Sloan asserts: Corresponding with the turn of the century, peacekeeping is now relied on by the Security Council not only as a means by which to keep the peace: it is now all too often required to restore the peace, and also to protect civilians.

As he points out, '[t]he presence of UN peacekeepers on the ground was once a welcome indicator that there was peace in the land following a period of conflict. Respected by civilians and militants alike, peacekeeping forces were present at the request of the state and charged with managing and facilitating an existing peace in a neutral, non-violent way' (Introduction). However, beginning in late 1999, the model radically changed. Such missions often enter territories where conflict and disorder rages. These peacekeeping forces are charged with using force beyond self-defence:

> The level of force that is authorised for the twenty-first century peacekeeping operations can include the use of 'all necessary means' – language that had traditionally been associated with enforcement operations, and which echoes the . . . language in Article 42 of the UN Charter. [Introduction]

Consent and impartiality become, in Dr Sloan's view, almost meaningless concepts.

The prototype, of course, was UNPROFOR, and the difficulties – indeed, inappropriateness – of this type of action did not escape widespread adverse comment. Nor was the UN itself unaware both of the problems and of the criticisms. Yet the Organization 'decided to revert to a system of militarised peacekeeping that had previously shown itself unworkable . . . [This was not based on a belief] that the Organization . . . [had] evolved . . . such that it had reached a stage where it could overcome the many problems of the past . . . Instead, [the decision] would appear to have been animated primarily by thinking of a more wishful nature'. (Introduction).

The Brahimi Report, prepared by the Panel established by Secretary-General Kofi Annan, argued that with sufficient safeguards and resources, UN peacekeeping forces could secure the restoration of peace and security in a country as well as maintaining it. Dr Sloan, however, in a very detailed and sustained analysis, shows that militarised peacekeeping operations in the twenty-first century are no more successful than they were in the twentieth; and he regards this as inevitable. The safeguards aren't there, the needed resources have not been forthcoming. As Dr Sloan forthrightly says, 'The Brahimi thesis pays insufficient attention to the fundamentally political nature of UN activities and the fundamentally selfish nature of Member States'.

Two arguments are advanced for nonetheless pressing on with this type of peacekeeping. The first is that things will gradually improve: Dr Sloan decimates this wishful thinking. The second is that, notwithstanding the problems, militarised peacekeeping must be continued, because without it the results would be even more disastrous. It is the firm rebuttal of this second contention that is one of the most interesting aspects of the book. This rebuttal runs like a thread throughout the book, but could be crystallised in the following way: All the problems that UN peacekeeping forces face are exacerbated where peacekeeping operations are militarised. That is true of the difficulties related to the establishment of (and offering of troops for) peacekeeping; of difficulties relating to the management of such an operation; and, of course, of relations with the host state. Dr Sloan agrees with former Secretary-General Annan that militarised peacekeeping operations serve as an 'alibi' for the Security Council not to fulfil its responsibilities. All of this is argued through in relation to specific operations and moments.

Dr Sloan has to face the big political question: problematic as militarised peacekeeping may be, has not the UN to do the very best it can, and not to turn away from unfolding tragedies? He offers a firm response: the hard evidence is that these undoubtedly decent intentions lead, when militarised peacekeeping has been chosen, to a worse, rather than better, outcome for the country and civilians concerned. The results have in fact often been calamitous – and qualitatively worse than if traditional peacekeeping had been in operation.

And, tellingly, this powerful book contends that there has now developed a routine – and unacceptable – response to the tragedies that have arisen through the inevitable inability of militarised peacekeeping to protect as was intended. First, says Dr Sloan, the UN attempts to minimise its role in the tragedy, and asserts the unawareness of the peacekeepers of the unfolding disaster. Then it admits that not everything that could have been done was done. Finally, the UN points out the hopelessness of charging a handful of peacekeepers with tasks that no one could reasonably have expected of them. All this is supported by detailed evidence and example.

Dr Sloan concludes that the tough but necessary choice is to admit as much, and to return to classic peacekeeping. In his view, all its shortcomings bring less havoc to those involved than does militarised peacekeeping.

This is a challenging, informative and important book.

Rosalyn Higgins

Acknowledgements

The present study is based on my PhD, which I defended in December 2007. It has been modified and updated to 1 April 2011.

I am deeply grateful to those who helped me with the PhD process. First and foremost, I owe a debt of gratitude to Professor Nigel White for his careful supervision. I am also grateful to Professor Peter Rowe and the late Professor Kaiyan Kaikobad for examining my PhD thesis. I am indebted to the numerous colleagues and friends who helped me to shape the thesis, in particular, the late, great Professor Tom Franck, Professor Richard Gardiner, Mr Eduardo Valencia-Ospina and Professor Iain Scobbie. I am also grateful to the numerous friends and family who provided me with support – be it academic or moral – throughout the PhD process. I am deeply indebted to Dr Catriona Drew, whose frank advice was enormously helpful.

I must also acknowledge the numerous colleagues at the University of Glasgow who gave excellent advice on the process of transforming the PhD into a book and encouragement in completing it. Included here are Doctors Mark Godfrey, Ruth Dukes and Gavin Anderson. Particular thanks to Professor Christian Tams for reading the work in draft and for his leadership and friendship. Much of the work on the book was done while I was a Visiting Scholar and Visiting Professor at the University of California, Hastings College of the Law in San Francisco. I thank colleagues at UC Hastings for welcoming me and providing me not only with an office and access to their excellent facilities, but also with invaluable advice on how to improve the book. Thanks to Professors Elizabeth Hillman, David Faigman, Evan Lee, Joel Paul and David Levine.

I am grateful to Hart Publishing, in particular to Mr Richard Hart, for his support, patience and unique ability to act quickly and with a minimum of red tape. Thanks also to Ms Ruth Massey, whose editorial expertise has given the book a level of polish and clarity that it otherwise would have lacked. I am also indebted to the editors of the *Hastings International and Comparative Law Review* and to the editors of the *Yearbook of International Peace Operations*, in particular Professor Boris Kondoch, for their encouragement and support in the preparation and publication of earlier articles in which I was able to develop and test some of the themes in this book.

Finally, a special expression of appreciation is due to Dame Rosalyn Higgins. That someone of her stature, and with her numerous commitments around the world, has been willing to find the time to advise me at all stages of this project is testament to her remarkable generosity. Her scholarship on peacekeeping (and, of course, beyond) has been invaluable in preparing this work. Her encouragement, beginning when she was my professor at the London School of Economics, was in large part responsible for my interest in international law. I am deeply grateful to her in so many ways and, in particular, for having done me the honour of writing a foreword to this book.

While I am in the debt of all of these persons, none of them is of course in any way responsible for any shortcomings or errors in this book, nor do they necessarily share the views expressed herein.

JS
April 2011

Table of Contents

Abbreviations

AMIB	African Union Mission in Burundi
ANC	National Congolese Army
CNDP	*Congrès National pour la Défense du Peuple* (DRC)
CPA	Comprehensive Peace Agreement (Sudan)
DFS	Department of Field Services, UN Secretariat
DPA	Department of Political Affairs, UN Secretariat
DPKO	Department of Peacekeeping Operations, UN Secretariat
DRC	Democratic Republic of the Congo
ECOFORCE	ECOWAS Force in Côte d'Ivoire (also known as ECOMICI)
ECOMICI	ECOWAS Mission in Côte d'Ivoire (also known as ECOFORCE)
ECOMIL	ECOWAS Mission in Liberia
ECOMOG	ECOWAS Military Observer Group (Liberia)
ECOWAS	Economic Community of West African States
EUFOR	European Union Force in Bosnia and Herzegovina
EUFOR Chad/CAR	European Union Force in Chad/Central African Republic
FARDC	Armed Forces of the Democratic Republic of the Congo
FDLR	*Forces démocratiques de libération du Rwanda*
FDN	*Forces Nationales de la Défense* (Burundi)
HNP	Haitian National Police
ICJ	International Court of Justice
ICRC	International Committee of the Red Cross
ICTY	International Criminal Tribunal for the former Yugoslavia
IEMF	Interim Emergency Multinational Force in Bunia, DRC (also known as 'Operation Artemis')
IFOR	Implementation Force in Bosnia and Herzegovina
INTERFET	International Force for East Timor
ISF	International Security Forces (East Timor)
JEM	Justice and Equality Movement (Sudan)
KFOR	Kosovo Force
LCA	Lusaka Ceasefire Agreement (DRC)
LRA	Lord's Resistance Army

MFO	Multinational Force and Observers (in the Sinai Peninsula)
MIF	Multinational Interim Force (Haiti)
MINUCI	United Nations Mission in Côte d'Ivoire
MINURCAT	United Nations Mission in Central African Republic and Chad
MINUSTAH	United Nations Stabilization Mission in Haiti
MIPONUH	United Nations Civilian Police Mission in Haiti
MISAB	*Mission interafricaine de surveillance des Accords de Bangui*
MNF	Multinational Force (in Haiti)
MONUC	United Nations Organization Mission in the Democratic Republic of the Congo
MONUSCO	United Nations Organization Stabilization Mission in the Democratic Republic of the Congo
NATO	North Atlantic Treaty Organization
OLA	Office of Legal Affairs, UN Secretariat
ONUB	United Nations Operation in Burundi
ONUC	United Nations Operation in the Congo
RRF	Rapid Reaction Force
RUF	Revolutionary United Front (Sierra Leone)
SFOR	Stabilization Force (Bosnia and Herzegovina)
SFRY	Socialist Federal Republic of Yugoslavia
SPLM/A	Sudan People's Liberation Movement/Army
TCCs	Troop Contributing Countries
UNAMET	United Nations Mission in East Timor
UNAMID	African Union/United Nations Hybrid Mission in Darfur
UNAMIR I	First United Nations Assistance Mission for Rwanda
UNAMIR II	Second United Nations Assistance Mission for Rwanda
UNAMIS	United Nations Advance Mission in Sudan
UNAMSIL	United Nations Mission in Sierra Leone
UNCI	United Nations Commission for Indonesia
UNCRO	United Nations Confidence Restoration Organization in Croatia
UNDOF	United Nations Disengagement Observer Force (in the Middle East)
UNDP	United Nations Development Programme
UNEF I	First United Nations Emergency Force (in the Suez)

UNEF II	Second United Nations Emergency Force (in the Suez)
UNFICYP	United Nations Force in Cyprus
UNHCR	United Nations High Commissioner for Refugees
UNIFIL	United Nations Interim Force in Lebanon
UNIIMOG	United Nations Iran-Iraq Military Observer Group
UNIKOM	United Nations Iraq-Kuwait Observation Mission
UNIPSIL	United Nations Integrated Peacebuilding Office in Sierra Leone
UNIOSIL	United Nations Integrated Office in Sierra Leone
UNIPOM	United Nations India-Pakistan Observer Mission
UNITAF	Unified Task Force (Somalia)
UNMEE	United Nations Mission in Ethiopia and Eritrea
UNMIBH	United Nations Mission in Bosnia and Herzegovina
UNMIH	United Nations Mission in Haiti
UNMIK	United Nations Interim Administration Mission in Kosovo
UNMIL	United Nations Mission in Liberia
UNMIS	United Nations Mission in Sudan
UNMISET	United Nations Mission of Support in East Timor
UNMIT	United Nations Integrated Mission in Timor Leste
UNMOGIP	United Nations Military Observer Group in India and Pakistan
UNMOP	United Nations Mission of Observers in Prevlaka
UNOB	United Nations Office in Burundi
UNOCI	United Nations Operation in Cote D'Ivoire
UNOGIL	United Nations Observation Group in Lebanon
UNOL	United Nations Peace-Building Support Office in Liberia
UNOMIL	United Nations Observer Mission in Liberia
UNOMSIL	United Nations Observer Mission in Sierra Leone
UNOSOM I	First United Nations Operation in Somalia
UNOSOM II	Second United Nations Operation in Somalia
UNOTIL	United Nations Office in Timor-Leste
UNPROFOR	United Nations Protection Force in Yugoslavia
UNPSG	United Nations Police Support Group in Croatia
UNSCOB	United Nations Special Committee on the Balkans
UNSF	United Nations Security Force in West New Guinea (also known as UNTEA)
UNSMIH	United Nations Support Mission in Haiti
UNTAES	United Nations Transitional Administration for Eastern Slavonia, Baranja and Western Sirmium

UNTAET	United Nations Transitional Administration in East Timor
UNTAG	United Nations Transition Assistance Group
UNTEA	United Nations Temporary Executive Authority (also known as UNSF)
UNTMIH	United Nations Transition Mission in Haiti
UNTSO	United Nations Truce Supervision Organization (in the Middle East)
UNYOM	United Nations Yemen Observation Mission
UPDF	Ugandan People's Defence Force
URUBATT	Ugandan Battalion

Table of Cases and Court Opinions

International Court of Justice

International Criminal Court

International Criminal Tribunal for the former Yugoslavia

Special Court for Sierra Leone

Table of Legislation

International Instruments

Sundry

United Nations

Security Council Resolutions

Peace Agreements and Analogous Instruments

National Legislation

Canada

United States

Chapter 1

Introduction

> [M]any feel that peacekeeping has become a panacea, with the deployment of United Nations forces considered proof that the Security Council is paying attention to a crisis, whether the troops are effective or not.
>
> Neil MacFarquhar (*New York Times*), referring to discussions with diplomats and UN officials in 2009[1]

OVER A FOUR-DAY period between 30 July and 2 August 2010, 242 individuals – reportedly ranging from a one-month-old baby boy to a 110-year-old great-great grandmother – were raped in and around the village of Luvungi, in the Eastern part of the Democratic Republic of the Congo (DRC).[2] To the embarrassment of the UN, the rapes took place some 20 miles from an armed unit of a UN peacekeeping mission, the United Nations Organization Stabilization Mission in the Democratic Republic of the Congo (MONUSCO), which, despite being authorised under Chapter VII of the UN Charter[3] to use 'all necessary means' – Security Council shorthand for the use of force beyond self-defence – to ensure the effective protection of the civilian population,[4] did nothing to prevent them.

This tragic incident is a recent example of the myriad problems associated with UN peacekeeping in the last decade, since the UN Security

[1] Neil MacFarquhar, 'In UN Peacekeeping, a Muddling of the Mission', *New York Times* (online), 11 February 2009.

[2] Michelle Faul, 'Congo Leaders: We Begged the UN to Protect Civilians', *Associated Press* (online), 1 September 2010. See also UN News Service, 'In Wake of Mass Rapes in DR Congo, UN Official Calls for End to Impunity', 31 August 2010, www.un.org/apps/news/story.asp?NewsID=35784# (accessed 1 April 2011).

[3] Chapter VII of the UN Charter comprises 13 articles (Arts 39–51) which relate to action by the Security Council with respect to threats to the peace, breaches of the peace and acts of aggression. Art 41 provides that the Security Council may 'decide what measures not involving the use of armed force are to be employed to give effect to its decisions, and it may call upon the Members of the United Nations to apply such measures'. According to Art 42: 'Should the Security Council consider that measures provided for in Article 41 would be inadequate or have proved to be inadequate, it may take such action by air, sea, or land forces as may be necessary to maintain or restore international peace and security.' Decisions taken under either article may bind UN Member States. See chapter 3, section 3 for a detailed discussion of Chapter VII measures.

[4] SC Res 1925 of 28 May 2010.

Council adopted a practice of routinely bestowing enforcement-type tasks, such as maintaining security and providing civilian protection, on its peacekeeping operations. The UN reacted to the rape in a way that has, by now, become familiar. First, it attempted to minimise its role in the tragedy. It asserted that its peacekeepers were unaware of the extent of the harm being caused until nearly two weeks after the events, when the Mission was informed about them by a humanitarian organization.[5] Even if true, a claim that the Mission was unaware of what was taking place nearby did little to absolve the Organization. However, there was some uncertainty as to how much the Organization did, in fact, know. It was later to emerge that the UN *had been* aware at the outset that at least one rape had occurred in the area, and the reaction of its Department of Safety and Security was to issue an alert on 30 July advising UN staff to stay away from the area. It is difficult to argue that the peacekeepers met their obligation to ensure civilian protection.

Second, the UN admitted that its peacekeepers had not done all they should have. In a statement of 7 September 2010, Atul Khare, Assistant Secretary-General in the UN Department of Peacekeeping Operations (DPKO), observed: 'Our actions were not adequate, resulting in unacceptable brutalisation of the population of the villages in the area. We must do better.'[6] In an address to the Security Council, Margot Wallström, the Secretary-General's Special Representative on Sexual Violence in Conflict, stated: '[W]e are all compelled to look in the mirror and face our collective responsibility for our inability to prevent the mass rapes.'[7]

Third, the UN pointed out the hopelessness of charging a handful of peacekeepers with tasks that no one could reasonably expect of them. In the case of Luvungi, the UN cited a lack of communication facilities (including a lack of something as basic as cell phones or high frequency radios) as one of the reasons for MONUSCO's failure to react immediately.[8] It also drew attention to the limited number of personnel covering an enormous territory: at the time of the rapes, there were 80 peacekeepers stationed in an area of over 300 square kilometres. In the words of Wallström, 'we are expected to do more at the same time with [fewer] peacekeepers'.[9]

[5] The UN's initial reaction was to deny that its peacekeepers were aware that the rapes were taking place. Later, however, a UN official conceded that a patrol of peacekeepers had been present in the area at the time the rapes were taking place.

[6] Unattributed, 'UN Outlines Steps to Boost Civilian Protection in DR Congo in Wake of Mass Rapes', United Nations (News Centre), 7 September 2010.

[7] United Nations, *Provisional Record of the 6378th Meeting of the Security Council* (UN Doc S/PV.6378), 7 September 2010.

[8] Unattributed, 'UN Security Council Renews Condemnation of Mass Rape in DR Congo', *Deutsche Presse-Agentur* (online), 17 September 2010.

[9] UN News Service (n 2).

1. THE CHANGED NATURE OF PEACEKEEPING

At the heart of MONUSCO's inability to meet the responsibilities assigned to it in its mandate is the fact that the UN peacekeepers in the DRC have been cast in a different role from that of the traditional peacekeeper. Corresponding with the turn of the century, peacekeeping is now relied upon by the Security Council not only as a means of keeping the peace; in some cases it is now charged with protecting civilians and restoring the peace (including through the use of 'all necessary means') when the peace breaks down. Moreover, the Security Council routinely invokes Chapter VII when establishing peacekeeping operations. This book will show that as peacekeeping has become more and more forceful and as its constitutional basis has become explicitly located in Chapter VII, such operations have, at times, taken on the character of enforcement operations. It will also show that despite these radical changes, the UN Secretariat has, somewhat disingenuously, continued to maintain that host state consent, non-use of force and impartiality are basic principles of peacekeeping operations.[10]

The term 'militarised peacekeeping' is used herein to refer to a peacekeeping operation that possesses enforcement characteristics – that is to say, is authorised, explicitly or implicitly, under Chapter VII and authorised to use force beyond self-defence. Depending on the circumstances, the consent of the host state may not be a legal prerequisite to the establishment of a militarised peacekeeping operation or to the assignment of certain tasks to it; similarly, impartiality may not be a legal requirement for some or all of its tasks.

The presence of UN peacekeepers on the ground was once a welcome indicator that there was peace in the land following a period of conflict. Respected by civilians and militants alike, peacekeeping forces were present at the request of the state and charged with managing and facilitating an existing peace in a neutral, non-violent way. At various stages of the endeavour, peacekeepers took on a number of different tasks, at times of a limited, non-participatory nature, and at other times featuring more pro-active involvement to secure lasting peace. What peacekeeping was not expected to do was to take sides in a post-conflict situation (or, *a fortiori*, in a conflict situation) or to take forceful measures to enforce the will of the Security Council.

While certain exceptions occurred, they tended to be damaging to the Organization. In the early 1960s, the Security Council modified the

[10] United Nations Department of Peacekeeping Operations and Department of Field Operations, *United Nations Peacekeeping Operations: Principles and Guidelines* ('Capstone Doctrine'), 2008, http://pbpu.unlb.org/pbps/Library/Capstone_Doctrine_ENG.pdf (accessed 1 April 2011), 31.

mandate of the United Nations Operation in the Congo (ONUC) such that it was charged with enforcement functions involving the use of offensive force to protect certain government interests, including assisting in preventing the Katangan province from seceding. This controversial operation was seen as an aberration in peacekeeping: an exception proving the rule that the distinction between peacekeeping and enforcement must be a rigid one.

Later, with the end of the Cold War and the lessening of East-West hostilities, a sense developed within the Organization that the conventional wisdom – that peacekeeping and enforcement ought not to coexist (as proven through ONUC) – was open to challenge. During the period 1992–95, the Organization once again bestowed enforcement-type tasks on peacekeeping operations. And, once again, the operations were generally not successful: they were not sufficiently equipped or staffed to undertake the complex, enforcement-related tasks demanded of them. Moreover, peacekeepers, once seen as impartial heroes, came to be seen as partisan. Sober in the realisation that forceful, partial peacekeeping did not work, it became clear within the UN that the best course was to return to the more traditional model of peacekeeping. There was agreement – supported in the near-unanimous writings of commentators – that peacekeeping operations worked best when they were keeping an existing peace through non-forceful means, rather than attempting to establish peace or secure its continuance through the use of enforcement-type measures.

Against this background, it may come as something of a surprise that the approach of assigning enforcement tasks to peacekeeping forces represents the current model for peacekeeping. Beginning in late 1999 and continuing to the time of writing, the mandates of peacekeeping operations are routinely established through the invocation of Chapter VII and are routinely charged with using force beyond self-defence. While the consent of the host state is generally still granted before a mandate is established or modified, the Security Council's invocation of Chapter VII, and the nature of the measures it authorises under that Chapter, call into question the legal necessity of such consent. The level of force that is authorised for these twenty-first century peacekeeping operations can include the use of 'all necessary means' – language that had traditionally been associated with enforcement operations, and which echoes the 'action . . . as may be necessary' language of Article 42 of the UN Charter. A requirement that the force be impartial – unless that term is defined so as to bear no resemblance to its normal meaning – has been all but cast aside.

The fact that the UN decided to revert to a system of militarised peacekeeping that had previously shown itself unworkable might suggest that the Organization was thought to have evolved in the years between its unsuccessful forceful peacekeeping activities in the mid-1990s and its resumption of militarised peacekeeping operations in the late 1990s, such that it had reached a stage where it could overcome the many problems of the past. Surprisingly, however, the arguments in favour of the UN reverting to militarised peacekeeping were not based on such factors. Instead, they would appear to have been animated primarily by thinking of a more wishful nature. It was considered to be so essential that peacekeepers protect those within their sphere of influence who were vulnerable in the face of a breach of security that peacekeeping mandates simply *had* to provide for this – whether or not the Organization had yet evolved such that it had the capacity to do so. The reasoning seemed to be that if the Security Council was to assign enforcement-type tasks to militarised peacekeeping operations then, *ipso facto*, the Security Council and Member States would ensure that such operations were sufficiently well-funded, well-organised and had sufficient personnel to undertake them successfully. Influential voices, including that of former Secretary-General Kofi Annan and the experts appointed to a panel established by him – the panel that produced the Brahimi Report[11] – persuasively argued that with sufficient safeguards and resources, as well as a certain amount of restraint on the part of the Security Council, militarised peacekeeping operations could be successful. With these changes, some UN peacekeeping operations were given the dual task of securing the restoration of peace and security in a country as well as maintaining it. Thus peacekeeping operations were, in addition to their other duties, charged with saving lives and preventing future genocides. But can such militarised peacekeeping operations work?

2. MILITARISED PEACEKEEPING: SLOUCHING TOWARDS CRISIS

This book will consider the changed nature of peacekeeping and argue that, generally speaking, militarised peacekeeping operations have not been successful. As with the Luvungi rapes discussed above, militarised peacekeeping operations are asked to do too much, thereby leading to frequent failure. Press reports and the nationals of countries where such peacekeepers are operating tend to blame the peacekeepers themselves, suggesting that they are not willing to risk their lives to perform their assigned functions, labelling them 'cowards' or 'tourists'. This is too easy a conclusion to draw. Even if some measure of fault may be found with the peacekeepers themselves in certain situations, this would represent only one element of a larger problem: peacekeeping operations are, by their very nature, ill-suited to carrying out enforcement-type functions. They do not have the necessary management structure, personnel or resources

[11] United Nations, *Identical Letters Dated 21 August 2000 from the Secretary-General to the President of the General Assembly and the President of the Security Council [Attaching Report of the Panel on UN Peacekeeping Operations (the 'Brahimi Report')]* (UN Docs A/55/305 and S/2000/809), 21 August 2000, para 21.

to carry out enforcement-type tasks and, as such, they almost invariably fail when they attempt them.

Through an analysis of UN practice with respect to militarised peacekeeping operations, this book will show that, aside from the rare success story, such operations are no more successful in the twenty-first century than they were in the twentieth. Moreover, it will show that there is no sign that the level of success of such operations is on any sort of upward trajectory. As the discussion of the DRC situation above shows, militarised peacekeeping operations continue to be fundamentally ill-suited to their military tasks, and their failure in this regard continues to damage the UN. According to interviews with a number of diplomats and other experts, UN peacekeeping 'appears to be slouching toward crisis once again'[12] due to a sharp rise in the number of peacekeeping commitments worldwide and a type of 'mission creep' whereby peacekeeping operations may be expected to restore security and protect civilians.

Surprisingly, the book's contention that twenty-first century militarised peacekeeping operations have generally been unsuccessful in carrying out the enforcement-type functions assigned to them is relatively uncontroversial. Few argue otherwise. Perhaps more surprising still is the fact that many – including those who readily accept that peacekeeping operations are generally unsuccessful in carrying out enforcement functions – argue that the UN must, nevertheless, continue with its current model of militarised peacekeeping. Arguments for the continued vesting of enforcement-type tasks tend to take two (somewhat overlapping) forms.

First, there is an argument that while militarised peacekeeping is not currently successful, it will eventually succeed if the lessons of the past are learnt, past successes are built upon, and the necessary fine-tuning takes place. This argument was summarised by Findlay, writing in 2002: '[T]he UN is not currently capable of conducting such operations but might, in time, be able to do so, providing its capacities are dramatically improved.'[13] He continued: '[T]he reflections of many observers on this issue are almost tautologous: UN peace-enforcement operations could succeed if they were provided with all the elements for success.'[14]

The thesis of the Brahimi Report is that peacekeeping must be reinvented such that it is authorised to ensure security and protect civilians. In order to do so, the Report argues, operations must be carefully planned, realistically mandated and vested with the necessary resources by Member States; moreover, the Security Council must exercise considerable restraint by waiting for resources to be available before establishing militarised peacekeeping operations. The UN appears to have accepted

[12] MacFarquhar (n 1).

[13] Trevor Findlay, *The Use of Force in UN Peace Operations* (Oxford, Oxford University Press for the Stockholm International Peace Research Institute (SIPRI), 2002) 381–82.

[14] ibid.

the first part of the thesis, while ignoring the second. The Brahimi thesis pays insufficient attention to the fundamentally political nature of UN activities and the fundamentally selfish nature of Member States. The UN is not currently, nor will it ever be, capable of administering a fighting force with the same level of skill as a state with a well-disciplined and well-resourced military. Because the UN relies on Member States to volunteer troops and resources, the planning of such operations will involve little more than guesswork. Discipline is difficult, if not impossible: if members of a peacekeeping operation disagree with the decisions of the force commander, little prevents them from taking the matter up with their national commander or state representatives and, if they gain the necessary support, simply disregarding the force commander.

Arguments that the Security Council ought to exercise restraint (and ensure that sufficient resources are available before assigning enforcement-type functions to peacekeeping operations) have gone unheeded; instead, the Security Council's approach has been to decide what result it would like – based on the politics of the day or, perhaps, a lingering sense of colonial obligation on the part of some of its Member States – and leave the Secretary-General and the Secretariat to attempt to cobble together a force with the scarce resources they have to hand. Frequently, though such a force will patently be unable to undertake the duties assigned to it, it will be established by the Security Council nonetheless.

An analysis of practice shows no indication of a trend towards greater state support for such operations. To the contrary, whereas in the early- to mid-1990s it was not uncommon for states with developed militaries, including Security Council permanent Member States, to contribute personnel to militarised peacekeeping operations, now very few peacekeeping forces come from such states. Developed states tend to participate in forceful peacekeeping only when their national interests are affected – for example, Australia's participation in UNTAET beginning in late 1999. Nor can there be said to be any favourable trends as regards Member States' willingness to volunteer equipment.

The question must then be asked: for how long must this, the UN's third experiment with militarised peacekeeping, be allowed to fail? When will it be time to acknowledge that the UN and its Member States are not going to change – that they are not going to provide the necessary capacity for successful missions? When will it be time to acknowledge that the UN is inherently incapable of undertaking militarised peacekeeping?

It is a central contention of this book that in 2011, over 10 years after the peacekeeping model was militarised, it is time to recognise that the militarised peacekeeping experiment has gone on long enough – that it is working no better than it did in the early 1960s or the early- to mid-1990s. It is time, moreover, to acknowledge that the militarised peacekeeping model is, simply put, beyond the capacity of the UN. As Michael Mandelbaum put it:

> The UN is a trade association of sovereign states. Just as a trade association of hospitals can issue resolutions on health care policy, the UN is an appropriate forum for passing resolutions expressing the will of the international community. However, where the execution of UN decrees is difficult or costly, responsibility must be assumed by sovereign states, acting under the authorization of the Security Council or the General Assembly. The UN can no more conduct military operations on a large-scale on its own than a trade association of hospitals can conduct heart surgery.[15]

For the UN to continue to establish militarised peacekeeping operations when it has become clear that they are – and are likely to continue to be – unsuccessful, is damaging not only to peacekeeping, but also to the UN more broadly.

A second argument is made by those who favour the assignment of enforcement-type functions to peacekeeping operations: even if operations frequently fail to carry out their enforcement-type functions, at least the UN has tried to do something to avert humanitarian crisis. The UN, and the Security Council more specifically, they would argue, cannot be seen to be inactive in the face of brutal violence being visited upon innocent civilians. This argument would appear to be motivated by the laudable belief that the UN must do everything it can to minimise civilian harm in the countries where peacekeepers are present. Even if a peacekeeping operation empowered to use enforcement-type powers is only sufficiently skilled and equipped to save one civilian life out of 100 or 1,000, it could be argued, that is better than a peacekeeping operation which is not so authorised and which, as a result, saves none.

A more pragmatic variation on the argument may be based on the perception that the UN must not *be seen* to be doing nothing in the face of atrocity. Here, adherents of militarised peacekeeping might argue that the Organization can better shoulder the disgrace that comes from a peacekeeping operation's inability to perform its enforcement-related tasks than it could the disgrace that comes from being seen to have done nothing in the face of a massive loss of life – as was the case when the peacekeeping operations in Rwanda in 1994 or Srebrenica in 1995 did little to protect civilians. In the words of Chesterman:

> The three peace operations in which troops under UN command engaged in the use of force on a significant scale – Congo from 1960–1963, Somalia in 1993, and Bosnia and Herzegovina from 1994–1995 – were traumatic experiences for the organization; the controversies to which they gave rise were surpassed only by two occasions on which force was not used at all: in Rwanda and Srebrenica.[16]

[15] Michael Mandelbaum, 'The Reluctance to Intervene' (1994) 95 *Foreign Policy* 3, 10–11.

[16] Simon Chesterman, 'The Use of Force in UN Peace Operations', August 2004, http://pbpu.unlb.org/pbps/Library/Chesterman%20External%20Paper%20(31-08-2004).pdf (accessed 1 April 2011).

The problem is clear: the cost to the UN of being seen to do nothing in the face of atrocities is dear.

There may be another, more cynical variant of the argument that the UN must not be seen to be doing nothing: assigning enforcement-type tasks to a peacekeeping operation – even where the peacekeeping operation is under-equipped and unable to carry out these tasks – provides the Security Council with an element of political cover, plausible deniability or, to use the word of former Secretary-General Annan, an 'alibi'.[17] It allows powerful states on the Security Council to point to the steps that the organ took to protect civilians on the ground or to authorise the use of offensive force against conduct that it has judged to be harmful. Whether or not those steps are successful – or could ever reasonably be successful – the establishment of a militarised peacekeeping operation provides the Security Council with the ability to argue that it did *something*, even if that something was almost certain to fail in its militarised aspects, and to argue that the responsibility, where failure does occur, falls to others, such as the Secretariat or the peacekeepers themselves.

The 'at least the UN is doing something' argument – whether motivated by a desire to save as many lives as possible, to avoid unfavourable publicity for the UN or to provide an alibi – is more complex than many acknowledge. In order to judge the merits of militarised peacekeeping, the *costs* of the undertaking must be considered alongside the possible benefits. This book will argue that there are four main costs involved in such operations (in addition to the increased financial costs to the Organization). First, with a militarised mandate comes an increase in loss of peacekeepers' lives. It may, of course, be argued that the loss of a small number of peacekeepers is a necessary sacrifice to assist a civilian population that is being attacked. Putting to one side the issue of whether this argument may be made in the circumstances of a particular mission, another factor must be borne in mind: because militarised peacekeeping is an endeavour which may be costly in terms of peacekeepers' lives, states will be more reluctant to volunteer troops. As noted, over recent years there has been a noticeable shift in the countries from which troops are being volunteered. This, in turn, may have an effect on the skills, training and equipment of the troops.

Second, when the UN is charged with enforcing security or protecting civilians, the expectations of the civilian population affected, as well as of observers generally, are raised. When the operation fails to achieve its objectives – as this book will argue it almost invariably does – the particular peacekeeping operation, peacekeeping generally and the UN overall are all brought into disrepute. The mass rapes in Luvungi, discussed

[17] As quoted by Jim Hoagland, 'Who Wants Peacekeeping? Put Up or Shut Up', *Washington Post*, 3 August 2000.

above, provide but one example of UN peacekeeping not meeting the demands placed upon it and of the stinging criticism of the UN that followed.

Third, the increased potential for militarised peacekeeping operations to use offensive force and to take sides undermines one of peacekeeping's greatest strengths: its reputation for non-violence and even-handedness. This can lead to the view that peacekeeping has been reinvented such that *all* missions may now use force to carry out all of the tasks within their mandates, regardless of the nature of the tasks in which they are engaged. Thus, peacekeepers who are engaging in functions for which force has not been authorised or is not necessary are more likely than ever to be perceived as the 'enemy' by various factions within a state, rather than international neutrals whose presence represents a time of peace.

Finally, when the Security Council assigns enforcement functions to a peacekeeping operation, it may serve to impede (or delay) the establishment of an enforcement force. The political pressure on the Security Council and Member States to do something effective in the face of a genocide or mass atrocity – something which, I will argue, can generally only be achieved through a state-led enforcement operation – will be diminished, at least until the militarised peacekeeping operation has proven itself to be a clear failure. With the United Nations Mission in Sierra Leone (UNAMSIL), for example, the Security Council, at the instigation of the UK (Sierra Leone's former coloniser), bestowed numerous enforcement-type responsibilities on an under-equipped, under-manned, poorly trained militarised peacekeeping force. It was only after the forces had proven themselves almost entirely incapable of maintaining order or protecting civilians – and scores of peacekeepers were kidnapped – that the UK agreed to send in an independent force for a limited period. If the assignment of unrealistic enforcement tasks to a militarised peacekeeping operation serves as an impediment to the Security Council taking efficacious steps, the suffering the militarised peacekeeping operation was designed to prevent may, in fact, be prolonged.

3. STRUCTURE OF THE BOOK

Following this introductory chapter, chapter 2 traces the development of peacekeeping and enforcement and asks the question: is peacekeeping the opposite of enforcement? Peacekeeping, which began as an uncontroversial Cold War compromise featuring a handful of observers present in a state, developed into a model featuring larger, better equipped operations and, most recently, into a Chapter VII-authorised endeavour, at times, overlapping with enforcement. Chapter 2 illustrates that host state consent, non-use of force and impartiality may no longer be said to be 'fundamental principles' of peacekeeping. The chapter also outlines the development of enforcement. What was envisioned in the UN Charter as a means to ensure international security through reliance by the Security Council on a UN force established pursuant to Article 43, has evolved such that the Security Council authorises willing states or groups of states to enforce its will. Moreover, the nature of the circumstances in which enforcement operations have been authorised by the Security Council has changed. Where force was once authorised to address the invasion of one state by another, it is now authorised to aid with internal disturbances, frequently in association with a peacekeeping operation with overlapping functions. In short, it will be shown that as peacekeeping has become more enforcement-like, enforcement has become more peacekeeping-like. Thus, it is no longer meaningful to refer to peacekeeping as the opposite of enforcement.

With that background, chapter 3 considers the legal basis of peacekeeping, including peacekeeping operations that have been given enforcement functions. The chapter outlines the restrictions that the UN Charter imposes on the Security Council's freedom to act, which may be lifted when it is engaging in enforcement action or where the affected state consents. The chapter examines the powers vested in the Security Council in Chapters VI and VII of the Charter, the prerequisites thereto and limitations thereupon, and considers their impact on the Security Council's ability to establish peacekeeping operations. The chapter shows that while certain restrictions on the Security Council's ability to function are lifted when it is taking enforcement measures, certain other restrictions come into play that may impact on its freedom to act.

Chapters 4–6 consider Security Council practice in relation to militarised peacekeeping. Chapter 4 considers such practice in the twentieth century, including an examination of UNEF I and ONUC in the Organization's early years, and an examination of four operations in the early 1990s: UNPROFOR in the former Yugoslavia, UNOSOM II in Somalia, UNAMIR II in Rwanda, and UNMIH in Haiti. The Security Council's twenty-first century practice in relation to militarised peacekeeping is considered in chapters 5 and 6. Chapter 5 considers militarised peacekeeping operations that were established at or around the turn of the century in Sierra Leone, East Timor and the DRC. Chapter 6 examines later twenty-first century militarised peacekeeping operations in Liberia, Côte d'Ivoire, Burundi, Haiti, Sudan, and the Central African Republic and Chad.

In chapters 4, 5 and 6, the circumstances in which each of the peacekeeping missions was established are considered, as are, where appropriate, the circumstances leading to each operation being made more forceful. The focus is not only on the level of force authorised in each operation but also on the level of force actually used. Where a state-led enforcement operation is established by the Security Council to aid militarised peacekeeping operations, these enforcement operations are examined. In analysing these peacekeeping operations, the question of whether or not the operation adhered to the 'fundamental principles' of peacekeeping – force only in self-defence or in defence-of-mandate, host state consent, impartiality – is examined. In addition, the difficult – but, as argued herein, highly relevant – issue of the Article of the UN Charter under which each operation was established is considered. Finally, general conclusions are offered, which consider the lessons learned from each operation.

In chapter 7, overall conclusions are drawn. It is argued that the force-only-in-self-defence/host-state-consent/impartiality model of peacekeeping (the three 'fundamental principles' of peacekeeping) is, in most respects, legally irrelevant in terms of militarised peacekeeping operations – despite attempts by the UN Secretariat to promote the view that those 'fundamental principles' are alive and well. Based upon the invocation of Chapter VII (implied with ONUC; express in subsequent operations) and the authorisation to use offensive force in order to restore international peace and security, militarised peacekeeping operations are frequently best characterised as an exercise by the Security Council of its enforcement powers under Article 42. Chapter 7 also considers the myriad problems associated with militarised peacekeeping. In view of the severity and insuperability of these problems, the book contends that the status quo is not sustainable. Peacekeeping must return to its roots in order for it to succeed. Enforcement-type tasks must be left to enforcement operations.

4. THE DEFINITION OF PEACEKEEPING

The term 'peacekeeping' is not found in the Charter of the United Nations. What has developed over the years is an extremely wide variety of interpretations of the concept. While those invoking the term – lawyers, diplomats, UN functionaries, scholars, journalists and others – may share the same general conception of peacekeeping, it is striking how far apart they will frequently be as to its exact particulars. Indeed, no agreement exists as to whether the first peacekeeping operation occurred in the late 1940s or in 1956.[18] The nature of operations covered by the term 'peacekeeping' is extremely varied and can include an operation with limited personnel and a limited mandate (such as to observe and report) through to an operation involving tens of thousands of personnel charged with maintaining security or even acting as a de facto government.

[18] Some exclude early observer missions from their definitions of peacekeeping, while others include them. To adherents to the former view, the United Nations Emergency Force in the Suez (UNEF I) in 1956 was the first example of UN peacekeeping. For adherence to the latter view, UN peacekeeping began sometime between 1946 and 1948, with the establishment of the United Nations Special Committee on the Balkans (UNSCOB), the United Nations Commission for Indonesia (UNCI) or the United Nations Troop Supervision Operation (in the Middle East) (UNTSO).

In the introduction to her seminal four-volume study on UN peacekeeping,[19] Dame Rosalyn Higgins highlighted the fact that peacekeeping is open to a variety of definitions, each of which may be permissible according to the purpose of the particular study. She observed:

> To some, peacekeeping is a broad concept, referring to the entire role of the UN in maintaining, or restoring, international peace. According to this definition any book on peacekeeping must refer not only to UN Forces, but to investigation committees, special representatives of the Secretary-General and diplomacy within the UN system. Others have suggested that peacekeeping is a term which has come to refer to UN Forces and observer groups which are operational on a territory with the consent of its government. Yet others have insisted that the term peacekeeping cannot include UN observers. There is, of course, no one 'correct' definition.[20]

Higgins's comments, first made in 1969, are all the more true in the twenty-first century, now that the range of functions assigned to peacekeeping operations has increased dramatically.

Definitional issues are further complicated by the fact that a decision by a politician, a diplomat representing a UN Member State or a member of staff at the UN Secretariat to characterise an operation as 'peacekeeping' is not taken in a vacuum. It may be motivated less by a concern for consistency or fidelity to an established meaning or set of characteristics than by what best suits the characteriser's objectives in relation to the particular mission. For example, if it is accepted that the label 'peacekeeping' carries with it a substantial limitation on the operation's ability to use force – something which many continue to believe despite evidence to the contrary – referring to an action as such may increase the likelihood that states will contribute forces to the operation[21] and that the affected state will consent to the operation's presence on its territory.[22] If it is accepted that the term 'peacekeeping' implies that an operation is 'non-enforcement' in

[19] Higgins's four-volume study of UN peacekeeping operations, published by Oxford University Press between 1969 and 1981, is among the most influential bodies of work on UN peacekeeping to date. Rosalyn Higgins, *United Nations Peacekeeping 1946–1967: Documents and Commentary, Vol I: The Middle East* (1969); *Vol II: Asia* (1970); *Vol III: Africa* (1980); *Vol IV: Europe 1946–1976* (1981).

[20] Higgins, ibid, vol I, ix.

[21] In some states, participation in an operation where force is used beyond self-defence may be constitutionally prohibited. On the situation in Japan see eg Akiho Shibata, 'Japanese Peacekeeping Legislation and Recent Developments in UN Operations' (1994) 19 *Yale Journal of International Law* 307. Further, the use of force beyond self-defence by a peacekeeping operation may be be considered to impact on a state's neutrality. See Katherine E Cox, 'Beyond Self-Defense: United Nations Peacekeeping Operations and the Use of Force' (1999) 27 *Denver Journal of International Law & Policy* 239, 271 and n 132, which refers to Austria, Switzerland, Finland and Sweden.

[22] As noted by Brian Urquhart, a former UN Under-Secretary-General, it is their non-violent nature 'that makes peacekeeping forces acceptable both to the governments and parties engaged in conflict, and to the governments that contribute the troops'. Quoted in Fou-Tchin Liu, *United Nations Peacekeeping and the Non-Use of Force* (Occasional Paper, International Peace Academy) (Boulder, Col, Lynne Rienner Publishers, 1992) 7.

nature, the operation's characterisation as peacekeeping will facilitate the establishment of the operation by the Security Council, some of whose permanent Member States have consistently voiced reluctance to see obligations imposed on sovereign states. Similarly, whether or not an operation is characterised as 'peacekeeping' may have an impact on the protection under international humanitarian law to which its personnel are entitled.[23]

Many observers turn to the UN itself for a definition of peacekeeping – and a listing of the missions that comport with this definition.[24] However, the UN does not speak with one voice on the issue, leading to inconsistencies in approach among the principal organs that have considered the matter; indeed there can be variance in approach within a single organ. Nor are the different organs' approaches to defining the term – or indicating which missions may be classed as peacekeeping – necessarily objective: certain organs of the UN are not above allowing political considerations to influence their characterisation of an operation as peacekeeping, or as something other than peacekeeping. For example, the Secretariat has been known to opt not to label an operation as 'peacekeeping' in order not to displease a host state that did not favour the term.[25]

The website of the UN Secretariat's Department of Peacekeeping Operations (DPKO) was restructured in late 2010/early 2011 and continues to stress that host state consent, non-use of force except in self-defence

[23] The Rome Statue of the International Criminal Court provides that where an individual intentionally directs attacks against personnel involved in a 'peacekeeping mission in accordance with the Charter of the United Nations', he or she is guilty of a war crime, as long as the peacekeepers are entitled to the protection given to civilians under the international law of armed conflict (Rome Statute of the International Criminal Court, adopted 17 July 1998, entered into force 1 July 2002 (2187 UNTS 90), Art 8(2)(b)(iii) in the context of international conflicts and Art 8(2)(e)(iii) in the context of non-international armed conflicts). Where a peacekeeper is a combatant he or she is not entitled to civilian protection. See discussion on this point in *Situation in Darfur, Sudan in the case of The Prosecutor v Bahar Idriss Abu Garda, Decision on the Confirmation of Charges (Public Redacted Version)* (No ICC-02/05-02/09), 8 February 2010 (PTC I), www.icc-cpi.int/iccdocs/doc/doc819602.pdf (accessed 1 April 2011). This provision was subsequently reproduced in Art 4(b) of the Statute of the Special Court for Sierra Leone (established by an Agreement between the United Nations and the government of Sierra Leone pursuant to Security Council Resolution 1315 (2000) of 14 August 2000). See discussion on this point in *Prosecutor v Issa Hassan Sesay, Morrison Kallon and Augustine Gbao* (Case No SCSL-04-15-T, Special Court for Sierra Leone, Trial Chamber I, 2 March 2009).

[24] For a list of peacekeeping missions between 1948 and 2011, according to the UN Secretariat, see www.un.org/en/peacekeeping/documents/operationslist.pdf (accessed 1 April 2011). See also United Nations, *The Blue Helmets: A Review of United Nations Peace-Keeping*, 3rd edn (New York, UN Sales No E.96.I.14, 1996) 296.

[25] Marrack Goulding, then UN Under-Secretary-General for Political Affairs, noted that while he considered the United Nations Observer Group for the Verification of the Elections in Haiti to be peacekeeping, it was not officially so called at the request of the Haitian authorities; nor was it established or financed as such (Marrack Goulding, 'The Evolution of United Nations Peacekeeping' (1993) 69 *International Affairs* 451, 456). Similarly, the government of Papua New Guinea refused to allow the United Nations Political Office in Bougainville (a 'peace-building mission' or 'political office') to carry on under its assigned name, preferring that it refer to itself as the United Nations Observer Mission in Bougainville on the basis that the latter name sounded less politically intrusive.

or in defence-of-mandate and impartiality are the three 'guiding principles' of peacekeeping[26] – this despite the fact that of the 10 peacekeeping operations established since October 1999, almost all have been established, at least in part, under Chapter VII of the Charter and vested with the authority to use force beyond self-defence in relation to at least some of their functions.[27] While certain of these characteristics are frequently present in peacekeeping operations – and, as will be discussed in chapter 3, find considerable legal support in the UN Charter – to characterise them as 'fundamental' or 'guiding' principles of peacekeeping is misleading in today's world.[28] These considerations notwithstanding, the UN provides a valuable source of understanding of the nature of UN peacekeeping.

No attempt will be made to provide a 'correct' definition of the term 'peacekeeping'. Nevertheless, certain types of operation will be excluded for the purposes of this book. First, this study will focus on *UN* peacekeeping. As such, a 'peacekeeping' operation such as the Multinational Force and Observers (MFO) in the Sinai Peninsula, established outside the auspices of the UN to supervise the implementation of the security provisions of the 1979 Egyptian-Israeli Treaty of Peace, falls outside its scope. Similarly, the African Union Mission in Sudan (AMIS) will not be classified as a peacekeeping operation for the purposes of this book; despite being endorsed by the UN Security Council ex post facto, it was established by the African Union, not the UN.[29] Second, for the purposes of this book an operation must have a physical presence in the state or states in question in order to be characterised as peacekeeping. Third, 'peacekeeping' operations must be primarily in aid of maintaining peace or preventing the recurrence of a breach of the peace, as broadly construed.[30] Thus, the term as used herein does not 'encompass low-level operations by the Organization involving technical assistance, even if that aid serves to help a state implement some type of solution to a conflict'.[31] Nor does it

[26] See the DPKO's definition of peacekeeping at www.un.org/en/peacekeeping/operations/peacekeeping.shtml (accessed 1 April 2011).

[27] See discussion in chapters 5 and 6.

[28] This is also discussed in chapters 4, 5 and 6, which consider UN practice.

[29] cf the approach taken by the International Criminal Court. In the *Abu Garda* case, it needed to determine whether AMIS was a 'peacekeeping mission in accordance with the Charter of the United Nations' for the purposes of the application of Art 8(2)(e)(iii) of the Rome Statute. It held that a requirement that the operation be established in accordance with the Charter was 'not tantamount to a requirement that the mission be established by the United Nations only, and shall be understood to encompass also missions that are otherwise foreseen by the UN Charter' (*Prosecutor v Abu Garda* (n 23) para 75). It referred to the fact that Art 52 of the UN Charter envisages a role for regional arrangements or agencies in relation to the maintenance of international peace and security (ibid, para 76).

[30] This may include operations with enforcement functions; the overlap between peacekeeping and enforcement will be considered in chapter 2 below.

[31] Steven Ratner, *The New UN Peacekeeping: Building Peace in the Lands of Conflict after the Cold War* (New York, St Martin's Press, 1995) 20. He conceded, however, that the line between a technical assistance operation that assists with elections or human rights and peacekeeping may not always be clearly drawn (ibid, 20–21).

include diplomacy or fact-finding missions;[32] while the functions of such missions may overlap with those of peacekeeping missions, they tend to be considerably narrower.[33] Finally, the concept of peacekeeping used in this book does not include operations that, while UN-authorised, are led by states or regional organizations.[34] The distinction between UN-led operations and state-led operations – and its significance – is discussed in detail in chapter 2.

[32] cf Boutros Boutros-Ghali in United Nations, *An Agenda for Peace: Preventive Diplomacy, Peacemaking and Peace-Keeping* (UN Doc A/47/277-S/24111), 17 June 1992, para 25.

[33] The point at which a fact-finding or investigative mission ends and a peacekeeping mission begins may be difficult to discern. For example, a diplomatic or fact-finding mission will likely contribute to the maintenance or restoration of peace; similarly, peacekeeping forces will frequently have diplomatic functions (ie resolving minor breaches of a ceasefire, etc), as well as fact-finding and reporting functions.

[34] A similar requirement is set out in *An Agenda for Peace* (n 32) at paras 20 and 44, which define peacekeeping as featuring UN personnel ('normally' at any rate) under the command of the Secretary-General. See also Roy Lee, formerly of the UN Office of Legal Affairs, who observed that 'UN peacekeeping operations do not include actions which are authorized by the Security Council but carried out by interested Member States or by an ad hoc multinational force. Roy S Lee, 'United Nations Peacekeeping: Development and Prospects' (1995) 28 *Cornell International Law Journal* 619, 621–22.

Chapter 2

Peacekeeping: The Opposite of Enforcement?

Insistence on clarifying the nature and meaning of peacekeeping is not merely a lawyer's obsession with clarity and legal definition; it is necessary because the legal character and nature of the operation has a direct bearing on the legal issues which arise and their resolution.

Ralph Zacklin, former United Nations
Assistant Secretary-General for Legal Affairs[1]

1. INTRODUCTION

IT HAS LONG been an article of faith for many that UN peacekeeping is of an entirely different nature from UN enforcement. In the words of former Secretary-General Pérez de Cuellar, peacekeeping is 'the opposite of enforcement'.[2] Where the differences between the two endeavours are elaborated – frequently, the different nature of each is taken as self-evident[3] – the following three characteristics are cited as being essential to a peacekeeping operation: it must be impartial, it must take place only with the consent of the host state(s), and it must use force only in self-defence.[4] Enforcement

[1] Ralph Zacklin, 'Managing Peacekeeping from a Legal Perspective' in Daniel Warner (ed), *New Dimensions of Peacekeeping* (Dordrecht, Martinus Nijhoff, 1995) 159–62, 159.

[2] Javier Pérez de Cuéllar, Nobel Lecture, 9 January 1989, http://nobelprize.org/nobel_prizes/peace/laureates/1988/un-lecture.html (accessed 1 April 2011).

[3] For example, one member of the UN's Office of Legal Affairs simply spoke in terms of 'peacekeeping' operations and 'non-peacekeeping' operations, with the latter category including enforcement (Roy S Lee, 'United Nations Peacekeeping: Development and Prospects' (1995) 28 *Cornell International Law Journal* 619, 621–22).

[4] Many authors and the UN Secretariat speak of 'consent of the parties' or 'consent of the host nation and/or the main parties to the conflict' when discussing the importance of consent. While it is indeed true that a peacekeeping operation generally is unable to succeed if it is attempting to carry out its mandate without the consent of all (significant) parties, the significance of consent of parties other than the host state is of a different nature to the consent of the host state, which may be *legally* required unless the Security Council is acting under Chapter VII in a binding way. The focus of this book is on the legal significance of consent. Thus when the 'fundamental principle' of consent is referred to herein, the focus is on the host state(s) rather than the other parties to the conflict. See discussion of this point in Christine Gray, 'Host-State Consent and United Nations Peacekeeping in Yugoslavia' (1996–97) 7 *Duke Journal of Comparative and International Law* 241, 243–45.

operations, on the other hand, are frequently thought to possess characteristics which are the mirror image: they are viewed as occurring without the consent of the host state, relying on considerable offensive force and taking sides to enforce a political solution decided upon by the Security Council. As we shall see, however, the distinction between peacekeeping and enforcement is not always plain.

During the Cold War, the East-West divide precluded the establishment of virtually all enforcement measures.[5] Because of their non-confrontational, non-enforcement character, peacekeeping operations were looked upon more favourably. Peacekeeping began as a gentler alternative to enforcement, whether created by the General Assembly (which, of course, does not possess the power to establish binding enforcement actions) or by the Security Council, through the exercise of its non-enforcement powers. Three elements – consent of the affected state, limited use of force and impartiality – came to be seen as fundamental to the peacekeeping endeavour through the legal guidance provided by Secretary-General Hammarskjöld in the late 1950s, after the establishment of the first United Nations Emergency Force (UNEF I) in 1956. From UNEF I onwards, however, these 'fundamental principles' were not all to be strictly observed. Currently it is the norm for the Security Council to invoke Chapter VII of the UN Charter[6] in relation to resolutions establishing aspects of peacekeeping operations (calling into question the legal need for host state consent), to vest operations with a mandate to use force beyond self-defence and to pay little regard to impartiality. In such circumstances, can the 'fundamental principles' be said to continue to play a central role in peacekeeping practice?

Despite evidence to the contrary, many commentators continue to consider the 'fundamental principles' as essential characteristics of peacekeeping operations. One expert, writing in 2006, considered that the three principles had 'acquired constitutional status', concluding that they 'continue to apply even if the peacekeeping context has radically changed'.[7] A similar approach was taken in a recent judgment of the Special Court for Sierra Leone,[8] which turned to the three 'fundamental principles' in order

[5] One exception was the authorisation to use force in reply to North Korea in 1950 (discussed below in section 3.1); however, that only came about as a result of a unique set of circumstances (the absence of the Soviet Union from the meeting room) which were not to be repeated.

[6] In certain circumstances, the Security Council, when acting under Chapter VII, is empowered to take binding enforcement measures, including measures involving the use of force. For a discussion of the powers and limitations found in Chapter VII of the UN Charter, see chapter 3, section 3.

[7] Nicholas Tsagourias, 'Consent, Neutrality/Impartiality and the Use of Force in Peacekeeping: Their Constitutional Dimension' (2006) 11 *Journal of Conflict and Security Law* 465, 466.

[8] The Special Court for Sierra Leone was established in 2002 by means of Agreement between the United Nations and the Government of Sierra Leone on the Establishment of a Special Court for Sierra Leone (16 January 2002, entered into force 12 April 2002 (2178 UNTS 138)).

to determine whether an operation was a 'peacekeeping mission in accordance with the Charter of the United Nations' – a *sine qua non* for attacks to be prosecutable by that Court as 'other serious violations of international humanitarian law', as provided in Article 4(b) of the Court's Statute.[9] A set of principles and guidelines prepared by the UN Secretariat's Department of Peacekeeping Operations (DPKO) in 2008 – at a time when the Security Council was routinely invoking Chapter VII in its resolutions establishing peacekeeping operations (or assigning certain tasks to them) and giving those operations the authority to use force beyond self-defence, sometimes in a way that was not (or did not have the appearance of being) impartial – describes consent of the parties, impartiality and non-use of force except in self-defence (or in defence-of-mandate) as being 'basic principles [that] have traditionally served *and continue* to set United Nations peacekeeping operations apart as a tool for maintaining international peace and security'.[10]

This chapter will begin by looking at how UN peacekeeping has changed over the years and will show that, over time, the 'fundamental principles' are no longer a defining feature of peacekeeping. It will conclude that the contention that the 'fundamental principles' serve to constrain the Security Council's peacekeeping practice in a meaningful way is largely misleading.

The chapter will then consider the changed nature of UN enforcement. Various Security Council actions that are widely considered to amount to enforcement will be examined, as will the role of the 'fundamental principles' of enforcement – basically the opposite of the 'fundamental principles' of peacekeeping. The chapter will show that, as with the influence of the 'fundamental principles' of peacekeeping, the influence of the 'fundamental principles' of enforcement have become less and less relevant as enforcement has changed over the years. Finally, the chapter will consider the concept of 'peace-enforcement' – a type of operation falling somewhere between peacekeeping and enforcement. The chapter will assert

[9] Statute of the Special Court for Sierra Leone (established by an Agreement between the United Nations and the Government of Sierra Leone pursuant to Security Council Resolution 1315 (2000) of 14 August 2000). There, despite the fact that the Security Council had invoked Chapter VII in assigning certain tasks to the operation and had authorised it to use considerable force, the Court found it to be a 'peacekeeping mission in accordance with the Charter of the United Nations'. *Prosecutor v Issa Hassan Sesay, Morrison Kallon and Augustine Gbao* (Case No SCSL-04-15-T, Special Court for Sierra Leone, Trial Chamber I, 2 March 2009) paras 213–35. The three 'fundamental principles' were also invoked in similar circumstances by the International Criminal Court in *Situation in Darfur, Sudan in the case of The Prosecutor v Bahar Idriss Abu Garda, Decision on the Confirmation of Charges (Public Redacted Version)* (Case No ICC-02/05-02/09), 8 February 2010 (PTC I), www.icc-cpi.int/iccdocs/doc/doc819602.pdf (accessed 1 April 2011), paras 68–76.

[10] United Nations Department of Peacekeeping Operations and Department of Field Operations, *United Nations Peacekeeping Operations: Principles and Guidelines* ('Capstone Doctrine'), 2008, http://pbpu.unlb.org/pbps/Library/Capstone_Doctrine_ENG.pdf (accessed 1 April 2011), 31 (emphasis added).

that the meaning of this term – and the nature of the operations envisaged as falling within it – is so imprecise as to render it of little value.

2. THE CHANGED NATURE OF PEACEKEEPING

Because of the fundamental differences that exist among peacekeeping operations – in mandate, in personnel levels, in authorisation to use force – it is frequently necessary to create categories of operations.[11] Included here is the practice of dividing peacekeeping into generations (first-, second- or third-generation peacekeeping)[12] or categorising operations through reliance on various adjectives signalling (frequently in a very imprecise way) their nature: 'traditional peacekeeping', 'complex peacekeeping', 'new peacekeeping', 'multifunctional peacekeeping', etc. Others reserve the term 'peacekeeping' for certain types of activities only, using other terms – often with the prefix 'peace' – to distinguish peacekeeping from other operations which they consider to be related to maintaining or restoring the peace but of a different character from peacekeeping.[13] Despite the desire of the coiners of such terms to simplify matters, the result has frequently been the opposite: categories overlap, terms are relied upon by different writers to mean different things; in short, confusion abounds.[14] For this reason, to the extent possible, this book will avoid invoking the various categories of peacekeeping – or at least will not do so

[11] An alternative approach is to rely on broad headings such as 'UN peace operations' or 'UN peace-related missions' to include not only peacekeeping (in all its forms) but also 'peace-enforcement', 'peace-making' and 'peace-building'. While this serves to avoid making difficult distinctions between the various forms of peacekeeping, this approach may be unhelpful where, as here, an author needs to distinguish between the functioning of the various operations.

[12] Some authors divide peacekeeping into as many as six generations (see Ramesh Chandra Thakur and Albrecht Schnabel, 'Cascading Generations of Peacekeeping: Across the Mogadishu Line to Kosovo and Timor' in Ramesh Chandra Thakur and Albrecht Schnabel (eds), *United Nations Peacekeeping Operations: Ad Hoc Missions, Permanent Engagement* (Tokyo, United Nations University Press, 2001) 3–25, 9–14.

[13] Included here are the terms 'peace-building', 'peace-enforcement' and 'peace-making'. For a discussion of these terms and their meanings (at the time, at any rate), see United Nations, *An Agenda for Peace: Preventive Diplomacy, Peacemaking and Peace-Keeping* (UN Doc A/47/277-S/24111), 17 June 1992.

[14] For example, the term 'traditional peacekeeping' (referred to by some as 'classic peacekeeping', 'old peacekeeping' or 'first generation peacekeeping') is used by many to refer to operations charged with interposition or monitoring functions and to distinguish such operations from 'non-traditional' peacekeeping operations (sometimes referred to as 'multifunctional peacekeeping', 'multidisciplinary peacekeeping' or 'integrated peacekeeping') where peacekeepers take on more hands-on responsibilities relating to the establishment of a lasting peace. However, the distinction between 'traditional' and 'non-traditional' peacekeeping overlaps to a considerable degree with the distinction between 'first-generation' and 'second-generation' peacekeeping, as well as the distinction between 'peacekeeping' and 'peace-building'. Yet others rely on a distinction between 'traditional peacekeeping' and 'non-traditional peacekeeping' to indicate that only the latter type of operation is authorised to use force beyond self-defence.

without a comprehensive explanation of how the term is being used – and will resist, again, to the extent possible, the temptation to create its own.

Having said that, it remains necessary for the purposes of charting the development of peacekeeping to distinguish between different types of operation. The discussion will consider the following four stages of peacekeeping: (1) peace observation missions, (2) UNEF I-type missions, (3) post-UNEF non-militarised missions, and (4) militarised peacekeeping. In discussing each category, the questions of whether and to what extent the 'fundamental principles' thought to be at the heart of peacekeeping's non-enforcement character have been adhered to will be considered.

2.1 Peace Observation Missions

While it was in the context of UNEF I, established in 1956, that Secretary-General Hammarskjöld set forth the 'fundamental principles' of peacekeeping, the principles were all very much in evidence in the UN's observation-focused peacekeeping operations that began in the late 1940s.[15] Given their limited mandates and the fact that peacekeepers tended to be unarmed, peacekeepers working for observer missions such as the United Nations Yemen Observation Mission (UNYOM) and the United Nations Troop Supervision Operation in the Middle East (UNTSO) had little occasion to consider the parameters of their ability to use force.[16] One early UN official, foreshadowing the Organization's future approach to force in peacekeeping missions, wisely reasoned that the less forceful peacekeepers were, the less likely they were to be targets.[17] Indeed, given the limited size of some early missions, peacekeepers would not have been able to use force even if they had wanted to.[18] Nevertheless, the personnel involved in such operations would have possessed the right to use force in self-defence.[19]

[15] Some do not consider observer missions to be 'true' peacekeeping operations; they regard them merely as antecedents to peacekeeping operations.

[16] Kjell Goldmann, *Peace-Keeping and Self-Defence* (Monograph No 7) (Paris, International Information Centre for Peace-Keeping Operations, 1968) 10.

[17] See Fou-Tchin Liu, *United Nations Peacekeeping and the Non-Use of Force* (Occasional Paper, International Peace Academy) (Boulder, Col, Lynne Rienner Publishers, 1992) 13, referring to a discussion with Ralph J Bunche, Deputy to the United Nations Mediator for Palestine in 1948.

[18] ibid.

[19] Hammarskjöld described the right of self-defence for UN peacekeepers as 'generally accepted' (United Nations, *Summary Study of the Experience Derived from the Establishment and Operation of the Force (Report of the Secretary-General)* (UN Doc A/3943), 9 October 1958, para 179) and 'inherent' (United Nations, *Note [Transmitting the Statement by the President of the Security Council Concerning the Item Entitled 'An Agenda for Peace: Preventive Diplomacy, Peacemaking and Peace-Keeping']* (UN Doc S/25859), 28 May 1993, 1). See also Trevor Findlay, 'The Use of Force by Peacekeepers Beyond Self-Defence: Some Politico-Legal Implications' in Alex Morrison, Douglas A Fraser and James D Kiras (eds), *Peacekeeping with Muscle: The Use of Force in International Conflict Resolution* (Clementsport, Nova Scotia, The Canadian Peacekeeping Press, 1997) 51–76, 73 endnote 5.

During these early operations, the consent principle was strictly observed. For example, the United Nations Special Committee on the Balkans (UNSCOB), a peacekeeping mission[20] that was to take place in Greece, Albania, Bulgaria and Yugoslavia, ultimately only took place in Greece as only that state would authorise its entry; with the exception of a single visit to Bulgaria, the operation did not enter the territory of the other three states.[21] Finally, the non-intrusive and non-military functions undertaken by observer missions meant that the operations were generally impartial – and were generally perceived as such. In short, this early type of peacekeeping mission was significantly different from enforcement.

2.2 UNEF I-Type Missions

With the establishment of the first United Nations Emergency Force in the Suez (UNEF I) by the General Assembly, the model of UN peacekeeping was modified.[22] The operation was given a mandate that was more comprehensive in nature and featured a considerably larger number of troops than the observation-focused operations that had come before it.[23] With the increase in size and functions of peacekeeping operations came the potential for an operation to have a greater impact on the situation in question. Secretary-General Hammarskjöld recognised that UNEF I was of a different nature from observer forces previously established by the UN. He described it as 'paramilitary in character and much more than an observers' corps'.[24] Despite this, he observed that it was to be 'in no

[20] The UN Secretariat took the view that UNSCOB was not peacekeeping (United Nations, *The Blue Helmets: A Review of United Nations Peace-Keeping* (New York, UN Sales No E.85.I.18, 1985). Many experts, however, do consider UNSCOB to be peacekeeping (see eg Rosalyn Higgins, *United Nations Peacekeeping: Documents and Commentary, Vol IV: Europe 1946–1976* (Oxford, Oxford University Press, 1981) 1–75).

[21] Higgins, ibid, 48.

[22] The functioning of the operation is discussed in chapter 4, section 2.

[23] At its maximum strength, UNEF I had 6,073 military personnel, supported by international and local civilian staff (www.un.org/en/peacekeeping/missions/past/unef1facts.html, accessed 1 April 2011). This may be contrasted with the observer mission UNYOM, for example, which at its maximum strength consisted of 189 military personnel supported by international and local staff (www.un.org/en/peacekeeping/missions/past/unyomfacts.html, accessed 1 April 2011).

[24] United Nations, *Second and Final Report of the Secretary-General on the Plan for an Emergency International United Nations Force Requested in Resolution 998 (ES-I), Adopted by the General Assembly on 4 November 1956* (UN Doc A/3302), 6 November 1956, para 12. See also the Secretary-General's 1958 *Summary Study* (n 19) on the experience of UNEF I in which he described that operation as 'paramilitary in character and much more than an observer corps, but . . . in no sense a military force exercising, through force of arms, even temporary control over the territory in which it is stationed; nor does it have military objectives, or military functions exceeding those necessary to secure peaceful conditions on the assumption that the parties to the conflict will take all the necessary steps for compliance with the recommendations of the General Assembly' (para 15).

way a military force temporarily controlling the territory in which it is stationed'.[25]

As noted, it was in the context of this operation that Hammarskjöld set out the 'fundamental principles' of peacekeeping and elaborated the meaning of each. Regarding impartiality, Hammarskjöld observed that the mission must be 'impartial, in the sense that it does not serve as a means to force settlement, in the interests of one party, of political conflicts or legal issues recognized as controversial'.[26] Moreover, he observed that UNEF I 'should not be used to enforce any specific political solution of pending problems or to influence the political balance decisive to such a solution'.[27] As Marrack Goulding, former Under-Secretary-General for Peacekeeping Operations, observed, the principle of impartiality arose from the fact that peacekeeping operations were 'interim arrangements set up, as UNEF [I] had been, without prejudice to the claims and positions of the parties'.[28] Despite this impartiality, he observed:

> Of course, the peacekeepers had to criticize, use pressure, mobilize international support, even in certain circumstances take more forceful action when a party violated agreed arrangements. But, beyond that, they could not take sides. Otherwise they themselves would violate the terms on which the operation had been accepted by the parties. This requirement for absolute impartiality sometimes obliged peacekeepers to maintain normal relations with a party whose behaviour was being censured by most of the international community and thus exposed them to the charge of condoning that behaviour.[29]

As to the use of force, Hammarskjöld observed that UNEF I should not have military functions exceeding those necessary to secure peaceful conditions on the assumption that the parties to the conflict would take all necessary steps to comply with the recommendations of the General Assembly.[30] In a 1958 Summary Study on the experience of UNEF I, Hammarskjöld noted that peacekeeping operations could 'never include combat activity'.[31] He recognised, nonetheless, that '[t]here will always remain, of course, a certain margin of freedom for judgement, as, for example, on the extent and nature of the arming of the units and of their right of self-defence'.[32] He continued:

> A reasonable definition [of when force may be used in self-defence] seems to have been established in the case of [UNEF I], where the rule is applied that

[25] *Second and Final Report* (n 24) para 12.

[26] United Nations, *Report of the Secretary-General on Compliance with General Assembly Resolution 1123 (XI)* (UN Doc A/3512), 24 January 1957, para 5.

[27] *Summary Study* (n 19) para 167.

[28] Marrack Goulding, 'The Evolution of United Nations Peacekeeping' (1993) 69 *International Affairs* 451, 454.

[29] ibid, 454–55.

[30] *Second and Final Report* (n 24) para 12.

[31] *Summary Study* (n 19) para 178.

[32] ibid.

> men engaged in the operation may never take the initiative in the use of armed force, but are entitled to respond with force to an attack with arms, including attempts to use force to make them withdraw from positions which they occupy under orders from the Commander, acting under the authority of the Assembly and within the scope of its resolutions. The basic element involved is clearly the prohibition against any *initiative* in the use of armed force. This definition of the limit between self-defence, as permissible for United Nations elements of the kind discussed, and offensive action, which is beyond the competence of such elements, should be approved for future guidance.[33]

In Hammarskjöld's view, while it should generally be recognised that a right to self-defence for peacekeeping missions exists, the right 'should be exercised only under strictly defined conditions'.[34] He stressed that:

> [A] wide interpretation of the right of self-defence might well blur the distinction between [peacekeeping] operations and combat operations, which would require a decision under Chapter VII of the Charter and an explicit, more far-reaching delegation of authority to the Secretary-General . . .[35]

Hammarskjöld struck a careful balance between an unrealistic, overly-literal conception of self-defence – one limiting the use of force to the defence of the peacekeeper's own person, or 'self' – and an overly-broad conception which would stray into 'offensive' or 'combat' operations. Under his conception of self-defence, a peacekeeper would be permitted to use reasonable force in response to force but never to initiate the use of force; moreover, a peacekeeper must possess a certain amount of discretion to defend more than just him- or herself in some circumstances. Similar approaches, which strike a balance between an overly-narrow approach and an overly-broad one, have been taken at the national level,[36] as well as by the drafters of the Rome Statute of the International Criminal Court.[37] Were the concept

[33] ibid, para 179.

[34] ibid.

[35] *Summary Study* (n 19) para 179.

[36] For example, the California Code provides that homicide is justified when committed 'in defense of habitation, property or person' against someone who endeavours to commit a violent felony or who intends to enter the habitation, in a violent, riotous or tumultuous manner, with a violent purpose (Cal Penal Code, Section 197(2) (West 2007)). Further, homicide is justified where it is relied upon (as a last resort) in defence of the actor's *own person or 'a wife or husband, parent, child, master, mistress, or servant of such person'* (emphasis added) where there are reasonable grounds to believe that a sufficiently serious felony is imminent (ibid, Section 197(3)). The Canadian Code provides that a person is justified in 'using force to defend himself *or any one under his protection* from assault, if he uses no more force than is necessary to prevent the assault or the repetition of it' (emphasis added) (Canadian Criminal Code, RSC 1985, c C-46, section 37(1)).

[37] Art 31(1)(c) of the Rome Statute of the International Criminal Court (adopted 17 July 1998, entered into force 1 July 2002 (2187 UNTS 90)) excludes criminal responsibility if at the time of the conduct '[t]he person acts reasonably to defend himself or herself *or another person* or, in the case of war crimes, property which is essential for the survival of the person or another person or property which is essential for accomplishing a military mission, *against*

to be limited strictly to defence of the 'self' of a peacekeeper who had been subjected to force, their fellow peacekeepers would be required simply to stand by and observe the forceful acts. Moreover, if the 'self' did not extend to the territory on which they operated, peacekeepers would be required to retreat when that territory was overrun by armed 'spoilers'.[38] Such a position would clearly be untenable.

Hammarskjöld linked the need for host state consent with the fact that UNEF I was not an enforcement force, noting that '[t]he use of military force by the United Nations other than that under Chapter VII of the Charter requires the consent of the States in which the force is to operate'.[39] He stressed that UNEF I would be stationed on Egyptian territory with that country's agreement as 'required under generally recognized international law'.[40] UNEF I, he observed, 'obviously should have no rights other than those necessary for the execution of its functions, in *co-operation with local authorities*'.[41] The importance of state consent was illustrated by the fact that UNEF I was located only on the territory of Egypt because Israel had not consented to the stationing of troops on its side of the armistice line.[42] Moreover, the essential nature of host state consent to the stationing and functioning of a peacekeeping operation established by the General Assembly was confirmed when UNEF I left the country in 1967, when consent to its presence there was revoked by the Egyptian government.[43]

Hammarskjöld saw UNEF I, an operation possessed of the 'fundamental principles' of peacekeeping, as 'other than' an enforcement operation. It was, he stressed, 'not established to undertake enforcement actions. While [UNEF I] has a military organization, it does not use all normal

an imminent and unlawful use of force in a manner proportionate to the degree of danger to the person or the other person or property protected' (emphasis added). Cf Cassese, who observed that '[t]he notion of self-defence as a ground for excusing criminal responsibility laid down in this provision seems to be excessively broad and at variance with existing international criminal law' (Antonio (indexed as 'a Caesius') Cassese, 'The Statute of the International Criminal Court: Some Preliminary Reflections' (1999) 10(1) *European Journal of International Law* 144, 154).

[38] 'Spoilers' are defined in the Brahimi Report as groups (including signatories to peace agreements) who renege on their commitments or otherwise seek to undermine a peace accord by violence (United Nations, *Identical Letters Dated 21 August 2000 from the Secretary-General to the President of the General Assembly and the President of the Security Council [Attaching Report of the Panel on UN Peacekeeping Operations* (UN Docs A/55/305 and S/2000/809), 21 August 2000, para 21).

[39] Report of the Secretary-General on Compliance (n 26).

[40] *Summary Study* (n 19) para 15.

[41] *Second and Final Report* (n 24) para 12 (emphasis added).

[42] Alexander Orakhelashvili, 'The Legal Basis of the United Nations Peace-Keeping Operations' (2003) 43 *Virginia Journal of International Law* 485, 521.

[43] See United Nations, *Report of the Secretary-General on the Withdrawal of the Emergency Force* (UN Doc A/6730/Add.3), 26 June 1967, para 32, as reproduced in Rosalyn Higgins, *United Nations Peacekeeping 1946–1967: Documents and Commentary, Vol I: The Middle East* (Oxford University Press, 1969) 344–62.

military methods in achieving the objectives defined for it by the General Assembly.'[44]

2.3 Post-UNEF I Non-Militarised Missions

Having traced the elaboration of the three 'fundamental principles' to UNEF I, it is important to underline that Hammarskjöld's emphasis on the non-enforcement nature of peacekeeping emerged in relation to an operation that was established by the General Assembly and not, as all subsequent peacekeeping operations but one would be, by the Security Council.[45] It was essential that UNEF I should not be of an enforcement nature lest it be *ultra vires* the General Assembly's powers. What, then, is the significance of the 'fundamental principles' where it is the Security Council that establishes a peacekeeping operation? And what is their significance if the Security Council establishes such a peacekeeping operation as an enforcement measure under Chapter VII?[46]

In his careful consideration of UNEF I, Hammarskjöld appeared to recognise that where a peacekeeping operation was established by the Security Council, the rules were potentially different. In support of his view that force could only be used in self-defence (and only where that concept was reasonably defined) he observed:

> [A] wide interpretation of the right of self-defence might well blur the distinction between operations [in the nature of UNEF I] and combat operations, which

[44] United Nations, *Report of the Secretary-General* (UN Doc A/3694 and Add.1), 9 October 1957, para 31. cf an earlier report, where the Secretary-General described the 'primary duty' of UNEF I as being 'to supervise and *enforce* the cease-fire to which the parties committed themselves in response to the request of the General Assembly in the resolution of 2 November' (United Nations, *Report of the Secretary-General on Compliance with General Assembly Resolution 1123 (XI)* (UN Doc A/3500), 15 January 1957, emphasis added).

[45] In the early history of the UN, when Cold War tensions meant that the Security Council was at times unable to act, the General Assembly was involved in the establishment of three UN peacekeeping operations. First, the United Nations Special Commission in the Balkans (UNSCOB) was established by the General Assembly after the situation was removed from the Agenda of the Security Council and transferred to the General Assembly in September 1947 as a result of a veto in the Security Council by the USSR. Second, the United Nations Emergency Force in the Suez (UNEF I) was established by the General Assembly after vetoes (this time by the British and the French) prevented the matter from being dealt with in the Security Council. Finally, the United Nations Security Force in West New Guinea/West Irian (UNTEA/UNSF) was established by the General Assembly in September 1962. This last situation, unlike the other two mentioned, went directly to the General Assembly. Since 1962, however, the General Assembly has not created a single peacekeeping operation. While there is nothing in law preventing the General Assembly from doing so again, in practical terms it is highly unlikely and the role of the General Assembly in this regard will be treated as being of historical interest only. For an excellent discussion of the constitutional basis of the General Assembly's role in peacekeeping, see Nigel D White, *The United Nations and the Maintenance of International Peace and Security* (Manchester, Manchester University Press, 1990) chs 3–6.

[46] This question is explored in depth in chapter 3, section 3.2 and in chapters 4–6.

> would require a decision under Chapter VII of the Charter and an explicit, more far-reaching delegation of authority to the Secretary-General.[47]

Similarly, after making it clear that consent was a prerequisite to the General Assembly stationing UNEF I in Egypt, he recognised that such consent would not be required if the Security Council were to establish such an operation under Chapter VII:

> [T]he General Assembly . . . could not request the Force to be stationed or operate on the territory of a given country without the consent of the Government of that country. This does not exclude the possibility that the Security Council could use such a Force within the wider margins provided under Chapter VII of the United Nations Charter. I would not for the present consider it necessary to elaborate this point further, since no use of the Force under Chapter VII . . . has been envisaged.[48]

As Bowett observed, this remark by the Secretary-General 'must be taken to mean that consent would not be necessary were the Security Council taking enforcement measures'.[49]

While the Secretary-General's remark was, at the time, an academic one, this was to change four years later with the establishment of the United Nations' next peacekeeping operation, the UN mission in the newly independent Congo, known by its French acronym, ONUC (l'Organisation des Nations Unis au Congo). This operation may be categorised as 'militarised peacekeeping' and will be dealt with in the next section of this chapter.[50] If the 'fundamental principles' of force only in self-defence, impartiality and host state consent in peacekeeping operations were the legacies of UNEF I, they were ignored or at least seriously strained with ONUC, leading to considerable speculation that the operation amounted to an enforcement measure under Chapter VII.[51]

It is perhaps because ONUC was something of a 'one-off' in terms of its disregard for the 'fundamental principles' that commentators continued to view Hammarskjöld's principles as setting out limitations on peacekeeping operations established subsequent to ONUC, even when established by the Security Council. The peacekeeping operations established after ONUC (up until the forceful operations established in the early 1990s) were not as forceful in nature as ONUC; however, they were not

[47] *Summary Study* (n 19) para 178.

[48] *Second and Final Report* (n 24) para 9. This Report was approved by the General Assembly without opposition (GA Res 1001 (ES-I) of 7 November 1956) and the paragraph was cited with approval by the ICJ in *Certain Expenses of the United Nations (Article 17, Paragraph 2, of the Charter), Advisory Opinion of 20 July 1962* [1962] ICJ Rep 151, 170–71.

[49] Derek W Bowett, *United Nations Forces: A Legal Study of United Nations Practice* (London, Stevens & Sons, 1964) 416.

[50] See section 2.4 below.

[51] For a discussion of whether ONUC amounted to an enforcement action against a state, see discussion of the operation in chapter 4, section 3.

as reluctant to use force as UNEF I had been. Hammarskjöld's restrictive approach to the use of force, elaborated in the context of UNEF I – namely, a peacekeeping mission (1) must not initiate the use of armed force and (2) must only use force in response to an attack with arms, including attempts to make peacekeepers withdraw from their positions – was not to be revived after UNEF I. Instead, the UN adopted an approach to the definition of self-defence that included defence-of-mandate: the right of a peacekeeping operation to use force in 'self-defence' was said to extend to situations where the mandate of the mission was being interfered with.

In early 1964, as ONUC was winding down, the United Nations Force in Cyprus (UNFICYP) was just getting under way.[52] At the insistence of troop-contributing states,[53] Secretary-General U Thant expanded the concept of self-defence for the mission. He observed:

> The expression self-defence includes the defence of the United Nations posts, premises and vehicles under armed attack, as well as support of other personnel of UNFICYP under armed attack. When acting in self-defence the principle of minimum force shall always be applied and armed force will only be used when all means of persuasion have failed. The decision as to when force is to be used rests with the Commander on the spot. Examples in which troops may be authorized to use force include attempts by force to compel them to withdraw from a position which they occupy under orders from their commanders, attempts by force to disarm them, and attempts by force to prevent them from carrying out their responsibilities as ordered by their commanders.[54]

Thant's concept of self-defence – clearly considerably broader than that set out by Hammarskjöld in relation to UNEF I – was invoked in relation to the establishment of UNEF II, which was established in 1973 to supervise the ceasefire between Egyptian and Israeli forces. Secretary-General Kurt Waldheim, in his report to the Security Council,[55] described a force that 'will be provided with weapons of a defensive character only. It shall not use force except in self-defence.'[56] He went on, however, to define self-defence as including 'resistance to attempts by forceful means to prevent [UNEF II] from discharging its duties under the mandate of the Security Council'.[57] In a resolution passed the same day, the Security Council approved this report.[58] According to the DPKO, an understand-

[52] SC Res 186 of 4 March 1964.

[53] Indar Jit Rikhye, 'The Use of Force in International Conflict Resolution' in Morrison et al (n 19) 19.

[54] United Nations, *Report by Secretary-General U Thant on the Deployment of UN Forces in Cyprus* (UN Doc S/5960), 10 September 1964.

[55] United Nations, *Report of the Secretary-General on the Implementation of Security Council Resolution 340 (1973)* (UN Doc S/11052/Rev.1), 27 October 1973.

[56] ibid, para 4(d).

[57] ibid.

[58] SC Res 341 of 27 October 1973.

ing that self-defence includes defence-of-mandate has existed in relation to all peacekeeping forces since 1973.[59]

Waldheim used similar language in his report calling for the establishment of the United Nations Interim Force in Lebanon (UNIFIL) in 1978.[60] In addition to adopting Waldheim's report[61] – and thereby his inclusion of defence-of-mandate within the concept of self-defence – the Security Council went one step further. With UNIFIL, the Security Council, for the first time,[62] specifically included defence-of-mandate as part of its definition of self-defence in a resolution. It 'recalled' that 'self-defence would include resistance to attempts by forceful means to prevent it from discharging its duties under the mandate of the Security Council'.[63] Thus, the UN's conception of self-defence as including defence-of-mandate became even more firmly entrenched.

Widening the definition of self-defence to include forceful actions to defend the mandate in effect authorises virtually any use of force, so long as an operation's mandate is sufficiently ambiguous or general in nature – as is frequently the case. For example, the Security Council mandated UNEF II to supervise its demand that a ceasefire be observed and to prevent a recurrence of the fighting.[64] Similarly, it mandated UNFICYP to 'use its best efforts to prevent a recurrence of fighting and, as necessary, to contribute to the maintenance and restoration of law and order and a return to normal conditions'.[65] Under a conception of self-defence that includes defence-of-mandate, any forceful action that would serve to achieve these very broad goals could be classed as self-defence – including, presumably, forceful disarmament or military engagement with any faction whose conduct was judged likely to reignite the conflict. Moreover, there would appear to be nothing to limit such force to action against spoilers or to prohibit its use against the government of the host state. In the words of White: 'Allowing a force to take positive action in defence of its purposes is no different from allowing it to enforce them.'[66]

Despite these post-UNEF I, non-militarised operations possessing a broad authority to use force, commanders in the field have tended to do so only very rarely. The UN's changed approach to the definition of self-defence 'did not in practice lead to a general pattern of more

[59] United Nations, *General Guidelines for Peacekeeping Operations* (United Nations (DPKO) (UN/210/TC/GG95)), on file with author, para 35.

[60] See United Nations, *Report of the Secretary-General on the Implementation of Security Council Resolution 425 (1978)* (UN Doc S/12611), 19 March 1978, para 4(d).

[61] SC Res 425 and SC Res 426, both adopted 19 March 1978.

[62] Christine Gray, *International Law and the Use of Force*, 3rd edn (Oxford, Oxford University Press, 2008) 303.

[63] SC Res 467 of 24 April 1980.

[64] SC Res 341 of 27 October 1973, endorsing *Report of the Secretary-General* (n 55).

[65] SC Res 186 of 4 March 1964, para 5.

[66] White (n 45) 201.

forceful response when UN forces were hampered by armed groups from performing their duties; nor did it lead to a general pattern of [increased] troop deployments and armament levels'.[67] Former Under-Secretary-General Goulding attributed peacekeepers' reluctance to use force to

> sound calculations related to impartiality, to their reliance on the continued cooperation of the parties and to the fact that their force's level of armament was based on the assumption that the parties would comply with their commitments. The peacekeepers could perhaps win the firefight at that first roadblock. But in the lands of the vendetta, might they not find themselves out-gunned in the third or fourth encounter?[68]

In addition, commanders would presumably have been aware that if they required their forces to engage in combat and significant casualties resulted, this would contribute to the possibility that states volunteering troops might withdraw them. So, while UNIFIL, for example, has a broad mandate (in that case to restore international peace and security and assist 'the Government of Lebanon in ensuring the return of its effective authority in the area'),[69] it refrained from using force to deploy in the area controlled by the Palestine Liberation Organization. As Murphy observed, the involvement of UNIFIL in functions and duties related to the maintenance of internal law and order 'could have had serious repercussions on the impartiality of the force by involving it in the internal conflict taking place alongside the international crisis caused by the Israeli invasion'.[70]

In short, depending on the nature of the mandate, a concept of self-defence that includes defence-of-mandate may denude the 'fundamental principle' of force only in self-defence of much of its meaning. Moreover, if this expanded authority to use force were exercised, the 'fundamental principle' of impartiality could be severely undermined. This expansion by the UN of its conception of self-defence to include defence-of-mandate is something of a sleight of hand: it allows the Security Council and the Secretariat to continue to emphasise that peacekeepers must adhere to the 'fundamental principle' of force only in self-defence – with the attendant suggestion of non-violence so highly valued by host states and troop-contributing states alike – while, at the same time, allowing 'the Security Council to give almost any task, however ill thought out or unrealistic, to a peacekeeping force, in the expectation that it could use force under the

[67] Adam Roberts, 'From San Francisco to Sarajevo: The UN and the Use of Force' (1995–96) 37(4) *Survival* 7, 14. See also Goulding (n 28), who noted that it was rare for peacekeepers 'to open fire on, for instance, soldiers at a roadblock who were denying passage to a United Nations convoy' (455); Ray Murphy, 'United Nations Peacekeeping in Lebanon and Somalia, and the Use of Force' (2003) 8(1) *Journal of Conflict and Security Law* 71, 83.

[68] Goulding (n 28) 455.

[69] SC Res 425 of 19 March 1978, para 3.

[70] Murphy (n 67) 84.

guise of self-defence and still retain its peacekeeping status'.[71] In practice, because force commanders were aware of the high cost of actually using offensive force to defend the mandate they very rarely did so.

2.4 Militarised Peacekeeping

In the history of UN peacekeeping there have been only three periods in which the UN has felt it necessary or appropriate to vest significant military force in peacekeeping operations, thereby departing from some or all of its 'fundamental principles'. After the first two occasions – with ONUC in 1960 and with two operations in the early 1990s – it moved swiftly back to a less militarised form of peacekeeping, with a renewed emphasis on the 'fundamental principles'. The third occasion began at around the turn of the century and continues today.

With such operations now firmly a part of the peacekeeping landscape, it has become necessary to distinguish them from peacekeeping operations that are not possessed of an authorisation under Chapter VII to use considerable force beyond self-defence. As a result, a number of terms have developed. The term 'Chapter VII peacekeeping' is frequently used, as the Security Council tends to – though does not always – invoke that Chapter in establishing such operations.[72] However, the term can be misleading, given that the establishment of a peacekeeping operation under Chapter VII is not, in and of itself, an indication that the operation is vested with the authority to use considerable military force.[73] Some commentators have relied on the terms 'multifunctional' peacekeeping and 'second-generation' (or, for others, 'third-generation') peacekeeping to signal an operation's forcefulness; however, as noted, there is little uniformity of use of these terms.[74]

This book will use the term 'militarised peacekeeping' to refer to an operation which is established or has some of its tasks established by the Security Council by means of an invocation of Chapter VII (express or implied) and which is authorised to use force beyond self-defence for at least some of its mandated tasks.[75]

[71] See Murphy, ibid, 72.

[72] In the context of ONUC there was no such explicit invocation of Chapter VII; however, there was an invocation of articles of the UN Charter contained in that Chapter and it is generally accepted to have been a Chapter VII measure. For a detailed discussion of the constitutional basis of ONUC see chapter 4, section 3.2.2.

[73] See discussion on this point in chapter 3, section 3.2.

[74] For example, some use the term 'multifunctional peacekeeping' to connote an operation with functions which are non-forceful in nature but which are broader in nature than those traditionally bestowed upon peacekeeping operations.

[75] Other terms in use that suggest a strengthened ability to use force include 'muscular peacekeeping' and 'robust peacekeeping'.

2.4.1 ONUC (1960–64)

In early July 1960, in the aftermath of its hasty transition to independence, disturbances broke out in the former Belgian Congo, resulting in attacks against Belgian nationals remaining there.[76] Belgium responded by sending in troops against the wishes of the Congolese Central Government. ONUC was established in the summer of 1960 as a peacekeeping operation in the image of UNEF I. Its initial mandate was for a force that would be impartial, would operate with the consent of the host state, and would use force only in self-defence. However, as the situation in the country deteriorated, the organ that established the operation – this time the Security Council, rather than the General Assembly which had established UNEF I – began to stray from the 'fundamental principles' such that ONUC ultimately 'became, through accident and design, involved in military operations that differed little from standard warfare'.[77]

ONUC, which is discussed in detail in chapter 4, was a highly controversial operation. The United Nations, which had planned for a peacekeeping force, found itself supervising what was, in effect, an enforcement force. The operation led to the death of over 100 peacekeepers and the wounding of over 100 more.[78] Moreover, the operation was extremely expensive, and this at a time when certain states were refusing to contribute to peacekeeping expenses.[79] That this operation might represent a new model of peacekeeping appears not to have been entertained.[80] Indeed, there was an unwillingness on the part of UN officials to even admit that force beyond self-defence had been used.[81] Instead, ONUC served as something of a cautionary tale, illustrating the perils associated with departing from the 'fundamental principles' of peacekeeping.

[76] See, generally, Georges Abi-Saab, *The United Nations Operation in the Congo 1960–1964* (Oxford, Oxford University Press, 1978). See also Trevor Findlay, *The Blue Helmets' First War? Use of Force by the UN in the Congo 1960–1964* (Clementsport, Nova Scotia, Canadian Peacekeeping Press, 1999).

[77] Trevor Findlay, *The Use of Force in UN Peace Operations* (Oxford, Oxford University Press for the Stockholm International Peace Research Institute (SIPRI), 2002) 83.

[78] ibid, 81–82.

[79] Rosalyn Higgins, *United Nations Peacekeeping 1946–1967: Documents and Commentary, Vol III: Africa* (Oxford, Oxford University Press, 1980) 274 ff.

[80] Without the unique set of circumstances surrounding ONUC – 'the interest of the major powers, the isolated location of the civil strife away from strategic areas of the superpowers' major interests, and the presence of one of the few issues, colonialism, upon which all but a handful of states agree' – the operation would not have been possible. Edwin Brown Firmage, 'Summary and Interpretation' in Richard A Falk (ed), *The International Law of Civil War* (Baltimore, Johns Hopkins University Press, 1971) 405–28, 422.

[81] Simon Chesterman, 'The Use of Force in UN Peace Operations', August 2004, http://pbpu.unlb.org/pbps/Library/Chesterman%20External%20Paper%20(31-08-2004).pdf) (accessed 1 April 2011), 8.

2.4.2 *An Agenda for Peace (1992–95)*

In the years immediately preceding Boutros Boutros-Ghali's appointment as Secretary-General, two events occurred which impacted significantly on UN peacekeeping.[82] The first was the end of the Cold War in the late 1980s. For almost the first time in its history, East-West rivalries (and the overuse of the veto that accompanied them) were not constantly interfering with the functioning of the Security Council. Second, and related, was the success of Operation Desert Storm in Iraq/Kuwait, an enforcement operation established by a newly-cooperative Security Council.[83] The Security Council's willingness to authorise an enforcement action in the face of aggression against Kuwait raised a spectre of hope that that organ would finally become the powerful, authoritative body that the drafters of the Charter had intended. In the aftermath of these events came 'what was perhaps the apogee of expectations for peacekeeping'.[84]

In one of his first tasks after taking up the Secretary-Generalship, Boutros-Ghali was requested by the Security Council (sitting for the first time at the Head of State or Head of Government level) to set forth his ideas on ways of strengthening and making more efficient peacekeeping and related activities.[85] The report that emerged, entitled *An Agenda for Peace*,[86] revealed the new Secretary-General's desire to engage in fresh thinking with regard to peacekeeping operations, including a willingness to challenge the 'fundamental principles'. In *An Agenda for Peace*, Boutros-Ghali attempted to clarify the concept of peacekeeping by distinguishing it from various related concepts, such as preventive diplomacy, peace-making and peace-building.[87] He proposed the use, if necessary, of peace-enforcement forces – a category of 'peace-making' featuring forces that were more heavily armed than peacekeeping forces.[88] Significantly, the Report provided the following, revised definition of peacekeeping:

> Peace-keeping is the deployment of a United Nations presence in the field, hitherto with the consent of all the parties concerned, normally involving United Nations military and/or police personnel and frequently civilians as well. Peace-keeping is a technique that expands the possibilities for both the prevention of conflict and the making of peace.[89]

[82] A third event may have also had an impact: in 1988 the United Nations was awarded a Nobel Peace Prize for its peacekeeping activities.

[83] For a discussion of the establishment of this operation, see below at nn 155–58 and accompanying text.

[84] Dennis C Jett, *Why Peacekeeping Fails* (New York, St Martin's Press, 1999) 3.

[85] United Nations, *Note by the President of the Security Council* (UN Doc S/23500), 31 January 1992, para 3.

[86] *An Agenda for Peace* (n 13).

[87] Boutros-Ghali characterised preventive diplomacy as a means to avoid a crisis and post-conflict peace-building as a means to 'prevent a recurrence' of the crisis (ibid, para 57).

[88] ibid, para 44.

[89] ibid, para 20.

An Agenda for Peace impacted on the 'fundamental principles' of peacekeeping in two important ways.[90] First, the insertion into the definition of the word 'hitherto' before the words 'with the consent of all the parties concerned' carried with it the implication that Boutros-Ghali did not necessarily consider host state consent to be an essential part of peacekeeping of the future. Second, he took the view that peacekeeping and peacemaking (including peace-enforcement) were 'mutually reinforcing'[91] and that there may be no 'dividing line' between them.[92] This left the impression that he considered the principle that peacekeepers must use force only in self-defence and the principle of impartiality to be somewhat outdated. In the words of Higgins, *An Agenda for Peace* opened the way to 'an enforcement element *within* peacekeeping operations – thus setting aside the long-standing distinction between enforcement and peace-keeping'.[93]

In the early years of Boutros-Ghali's five-year term, this new vision of peacekeeping was relied upon in peacekeeping operations established in the former Yugoslavia and Somalia.[94] Each operation was militarised, severely testing the 'fundamental principles' of peacekeeping. As with ONUC, each militarised operation began as non-militarised peacekeeping (or had a predecessor that did), only to encounter violent conditions on the ground, leading the Security Council to modify the mandates of the operations such that they became de facto enforcement operations. As we shall see in chapter 4, these two peacekeeping operations proved to be extremely problematic and in some respects seriously damaged the reputation of the UN. The lesson to emerge from the operations was that militarised peacekeeping did not work.

In January 1995, Boutros-Ghali produced *Supplement to An Agenda for Peace*, in which he reversed his position to a considerable degree.[95] First, he emphasised the importance of the 'fundamental principle' of consent: peacekeeping 'can be employed only with the consent of the parties to the conflict . . . Sanctions and enforcement, on the other hand, are coercive measures and thus, by definition, do not require the consent of the party concerned.'[96] Second, he moved away from his earlier willingness to blur the concepts of peacekeeping and enforcement, positing that

[90] For an extremely helpful discussion of the impact of *An Agenda for Peace* on the use of force in peacekeeping, see Rosalyn Higgins, 'Peace and Security: Achievements and Failures' (1995) 6 *European Journal of International Law* 445–60.

[91] *An Agenda for Peace* (n 13) para 3; see also para 21.

[92] ibid, para 45.

[93] Higgins (n 90) 450.

[94] The operations will be considered in detail in chapter 4 below.

[95] United Nations, *Supplement to An Agenda for Peace: Position Paper of the Secretary-General on the Occasion of the Fiftieth Anniversary of the United Nations* (UN Doc A/50/60-S/1995/1), 3 January 1995. While Boutros-Ghali asserted that he was not retreating from his position in *An Agenda for Peace*, arguing that '[m]ost of the ideas in "An Agenda for Peace" have proved themselves' (para 6), it is clear that his concept of peacekeeping changed considerably.

[96] See para 23 of *Supplement to An Agenda for Peace* (ibid).

'[p]eace-keeping and the use of force (other than in self-defence) should be seen as alternative techniques and not as adjacent points on a spectrum, permitting easy transition from one to the other'.[97] He observed:

> Three particularly important principles are the consent of the parties, impartiality and the non-use of force except in self-defence. Analysis of recent successes and failures shows that in all the successes those principles were respected and in most of the less successful operations one or other of them was not . . . There are three aspects of recent mandates that, in particular, have led peace-keeping operations to forfeit the consent of the parties, to behave in a way that was perceived to be partial and/or to use force other than in self-defence. These have been the tasks of protecting humanitarian operations during continuing warfare, protecting civilian populations in designated safe areas and pressing the parties to achieve national reconciliation at a pace faster than they were ready to accept. The cases of Somalia and Bosnia and Herzegovina are instructive in this respect. In both cases, existing peace-keeping operations were given additional mandates that required the use of force and therefore could not be combined with existing mandates requiring the consent of the parties, impartiality and the non-use of force. It was also not possible for them to be executed without much stronger military capabilities than had been made available . . . *[N]othing is more dangerous for a peace-keeping operation than to ask it to use force when its existing composition, armament, logistic support and deployment deny it the capacity to do so.* The logic of peace-keeping flows from political and military premises that are quite distinct from those of enforcement; and the dynamics of the latter are incompatible with the political process that peace-keeping is intended to facilitate. To blur the distinction between the two can undermine the viability of the peace-keeping operation and endanger its personnel (emphasis added).[98]

In short, Boutros-Ghali recognised that the UN's experiment with militarised peacekeeping had been a failure, due to the move away from the 'fundamental principles' of peacekeeping and the UN's lack of military capability.

UN peacekeeping emerged from this, its second forceful period, in something of a crisis.[99] Much like the introspectiveness that came about after ONUC in the Congo, much soul-searching took place within the Organization as a result of the problems with the missions in the early

[97] ibid, para 36. At para 33 he stressed the importance of force being used only in self-defence if a peacekeeping mission was to be successful. See also the introduction by Boutros-Ghali in United Nations, *The Blue Helmets: A Review of United Nations Peace-Keeping*, 3rd edn (New York, UN Sales No E.96.I.14, 1996) 6.

[98] *Supplement to an Agenda for Peace* (n 95) paras 33–35.

[99] Writing in 1995, Tharoor noted that '[p]eace-keeping today is . . . in flux, if not in crisis' (Shashi Tharoor, 'The Changing Face of Peace-Keeping and Peace-Enforcement' (1995–96) 19 *Fordham International Law Journal* 408, 426). Another observer spoke of the 'death of peacekeeping' during this period, and noted that when the Under-Secretary-General for Peacekeeping, Bernard Miyet, was appointed in 1997, 'many people called him the "commissioner of liquidation" of UN peacekeeping' (A Williams, *The United Nations and Peace Operations* in Dean Rusk Lectures at the Dean Rusk Center, University of Georgia School of Law, 2003, 24 at 29).

1990s. A clear sense that militarised peacekeeping could not succeed was evident not just from the writings of the Secretary-General, but from the documentation and guidance prepared by the Secretariat at the time.[100] A Commission of Inquiry established to consider the attacks against UNOSOM II[101] made its view plain when it recommended that the UN 'refrain from undertaking further peace-enforcement actions within the internal conflicts of states'.[102] The conclusion that peacekeeping operations should not be vested with enforcement-type powers was almost universally endorsed by UN scholars.[103] As noted by Chesterman, the operations in Somalia and the former Yugoslavia 'confirmed the emerging view that forces under UN command were unsuited to war-fighting'.[104]

2.4.3 *Twenty-First Century Peacekeeping (October 1999–Present)*

In 1997 Kofi Annan became Secretary-General of the UN. By October 1999, with Annan beginning his third year in office, a change had occurred in peacekeeping practice such that peacekeeping operations were, once again, becoming militarised. From October 1999 up to the time of writing, the Security Council has authorised the use of force beyond self-defence in nine of the 10 countries or regions in which it has established peacekeeping operations, in relation to some or all of their tasks.[105] A variety of

[100] See eg *General Guidelines for Peacekeeping Operations* (n 59); *The Blue Helmets* (n 97); and DPKO's *1997 Peacekeeping Training Manual*, 2nd edn (New York, United Nations), as referred to in Findlay (n 77) 323–26.

[101] United Nations, *Note by Secretary-General, Appendix: Report of the Commission of Inquiry Established Pursuant to Security Council Resolution 885 (1993) to Investigate Armed Attacks on UNOSOM II Personnel which Led to Casualties Among Them* (UN Doc S/1994/653), 1 June 1994.

[102] ibid, 48. See also Gray (n 62) 302, who observed a trend in at least one Member State (see the US President's Decision Directive on Reforming Multilateral Peace Operations (1994) 33 *ILM* 795) as well as in some regional organisations such as the Commission on Security and Cooperation in Europe (CSCE, (1992) 31 *ILM* 1385) or the Commonwealth of Independent States (CIS, (1996) 35 *ILM* 738), of adhering to a more traditional concept of peacekeeping whereby force is not used except in self-defence.

[103] See eg Higgins (n 90) 449. See also Gray (n 62) 302; Findlay (n 77) 315; Tharoor (n 99) 408; Yasushi Akashi, 'The Use of Force in a United Nations Peace-Keeping Operation: Lessons Learnt from the Safe Areas Mandate' (1995–96) 19 *Fordham International Law Journal* 312, 320; Chesterman (n 81) 9.

[104] Chesterman (n 81) 9.

[105] The 10 countries or regions and 14 the associated peacekeeping missions are: (1) Sierra Leone (United Nations Mission in Sierra Leone (UNAMSIL), Oct 1999–Dec 2005); (2) East Timor (United Nations Transitional Administration in East Timor (UNTAET), Oct 1999–May 2002, United Nations Mission of Support in East Timor (UNMISET), May 2002–May 2005, and United Nations Integrated Mission in Timor Leste (UNMIT) Aug 2006–present); (3) Democratic Republic of the Congo (United Nations Organization Mission in the Democratic Republic of the Congo (MONUC), Nov 1999–Jun 2010, and United Nations Organization Stabilisation Mission in the Democratic Republic of the Congo (MONUSCO), Jul 2010–present); (4) Ethiopia and Eritrea (United Nations Mission in Ethiopia and Eritrea (UNMEE), Jul 2000–Jul 2008); (5) Liberia (United Nations Mission in Liberia (UNMIL), Sep 2003–present); (6) Côte d'Ivoire (United Nations Operation in Cote d'Ivoire (UNOCI), Apr 2004–present); (7) Haiti (United Nations Stabilization Mission in Haiti (MINUSTAH), Apr 2004–present);

factors in the late 1990s would appear to have influenced the UN's move towards an increased use of force in peacekeeping missions. They are interlinked and, for the most part, tend to reflect the influence of Secretary-General Annan who, affected perhaps by a sense of remorse relating to his involvement in the UN's management of events in Srebrenica and Rwanda,[106] appeared to favour the view that there was nothing inherently wrong in vesting peacekeeping missions with enforcement powers, so long as the level of force authorised was such that operations could succeed in their militarised operations.[107]

First, in late 1999, two highly critical reports detailing the UN's failures in Srebrenica[108] and Rwanda[109] were issued within a month of each other, bringing the role of UN peacekeeping into the spotlight. As will be discussed in detail in chapter 4, each operation featured a massive loss of life which the peacekeeping force present on the ground had done little to prevent. A second event that may have influenced the Organization's view that there was considerable scope for increased forcefulness in peacekeeping was the bombing campaign in Kosovo that took place between March and June of 1999. The campaign was undertaken by NATO, *without* the authorisation of the Security Council, to protect the humanitarian interests of the ethnic Albanian population there. The Security Council's inability to reach agreement on a forceful action authorisation graphically illustrated the limitations on its ability to protect vulnerable people and

(8) Burundi (United Nations Operation in Burundi (ONUB), May 2004–Dec 2006); (9) Sudan (United Nations Mission in the Sudan (UNMIS), Mar 2005–present, and African Union/ United Nations Hybrid Mission in Darfur (UNAMID), Jul 2007–present); (10) Central African Republic and Chad (United Nations Mission in Central African Republic and Chad (MINURCAT), Sep 2007–31 Dec 2010). Only with UNMEE did the Security Council not rely on Chapter VII at any stage of the operation.

[106] Annan had been Assistant Secretary-General for Peacekeeping Operations from March 1992 to February 1993 and Under-Secretary-General from March 1993 to December 1996 before becoming Secretary-General in January 1997. As noted by Findlay, Annan's view of the UN's obligations in the sphere of peacekeeping was more expansive than that of any previous Secretary-General. Findlay observed that the most telling factor in this regard 'seems to have been the fact that as Under Secretary-General for Peacekeeping Operations he was partly responsible for the Bosnia and Rwanda tragedies which, in his view, had so tarnished the UN's credibility and moral standing' (Findlay (n 77) 236).

[107] For a detailed discussion of the events leading up to the resumption of militarised peacekeeping, see James Sloan, 'UN Peacekeeping under Kofi Annan: Recourse to Force' (2007) 12 *Yearbook of International Peace Operations* 51.

[108] In GA Res of 30 November 1998, the General Assembly requested that the Secretary-General prepare a comprehensive report on the events relating to the safe area in Srebrenica. Annan considered this to be 'an opportunity to explain why the United Nations failed to deter the Serb attack on Srebrenica and the appalling events that followed' (United Nations, *Report of the Secretary-General Pursuant to General Assembly Resolution 53/35: The Fall of Srebrenica* (UN Doc A/54/549), 15 November 1999, para 3).

[109] United Nations, *Letter Dated 15 December 1999 from the Secretary-General Addressed to the President of the Security Council [Enclosing the 'Report of the Independent Inquiry into the Actions of the United Nations During the 1994 Genocide in Rwanda', 15 December 1999]* (UN Doc S/1999/1257), 16 December 1999.

led the Secretary-General to seek alternative methods of protection.[110] It was shortly after this intervention that an International Commission on Intervention and State Sovereignty was established by Annan. It produced the influential report, *The Responsibility to Protect*,[111] a central theme of which was that 'sovereign states have a responsibility to protect their own citizens from avoidable catastrophe, but . . . when they are unwilling or unable to do so, that responsibility must be borne by the broader community of states'.[112] A third factor – closely related to the second – which contributed to the UN's change in attitude regarding militarised peacekeeping was the UN's emerging focus on the protection of civilians in armed conflicts in the late 1990s. In 1999 the Security Council expressed its 'willingness to consider how peacekeeping mandates might better address the negative impact of armed conflict on civilians'.[113] Subsequently, the Security Council affirmed

> its intention to ensure, where appropriate and feasible, that peacekeeping missions are given suitable mandates and adequate resources to protect civilians under imminent threat of physical danger, including by strengthening the ability of the United Nations to plan and rapidly deploy peacekeeping personnel, civilian police, civil administrators, and humanitarian personnel, utilizing the stand-by arrangements as appropriate.[114]

[110] William J Durch et al, *The Brahimi Report and the Future of UN Peace Operations* (Washington, DC, Henry L Stimson Center, 2003), www.stimson.org/fopo/pubs.cfm?ID=90 (accessed 1 April 2011), 22.

[111] See United Nations, *The Responsibility to Protect*, www.iciss.ca/report-en.asp accessed 1 April 2011). See, generally, Susan C Breau, 'The Impact of *The Responsibility to Protect* on Peacekeeping' (2006) 11(3) *Journal of Conflict and Security Law* 429; Christine Gray, 'A Crisis of Legitimacy for the UN Collective Security System?' (2007) 56 *International and Comparative Law Quarterly* 157, part VI.

[112] *Responsbility to Protect*, ibid, viii. In its Resolution on the outcome of the 2005 World Summit, the General Assembly (though not making any specific reference to the *Responsibility to Protect* report) gave a limited endorsement of the concept of a 'responsibility to protect populations from genocide, war crimes, ethnic cleansing and crimes against humanity'. It acknowledged the need in some instances 'to take collective action . . . through the Security Council, in accordance with the Charter, including Chapter VII, . . . should peaceful means be inadequate and [where] national authorities are manifestly failing to protect their populations from genocide, war crimes, ethnic cleansing and crimes against humanity' (United Nations, *2005 World Summit Outcome Document [Resolution of the General Assembly]* (UN Doc A/RES/60/1), 24 October 2005, para 139). In April 2006, the Security Council reaffirmed the 'provisions of . . . the World Summit Outcome Document regarding the responsibility to protect populations from genocide, war crimes, ethnic cleansing and crimes against humanity' (SC Res 1674 of 28 April 2006, para 4).

[113] SC Res 1265 of 17 September 1999, para 11.

[114] SC Res 1296 of 19 April 2000, para 13. This Resolution was cited by the Secretary-General as the basis upon which 'the mandates of peacekeeping operations have been broadened to allow troops to physically protect civilians under imminent threat of violence' (United Nations, *Report of the Secretary-General to the Security Council on the Protection of Civilians in Armed Conflicts* (UN Doc S/2004/431), 28 May 2004, para 8). Since then, the Security Council has reaffirmed its commitment to civilian protection in a number of resolutions and statements of its President, including SC Res 1325 of 31 October 2000, SC Res 1612 of 26 July 2005, SC Res 1674 of 28 April 2006, SC Res 1738 of 23 December 2006, SC Res 1820 of 19 June 2008, SC Res 1882 of 4 August 2009, SC Res 1888 of 30 September 2009,

The theme of civilian protection has been the subject of numerous reports by the Secretary-General,[115] and the role of peacekeepers in this regard has been recognised by the General Assembly's Special Committee on Peacekeeping Operations.[116]

The three factors outlined above would appear to have contributed to Annan's decision to convene the Panel on United Nations Peace Operations in March 2000 'to undertake a thorough review of the United [Nations'] peace and security activities, and to present a clear set of specific, concrete and practical recommendations to assist the United Nations in conducting such activities better in the future'.[117] The panel's report, which came to be known as the Brahimi Report (its Chairman was Lakhdar Brahimi), was released on 21 August 2000. The Report expressed a deep sense of regret at the UN's failures in Rwanda and Srebrenica, noting that '[n]o failure did more to damage the standing and credibility of United Nations peacekeeping in the 1990s than its reluctance to distinguish victim from aggressor'.[118]

The Report's treatment of the 'fundamental principles' warrants close examination. It begins by labelling consent of the parties, use of force only in self-defence and impartiality as the 'bedrock principles of peacekeeping' and asserting that they should remain as such.[119] However, the Report then goes on to undermine these bedrock principles, either by linking adherence to them with certain operational difficulties experienced by some peacekeeping missions (as it does with consent) or by redefining them, such that they bear little resemblance to how they had previously been understood (as it does with force only in self-defence and impartiality).

SC Res 1889 of 2009 5 October 2009, and SC Res 1894 of 11 November 2009. In this last Resolution, it reaffirmed its 'practice of ensuring that mandates of UN peacekeeping and other relevant missions include, where appropriate and on a case-by-case basis, provisions regarding the protection of civilians' (para 19). In 2002 the Security Council produced an Aide Mémoire in order to facilitate the Council's consideration of civilian protection, including at the time of the establishment or renewal of peacekeeping mandates (United Nations, *Statement by the President of the Security Council [Annexing an Aide Mémoire on the Protection of Civilians in Armed Conflicts]* (UN Doc S/PRST/2002/6), 15 March 2002). For the most recent update of this Aide Mémoire, see United Nations, *Statement by the President of the Security Council [Annexing the Third Edition of an Aide Mémoire on the Protection of Civilians in Armed Conflicts]* (UN Doc S/PRST/2009/1), 14 January 2009. In addition, the Security Council has established an informal Expert Group on the Protection of Civilians.

[115] See eg United Nations, *Report of the Secretary-General on the Protection of Civilians in Armed Conflict* (UN Doc S/2010/579), 11 November 2010. This was the eighth such report of the Secretary-General.

[116] See eg its 2010 report where it recognised, inter alia, the 'protection of civilians under imminent threat of physical violence, without prejudice to the primary responsibility of the host Government' as an important mandated task of peacekeeping operations (United Nations, *Report of the Special Committee on Peacekeeping Operations: 2010 Substantive Session (22 February–19 March 2010)* (UN Doc A/64/19), 2010, para 143).

[117] Brahimi Report (n 38) para 21.

[118] ibid, ix.

[119] ibid, para 48.

In terms of the 'bedrock peacekeeping principle' of consent, the panel highlighted various problems – for example, parties may grant consent only to withdraw it when it serves their interests, or they may use consent to limit an operation's freedom of movement. Thus, the Report implied that the consent requirement (at least one which is interpreted strictly) may be detrimental to a mission's success.[120]

As regards the use of force, the panel noted that peacekeepers must be 'capable of defending themselves, other mission components and the mission's mandate, with robust rules of engagement'.[121] Most significantly, the panel called for peacekeepers to be vested with an obligation to protect civilians, within their means.[122] In order to achieve this modified concept of 'self-defence', the Report recommended that peacekeeping missions be given mandates that were more forceful than they had tended to be historically. It observed:

> Rules of engagement should not limit contingents to stroke-for-stroke responses but should allow ripostes sufficient to silence a source of deadly fire that is directed at United Nations troops or at the people they are charged to protect and, in particularly dangerous situations, should not force United Nations contingents to cede the initiative to their attackers.[123]

The Brahimi Report called for bigger, better equipped, more confrontational[124] forces that would be able to pose a credible deterrent – forces which were 'sized and configured so as to leave no doubt in the minds of would-be spoilers' that peacekeeping was no longer 'non-threatening'[125] in character.

Having called for an expansion of the concept of self-defence to include not just defence-of-mandate – as noted above, a concept which itself may amount to an authorisation to use force in almost unlimited circumstances – but also defence of civilians, and having sketched out the need for confrontational, threatening peacekeeping forces vested with robust rules of engagement, the Report went on to imply (though without explicitly so stating) that peacekeepers should not engage in enforcement-type activities: The panel 'recognizes that the United Nations does not wage war. Where enforcement action is required, it has consistently been entrusted to coalitions of willing States, with the authorization of the Security Council, acting under Chapter VII of the Charter.'[126] Given the size and

[120] ibid, para 48.
[121] ibid, para 55.
[122] Peacekeepers 'who witness violence against civilians should be presumed to be authorised to stop it, within their means, in support of basic United Nations principles and . . . consistent with "the perception and the expectation of protection created by [an operation's] very presence"' (ibid, para 62). The quoted passage within the larger quotation comes from *Letter Dated 15 December 1999* (n 109) 15.
[123] Brahimi Report (n 38) para 49.
[124] ibid, para 1.
[125] ibid, para 51.
[126] ibid, para 53.

level of robustness envisioned for peacekeeping operations by the Report and the circumstances in which such operations would be expected to use force, there is something of a disconnect – perhaps even an element of disingenuousness – about the Report's characterisation of self-defence as a 'bedrock principle' of peacekeeping and its implication that such peacekeeping operations would not engage in enforcement-type activities.

As regards the 'bedrock principle' of impartiality, this too was redefined in the Report such that it bore little resemblance to its normal meaning. According to the Report, impartiality in peacekeeping operations must mean 'adherence to the principles of the Charter and the objectives of a mandate that is rooted in those Charter principles'.[127] Extraordinarily, the Report linked its revised definition of impartiality to an obligation on the part of peacekeepers to use force, warning that, in some cases, 'peacekeepers may not only be operationally justified in using force but morally compelled to do so'.[128] It observed that impartiality 'is not the same as neutrality or equal treatment of all parties in all cases for all time', something which the Report concluded may amount to 'appeasement'.[129]

The ambiguous way in which the Brahimi Report dealt with the 'fundamental principles' of peacekeeping did not go unnoticed by certain members of the General Assembly, who saw its findings as a potential intrusion on state sovereignty.[130] The General Assembly's reception of the Report was somewhat muted.[131] For its part, the Security Council was more supportive, welcoming the Report and endorsing some of its recommendations.[132] More significant, however, has been the Security Council's

[127] ibid, para 50.

[128] ibid, para 50.

[129] ibid, para 50. The use of the term – with its associations of inaction in the face of Nazi atrocities – sends a clear signal that the non-use of force by peacekeepers may, in certain cases, be morally reprehensible.

[130] This was particularly the case with developing states (see Durch et al (n 110) 7–8). It may have been with a view to reassuring these states that the Secretary-General observed that he did not consider the Brahimi Report's recommendations to 'turn the United Nations into a war-fighting machine or to fundamentally change the principles according to which peacekeepers use force' and that '[t]he Panel's recommendations regarding the use of force apply only to those operations in which armed United Nations peacekeepers have deployed with the consent of the parties concerned'. United Nations, *Report of the Secretary-General on the Implementation of the Report of the Panel on United Nations Peace Operations* (UN Doc A/55/502), 20 October 2000, para 7(f).

[131] It decided to 'take note' of the Report, an action described by Durch and Holt (n 110) as 'a polite but noncommittal acknowledgment'.

[132] SC Res 1318 of 7 September 2000 and SC Res 1327 of 13 November 2000. It recognised the 'critical importance of peacekeeping operations having, where appropriate and within their mandates, a credible deterrent capability' (SC Res 1327, Annex I) and undertook to 'ensure that the mandated tasks of peacekeeping operations are appropriate to the situation on the ground, including such factors as the prospects for success, the potential need to protect civilians and the possibility that some parties may seek to undermine peace through violence' (SC Res 1327, Annex II). Moreover, it emphasised that the rules of engagement for UN peacekeeping 'should . . . support the accomplishment of the mission's mandate' (SC Res 1327, Annex II).

practice: as noted, since October 1999, peacekeeping operations[133] have been established in 10 countries or regions and, of these, only one has not been authorised to use force beyond self-defence at some stage of its functioning.[134] It is now routine for the Security Council to invoke Chapter VII when establishing or modifying UN peacekeeping mandates (or in relation to certain tasks assigned to them), with no requirement that the force only be used in self-defence – something that was previously almost unknown.[135] Such was the level of force envisaged for peacekeepers that, in 2000, the Secretary-General spoke of the need to distinguish between 'peacekeepers as civilians' and 'peacekeepers turned combatants'.[136]

2.5 Conclusion on the Changed Nature of Peacekeeping

The above discussion reveals the origins of the three 'fundamental principles' of peacekeeping – and shows the UN to have moved away from them almost immediately after they were identified. Even where peacekeeping operations were not militarised, the 'fundamental principle' of force only in self-defence was defined to include defence-of-mandate, opening the door to the use of virtually unlimited force where the mandate was written in general terms. While force in defence-of-mandate was only infrequently used in practice, this would not appear to have been based on the view that the use of such force would be beyond the scope of an operation's mandate; rather it appears to have been due to the knowledge of the commanders on the ground that if such force were used, the 'fundamental principle' of impartiality would be imperilled (or at least would be perceived to be imperilled) and there would be a heightened risk that the 'fundamental principle' of host state consent would be withdrawn.

[133] Several other operations, described as 'political and peace-building' missions rather than 'peacekeeping' by DPKO, were established during the period in question. In light of the fact that none of these missions have been authorised to use force beyond self-defence, I will not consider them herein.

[134] Also during this period, the UN peacekeeping mission in Lebanon was given a retrospective upgrade in terms of the amount of force it was authorised to use. Chapter VII, however, was not invoked.

[135] Prior to October 1999, Chapter VII had only been explicitly invoked in relation to the functioning of three peacekeeping operations: UNOSOM II, the United Nations Iraq-Kuwait Observer Mission (UNIKOM) in the aftermath of the Gulf War (SC Res 689 of 9 April 1991), and UNPROFOR. In the case of UNIKOM and UNPROFOR, the Chapter VII authorisation was tempered by a – somewhat incongruous – call for the operations to use force only in self-defence (see United Nations, *Report of the Secretary-General on the Implementation of Paragraph 5 of Security Council Resolution 678 (1991)* (UN Doc S/22545), 5 April 1991 regarding UNIKOM and see SC Res 836 of 4 June 1993 regarding UNPROFOR). While the Security Council had invoked Chapter VII in resolutions establishing three other peacekeeping missions – UNCRO and UNTAES in Croatia and UNMIK in Kosovo – its use of Chapter VII was in relation to the use of force by state-led directed at the support operations established in the same resolutions.

[136] *Report of the Secretary-General on the Establishment of the Special Court* (UN Doc S/2000/915), 4 October 2000, para 16.

As the discussion in chapters 4, 5 and 6 will show, UN practice in terms of militarised peacekeeping is such that all three 'fundamental principles' have been tested or ignored to varying degrees. Indeed, in the twenty-first century, the 'fundamental principles' of peacekeeping, never strictly observed, are frequently honoured more in the breach than in the observance.

3. THE CHANGED NATURE OF ENFORCEMENT

Unlike the term 'peacekeeping', 'enforcement' can be found in the UN Charter;[137] however, it is not defined therein. As such, as with peacekeeping, there is no universally accepted definition of enforcement. The UN Security Council does not favour relying on the word 'enforcement' when authorising such measures.[138] Nor does it tend to indicate the article of the Charter under which it is acting: it has never specifically invoked Article 42; indeed, the Security Council did not even invoke Chapter VII in resolutions until the late 1960s.[139] As such, there may frequently be scope for disagreement as to whether or not an authorisation by the Security Council to use force was intended to amount to an Article 42 enforcement operation.

The procedure by which the Security Council is to enforce its will against states is set out in Chapter VII of the Charter: once the Security Council has determined that there is a threat to or breach of the peace or an act of aggression under Article 39[140], it may decide to pursue non-forceful enforcement measures (such as sanctions) under Article 41[141] and/or, where necessary, forceful action pursuant to Article 42 'by air, sea, or land forces as may be

[137] At Arts 2(5), 2(7), 5, 45, 50 and 53.

[138] An exception is the Security Council's authorisation of the NATO-led multinational International Force (IFOR) in Bosnia and Herzegovina. The Security Council authorised Member States acting as part of the force to 'take all necessary measures to effect the implementation of and ensure compliance with Annex 1-A of the [Dayton] Peace Agreement' and stressed that parties were subject to 'such enforcement action by IFOR as may be necessary to ensure implementation of that Annex and the protection of IFOR' (SC Res 1031 of 15 December 1995). Similar wording was used when IFOR became the multinational Stabilisation Force (SFOR) a year later (SC Res 1088 of 12 December 1996) and when the NATO-led SFOR was later taken over by an EU-led force, EUFOR (SC Res 1575 of 22 November 2004).

[139] Security Council, *Special Research Report: Security Council Action Under Chapter VII: Myths and Realities*, June 2008, www.securitycouncilreport.org/site/pp.aspx?c=glKWLeMTIsG&b=4202671 (accessed 1 April 2011), section 2.

[140] Art 39 provides: 'The Security Council shall determine the existence of any threat to the peace, breach of the peace, or act of aggression and shall make recommendations, or decide what measures shall be taken in accordance with Articles 41 and 42, to maintain or restore international peace and security.'

[141] Art 41 provides: 'The Security Council may decide what measures not involving the use of armed force are to be employed to give effect to its decisions, and it may call upon the Members of the United Nations to apply such measures. These may include complete or partial interruption of economic relations and of rail, sea, air, postal, telegraphic, radio, and other means of communication, and the severance of diplomatic relations.'

necessary to maintain or restore international peace and security'.[142] It is this latter type of measure – known as an 'enforcement action' or simply 'enforcement'[143] – that is being contrasted with peacekeeping herein.[144] The Charter envisions the Security Council taking forceful measures through reliance upon forces that have been pre-committed for this purpose by Member States pursuant to agreements under Article 43 of the Charter.[145] The Charter is clear that an Article 42 enforcement action features: (1) no requirement for state party consent to an action on its territory,[146] (2) a level of force beyond self-defence, and (3) no requirement of impartially (ie, no requirement that it refrain from 'serv[ing] as a means to force settlement, in the interests of one party, of political conflicts or legal issues recognized as controversial');[147] rather, its objective *is* to enforce the way forward deemed necessary by the Security Council to restore international peace and security. In effect, it might be posited that enforcement actions have their own 'fundamental principles' which are direct opposites to the 'fundamental principles' of peacekeeping. Whether such principles are, in fact, fundamental to enforcement will be considered below, along with the scope of the principles.

While the process for establishing an enforcement action as envisaged in the Charter is relatively clear, matters have not unfolded as intended: Article 43 agreements, providing for the establishment of a standing force available to the Security Council on an on-call basis, have never been reached and no such standing force exists. According to those who take the view that the concept of a UN enforcement action is limited to a UN-led activity decided upon under Article 42 and carried out by a force established under Article 43, there has been no instance of UN enforcement action in the UN's history.[148] Practice, however, has resulted in the development of a variation on the type of enforcement action envisaged in the Charter, despite the absence of Article 43 agreements.[149] Enforcement is now widely accepted as

[142] The full text of Art 42 provides: 'Should the Security Council consider that measures provided for in Article 41 would be inadequate or have proved to be inadequate, it may take such action by air, sea, or land forces as may be necessary to maintain or restore international peace and security. Such action may include demonstrations, blockade, and other operations by air, sea, or land forces of Members of the United Nations.'

[143] Other writers use terms such as 'military enforcement', 'collective security' or 'collective enforcement'.

[144] Non-forceful sanctions under Art 41 are also referred to by some as 'enforcement' measures. They will be discussed further in chapter 3.

[145] See Arts 43 and 48(1) of the UN Charter.

[146] By signing the Charter states have, in effect, pre-consented to the presence of a Security Council authorised force on their territory (see Arts 25 and 48 of the UN Charter).

[147] *Report of the Secretary-General* (n 26) para 5.

[148] See eg Hans Kelsen, *Recent Trends in the Law of the UN: A Supplement to the Law of the United Nations* (London, Stevens, 1951) 932–37. Cf Bowett (n 49) 33–34. In more recent times few commentators have taken this position, presumably due to Security Council practice.

[149] While some have argued that it was the intention of the drafters that no enforcement actions would take place until the Article 43 agreements were drafted (as evidenced by the transitional security arrangements in Art 106 of the Charter), it is generally accepted that, based on Security Council practice, whether or not such a link may at one time have

including operations where an authorisation to use force is granted by the Security Council, but the leadership of the force is delegated to a state or a coalition of states which volunteer to participate. Such operations are sometimes referred to as 'delegated enforcement actions' (command and control responsibilities are, in effect, delegated by the Security Council to the states that have volunteered to participate) to distinguish them from the type of enforcement action envisaged in the Charter; more often, such operations are simply referred to as 'enforcement'.

As this section will show, enforcement has evolved over the years, particularly since the end of the Cold War. For the purposes of charting the development of enforcement, operations will be considered in three categories: (1) full-blown enforcement, (2) sanctions-related enforcement, and (3) quasi-enforcement.[150] In each category, the question of whether and to what extent each type of enforcement operation has adhered to the 'fundamental principles', thought to be at the heart of its enforcement character, will be addressed. As we shall see with enforcement, as with peacekeeping, what may be perceived as 'fundamental principles' are not always present.

3.1 Full-Blown Enforcement

The term 'full-blown enforcement' is used to refer to an authorisation to use force to expel forces from a state that has been invaded by another state. The UN Security Council has authorised such use of force on only two occasions. The first occurred following the armed attack on

existed, it no longer does. See eg Rosalyn Higgins, 'A General Assessment of United Nations Peace-Keeping' in Antonio Cassese (ed), *United Nations Peace-Keeping: Legal Essays* (The Netherlands, Sijthoff & Noordhoff, 1978) 1–14, 3. See also Thomas Franck, who noted that, '[t]extually, Article 42 can stand on its own feet and it now may be said to do so as a result of Council practice' (Thomas M Franck, *Recourse to Force: State Action Against Threats and Armed Attacks* (Cambridge, Cambridge University Press, 2002) 26). See further Simon Chesterman, *Just War or Just Peace? Humanitarian Intervention and International Law* (Oxford, Oxford University Press, 2001) 119. For a careful discussion of the change in position on this issue, see Rosalyn Higgins, 'International Law and the Avoidance, Containment and Resolution of Disputes (General Course on Public International Law)' (1991) 230 *Recueil des Cours* ch XV.

[150] For the purposes of this book, the term 'full-blown enforcement' will be used to refer to invasion-related enforcement operations in the Korean peninsula or Iraq/Kuwait and the term 'quasi-enforcement' will be used to refer to security-related operations such as UNITAF in Somalia or *Opération Turquoise* in Rwanda. The terms are borrowed from Hilaire McCoubrey and Nigel D White, *The Blue Helmets: Legal Regulation of United Nations Military Operations* (Aldershot, Dartmouth, 1996) 55. Some commentators refer to Korea or Iraq/Kuwait-type operations as 'pure enforcement' or 'full-scale enforcement'. See eg Jane Boulden, *Peace Enforcement: The United Nations Experience in Congo, Somalia, and Bosnia* (Praeger, 2001) 3. The term 'peace support operations' has been used by some European governments to indicate a mission of the type referred to herein as 'quasi-enforcement' (see Nigel D White, 'Empowering Peace Operations to Protect Civilians: Form Over Substance?' (2009) 13 *Journal of International Peacekeeping* 327, 345 ff).

the Republic of Korea by forces from North Korea in 1950. The Security Council determined that this act constituted a 'breach of the peace'[151] (one of the events specified in Article 39 as warranting Security Council action under Chapter VII), thereby opening the door for it to act under Chapter VII. It recommended that UN Member States 'furnish such assistance to the Republic of Korea as may be necessary to repel the armed attack and to restore international peace and security in the area'.[152] The Security Council did not elaborate further on the operation's constitutional basis, causing some controversy at the time.[153] It is now, however, generally accepted that the use of force in the context of the Korean situation constituted an enforcement action under Article 42.[154]

The second instance of the Security Council authorising full-blown force occurred in response to Iraq's invasion of Kuwait on 2 August 1990. On the same day, the Security Council passed Resolution 660 condemning the invasion, determining that there existed 'a breach of international peace and security' and – '[a]cting under Article[s] 39 and 40 of the Charter of the United Nations' – demanding Iraq's unconditional withdrawal.[155] On 29 November 1990, the Security Council authorised Member States cooperating with the government of Kuwait 'to use all necessary means to uphold and implement resolution 660 (1990) and all subsequent resolutions and to restore international peace and security to the area'.[156] While the Security Council indicated that it was acting under Chapter VII, it did not specify the particular article it was relying upon in authorising the use of force, leading, once again, to controversy regarding the constitutional basis of the force.[157] However, most commentators consider the force to represent an Article 42 enforcement action.[158]

[151] SC Res 82 of 25 June 1950. See also SC Res 83 of 27 June 1950 and SC Res 84 of 7 July 1950.

[152] SC Res 83, ibid.

[153] For various opinions on the characterisation of the force see the sources cited in Rosalyn Higgins, *The Development of International Law through the Political Organs of the United Nations* (Oxford, Oxford University Press, 1963) 224 n 79.

[154] See eg Franck (n 149) 24–25; Chesterman (n 149) 116 and n 36; Rosalyn Higgins, *United Nations Peacekeeping 1946–1967: Documents and Commentary, Vol II: Asia* (Oxford, Oxford University Press, 1970) 178; Higgins, *United Nations Peace-keeping* (n 149) 3. Bowett, while considering the Korean action to be an 'unequivocal United Nations enforcement action', regarded it as 'enforcement action authorised by recommendations under Article 39' (Bowett (n 49) 267 and 34, respectively). For the view that it was not an enforcement action see Kelsen (n 148) 932–37; Jochen Frowein and Nico Krisch, 'Article 42' in Bruno Simma (ed), *The Charter of the United Nations: A Commentary*, 2nd edn, vol 1 (Oxford, Oxford University Press, 2002) 749–59, 751 para 4.

[155] SC Res 660 of 2 August 1990.

[156] SC Res 678 of 29 November 1990. The resolution gave Iraq a 'pause of goodwill' until 15 January 1991 to give it the opportunity to comply with the earlier resolutions.

[157] Some argued that the matter was an exercise of collective self-defence under Art 51 of Chapter VII. See discussion of this view in Oscar Schachter, 'United Nations Law in the Gulf Conflict' (1991) 85 *American Journal of International Law* 452, 457.

[158] See eg Franck (n 149) 26. See also Rosalyn Higgins, *Problems and Process: International Law and How We Use It* (Oxford, Clarendon Press, 1994) 266.

In each operation the three 'fundamental' elements of enforcement were present (and it was on the basis of these elements that experts characterised the two operations as enforcement): first, each action was directed against the state, rather than taking place with its consent;[159] second, each action was authorised to use (and did use) considerable force;[160] and third, neither operation was impartial.[161]

3.2 Sanctions-Related Enforcement

The second category of operations comprises Security Council authorisations to use force for the specific purpose of enforcing Article 41 (ie non-forceful) sanctions. The first enforcement measure of this type came about after the Smith regime in Southern Rhodesia illegally proclaimed independence in 1965.[162] In reply, the Security Council called on states to 'do their utmost in order to break all economic relations with Southern Rhodesia', including observing an oil embargo.[163] In April of the following year, it came to light that oil was secretly being pumped to Rhodesia through a pipeline originating in the Mozambican city of Beira.[164] The Security Council adopted Resolution 221, calling upon Portugal (which had administrative control over Mozambique at the time) not to permit the use of the pipeline.[165] It called on all states to 'ensure the diversion of their vessels reasonably believed to be carrying oil for Southern Rhodesia which may be en route for Beira';[166] furthermore, it called on the UK to 'prevent, by the use of force if necessary, the arrival at Beira of vessels reasonably believed to be carrying oil destined for Southern Rhodesia', and empowered the UK to 'arrest and detain the tanker known as the *Joanna V* upon her departure from Beira in the event her oil cargo is discharged there'.[167]

[159] Bowett (n 49) 32–36. See also Higgins (n 158) 266.

[160] Higgins, *Vol II* (n 154) 177. See also Higgins (n 158) 266.

[161] Goulding (n 28) contrasted the enforcement force in Korea with peacekeeping: '[P]eacekeepers must be impartial between the parties. They were not there to advance the interests of one party against those of the other. It was not like Korea where the United States and its allies had been authorized by the Security Council to use force against North Korea for the benefit of South Korea' (454).

[162] The Security Council called on states not to recognise the 'illegal racist minority régime' in Southern Rhodesia (SC Res 216 of 12 November 1965).

[163] SC Res 217 of 20 November 1965.

[164] Danesh Sarooshi, *The United Nations and the Development of Collective Security: The Delegation by the UN Security Council of its Chapter VII Powers* (Oxford, Oxford University Press, 1999) 195–96.

[165] SC Res 221 of 9 April 1966.

[166] ibid.

[167] ibid. Unconfirmed reports reached the Security Council that the *Joanna V* and another Greek-registered tanker, *The Manuela*, had been chartered to carry oil to be secretly pumped to Rhodesia through the pipeline at Beira. Sarooshi (n 164) 195–96.

The Security Council characterised the situation as a 'threat to the peace', thereby signalling its reliance on Chapter VII; however, it did not indicate under which article it was acting when it authorised the use of force.[168] While there were differing views on the point, the authorisation is generally accepted to be an exercise of the Security Council's Article 42 powers.[169]

From the Southern Rhodesia situation up to the end of the Cold War, the Security Council did not authorise any force of a similar nature. However, in 1990, the Security Council called on Member States that were cooperating with the government of Kuwait and which had maritime deployments in the area 'to use such measures commensurate to the specific circumstances as may be necessary under the authority of the Security Council to halt all inward and outward maritime shipping'[170] in order to ensure implementation of the economic sanctions it had earlier imposed on Iraq.[171] The Security Council did not invoke Chapter VII or any article contained in that Chapter in relation to the authorisation to use force; nor did it characterise the situation as a 'threat to the peace, breach of the peace or act of aggression'. It did, however, recall a number of earlier resolutions in which it had characterised the situation as a breach of international peace and security[172] and had invoked Chapter VII.[173] As a result, there was disagreement as to whether the authorisation to use force amounted to an enforcement action under Article 42. Some suggested that, given the limited circumstances under which the use of force had been authorised, the authorisation was less in the nature of Article 42 enforcement and more an authorisation impliedly permitted under Article 41.[174] Given

[168] While not specifically invoked, it was uncontroversial that the Security Council's imposition of economic sanctions was based on Art 41 of the Charter.

[169] Among those who took the view that it was an exercise of Art 42 see Higgins (n 158) 260; Sarooshi (n 164) 198–200 nn 120 and 121 and the jurists cited therein; Frowein and Krisch (n 154) 757, para 21 and Jochen Frowein and Nico Krisch, 'Article 41' in Simma (n 5) 735–749, 740, para 11. For the view that the operation was more in the nature of a recommendation under Art 39 see Vera Gowlland-Debbas, *Collective Responses to Illegal Acts under International Law: United Nations Actions in the Question of Southern Rhodesia* (Dordrecht, Martinus Nijhoff, 1990) 417. See also JES Fawcett, 'Security Council Resolutions on Rhodesia' (1965–66) 41 *British Yearbook of International Law* 121 who observed that 'the choice lies between Articles 39 and 42, but there are serious difficulties with either, and the conclusion may perhaps be that it was anomalous, and outside the Charter'.

[170] SC Res 665 of 25 August 1990.

[171] SC Res 661 of 6 August 1990. While not specifically invoked, the sanctions would appear to have been based on the Security Council's powers under Art 41 (see Schachter (n 157) 453).

[172] SC Res 660 of 2 August 1990.

[173] SC Res 660 of 2 August 1990, SC Res 661 of 6 August 1990, and SC Res 664 of 18 August 1990.

[174] Higgins, *Recueil des Cours* (n 149) 329 observed that 'the implication was that force could be authorized to implement economic sanctions without that use of force being viewed as military sanctions under Article 42. Just as a minimal use of force by United Nations Peacekeeping operations may be authorized by reference to Article 40 of the Charter, so limited force may apparently be authorized by reference to Article 41 – even though neither

the clear prohibition on the use of force in Article 41, however, the better view is that the authorisation was an Article 42 enforcement measure, albeit one where force of a limited nature was authorised.[175] The Security Council has subsequently authorised the use of force to ensure compliance with Article 41 sanctions on a number of occasions.[176]

This type of authorisation to use force shares many similarities with the Security Council's authorisation to engage in full-blown enforcement action. With both types of authorisation, the Security Council generally makes a finding of a threat to or breach of international peace and security (sometimes accompanied by a specific invocation of Article 39); Chapter VII is generally relied upon (implicitly or explicitly); and force is to be used by Member States, not acting under UN command.

However, sanctions-related enforcement is of a different nature from full-blown enforcement in two important respects. First, whereas in the Korea and Iraq/Kuwait situations the force was authorised against the particular invading state, sanctions-related enforcement operations feature force that is authorised against *any* state whose vessels ignored the embargoes. This question of who the threat of force was directed against is closely related to the question of consent. In terms of full-blown enforcement operations, it is axiomatic that an invading state would not consent to an action, the objective of which was to force that state to withdraw from the territory it had invaded. Were it otherwise, the invading state would simply withdraw and the need for force would be obviated. When it comes to sanctions-related authorisations, however, vessels registered to any state are subject to the possible use of force and not all such states are non-consenting. Presumably, most states would have no objection to an authorisation to use force to enforce Security Council sanctions – certainly those states on the Security Council that vote in favour of a resolution authorising the force do not. In the case of the sanctions against Southern Rhodesia, Greece, the state of registry of the *Joanna V*, was not opposed to the ship being intercepted by the UK, so long as the action

Article envisages that possibility.' See discussion in chapter 3 on the issue of the parameters of the Security Council's powers under Art 41.

175 Frowein and Krisch, 'Article 41' (n 169) 740 para 11.

176 For example, in 1992, the Security Council, '[a]cting under Chapters VII and VIII of the Charter, call[ed] upon States, nationally or through regional agencies or arrangements, to use such measures as may be necessary to ensure strict implementation of' an earlier-established weapons embargo in Somalia (SC Res 794 of 3 December 1992, para 16). In the same year, the Security Council indicated that it was acting under Chapters VII and VIII when it called on states to ensure adherence to the embargo in place in Serbia and Montenegro (SC Res 787 of 16 November 1992, para 12). In 1993 and again in 1994, the Security Council called upon Member States to 'use such measures commensurate with the specific circumstances as may be necessary under the authority of the Security Council' to ensure strict implementation of sanctions imposed against the non-democratic government in Haiti (SC Res 875 of 16 October 1993, SC Res 917 of 4 May 1994).

was UN authorised.[177] The fact that sanctions-related enforcement – unlike full-blown enforcement – features an authorisation of force which is not necessarily opposed by the states whose vessels are the object of the enforcement measure indicates that such a measure is not seen to be against their interests.

Second, the character of the force authorised in relation to the upholding of sanctions tends to be of a much more limited nature than the force authorised in response to the invasion of a state. In terms of sanctions-related enforcement, the force is limited to circumstances where the sanctions are violated;[178] the authorisations to use force in the Korea and Iraq situations were virtually unlimited. The force authorised in those latter situations – respectively, 'such assistance . . . as may be necessary to repel the armed attack . . . and to restore international peace and security in the area'[179] and 'all necessary means to uphold and implement resolution 660 (1990) and all subsequent resolutions and to restore international peace and security to the area'[180] – was sweeping in nature. The wording bears a strong resemblance to the language of Article 42 of the UN Charter: 'such action . . . as may be necessary to maintain or restore international peace and security'.

In sum, the advent of sanctions-related enforcement saw the 'fundamental principles' of enforcement being undermined somewhat. While it is still true to say that state consent is not required, it is not necessarily the case – as it would be with full-blown enforcement – that the existence of the consent of a state whose vessels may be the object of the use of force is a counter-indicant to an operation being classified as enforcement. As to force, while it is certainly the case that it may be used beyond self-defence, the force authorised is limited to preventing breaches of the Article 41 sanctions. Finally, it is difficult to categorise the use of force against a vessel breaching sanctions as partial: the interests of one party are not being advanced over those of another through the use of force; instead, all states are subject to the same requirement to adhere to the same binding economic sanctions previously established by the Security Council.

[177] Sarooshi (n 164) 196.

[178] For example, in relation to Southern Rhodesia, the Security Council authorised 'the use of force if necessary . . . to arrest and detain the tanker known as the *Joanna V* upon her departure from Beira in the event her oil cargo is discharged there' (SC Res 221 of 9 April 1966). Regarding the authorisation relating to sanctions in Iraq/Kuwait, the Security Council spoke of 'such measures commensurate to the specific circumstances as may be necessary . . . to halt all inward and outward maritime shipping' (SC Res 665 of 25 August 1990).

[179] SC Res 82 of 25 June 1950.

[180] SC Res 678 of 29 November 1990.

3.3 Quasi-Enforcement

The end of the Cold War brought with it a 'reinvented' version of enforcement.[181] Beginning in the early 1990s, the Security Council began a practice of authorising operations to use force to restore peace and security within a state, frequently in order to facilitate the work of a peacekeeping operation. The first such authorisation took place in August 1992 when the Security Council, faced with a situation it characterised as a threat to international peace and security,[182] authorised a NATO-led force to use 'all necessary means' to facilitate the distribution of humanitarian aid by the UN in the former Yugoslavia.[183] The United Nations Protection Force in Yugoslavia (UNPROFOR), a peacekeeping mission established in February 1992 'to create the conditions of peace and security required for the negotiation of an overall settlement of the Yugoslav crisis',[184] was already present on the ground. Similarly, in December 1992, after finding the situation in Somalia to be a threat to international peace and security, the Security Council authorised a US-led force – the Unified Task Force or UNITAF – to use 'all necessary means' to establish a secure environment for humanitarian relief operations in Somalia.[185] The first United Nations Mission in Somalia (UNOSOM I) had been unable to distribute humanitarian aid due to the violence occurring in the country.[186] The Security Council has subsequently established a number of quasi-enforcement operations,[187] either to restore peace and security in advance of the

[181] Niels Blokker, 'Is the Authorization Authorized? Powers and Practice of the UN Security Council to Authorize the Use of Force by "Coalitions of the Able and Willing"' (2000) 11(3) *European Journal of International Law* 541, 543.

[182] For a discussion of the expansion by the Security Council of what amounts to a 'threat to the peace, breach of the peace, or act of aggression' under Art 39, and its tendency to find the existence of such threats, breaches or acts, see chapter 3, section 3.2.1.

[183] SC Res 770 of 13 August 1992. NATO was not mentioned; rather the resolution referred to '[s]tates [acting] nationally or through regional agencies or arrangements'.

[184] SC Res 743 of 21 February 1992, para 5.

[185] SC Res 794 of 23 December 1992.

[186] For a discussion of the violence to which UNOSOM I was subject, see United Nations, *Letter Dated 24 November 1992 from the Secretary-General Addressed to the President of the Security Council* (UN Doc S/24859), 27 November 1992.

[187] Including operations in Haiti ('Operation Uphold Democracy'), SC Res 940 of 31 July 1994; Rwanda ('*Opération Turquoise*'), SC Res 929 of 22 June 1994; Eastern Zaire ('Temporary Multinational Force'), SC Res 1080 of 15 November 1996 (authorised but not implemented); Albania ('a temporary and limited multinational force'), SC Res 1101 of 28 March 1997; Central African Republic ('Inter-African Mission to Monitor the Implementation of the Bangui Agreements' (MISAB)), SC Res 1125 of 6 August 1997; Guinea Bissau (ECOMOG Mission to Guinea Bissau), SC Res 1216 of 21 December 1998; Kosovo (KFOR), SC Res 1244 of 10 July 1999; East Timor ('INTERFET'), SC Res 1264 of 15 September 1999; Cote d'Ivoire ('ECOFORCE' or 'ECOMICI'), SC Res 1464 of 4 February 2003; DRC ('Interim Emergency Multinational Force in Bunia' or 'Operation Artemis'), SC Res 1484 of 30 May 2003; Cote d'Ivoire ('Operation Licorne'), SC Res 1464 of 4 February 2003; Liberia ('ECOWAS mission in Liberia (ECOMIL)' or 'the Multinational Force'), SC Res 1479 of 1 August 2003; Iraq ('Multinational Force (MNF) in Iraq'), SC Res 1511 of 16 October 2003; Haiti ('Multinational

emplacement of a peacekeeping operation or to rescue a peacekeeping operation in circumstances where security has broken down.

This type of Security Council authorisation shares features with the full-blown enforcement actions used in the Korean and Iraq/Kuwait situations: each involves the Security Council acting under Chapter VII based on a finding of a threat to the peace, breach of the peace or act of aggression; each features an authorisation (express or implied) to use force (frequently, 'all necessary measures'); each delegates leadership of the force to a state or group of states.[188] However, there are several fundamental differences. First, quasi-enforcement operations tend to address a threat to peace and security *within* a state, rather than a threat or breach involving two or more states. Second, they tend to be in support of a peacekeeping operation, which functions alongside them or which is deployed (or re-deployed) after security has been restored by the quasi-enforcement operation.[189] Third (and closely related to the second point), while quasi-enforcement operations, like full-blown enforcement operations, tend to feature an authorisation by the Security Council to use 'all necessary means', the force required to achieve the objectives of a quasi-enforcement operation is of a more limited nature than that required in a full-blown enforcement operation. Instead of being in relation to the 'war-like' objective[190] of expelling an invading state, the authorisation to use force for a

Force (MNF)', SC Res 1529 of 29 February 2004; DRC ('EUFOR Chad/CAR') SC Res 1671 of 25 April 2006. Additional forceful operations led by states or groups of states have been established *independently* of the Security Council, such as ECOMOG in Sierra Leone and Liberia. Such operations are – initially at any rate – of dubious legality; however, they are sometimes later endorsed by the Security Council, arguably endowing them with *ex post facto* legality.

[188] McCoubrey and White (n 150) 55 argued that UNITAF-type operations feature more of a 'constitutional bridge', ie, a stronger reporting relationship, between the leadership of the operation and the Security Council than is the case with operations such as took place in Korea or Iraq/Kuwait.

[189] The Italian-led force authorised by the Security Council to provide humanitarian assistance and security in the face of political turmoil in Albania in 1997 (SC Res 1101 of 28 March 1997) is an example of what appears to be a quasi-enforcement operation established in circumstances where there was no link to a peacekeeping operation. There, the force, referred to as a 'temporary and limited multinational force', was mandated to 'facilitate the safe and prompt delivery of humanitarian assistance, and to help create a secure environment for the missions of international organizations in Albania, including those providing humanitarian assistance'. Although the Security Council invoked Chapter VII in authorising participating states 'to ensure the security and freedom of movement of the personnel of the said multinational protection force', it made no mention of the use of force or of 'all necessary means'.

[190] A distinction exists in military doctrine between full-scale military operations and operations with more limited objectives. For example, in the US, operations where force is used – frequently in aid of a UN peacekeeping operation – to achieve objectives such as arms control, restoration of security or humanitarian assistance are referred to as 'Military Operations Other Than War' or 'MOOTWA'. The term 'war' is reserved for 'large-scale, sustained combat activities to achieve national objectives or protect national interests'. See Joint Chiefs of Staff, *Joint Doctrine for Military Operations Other than War* (United States Government Joint Pub 3-07, 16 June 1995), www.bits.de/NRANEU/others/jp-doctrine/jp3_07.pdf (accessed 1 April 2011), 13.

quasi-enforcement operation tends to be in order to restore security.[191] The absence of 'war-like' objectives is indicated by the fact that quasi-enforcement operations tend to be of an extremely limited duration[192] – with a 'prompt transition' to a peacekeeping force frequently envisaged[193] – and the fact that quasi-enforcement operations tend to feature fewer personnel and far less equipment than quasi-enforcement operations.

A final important distinction between the two types of operation must be noted. The Security Council's objective in authorising a quasi-enforcement operation to use force is not to modify the behaviour of the state. Instead, the target is generally rebels or criminals within the state. For this reason, this type of operation almost always features the consent of the government of the host state.[194] Indeed, the Security Council would not authorise the establishment of INTERFET in 1999 without the host state's consent.[195]

Turning again to the 'fundamental principles' of enforcement, we see

[191] For example, UNITAF was 'to establish as soon as possible a secure environment for humanitarian relief operations in Somalia' (SC Res 794 of 3 December 1992, para 10).

[192] The duration of an operation may be linked with its objectives. While it would make sense to expect the force in South Korea to remain there until the Northern forces were expelled, the objective of UNITAF was the less measurably winnable one of restoring security such that humanitarian aid could be distributed. Arguably, the objective of the full restoration of security could never be met – and even if it had been, there would have been every risk that the country would have reverted to its pre-enforcement security situation as soon as UNITAF left.

[193] According to the Security Council, it was required to provide reports to the Security Council to enable it 'to make the necessary decision for a prompt transition to continued peacekeeping operations' (SC Res 974 of 3 December 1992). According to the Secretary-General, 'the purpose of [UNITAF] was to resolve the immediate security problem . . . [I]t would be replaced by a United Nations peace-keeping operation . . . as soon as the irregular groups had been disarmed and the heavy weapons of the organized factions brought under international control' (United Nations, *Letter Dated 29 November 1992 from the Secretary-General Addressed to the President of the Security Council* (UN Doc S/24868), 30 November 1992, 5).

[194] With its resolution authorising the NATO-led force in Bosnia and Herzegovina, the Security Council emphasised the request from the government for Chapter VII measures (SC Res 770 of 13 August 1992, which referred to United Nations, *Letter Dated 10 August 1992 from the Permanent Representative of Bosnia and Herzegovina to the United Nations addressed to the President of the Security Council* (UN Doc S/24401), 10 August 1992). Similarly, the Security Council, in authorising the use of 'all necessary means' by the MNF (or 'Operation Uphold Democracy') in Haiti, described the Cédras regime as an 'illegal' regime and referred to Aristide as 'the legitimately elected president' (SC Res 940 of 31 July 1994). The Security Council also referred to a request by Aristide for intervention (United Nations, *Letter Dated 29 July 1994 from the Permanent Representative of Haiti to the United Nations Addressed to the Secretary-General (Annexing 'Letter Dated 29 July 1994 from the President of the Republic of Haiti Addressed to the Secretary-General')* (UN Doc S/1994/905), 29 July 1994). The exception here was UNITAF in Somalia, where the force was authorised without the consent of any government as 'no government exist[ed] in Somalia that could request and allow such use of force' (*Letter Dated 29 November 1992* (n 193) 3). It could also be argued that as the government in Rwanda had limited control at the time that it consented to the establishment of *Opération Turquoise*, the quality of that consent may have been diminished (SC Res 929 of 22 June 1994). Each situation will be considered in detail in chapter 4 below.

[195] Findlay (n 77) 287.

that while offensive force is authorised and used in quasi-enforcement operations, it is of a far more limited nature than the force used in a full-blown enforcement action. Secondly, while host state consent is not a legal requirement for quasi-enforcement operations (given their apparent establishment under article 42 of Chapter VII), host states generally do consent – and the Security Council (at least in the case of INTERFET) has shown itself to consider the existence of consent to be an important factor in its decision-making. Finally, while quasi-enforcement operations may be said to lack impartiality given that they tend to side with the state against certain rebel forces within that state, it is of a different nature from the type of inter-state partiality that was evident in Korea or Iraq/Kuwait, given that with the former the objective tends to be humanitarian.

3.4 Conclusions on the Changed Nature of Enforcement

The foregoing discussion indicates considerable differences among the three categories of enforcement operations in terms of observance of the 'fundamental principles' of enforcement. First, full-blown enforcement operations are possessed of a war-like goal: regaining territory which the Security Council determines has been illegally taken. These operations rely on considerable offensive force to achieve their objective. In terms of sanctions-related enforcement operations, force is authorised only in very narrowly tailored circumstances (to prevent UN sanctions from being breached), and only for a limited time (until the breach is averted). Moreover, while quasi-enforcement operations tend to be authorised to use 'all necessary means', their goal is to restore security, generally to aid a peacekeeping operation. Many of the functions of such operations are not forceful at all. Instead, they tend to overlap with the peacekeeping operations they are frequently there to aid.

Second, full-blown enforcement operations take place not only without the consent of the recalcitrant state but in opposition to it. In sanctions-related enforcement operations, the states whose ships or nationals might be the object of the use of force are not necessarily opposed to the authorisation. Quasi-enforcement operations, on the other hand, do not generally use force against the host state – rather the target of the force is rebels or spoilers within the state – and such operations generally take place with the consent of the host state.

Third, a full-blown enforcement operation does not act impartially. To the contrary, the objective of such an operation is to enforce a specific political solution, namely, the withdrawal of one country from another. However, it is difficult to classify either sanctions-related enforcement or quasi-enforcement as not 'impartial' in the way the word was used by Hammarskjöld: action which is not designed 'to enforce any specific political solution of pending problems or to influence the political balance decisive to such a solution'.[196] The objective of a sanctions-related enforcement operation is to ensure that a previously established sanctions regime is enforced. While the sanctions regime was put in place to bring about a particular political solution previously decided upon by the Security Council, it applies equally to all states (and their vessels). As for quasi-enforcement operations, while they may be said to lack impartiality in that the Security Council generally authorises such operations to use force against one set of actors (rebels and criminals) and not another (the host state itself), they are not partial in the sense of enforcing a specific political solution. Instead, their objective is to restore security with a view to protecting the country's citizens from violence or allowing them to receive humanitarian aid.

The above discussion makes clear that quasi-enforcement operations are assigned tasks that are peacekeeping-like in nature – so much so that some writers have characterised certain quasi-enforcement operations as UN peacekeeping[197] or 'essentially' UN peacekeeping.[198] Others have used the term 'peace-enforcement' to include militarised peacekeeping operations (or a version thereof) as well as quasi-enforcement operations.[199] While a tendency to classify quasi-enforcement operations and militarised peacekeeping operations as similar in nature may be understandable[200] – after all, their functions overlap to a considerable degree and both types of operation have a Chapter VII basis – maintaining a distinction between UN-led militarised peacekeeping and state-led quasi-enforcement is

[196] *Summary Study* (n 19) para 167. If one were to opt for the Brahimi Report's definition of impartiality, ie, 'adherence to the principles of the Charter and to the objectives of a mandate that is rooted in those Charter principles', it would appear that the operations in both Korea and Iraq/Kuwait were impartial. However, as noted, this definition bears little resemblance to most conceptions of the term.

[197] See eg Dominik Zaum, 'The Security Council, the General Assembly, and War: The Uniting for Peace Resolution' in Vaughan Lowe et al (eds), *The United Nations Security Council and War: The Evolution of Thought and Practice since 1945* (New York, Oxford University Press, 2008) 154–74, 170.

[198] See Trevor Findlay, 'Introduction' in Trevor Findlay (ed), *Challenges for the New Peacekeepers (SIPRI Research Report No 12)* (Oxford, Oxford University Press, 1996) 13, who noted: 'On occasion, a non-UN multinational force has been authorized by the [Security Council] essentially to conduct a peacekeeping operation, but under a Chapter VII mandate, as in the case of Opération Turquoise by France in Rwanda and the [US-led Multinational Force] in Haiti.'

[199] The term 'peace-enforcement' is discussed immediately below.

[200] As noted by Niels Blokker ('The Security Council and the Use of Force: On Recent Practice' in Niels Blokker and Nico Schrijver (eds), *The Security Council and the Use of Force: Theory and Reality – A Need for Change?* (Dordrecht, Martinus Nijhoff, 2005) 1–29, 15): 'The concepts of peacekeeping and authorizations to coalition [*sic*] of the able and willing to use force are not always fully distinguishable. The mandates of coalitions of the able and willing authorized to use force may also include peacekeeping tasks . . . In practice the distinction . . . has become blurred to a certain extent, in particular since UN peacekeeping operations have been created under Chapter VII of the Charter and have received permission to use force on a larger scale than classical peacekeeping operations.'

essential in order to clearly understand the differences – and similarities – between the two types of operation.

4. THE CHANGED NATURE OF PEACE-ENFORCEMENT

4.1 *An Agenda for Peace*

The term 'peace-enforcement' was popularised by Boutros-Ghali in *An Agenda for Peace*. There, he envisioned peace-enforcement – a sub-category of 'peace-making'[201] – as overlapping with peacekeeping.[202] Boutros-Ghali was careful to stress that the concept of 'peace-enforcement' was different from that of enforcement. The most significant difference was that peace-enforcement operations were to be limited in their use of force to achieve the objective of maintaining or re-establishing ceasefires. Moreover, Boutros-Ghali characterised peace-enforcement as a provisional measure under Article 40.[203] According to him, peace-enforcement would feature UN-led forces, more heavily armed and more extensively trained than peacekeeping forces, charged with restoring and maintaining previously agreed ceasefires.[204]

4.2 Late 1990s

By the end of the 1990s, Boutros-Ghali's concept of peace-enforcement had 'long since fallen by the wayside'.[205] By this stage, the term 'peace-enforcement' had come to refer to an imprecise concept which fell into the 'grey area' between peacekeeping and enforcement.[206] Boulden's definition, which considered the extent to which the 'fundamental principles' of peacekeeping and the 'fundamental principles' of enforcement were

[201] *An Agenda for Peace* (n 13) paras 44–45. Some commentators use the terms 'peace-enforcement' and 'peace-making' interchangeably. Confusingly, however, in his follow-up report, *Supplement to An Agenda for Peace* (n 95), Boutros-Ghali described peace-making and peace-enforcement as being different in nature, with the former requiring the consent of the host state and the latter being 'a coercive measure . . . and thus, by definition, . . . not requir[ing] the consent of the party concerned' (para 23).

[202] Boutros-Ghali observed that '[p]eace-keeping is a technique that expands the possibilities for both the prevention of conflict and the *making* of peace' (*An Agenda for Peace* (n 13) para 20, emphasis added) and indicated that he considered peace-enforcement to occur at the same stage in the conflict as peacekeeping (para 57).

[203] ibid, para 44.

[204] ibid.

[205] Boulden (n 150) 3. Boutros-Ghali's comment in 1993 that peace-enforcement went 'beyond peacekeeping to the extent that the operation would be deployed without the express consent of the two parties' while retaining 'many of the features of peacekeeping' suggests that he had moved away from the concept as he outlined it in *An Agenda for Peace* almost immediately (Boutros Boutros-Ghali, 'Empowering the United Nations' (1992–93) 71 *Foreign Affairs* 89, 94).

[206] Boulden (n 150) 2.

present in order to distinguish peace-enforcement from those two entities, was typical.[207] For her, peacekeeping featured the principles of impartiality, the use of force only in self-defence and consent; enforcement[208] lacked impartiality, did not require host state consent and featured a 'full use of force authorisation';[209] and peace-enforcement fell somewhere in between. Peace-enforcement operations, she posited, were a means 'to bring about or ensure compliance with some aspect of a Security Council mandate or an agreement among the parties'.[210] They were authorised under Chapter VII of the UN Charter and possessed of the following characteristics:

(1) they could use force beyond self-defence;[211]
(2) they did not require the consent of the parties, though such consent was desirable; and
(3) they were intended to be impartial, with no judgement as to the claims or positions of the parties to the conflict and no action taken against any one state or party.[212]

Moreover, whereas peacekeeping is a UN-authorised, UN-led endeavour[213] and enforcement (in practice, as opposed to how it was envisaged in the Charter) is generally agreed to refer to an operation which is authorised by the UN but led by a state or a coalition of states, the term 'peace-enforcement' was said to cover UN-authorised forces which were *either* UN-led – Boulden gives the examples of ONUC, UNOSOM II and UNPROFOR – or led by a state or a coalition – such as the US-led UNITAF in Somalia in 1992/3 or the French-led *Opération Turquoise* in Rwanda in 1994.

[207] A similar approach was taken by Ralph Zacklin, UN Assistant Secretary-General for Legal Affairs, until May 2006. He observed that peace-enforcement operations are 'usually multinational forces under unified command, which do not rely on the consent of the host state, are purely military in nature and are authorized by the Security Council as enforcement operations under Chapter VII' (Ralph Zacklin, 'The Use of Force in Peacekeeping Operations' in Blokker and Schrijver (n 200) 91–106, 91–92).

[208] Boulden (n 150) 3 uses the term 'full-scale enforcement' to refer to what I have called 'full-blown' enforcement.

[209] ibid, 3.

[210] ibid, 3.

[211] See Findlay (n 77) 85–86, who takes the view that a peace-enforcement operation is more limited in its use of force than an enforcement operation. He described ONUC as 'having obtained elements of what might today be considered a peace enforcement mandate' but going on 'to actually conduct an enforcement operation – in the sense of defeating a breakaway regime and reasserting the authority of the central government – while all along denying that it was doing more than acting in self-defence and preserving its freedom of movement'.

[212] Boulden (n 150) 3.

[213] See discussion in chapter 1, section 4. Cf *Situation in Darfur, Sudan in the case of The Prosecutor v Bahar Idriss Abu Garda, Decision on the Confirmation of Charges (Public Redacted Version)* (No ICC-02/05-02/09), 8 February 2010 (PTC I), www.icc-cpi.int/iccdocs/doc/doc819602.pdf (accessed 1 April 2011), paras 75–76, where the Pre-Trial Chamber considered that an operation established and led by a regional organisation could amount to peacekeeping.

We see in this reliance on the term 'peace-enforcement' an attempt to define the grey area that lies between enforcement actions as they used to be – ie full-blown enforcement that adhered to the 'fundamental principles' of enforcement – and peacekeeping operations as they used to be – ie the non-militarised type of peacekeeping that adhered quite strictly to the 'fundamental principles' of peacekeeping. Given that, as this chapter has shown, models of peacekeeping and enforcement that adhere to their respective 'fundamental principles' are no longer the only models in existence, the approach loses much of its value. Indeed, militarised peacekeeping as well as quasi-enforcement operations may meet Boulden's criteria for peace-enforcement, thereby denuding the term of much of its value.

4.3 Twenty-First Century Peace-Enforcement

As militarised peacekeeping has become the norm in the twenty-first century, the UN Secretariat has attempted to draw a line between it and peace-enforcement. The drafters of the 2008 Capstone Doctrine,[214] created by the DPKO and the Department of Field Services (DFS), see peace-enforcement as something different from militarised peacekeeping;[215] however, they (unlike Boulden) do not appear to draw a distinction between enforcement (whether 'full-blown' or otherwise) and peace-enforcement. They define peace-enforcement as involving

> the application, with the authorization of the Security Council, of a range of coercive measures, including the use of military force. Such actions are authorized to restore international peace and security in situations where the Security Council has determined the existence of a threat to the peace, breach of the peace or act of aggression. The Security Council may utilize, where appropriate, regional organizations and agencies for enforcement action under its authority.[216]

This definition, like Boulden's, encompasses both UN-led and state-led operations. The drafters observe that since the mid-1990s, peace-enforcement action has been taken by 'ad hoc coalitions of Member States or regional organizations acting under United Nations Security Council authorization'.[217] This observation would appear to suggest that, in the view of the drafters of the Capstone Doctrine, (1) certain UN-led operations taking place before the mid-1990s *were* peace-enforcement – the

[214] United Nations Department of Peacekeeping Operations and Department of Field Operations, *United Nations Peacekeeping Operations: Principles and Guidelines* ('Capstone Doctrine'), 2008, http://pbpu.unlb.org/pbps/Library/Capstone_Doctrine_ENG.pdf (accessed 1 April 2011).

[215] The Capstone Doctrine uses the term 'robust peacekeeping' to describe peacekeeping operations authorised to use force beyond self-defence.

[216] Capstone Doctrine (n 214) 18.

[217] ibid, p 49 endnote 20.

Capstone Doctrine gives no examples, but ONUC, UNPROFOR and UNOSOM II, being the most enforcement-like operations occurring before the mid-1990s, may be what the drafters had in mind – and (2) none of the militarised peacekeeping operations undertaken since the mid-1990s, being UN-led, are thought by the drafters to be peace-enforcement.

The Capstone Doctrine's approach leaves considerable scope for confusion as to whether a UN-authorised, UN-led operation established under Chapter VII, or with certain of its tasks authorised thereunder, in response to a threat to international peace and security and vested with the authority to use considerable force is a peace-enforcement operation or a militarised peacekeeping operation. As the drafters themselves recognised, the line between the two concepts has 'become increasingly blurred'.[218] Nevertheless, the drafters insist that militarised peacekeeping and peace-enforcement are distinct on two bases:

(1) Whereas militarised peacekeeping involves the use of force 'at the tactical level',[219] 'peace enforcement may involve the use of force at the strategic or international level, which is normally prohibited for Member States under Article 2(4) of the Charter unless authorized by the Security Council'.[220]
(2) Whereas militarised peacekeeping takes place with the 'consent of the host authorities and/or the main parties to the conflict',[221] 'peace enforcement does not require the consent of the main parties'.[222]

Unfortunately, neither basis provides much in the way of clarity.

The distinction based on the use of force is unsatisfactory on two levels. First, the observation that 'force at the strategic or international level' is 'normally prohibited for Member States under Article 2(4) of the Charter unless authorized by the Security Council' is odd. Surely the use of force, whether 'at the tactical level' or at the 'strategic or international level', will be equally prohibited under Article 2(4) where it goes beyond self-defence.[223] Second, the drafters do not provide any meaningful elaboration as to how the use

[218] ibid, 18.
[219] ibid, 19.
[220] ibid.
[221] ibid, 19 and 34.
[222] ibid, 34. The fact that the drafters speak of the need for 'consent of the host authorities and/or the main parties to the conflict' in relation to militarised peacekeeping, and refer to the absence of the need for 'consent of the main parties' in relation to peace-enforcement, would appear to suggest that consent of the 'host authorities' is viewed as necessary in both types of operation. However, this does not appear to be the drafters' intention, given that such a position does not comport with the statement that '[t]he Security Council may take enforcement action without the consent of the main parties to the conflict, if it believes that the conflict presents a threat to international peace and security. This, however, would be a peace enforcement operation' (ibid, endnote 20 at 43).
[223] See discussion of Art 2(4) and its prohibition of the threat or use of force in chapter 3, section 2.22.

of force at the 'tactical' level differs from its use at the 'strategic' or 'international' level.[224] As noted, the drafters of the Capstone Doctrine appear to acknowledge that certain UN-led operations pre-mid-1990s may be classed as peace-enforcement. If this is the case, presumably UNOSOM II would be the clearest candidate.[225] However, it is not at all clear why the force used by UNOSOM II (assuming it is viewed by the drafters as a peace-enforcement operation) was at the 'strategic or international' level or in any other way different from the force used by, say, MONUC after 2003, which – if my inference discussed above is correct – the drafters would not appear to consider peace-enforcement. Nor is it clear why the EU-led Interim Emergency Multinational Force in Bunia (IEMF or 'Operation Artemis'), which was authorised to 'take all necessary measures to fulfil its mandate'[226] and which would appear to meet the drafters' definition of peace-enforcement, was any more 'strategic' or 'international' and any less 'tactical' in its use of force than the fortified MONUC that replaced it,[227] which the drafters – again, if my inference is correct – do not consider peace-enforcement.

The second test posited to distinguish militarised peacekeeping from peace-enforcement – looking to whether or not host state consent is required – is also problematic. First, host state consent is not legally required to establish a militarised peacekeeping operation (or to assign certain tasks to such an operation) if the Security Council intends to take a binding decision under Chapter VII. A comparison between various militarised peacekeeping operations and what the drafters of the Capstone Doctrine would consider peace-enforcement operations reveals that there are similarities between them: in each case the Security Council tends to authorise the operations by means of an explicit invocation of Chapter VII and a finding of a 'threat to international peace and security', and in each case it frequently authorises the use of 'all necessary measures'.[228] An additional complica-

[224] A Joint Report by the UNDP and the Department of Field Services (DFS) of March 2010 sheds some light on the differences. It describes tactical-level military tasks as including 'activities related to the protection of civilians, patrolling, checkpoint duties, humanitarian aid support and assistance to national security forces'. At the strategic level 'the activities of UN military peacekeeping personnel comprise the development of strategic military guidance, military planning, force generation, current operations and the provision of support to [Troop Contributing Countries], including operational advice' (United Nations, *DPKO/DFS Guidelines: Integrating a Gender Perspective into the Work of the United Nations Military in Peacekeeping Operations*, March 2010, www.un.org/en/peacekeeping/documents/dpko_dfs_gender_military_perspective.pdf (accessed 1 April 2011), 29 and 10 respectively).

[225] Boutros-Ghali referred to UNOSOM II as 'the first peace-enforcement operation authorized and commanded by the United Nations' (United Nations, *The United Nations and Somalia: 1992–1996* (Blue Book Series) (New York, UN Sales No E.96.I.8, 1996) 43).

[226] SC Res 1484 of 30 May 2003, para 4.

[227] MONUC was authorised under Chapter VII to use 'all necessary means to fulfil its mandate in the Ituri district and, as it deems it within its capabilities, in North and South Kivu' (SC Res 1493 of 28 July 2003, para 26).

[228] The Capstone Doctrine (n 214) notes: 'The Security Council may take enforcement action without the consent of the main parties to the conflict, if it believes that the conflict presents a threat to international peace and security. This, however, would be a peace

tion in attempting to distinguish militarised peacekeeping from peace-enforcement based on the need for host state consent is that, even accepting that host state consent is required for militarised peacekeeping but not for peace-enforcement, with each type of operation consent is almost always obtained. One is left, therefore, to argue that when a host state consents to a militarised peacekeeping operation the state's consent is a legal prerequisite, whereas when a host state does exactly the same thing in relation to a peace-enforcement operation, its action is legally irrelevant.[229]

4.4 Conclusion on the Changed Nature of Peace-Enforcement

The term 'peace-enforcement' has been defined in a number of ways in its short life, none of which is sufficiently precise to afford it much value. If the term is relied upon to refer to a type of operation that lies in the grey area between peacekeeping operations and enforcement operations, it provides little in the way of precision, given that peacekeeping operations (through the development of militarised peacekeeping) and enforcement operations (through the development of quasi-enforcement) have each evolved such that they both extend into this grey area. Nor does the term provide sufficient clarity when it is relied upon to distinguish between a militarised peacekeeping operation and an enforcement action based on the character of the force; the difference between a 'tactical' use of force and one that is 'strategic' is not self-evident. It would seem that the one essential characteristic of a peace-enforcement operation (according to the Capstone Doctrine, at any rate) is that host state consent is not a legal requirement. However, as will be discussed more fully in chapter 3, where a peacekeeping operation is established by the Security Council with the intention of binding Member States, host state consent is equally unnecessary. Moreover, the fact that the term is used to include both UN-led operations with enforcement functions and state-led operations with enforcement functions serves to blur the two types of operation.

As such, the term 'peace-enforcement' will be avoided in this study. Where an operation is state- or coalition-led and authorised by the Security Council under Chapter VII (implicitly or explicitly) in response to a threat to international peace and security to use force beyond self-defence, it will be referred to herein as enforcement or, where appropriate, quasi-

enforcement operation. It may also take enforcement action for humanitarian or protection purposes; where there is no political process and where the consent of the major parties may not be achievable, but where civilians are suffering' (p 43 endnote 20).

[229] While it is undoubtedly true that host state consent is of considerable importance in ensuring the success of a quasi-enforcement operation, this point may equally be made in relation to militarised peacekeeping.

enforcement.[230] Where an operation is UN-led and it or some of its tasks are authorised by the Security Council under Chapter VII (implicitly or explicitly) in response to a threat to international peace and security to use force beyond self-defence, it will be referred to as militarised peacekeeping. Whether or not host state consent is legally required for the establishment (or modification) of an operation – be it UN-led or state-led – will depend upon the Security Council's intention in relation to the particular operation.

5. CONCLUSION

The distinction between peacekeeping and enforcement is firmly rooted in the literature; peacekeeping is characterised as something 'other' than enforcement. Each type of operation has been viewed as possessing its own set of 'fundamental' principles, providing opposing approaches in relation to host state consent, the use of force and impartiality. However, as has been shown, in practice the two endeavours overlap to such a degree that many peacekeeping operations share many of the characteristics of enforcement operations and many enforcements operations have much in common with peacekeeping. Peacekeeping may no longer be seen as the opposite of enforcement; instead the two types of operation overlap to a remarkable degree – so much so that an attempt to clarify the grey area that lies between the two through use of the term 'peace-enforcement' is of ever diminishing value.

Despite the changed nature of each endeavour, there continues to be a desire on the part of the UN to maintain that peacekeeping continues to be the opposite of enforcement. In each of the three phases of militarised peacekeeping – including the current one – the UN has been at pains to downplay the enforcement nature of operations and to emphasise adherence to the 'fundamental principles' of peacekeeping. In the case of ONUC, for example, UN officials denied that force beyond self-defence was actually being used. With UNPROFOR, in the same Security Council Resolution that authorised the establishment of a rapid reaction force consisting of thousands of heavily armed troops as 'an integral part' of that peacekeeping operation, the Security Council stressed that its 'impartiality [would] be maintained'.[231] It was only by redefining impartiality and self-defence that the Brahimi Report was able to posit the view that force only in self-defence or in defence-of-mandate, impartiality and consent were the 'bedrock principles' of peacekeeping in the twenty-first century. Similarly, the General Assembly's Special Committee on Peacekeeping

[230] Where an operation is in the nature of a full-blown enforcement operation or a sanctions-related enforcement operation, that terminology will be used.

[231] SC Res 998 of 16 June 1995.

Operations continues annually to stress the importance of the 'fundamental principles'. In its 2010 Report it observed that:

> [R]espect for the basic principles of peacekeeping, such as the consent of the parties, impartiality and the non-use of force except in self-defence and in the defence of a mandate authorized by the Security Council, is essential to [a peacekeeping operation's] success.[232]

The literature emerging from the UN Secretariat also continues to stress that the three elements are characteristic of peacekeeping operations. In its Capstone Doctrine, the UN Secretariat described consent of the parties, impartiality and the non-use of force except in self-defence (and in defence-of-mandate) as 'basic' principles.[233]

It is doubtless the case that it is in the Organization's interests that peacekeeping is perceived to be a non-forceful, impartial, non-intrusive concept. Member States that see it as such are more willing to donate troops, host states are more willing to consent to operations, and Member States of the Security Council are less likely to see the establishment of peacekeeping operations as a threat to state sovereignty.[234] However, continued emphasis on these characteristics despite the reality of its practice can lead to considerable confusion. Moreover, it is not without cost to the Organization. Findlay made the following observation in relation to the UN's characterisation of ONUC:

> Even its 'prevention of civil war' mandate was played down. This deliberate playing down of the significance of ONUC's military operations by two successive secretaries-general and their staffs was clearly designed to avoid further controversy . . . None of this, however, was particularly helpful to the orderly development of UN peace operations. Indeed it discredited that endeavour by demonstrating that political machinations could ultimately render Security Council resolutions and peacekeeping mandates and norms irrelevant.[235]

[232] *Report of the Special Committee on Peacekeeping Operations* (n 116) para 23.

[233] Capstone Doctrine (n 214) 31.

[234] Goulding (n 28) describes peacekeeping operations as possessing 'United Nationsness' and contrasts them with 'enforcement operations in Korea or (subsequently) Kuwait and Somalia where the Security Council's role has only been to authorize certain member states to undertake military action for a specific purpose'. He continues: 'It was this United Nationsness which had made United Nations peacekeeping operations acceptable to member states who would not otherwise have accepted foreign troops on their territory' (454).

[235] Findlay (n 77) 85–86.

Chapter 3

The Peacekeeping Powers of the Security Council and the Limitations Thereupon

> The United Nations is the creature of a treaty, and as such it exercises authority legitimately only insofar as it deploys powers which the treaty parties have assigned to it. Or, to borrow a phrase from the jurisprudence of the United States Supreme Court, the Charter creates a governance of limited enumerated powers. These may be modestly augmented by a 'penumbra' of other powers which are necessarily incidental to the effective implementation of the enumerated ones.
>
> Professor Thomas Franck[1]

1. INTRODUCTION

THE SECURITY COUNCIL'S powers are not without limit. As a creature of treaty, the primary source of its powers – and the limitations thereupon – is the UN Charter. And the nature and extent of these limitations will be affected by the character of measures taken by the Security Council. As this chapter will show, certain restrictions on the Security Council's functioning – for example, an inability to interfere in matters normally within the domestic jurisdiction of a state – are lifted only when it is engaging in enforcement under Chapter VII. At the same time, however, the powers of the Security Council to establish enforcement measures are more limited than its powers to establish measures that do not amount to enforcement. Thus, as the line between peacekeeping and enforcement blurs, the importance of understanding the constitutional basis of a Security Council action becomes ever more important.

The fact that the UN Security Council has only rarely indicated the constitutional basis of the peacekeeping missions established by it makes arriving at such an understanding difficult. The Security Council has

[1] Thomas M Franck, *Fairness in International Law and Institutions* (Oxford, Clarendon Press, 1995) 219–20.

never explicitly invoked Chapter VI when establishing peacekeeping operations, and only after the Cold War did it begin to indicate that it was acting under Chapter VII. Even where the Security Council indicates that it is relying upon Chapter VII when establishing an operation or assigning certain tasks to an operation, it almost always remains silent as to the particular article of that Chapter under which it is acting. As a result, there will frequently be considerable uncertainty as to the constitutional basis of a peacekeeping operation and, in particular, whether or not, in establishing it, the Security Council intended to exercise its enforcement powers.

Regard must therefore be had to various indications of the Security Council's intent. Whether the Security Council has taken an obligatory Chapter VII measure will depend primarily upon the wording of the relevant resolution. Indicators of intent within the resolution may include: a finding of a threat to the peace, breach of the peace or act of aggression; the express or implied invocation of Chapter VII (or an article thereunder); the use of language signalling an intention to bind (such as 'decides'); or an authorisation to use 'all necessary means' or similar language signalling an authorisation to use force beyond self-defence which must have its basis in Chapter VII.[2] Finding the intention of the Security Council in a particular resolution may require that we look beyond the four corners of the document:

> The interpretation of Security Council resolutions may require the Court to analyse statements by representatives of members of the Security Council made at the time of their adoption, other resolutions of the Security Council on the same issue, as well as the subsequent practice of relevant United Nations organs and of States affected by those given resolutions.[3]

Moreover, whether or not a host state has consented to Security Council measures may be an important factor.[4]

This chapter will consider the impact that the constitutional basis on which the Security Council establishes or revises the mandate of a peacekeeping operation (or certain of its tasks) has on the Security Council's powers in relation to that operation. In chapters 4–6, the constitutional basis of

[2] 'The language of a resolution of the Security Council should be carefully analysed before a conclusion can be made as to its binding effect. In view of the nature of the powers under Article 25, the question whether they have been in fact exercised is to be determined in each case, having regard to the terms of the resolution to be interpreted, the discussions leading to it, the Charter provisions invoked and, in general, all circumstances that might assist in determining the legal consequences of the resolution of the Security Council.' *Legal Consequences for States of the Continued Presence of South Africa in Namibia (South West Africa) notwithstanding Security Council Resolution 276 (1970)*, Advisory Opinion of 21 June 1971 [1971] ICJ Rep 16, 53.

[3] *Accordance with International Law of the Unilateral Declaration of Independence in Respect of Kosovo*, Advisory Opinion of 22 July 2010, www.icj-cij.org/docket/files/141/15987.pdf (accessed 1 April 2011), 34–35.

[4] See discussion of the *Certain Expenses* case in chapter 4, section 3.

particular militarised peacekeeping operations (or operations which might potentially be characterised as militarised) and the impact that this basis has on the functioning of such operations will be considered.

It must be noted, however, that some commentators and international judges consider a focus on the constitutional basis of peacekeeping operations to be largely irrelevant.[5] A recent decision of the Special Court for Sierra Leone put it this way: 'Commentators have noted that the legal basis for peacekeeping missions is of no practical significance as peacekeeping missions are deployed with the consent of the parties and their legitimacy is no longer questioned.'[6] Neither of these arguments is convincing. The first disregards the fact that a number of important factors depend on whether a peacekeeping mission involves an exercise of the Security Council's Chapter VII powers, including, in certain cases, its enforcement powers. The second argument is short-sighted in view of the changing nature of peacekeeping. Each will be considered in turn.

To argue because operations always feature host state consent the constitutional basis of an operation irrelevant is incorrect for a number of reasons. First, while host state consent has generally been forthcoming with regard to the establishment of peacekeeping operations or modification of their mandates, this has not always been the case.[7] Second, even where host state consent has been granted, the issue of whether or not it is a legal prerequisite to the presence of peacekeeping forces may be relevant: it may impact on related questions such as the state's ability to withdraw consent[8] and the Security Council's ability (and willingness) to modify a mandate without seeking renewed consent from the host

[5] See eg Michael Bothe, 'Peace-Keeping' in Bruno Simma (ed), *The Charter of the United Nations: A Commentary*, 2nd edn, vol 1 (Oxford, Oxford University Press, 2002) 648–700, para 84: 'Whether a situation falls under Chapter VI or VII, is . . . primarily of significance for the formal powers of the [Security Council]. In practical terms, however, the problem is not relevant, as these peace-keeping forces have never been imposed upon the parties to a conflict; the agreement of all the parties concerned was sought and given in all cases.'

[6] *Prosecutor v Issa Hassan Sesay, Morrison Kallon and Augustine Gbao* (Case No SCSL-04-15-T, Special Court for Sierra Leone, Trial Chamber I, 2 March 2009), para 222. In a footnote, the Special Court relied on Christine Gray, *International Law and the Use of Force*, 3rd edn (Oxford, Oxford University Press, 2008) 261; and Marten Zwanenburg, *Accountability of Peace Support Operations* (Dordrecht, Martinus Nijhoff, 2005) 11–12.

[7] UNOSOM II, discussed in chapter 4, sections 4.1.2 and 4.2, is a clear exception. In addition, consent issues arise in relation to other peacekeeping operations, including ONUC in the Congo (discussed in chapter 4, section 3), UNPROFOR in the former Yugoslavia (discussed in chapter 4, sections 4.1.1 and 4.2), and UNOCI in Côte d'Ivoire (discussed in chapter 6, section 3).

[8] As Bowett observed: 'The fact that a State has consented to the presence of the Force does not of itself imply that the State retains the right to withdraw such consent and unilaterally terminate the mission . . . [S]ubject to any agreement with the host State and to . . . considerations of an estoppel and good faith, the United Nations has the exclusive right to terminate the mission . . . in all cases where the presence of the Force is not dependent in law entirely on the consent of the host State.' Derek W Bowett, *United Nations Forces: A Legal Study of United Nations Practice* (London, Stevens & Sons, 1964) 422.

state.[9] In order to address the issue, the constitutional basis on which the Security Council has established a peacekeeping operation or certain of its tasks must be known.

Third, the question of whether an operation was established by the Security Council under Chapter VII is significant because that Chapter provides the only Charter basis for the Security Council to authorise the use of offensive force. Given that peacekeeping operations are now routinely authorised to use force substantially beyond self-defence, the constitutional basis of an operation may be relevant to the legality of its use of force.

A fourth reason is illustrated by the *RUF* case, which was heard before the Special Court for Sierra Leone – the very Court that cited, with approval, the view of commentators that the legal basis was of no practical significance. There, the Court had to determine whether UNAMSIL peacekeepers in Sierra Leone were entitled to civilian protection or whether the forceful nature of the operation meant that they were, in effect, combatants participating in an enforcement operation. Despite its suggestion that the legal basis of peacekeeping was irrelevant, the Special Court for Sierra Leone expended considerable energy in attempting to establish the constitutional basis of UNAMSIL in its judgment.[10]

The second strand of the argument that the constitutional basis of peacekeeping operations is irrelevant – that the legitimacy of such operations is no longer questioned – ignores the changing nature of the endeavour. While it is certainly true that the time to argue that traditional peacekeeping operations are illegal has long since passed – peacekeeping operations have existed for over 50 years without an outpouring of condemnation from states and, arguably, with an endorsement by the ICJ in the *Certain Expenses* case[11] – that is not to say that every operation characterised as peacekeeping will necessarily be intra vires the Security Council's powers. As the Security Council continues to charge peacekeeping forces with ever wider tasks that are not in the nature of those traditionally carried out by peacekeeping forces – including civilian protection and the restoration of security through reliance on the use of offensive force – an examination of the legal basis of its operations is more relevant than ever before.

[9] In August 2006 the Security Council passed a resolution (SC Res 1706 of 31 August 2006) which came close to modifying the mandate of a peacekeeping mission without the host state's consent. See the discussion of the United Nations Mission in Sudan (UNMIS) in chapter 6, section 6. Moreover, in Côte D'Ivoire, there is little evidence of host state consent for the modification of the mandate of the peacekeeping operation there. See the discussion of the United Nations Operation in Côte d'Ivoire (UNOCI) in chapter 6, section 3.

[10] James Sloan, 'Peacekeepers Under Fire: Prosecuting the RUF for Attacks against the UN Assistance Mission in Sierra Leone' (2010) 9 *Law and Practice of International Courts and Tribunals* 242–93. For a discussion of UNAMSIL see chapter 5, section 2.

[11] *Certain Expenses of the United Nations (Article 17, Paragraph 2, of the Charter)*, Advisory Opinion of 20 July 1962 [1962] ICJ Rep 151. This case is discussed in detail in chapter 4, sections 2 and 3.

Thus, this book takes the view that the constitutional nature of a peacekeeping operation – whether or not it has host state consent – may be highly relevant and may impact on whether the Security Council possesses the legal authority to take certain measures. This chapter will first examine the purposes and principles of the United Nations (set out in Articles 1 and 2 of the UN Charter) and consider how the limitations contained therein impact on the Security Council's peacekeeping powers, both when it charges such operations with enforcement powers and when it does not. Next it will consider the Security Council's powers to take measures in relation to peace and security, as provided in Chapters VI and VII. In its examination of Chapter VII, the chapter will distinguish between those powers that are of an enforcement nature and those that are not. Finally, the chapter will consider whether the Security Council possesses any implied peacekeeping or enforcement powers.

2. PURPOSES AND PRINCIPLES OF THE UN

Unlike Chapters VI and VII of the UN Charter, which focus on the powers of the Security Council, the purposes and principles set out in Chapter I affect the functioning of the whole of the Organization, as well as its membership. Article 1 sets out, in broad terms, the purposes of the UN, and in Article 2 the principles of the Organization are elaborated. In these two articles the drafters of the UN Charter set out the reasons for the establishment of the Organization, their goals and the limits of the authority they were willing to vest in the Organization and its organs. The nature of these provisions, as well as their position at the beginning of the UN Charter, shows them to be an extremely important aspect of the legal regime envisaged therein. Moreover, the purposes and principles are invoked in several articles throughout the Charter, affecting or limiting the functioning of the organs of the Organization. Of particular importance in this regard is Article 24, which provides that the Security Council acts on behalf of Member States when carrying out the duty to maintain international peace and security, but stipulates that the Security Council shall act in accordance with the purposes and principles of the UN in so doing.[12] A 2010 report of the General Assembly's Special Committee on Peacekeeping Operations

[12] A link between the Security Council acting in accordance with the purposes and principles and the binding nature of its decisions has been recognised by the ICJ. The Court found that 'decisions made by the Security Council . . . adopted in conformity with the purposes and principles of the Charter and in accordance with its Articles 24 and 25 . . . are consequently binding on all States Members of the United Nations which are thus under the obligation to accept and carry them out' (*Namibia* case (n 2) 52–53). See also Judge Weeramantry's dissenting opinion in *Questions of Interpretation and Application of the 1971 Montreal Convention Arising from the Aerial Incident at Lockerbie (Libya v US: Libya v UK)*, Provisional Measures [1992] ICJ Rep 3, 61.

highlighted the continuing need for the Organization to comply with the UN's purposes and principles when engaging in peacekeeping:

> The Special Committee stresses that peacekeeping operations should strictly observe the purposes and principles enshrined in the Charter. It emphasizes that respect for the principles of the sovereignty, territorial integrity and political independence of States and non-intervention in matters that are essentially within the domestic jurisdiction of any State is crucial to common efforts, including peacekeeping operations, to promote international peace and security.[13]

This section will discuss the UN's purposes and principles and, in particular, the restrictions they place on the functioning of the Organization's peacekeeping practice, especially as regards the sovereignty, territorial integrity and political independence of states. It will show that these three restrictions overlap to a considerable degree with the 'fundamental principles' of peacekeeping: force only in self-defence, consent of the host state and impartiality. As we shall see, whether these restrictions will limit the Security Council's freedom of action in establishing a peacekeeping operation will depend on the character of the operation, in particular whether or not it amounts to an enforcement operation.

2.1 Article 1: Purposes

Broadly put, the four purposes of the United Nations are:

(1) to maintain international peace and security (Article 1(1));
(2) to develop friendly relations among nations (Article 1(2));
(3) to achieve international cooperation in solving international problems and encouraging respect for human rights and fundamental freedoms (Article 1(3)); and
(4) to be a centre for harmonising the actions of nations in the attainment of these common ends (Article 1(4)).

The nature and wording of the purposes suggests that they are meant to offer 'broad-brush' guidance regarding the reasons for the establishment of the Organization.[14] The specific powers entrusted to the Organization – and certain limitations thereupon – are located elsewhere in the Charter.[15]

Despite their broad-brush nature, the UN's purposes may impact on the Security Council's peacekeeping practice. The existence of provisions

[13] United Nations, *Report of the Special Committee on Peacekeeping Operations: 2010 Substantive Session (22 February–19 March 2010)* (UN Doc A/64/19), para 22.

[14] See Rüdiger Wolfrum, 'Article 1' in Simma (n 5) 39–46, 40 para 4.

[15] cf John W Halderman, 'Legal Basis for United Nations Armed Forces' (1962) 56 *American Journal of International Law* 971, who argued that Art 1(1) provided the legal basis for ONUC. See discussion later in this chapter at text accompanying n 233.

throughout the Charter requiring compliance with the purposes and principles gives them a certain legal grounding.[16] In particular, Article 2, which sets out the Organization's principles, provides the following link between the limitations contained in the principles and the UN's purposes: 'The Organization and its Members, in pursuit of the Purposes stated in Article 1, shall act in accordance with the following Principles . . .' The UN's purposes are again invoked in Article 2(4), which prohibits any use of force which is inconsistent with those purposes. The impact that the purposes may have on the Organization's ability to act was recognised by the ICJ in the *Certain Expenses* case, where it considered whether peacekeeping-related expenditures were compatible with the purposes of the UN. It observed that the 'purposes are wide indeed, but neither they nor the powers conferred to effectuate them are unlimited'. Nevertheless, it took the view that 'when the Organization takes action which warrants the assertion that it was appropriate for the fulfilment of one of the stated purposes of the United Nations, the presumption is that such action is not *ultra vires* the Organization'.[17]

2.1.1 *Article 1(1): To Maintain International Peace and Security*

For the purposes of this study, Article 1(1) warrants further analysis. It provides that the first purpose of the United Nations is:

> to maintain international peace and security, and to that end: to take effective collective measures for the prevention and removal of threats to the peace, and for the suppression of acts of aggression or other breaches of the peace, and to bring about by peaceful means, and in conformity with the principles of justice and international law, adjustment or settlement of international disputes or situations which might lead to a breach of the peace.

In the words of the ICJ in the *Certain Expenses* case: 'The primary place ascribed to international peace and security [in Article 1(1)] is natural, since the fulfilment of the other purposes will be dependent upon the attainment of that basic condition.'[18] ICJ President Schwebel observed that '[t]he drafters of the Charter above all resolved to accord the Security

[16] See discussion in this chapter above at n 12 and accompanying text.

[17] *Certain Expenses* (n 11) 168. In his separate opinion, Judge Spender made the following observation: 'A general rule is that words used in a treaty should be read as having the meaning they bore therein when it came into existence. But this meaning must be consistent with the purposes sought to be achieved' (189). This view was confirmed by the ICJ in the *Oil Platforms* case where it observed that, 'according to customary international law as expressed in Article 31 of the Vienna Convention on the Law of Treaties of 23 May 1969, a treaty must be interpreted in good faith in accordance with the ordinary meaning to be given to its terms in their context and in the light of its object and purpose'. *Oil Platforms (Islamic Republic of Iran v United States of America),* Preliminary Objection, Judgment [1996] ICJ Rep 803, 812.

[18] *Certain Expenses* (n 11) 168.

Council alone extraordinary powers. They did so in order to further realization of the first Purpose of the United Nations.'[19]

Article 1(1) refers to two methods of maintaining international peace and security, one of which corresponds to the Security Council's enforcement powers (use of collective measures to prevent and remove threats to the peace and to suppress aggression or other breaches) and one to its non-enforcement powers (peaceful adjustment of disputes). When the Organization is exercising these latter powers, Article 1(1) stipulates that actions must be 'in conformity with the principles of justice and international law'. No such requirement is provided where an operation is of an enforcement character, leading some to take the view that such Security Council actions are not so limited.[20] It has been argued, however, that such a view does not appear to comport with the wishes of the drafters.[21] Moreover, an argument may be made that recent practice suggests that the Security Council, and the United Nations more broadly, favours acting in compliance with the principles of justice and international law, regardless of the character of the operation.[22]

[19] He continued: '[Articles 1(1), 24(1) and (2) and 25 of the Charter] – the very heart of the Charter's design for the maintenance of international peace – manifest the plenitude of the powers of the Security Council, which are elaborated by the provisions of Chapters VI, VII, and VIII of the Charter. They also demonstrate that the Security Council is subject to the rule of law; it shall act in accordance with the Purposes and Principles of the United Nations and its decisions must be adopted in accordance with the Charter.' *Libyan Arab Jamahiriya v US* [1988] ICJ Rep 115, Dissenting Opinion of President Schwebel, 166–67. Note, however, the exception discussed by President Schwebel at n 20 below.

[20] See the Dissenting Opinion of President Schwebel, who, despite acknowledging the importance of the purpose of the Organization as provided in Art 1(1), held that the Security Council may 'lawfully decide upon measures which may in the interests of the maintenance or restoration of international peace and security derogate from the rights of a State under international law'. In addition to relying on Art 103 in support of this contention, he relied on the fact that the reference in Art 1(1) to the principles of justice and international law 'designedly relates only to adjustment or settlement by peaceful means, and not to the taking of effective collective measures for the prevention and removal of threats to and breaches of the peace. It was deliberately so provided to ensure that the vital duty of preventing and removing threats to and breaches of the peace would not be limited by existing law. (See the Report on the Preamble, Purposes and Principles, *United Nation Conference on International Organization (UNCIO)*, Vol. 6, pp. 453–54, and the observations of Lord Halifax, p 25.)' (*Libyan Arab Jamahiriya* case, ibid, Dissenting Opinion of President Schwebel, 166–67.) See also LM Goodrich, E Hambro and AP Simmons, *The Charter of the United Nations*, 3rd edn (Columbia University Press, 1969) 27–28; TD Gill, 'Legal and Some Political Limitations on the Power of the UN Security Council to Exercise its Enforcement Powers under Chapter VII of the Charter' (1995) 26 *Netherlands Yearbook of International Law* 33, 65.

[21] Dapo Akande, 'The International Court of Justice and the Security Council: Is there Room for Judicial Control of Decisions of the Political Organs of the United Nations?' (1997) 46 *International and Comparative Law Quarterly* 309, 317–21. Cf the statement of President Schwebel at n 20 immediately above.

[22] See eg United Nations, *Secretary-General's Bulletin: Observance by United Nations Forces of International Humanitarian Law* (UN Doc ST/SGB/1999/13), 6 August 1999, which provides that, inter alia, a UN enforcement operation would be bound by international humanitarian law obligations. See also United Nations, *Statement by the President of the Security Council* (UN Doc S/PRST/2003/15), 30 September 2003, where the Security Council reaffirmed the vital importance of justice and the rule of law, and recalled its 'repeated emphasis' on

Compliance with the 'principles of justice and international law' as called for in Article 1(1) would, of course, include customary international law. Among the most important customary international law rules relevant to peacekeeping are the principles of sovereign equality, non-use of force and non-intervention in domestic affairs. As we shall see immediately below, customary international law rules correspond with certain of the principles set out in Article 2.[23]

2.2 Article 2: Principles

The wording of Article 2 is of a different nature from that of Article 1. The mandatory nature of Article 2 is evident from the word 'shall', which appears in the *chapeau* and re-appears in all paragraphs with the exception of 2(1). Unlike Article 1, Article 2 is unambiguously prescriptive. The principles set out therein impose certain limits on the Organization and the Member States comprising it.[24] The principles tend to reflect a tension between two conflicting desires on the part of the drafters of the UN Charter. On the one hand, the principles emphasise sovereign equality, non-interference and the non-use of force, indicating a desire on the part of the drafting states to retain as much control over their sovereignty as possible and to ensure that the UN was not authorised to intervene unduly. On the other hand, the principles show a recognition on the part of the drafting states that if the Security Council is successfully to maintain peace and security, the enforcement powers vested in it must not be unduly impeded.

This tension was resolved in large part by limiting the Organization's authority to take measures without the consent of Member States to situations where the Security Council is acting under Chapter VII to restore international peace and security. Three of the Organization's seven principles, all closely linked, are of particular relevance as regards the establishment of peacekeeping operations and their emplacement in sovereign states: Article 2(1), guaranteeing sovereign equality, Article 2(4), providing for the non-use of force, and Article 2(7), precluding the Organization

them in relation to peacekeeping operations. In a 2006 Presidential Statement, the Security Council reaffirmed its commitment to the Charter and to international law (United Nations, *Statement by the President of the Security Council* (UN Doc S/PRST/2006/28), 22 June 2006).

[23] Additional customary international law rules relevant to peacekeeping not discussed here include those relating to the conduct of hostilities (see eg Ray Murphy, *UN Peacekeeping in Lebanon, Somalia and Kosovo* (Cambridge, Cambridge University Press, 2007) ch 5) and requirements relating to the delegation of powers (see eg Danesh Sarooshi, *The United Nations and the Development of Collective Security: The Delegation by the UN Security Council of its Chapter VII Powers* (Oxford, Oxford University Press, 1999).

[24] An exception here is Art 2(5), which imposes a positive obligation on Member States to provide the UN with 'every assistance in any action it takes in accordance with the present Charter'.

from interfering in matters which are essentially within a state's domestic jurisdiction. Each will be considered in turn.

2.2.1 *Article 2(1): Sovereign Equality*

Article 2(1) of the UN Charter provides that the Organization 'is based on the principle of sovereign equality of all its members'. This principle has been said by the ICJ to be a guarantee of the customary international law right of states to respect for their sovereignty.[25] The Court, moreover, made it clear that the principle of respect for state sovereignty is closely linked with the principle of non-intervention.[26] On its face, this provision would appear to preclude the imposition of a UN force – whether peace-keeping or enforcement in nature – in a state.

While no exceptions to the rights guaranteed in Article 2(1) are provided in the article, it is clear that where a state consents to a UN operation entering its territory and assuming certain functions (or where it requests that it does so), it may not claim to have had its rights under Article 2(1) breached.[27] Moreover, based on the structure of the UN Charter as a whole, it is clear that a second exception exists: the rights guaranteed in Article 2(1) do not preclude the Security Council from carrying out legitimate measures to restore international peace and security.

2.2.2 *Article 2(4): Non-Use of Force*

The prohibition on the use of force is primarily provided for in Article 2(4).[28] This principle has been said by the ICJ to be closely linked with that of sovereign equality of states, guaranteed in Article 2(1).[29] Article 2(4) provides that 'All Members shall refrain in their international relations from the threat or use of force against the territorial integrity or political independence of any state, or in any other manner inconsistent with the Purposes of the United Nations'. Although this prohibition is not specifically directed at the UN, its activities are affected by the provision.[30]

[25] *Military and Paramilitary Activities in and against Nicaragua (Nicaragua v United States of America)*, Merits, Judgment [1986] ICJ Rep 14, 111. While the Court was addressing sovereign equality as a principle of customary international law, its reasoning applies equally to the concept as guaranteed in the Charter. See Robert Jennings and Arthur Watts, *Oppenheim's International Law*, 9th edn, vol 1 (London, Longman, 1992) 428 para 128.

[26] *Nicaragua* case, ibid, 111. In addition, the ICJ observed that the concept of non-intervention 'has been presented as a corollary of the principle of sovereign equality of states' (ibid, 106).

[27] See below, nn 47–51 and accompanying text for a discussion on this point in relation to Art 2(7).

[28] The requirement set out in Art 2(3) that states settle their disputes peacefully is also relevant.

[29] *Nicaragua* case (n 25) 111.

[30] The *chapeau* of Art 2 provides that '*The Organization* and its Members . . . shall act in accordance with . . . the Principles' (emphasis added). The Art 2(4) prohibition on the use of force is frequently referred to by state representatives as being a *jus cogens* norm (*Nicaragua* case (n 25) 100–01).

While some take a narrow view of the type of force prohibited in the paragraph,[31] it is broadly accepted that the prohibition is of a general nature.[32] That is to say, Article 2(4) could be infringed by any sort of forcible trespass, including one not intended to deprive that state of part of its territory or where the invading troops are meant to withdraw immediately after completing a temporary and limited operation.[33] Therefore, depending on the particulars of an operation – such as whether it is armed and in what circumstances and against whom it is authorised to use force – it has been asserted that a peacekeeping operation, if unauthorised by the host state, could amount to a use of force.[34]

While not spelled out in the text of Article 2(4), it is clear from the UN Charter as whole that an exception to the prohibition on the use of force exists where the Security Council engages in enforcement action under Article 42. A second exception is provided by Article 51, where the 'inherent right of individual or collective self-defence if an armed attack occurs' is recognised. In addition, a third exception exists: if an operation is present with the consent of the host state (or at its request), it will not amount to a use of force against that state's territorial integrity or political independence, as proscribed by Article 2(4). A peacekeeping force operating with the consent of the host state is akin to a state entering another state at the host state's invitation. The general rule in such circumstances is that 'normally if one state requested assistance from another, then clearly that intervention could not be dictatorial and therefore unlawful'.[35] The General Assembly's Definition of Aggression provides, *inter alia*, that the following act qualifies as aggression:

> The use of armed forces of one State which are within the territory of another State with the agreement of the receiving State, *in contravention of the conditions provided for in the agreement or any extension of their presence in such territory beyond the termination of the agreement*.[36]

The exception spelled out in the italicised passage shows the General Assembly's recognition of the right of a state to invite a foreign force, including a peacekeeping force, onto its territory.[37]

[31] See eg Derek W Bowett, *Self-Defence in International Law* (Manchester, Manchester University Press, 1958) 152.

[32] See Simon Chesterman, *Just War or Just Peace? Humanitarian Intervention and International Law* (Oxford, Oxford University Press, 2001) 48–52.

[33] Albrecht Randelzhofer, 'Article 2(4)' in Simma (n 5) 112–36, 123–24 paras 35–37.

[34] Jennings and Watts (n 25) 428 para 128.

[35] See Gray (n 6) 81, relying on a UK Foreign Policy Document from 1984 ('UK Materials on International Law' (1986) 57 *British Yearbook of International Law* 614).

[36] GA Res 3314 (XXIX) of 14 December 1974, Annex Art 3(e), 'Definition of Aggression' (emphasis added).

[37] Gray (n 6) 81. Cf Bowett (n 8) 191, who stated that '[p]rima facie the United Nations have no power to intervene in a civil war within a state, and it is believed that this remains the position even when a request for assistance has been made to the United Nations by the authorities generally recognized as the lawful government'.

2.2.3 *Article 2(7): Non-Intervention in Domestic Matters*

Article 2(7) sets out the principle that nothing in the UN Charter authorises the UN to intervene in matters that are 'essentially within the domestic jurisdiction of any state'.[38] This too has been said by the ICJ to be closely linked with the principle of sovereign equality.[39] An ever-broadening involvement of the Security Council in what might traditionally have been considered matters within the domestic jurisdiction of states has led some to suggest that Article 2(7) is not fulfilling its purpose[40] or that it has become obsolete.[41] However, even accepting that the concept of domestic jurisdiction has become narrower over time[42] and that the impact of Article 2(7) has diminished, the article has certainly not fallen into desuetude. Article 2(7) still serves as an important limitation on the UN involving itself in matters which are essentially domestic in nature.[43] While the Security Council's discretion in relation to whether a matter it is dealing with falls outside a state's domestic jurisdiction at Article 2(7) is broad, it must be exercised in a manner that is '*bona fide* and *intra vires*'.[44]

There has been a tendency on the part of the Security Council to find that the effects (or even the *potential* effects) of events within a state – such as the risk of transborder population flows or the risk that the conflict may escalate to include neighbouring states – amount to a threat to *international* peace and security.[45] While the Security Council's characterisation of a dispute as a threat to international peace allows it to invoke Article 39 – the gateway to its Chapter VII powers – this characterisation does not change the nature of the functions carried out by a peacekeeping operation established to address the threat. That is to say, it does not mean that none of the activities of the peacekeeping operation may be classed as trespassing on matters 'essentially within the domestic jurisdiction'. Thus, even where a peacekeeping operation was established pursuant to a finding of a threat to international peace and security, its activities will still need to comport with Article 2(7) – absent the existence of an

[38] The Art 2(4) prohibition on the threat or use of force 'in their international relations' is also a reflection of the drafting states' emphasis on non-interference. As noted by Gray (n 6) 67, '[i]nternal conflicts were seen as a domestic matter except in so far as they might constitute a threat to international peace and security under Chapter VII of the UN Charter'.

[39] *Nicaragua* case (n 25) 111.

[40] Georg Nolte, 'Article 2(7)' in Simma (n 5) 148–71, 150 para 3.

[41] See *ibid*, 149–50 para 1 and the footnotes referred to therein.

[42] On the fluidity of the concept of domestic jurisdiction see Rosalyn Higgins, *The Development of International Law through the Political Organs of the United Nations* (Oxford, Oxford University Press, 1963) 61. See also Thomas M Franck, *Recourse to Force: State Action against Threats and Armed Attacks* (Cambridge, Cambridge University Press, 2002) 220.

[43] Nigel D White, *The United Nations and the Maintenance of International Peace and Security* (Manchester, Manchester University Press, 1990) 92.

[44] Franck (n 1) 219.

[45] For a discussion of Art 39 and Security Council practice thereunder see below, section 3.2.1.

exception. Whether or not peacekeeping operations trespass on states' domestic jurisdiction will depend on the tasks assigned to them. If, for example, an operation is tasked with reporting to the Security Council, this is not likely to be an 'essentially domestic' act; however, many other peacekeeping functions – including, say, distributing humanitarian aid, facilitating an election or restoring security – might well be.[46]

As with the other two principles of Article 2 discussed above, there are certain exceptions to the Article 2(7) prohibition. First, Article 2(7) itself specifically provides an exception to its application where the Security Council is engaging in 'enforcement measures under Chapter VII'. Second, though not set out in the text of Article 2(7), an exception to the limitation on interference in matters which are essentially within the domestic jurisdiction exists where the state consents to such interference. Consent precludes the characterisation of UN action as 'intervention' in the internal affairs of a state and any violation of Article 2(7) that might otherwise have resulted from the deployment of an operation will not arise.[47] Given that the original purpose of Article 2(7) was to protect the sovereignty of Member States,[48] there is no basis for a state to claim that this has been jeopardised in a situation where the UN has 'intervened' in a state's domestic affairs by putting in place a peacekeeping operation with the state's consent. One observer put it this way: '[P]rohibited intervention should be understood as intervention against the will of the state.'[49] Such a view of matters is not precluded by the wording of the text of Article 2(7);[50] moreover, it is supported by Security Council practice.[51]

[46] Higgins appeared to take a broad view of the concept of domestic jurisdiction. She noted that the very intrusive and forceful activities of ONUC (for a discussion of the activities of ONUC, see chapter 4) did not amount to interference with matters of an essentially domestic nature, observing that, after all, ONUC did not deal with matters such as convening parliament or imposing a constitution. Rosalyn Higgins, *United Nations Peacekeeping 1946–1967: Documents and Commentary, Vol III: Africa* (Oxford, Oxford University Press, 1980) 58.

[47] Steven Ratner, *The New UN Peacekeeping: Building Peace in the Lands of Conflict after the Cold War* (New York, St Martin's Press, 1995) 33. See also Joseph P Bialke, 'United Nations Peace Operations: Applicable Norms and the Application of the Law of Armed Conflict' (2001) 50 *Airforce Law Review* 1, 13 and n 62. See also R Simmonds, *Legal Problems Arising from the United Nations Military Operations in the Congo* (The Hague, Martinus Nijhoff, 1968) 61–62, who observed in relation to ONUC that 'it could scarcely be argued [in the face of the existence of a request, or consent, by the Congolese authorities] that the sending of the Force constituted "intervention"'.

[48] Franck (n 1) 220. See also Nolte (n 40) 150 para 3.

[49] David Wippman, 'Military Intervention, Regional Organizations, and Host-State Consent' (1996) 7 *Duke Journal of Comparative and International Law* 209, 210. Cf Frank (n 1) 228, who observed that 'it is surely not credible as a matter of law to say that intervention in a civil war is not intervention whenever it follows a government request'. However, the point being made here is a different one: while it may be an intervention, it is an intervention of a nature not contemplated by Art 2(7) – ie, an intervention by invitation – and therefore not proscribed by it.

[50] cf Franck (n 42) 41.

[51] ibid.

2.3 Conclusions on Purposes and Principles

It is clear, based on the foregoing, that the three UN principles set out at paragraphs (1), (4) and (7) of Article 2 all place restrictions on the conduct of the Organization in establishing peacekeeping forces. It is also clear that there are two relevant exceptions to the applicability of the principles: where there is host consent and where the Security Council is engaging in enforcement measures under Chapter VII of the Charter. Moreover, while '[p]rinciples such as those of the non-use of force, non-intervention, respect for the independence and territorial integrity of States . . . continue to be binding as part of customary international law' despite having been incorporated into treaties such as the Charter,[52] where a state invites an entity onto its territory there can be no claim that they have been violated.

The next section considers the possible constitutional bases of peacekeeping operations, including their establishment as enforcement measures under Chapter VII of the Charter.

3. SECURITY COUNCIL POWERS

Many commentators divide peacekeeping into 'Chapter VI peacekeeping' and 'Chapter VII peacekeeping'. While exactly what is meant by each term will vary, 'Chapter VI peacekeeping' generally connotes those operations that are not empowered to use force beyond self-defence and 'Chapter VII peacekeeping' generally refers to operations that are so empowered – such as the militarised peacekeeping operations described above. Moreover, because Chapter VII is the Chapter of the UN Charter under which the Security Council may establish binding measures, the use of the term 'Chapter VII peacekeeping' may carry with it the suggestion that the Security Council is not (or not as strictly) reliant on the consent of the host state.

The Chapter VI/Chapter VII dichotomy is something of an oversimplification. While it is indeed the case that Chapter VI does not envisage forceful action, it is *not* the case that all measures taken under Chapter VII (nor even all 'enforcement' measures under that Chapter) are forceful in nature. Nor are all measures taken by the Security Council under Chapter VII binding.[53] Not all measures taken by the Security Council under

[52] *Case Concerning Military and Paramilitary Activities in and Against Nicaragua*, Judgment of 26 November 1984 [1984] ICJ Rep 390, 424.

[53] As the ICJ has observed, Art 25 (which obliges states to 'accept and carry out the decisions of the Security Council') 'is not confined to decisions in regard to enforcement action but applies to "the decisions of the Security Council" adopted in accordance with the Charter' (*Namibia* case (n 2) 52–53). See Rosalyn Higgins, 'A General Assessment of United Nations Peace-Keeping' in Antonio Cassese (ed), *United Nations Peace-Keeping: Legal Essays* (The Netherlands, Sijthoff & Noordhoff, 1978) 1–14, 4, who took the view that nothing prevents the Security Council from taking binding decisions under Chapter VI if it clearly indicates an intention to do so.

Chapter VII amount to enforcement[54] and not all Chapter VII enforcement measures are mandatory in nature as regards all states.[55]

In light of this, the following discussion will first consider the Security Council's Chapter VI powers in relation to peacekeeping and will then turn to its Chapter VII powers in this regard; as to the latter, the discussion will consider whether or not an exercise of power based in a particular article amounts to enforcement.

3.1 Chapter VI Powers

The Security Council's powers with regard to dealing with disputes are set out in Chapters VI – entitled 'Pacific Settlement of Disputes', and VII – entitled 'Action with Respect to Threats to the Peace, Breaches of the Peace, and Acts of Aggression'. Chapter VI envisages the Security Council[56] acting in a supportive or facilitative role by aiding the parties to a dispute to reach a peaceful settlement. It makes provision for the Security Council to investigate a dispute in order to determine whether it is likely to endanger international peace and security and, in certain cases, to recommend methods of adjustment or terms of settlement. As noted, the Security Council has never invoked Chapter VI as a basis for the establishment of a peacekeeping operation; however, a former Secretary-General has indicated his view that Chapter VI provided the basis for at least one such operation.[57]

None of the six articles of Chapter VI (Articles 33–38) envisages the establishment of peacekeeping operations, and none lends itself particularly well to providing a constitutional basis for UN peacekeeping. Nevertheless, the following articles of Chapter VI have been said by some commentators to provide a basis for certain peacekeeping operations established by the Security Council:[58]

[54] Higgins, ibid, 4. Cf Georg Ress and Jürgen Bröhmer, 'Article 53' in Simma (n 5) 854–90, 860 para 3: 'The negotiations at the San Francisco Conference support the view that all measures under Chapter VII, without exception, are enforcement measures.'

[55] For example, the Security Council may only *recommend* that Member States participate in a coalition of the willing to address a threat to or breach of international peace, established as an enforcement measure under Art 42.

[56] As well as, in more limited ways, the Secretary-General (Art 33(1)), the General Assembly (Art 35) and the ICJ (Art 36(3)).

[57] Secretary-General Hammarskjöld observed that in creating UNOGIL the Security Council had 'acted entirely within the limit of Chapter VI of the Charter'. United Nations, *Summary Study of the Experience Derived from the Establishment and Operation of the Force (Report of the Secretary-General)* (UN Doc A/3943), 9 October 1958, Annex A.i.65 para 180.

[58] The ICJ cited Art 35 – which allows any member of the UN to bring a dispute or situation to the attention of the Security Council or the General Assembly – in conjunction with Art 11(2) – which grants the General Assembly the power to discuss questions relating to the maintenance of international peace and security and, with certain limitations, to make recommendations with regard to such questions to the Security Council or concerned

(1) Article 33(2), which provides that the Security Council 'shall, when it deems necessary, call upon parties to settle their dispute' by various means listed in Article 33(1);[59]
(2) Article 34, which empowers the Security Council to investigate certain disputes;[60]
(3) Article 36(1), which provides that the Security Council may 'recommend appropriate procedures or methods of adjustment'.[61]

Regardless of which article of Chapter VI is invoked, two characteristics must be noted: first, Chapter VI measures are generally recommendatory only;[62] and second, Chapter VI provides for non-forceful measures.

It is because of its recommendatory nature that some have been reluctant to rely on Chapter VI as a basis for peacekeeping. According to McCoubrey and White, this characteristic makes Chapter VI ill-suited to providing a basis for the 'concrete military presence' that is a part of peacekeeping.[63] However, on the basis that peacekeeping 'is closer to or [more] linked to pacific settlement' than to Chapter VII action, they concede that peacekeeping 'can be seen as a power derived from article 36(1) of Chapter VI'.[64] For Higgins, there is little point in relying on Chapter VI:

states or both – as a basis for the General Assembly to establish peacekeeping operations. It observed: '[Article 11(2)] applies not merely to general questions relating to peace and security, but also to specific cases brought before the General Assembly by a State under Article 35 . . . by means of recommendations to States or to the Security Council, or to both, to organize peacekeeping operations, at the request, or with the consent, of the States concerned.' *Certain Expenses* (n 11) 164.

[59] Among the various means listed, peacekeeping could perhaps be said to fall within the categories of 'mediation', 'negotiation' 'conciliation' or 'other peaceful means of their own choice'. For example, Tomuschat observed that a peacekeeping force can 'serve to mediate in a power struggle between adversary factions within a nation'. Christian Tomuschat, 'Article 33' in Simma (n 5) 583–94, 589 para 28.

[60] For example, White (n 43) 186 suggested that the United Nations Observer Group in Lebanon (UNOGIL) could have been established under Art 34, given that its functions 'probably remained as investigatory and observational', making it 'different from most other types of peacekeeping forces'.

[61] See eg Oscar Schachter, 'Authorized Uses of Force by the United Nations and Regional Organizations' in Lori Damrosch and David Scheffer (eds), *Law and Force in the New International Order* (Boulder, Col, Westview, 1991) 81, who wrote that '"observational" peacekeeping activities such as truce supervision . . . were all authorized by the Security Council and it was implicitly understood that they fell within the Council's general authority under Article 24 as well as under Article 36'. See also White (n 43) 181–212.

[62] Art 34 is thought to be an exception in this respect. See Theodor Schweisfurth, 'Article 34' in Simma (n 5) 594–608, 605–06 paras 34–35.

[63] Peacekeeping 'constitutes a concrete military presence and therefore does not simply consist of mere recommendations for settlement or the establishment of basic fact-finding missions as is found in Chapter VI'. Hilaire McCoubrey and Nigel D White, *The Blue Helmets: Legal Regulation of United Nations Military Operations* (Aldershot, Dartmouth, 1996) 50–51.

[64] ibid. It would appear that the 'derived' power referred to by McCoubrey and White is akin to an implied power; see the discussion of implied powers in section 4 below.

> Understandably, and very probably also correctly, the Council has usually felt that there is little to be gained from [taking action under Chapter VI], as any recommended settlement has to be one which both parties can agree upon between themselves.[65]

Some commentators have ruled out Chapter VI as a basis for peacekeeping because with peacekeeping the use of force is not entirely excluded.[66] According to Ciobanu, 'only by a stretch of the imagination could one tentatively suggest that the competence of the Security Council in the peaceful settlement of disputes includes, if necessary, the use of armed force'.[67] While this logic is sound if applied to a peacekeeping operation that goes *beyond* self-defence, it must be incorrect to argue that an operation's right to use force *in* self-defence would turn it into a forceful measure, thereby removing it from the scope of Chapter VI. As has been noted previously, all peacekeepers, regardless how pacific their objectives, possess the right to defend themselves in the face of an attack.[68] What *is* true, however, is that Chapter VI envisages pacific measures for the settlement of disputes; as such, any peacekeeping operation where force is used *beyond* self-defence may not have its constitutional basis exclusively therein.[69]

3.2 Chapter VII Powers

It has been observed that 'the powers of the [Security Council] under Chapter VII of the Charter are extremely far-reaching and subject to very

[65] Rosalyn Higgins, 'The Place of International Law in the Settlement of Disputes by the Security Council' (1970) 64 *American Journal of International Law* 1, 13. Elsewhere, Higgins observed that she had 'always . . . been uncomfortable with the contention that Chapter VI provides a satisfactory basis for peacekeeping'. Rosalyn Higgins, *United Nations Peacekeeping: Documents and Commentary, Vol IV: Europe 1946–1976* (Oxford, Oxford University Press, 1981) 144. Nevertheless, she conceded that it was 'plausible' that Chapter VI could provide the constitutional basis for UNFICYP based on 'both the wording of the resolutions and the absence of certain Chapter VII indications' (ibid).

[66] Dan Ciobanu, 'The Power of the Security Council to Organize Peace-Keeping Operations' in Cassese (n 53) 15–54, 16–17. See also Katherine E Cox, 'Beyond Self-Defense: United Nations Peacekeeping Operations and the Use of Force' (1999) 27 *Denver Journal of International Law & Policy* 239, 248: '[I]nsofar as UN peacekeeping forces are entitled to use force in self-defense they cannot be regarded as purely pacific means of dispute settlement under Chapter VI.'

[67] Ciobanu, ibid, 16–17. In support of this, he relied the title of Chapter VI – '*Pacific* Settlement of Disputes'.

[68] See chapter 2, section 2.1, n 19.

[69] Certain functions of a peacekeeping operation may be such that they cannot fall under Chapter VI, while other elements, such as policing or elections-focused tasks, may. Nigel D White, 'UN Peacekeeping – Development or Destruction?' (1994) 12(1) *International Relations* 129, 137.

few express limitations'.[70] However, it is almost universally agreed that such limitations do exist;[71] they will be the focus of this section.

In the words of the ICJ in the *Kosovo* Advisory Opinion: '*Within the legal framework of the United Nations Charter*, notably on the basis of Articles 24, 25 and Chapter VII thereof, the Security Council may adopt resolutions imposing obligations under international law.'[72] Three types of measures may be taken by the Security Council to maintain or restore international peace and security under Chapter VII without the consent of the affected states: (1) mandatory provisional measures under Article 40; (2) enforcement measures under Article 41; and (3) enforcement measures under Article 42. This section will examine the Security Council's powers under each article – and the associated prerequisites and restrictions. First, however, let us consider a general prerequisite for Security Council action under Chapter VII: the invocation of Article 39.

3.2.1 Powers under Article 39

Article 39 is the gateway to Chapter VII action – whether or not such action constitutes enforcement. It provides that where the Security Council finds a threat to the peace, breach of the peace or act of aggression (the 'triggering events'), it is obliged to ('shall'[73]) act in one of two

[70] Jochen Frowein and Nico Krisch, 'Introduction [to Chapter VII]' in Simma (n 5) 701–16, 705 para 11. They attribute this to the drafters of the UN Charter possessing the 'primordial goal of ensuring rapid and effective action to maintain international peace and security'.

[71] On the limits of the powers of the Security Council see eg Bardo Fassbender, '*Quis judicabit?* The Security Council, its Powers and its Legal Control: Review Essay' (2000) 11 *European Journal of International Law* 219; Gabriël H Oosthuizen, 'Playing the Devil's Advocate: The United Nations Security Council is Unbound by Law' (1999) 12 *Leiden Journal of International Law* 549; Dapo Akande, 'The International Court of Justice and the Security Council: Is there Room for Judicial Control of Decisions of the Political Organs of the United Nations?' (1997) 46 *International and Comparative Law Quarterly* 309; Gill (n 20); Ian Brownlie, 'The Decisions of Political Organs of the United Nations and the Rule of Law' in Ronald St John Macdonald (gen ed), *Essays in Honour of Wang Tieya* (Dordrecht, Martinus Nijhoff, 1994) 91; Mohammed Bedjaoui, *The New World Order and the Security Council: Testing the Legality of its Acts* (Dordrecht, Martinus Nijhoff, 1994); Vera Gowlland-Debbas, 'Security Council Enforcement Action and Issues of State Responsibility' (1994) 43 *International and Comparative Law Quarterly* 55; Thomas M Franck, 'The "Powers of Appreciation": Who is the Ultimate Guardian of UN Legality?' (1992) 86 *American Journal of International Law* 519.

[72] *Accordance with International Law of the Unilateral Declaration of Independence in Respect of Kosovo*, Advisory Opinion of 22 July 2010, www.icj-cij.org/docket/files/141/15987.pdf (accessed 1 April 2011), 32 (emphasis added). Later, the Court observed: 'Resolution 1244 (1999) was expressly adopted by the Security Council on the basis of Chapter VII of the United Nations Charter, and therefore clearly imposes international legal obligations.'

[73] Cf Jochen Frowein and Nico Krisch, 'Article 39' in Simma (n 5) 717–29, 719 para 3, who observed that 'both the history of the Charter and subsequent State practice show that the [Security Council] is under no obligation to make a determination under [Art] 39, even if it considers that a threat to or breach of the peace exists – [Art] 39 empowers, but does not oblige the [Security Council] to act'. See also Gowlland-Debbas (n 71) 62, who observed that the Security Council could follow its determinations under Art 39 'by total inaction' if it so chose.

ways:[74] it must either 'make recommendations, or decide what measures shall be taken in accordance with Articles 41 and 42, to maintain or restore international peace and security'.

As a prerequisite to acting under Chapter VII, the Security Council must find that a triggering event has occurred. The Security Council has not always made such a finding explicitly – nor has it always made an explicit reference to Article 39. It is generally accepted that there is no need for any such explicit reference so long as the Security Council's intention is clear;[75] however, the Security Council's recent practice has been to explicitly determine that a situation poses 'a threat to international peace and security' when it passes a resolution that is based in Chapter VII. While the Charter does not define 'threat to the peace', 'breach of the peace' or 'act of aggression',[76] the wording makes it clear that 'threat to the peace' has the lowest threshold, requiring the least forcefulness. Among the three triggering events, threats to the peace have been found to exist by the Security Council far more frequently than breaches of the peace or acts of aggression[77] – even in situations which many would regard as being more in the nature of 'aggression'.[78] As such, the focus here will be on the category of 'threat to the peace'.[79]

3.2.1.1 Prerequisites to the Security Council Finding a Threat to the Peace

The Security Council's discretion to make a determination that a disagreement constitutes a 'threat to the peace' under Article 39, while considerable,[80] is not unlimited.[81] For there to be a finding of a threat there must be at least some evidence of a disagreement – apparently of a character which is of

[74] Nothing, of course, precludes the Security Council from acting in both ways concurrently as it did with Iraq in 1990/91. See Gowlland-Debbas (n 71) 62 and n 28.

[75] Higgins (n 42) 236; Tarcisio Gazzini, *The Changing Rules on the Use of Force in International Law* (Melland Schill Studies in International Law) (Manchester, Manchester University Press, 2005) 7 n 2.

[76] According to Gowlland-Debbas (n 71) 61 and n 22, 'At the San Francisco Conference it was deliberately decided not to accept any definition of the terms since it was considered unwise to bind the Security Council'.

[77] Frowein and Krisch (n 73) 722 para 16.

[78] For example, neither the invasion of South Korea by North Korea nor the invasion of Kuwait by Iraq was characterised as 'aggression' by the Security Council.

[79] For a thorough discussion of the other two categories of disturbance under Art 39, see White (n 43) 41–49.

[80] 'It is generally agreed that the Security Council has full competence under Chapter VII to determine that a factual situation constitutes a threat to international peace and security and that it may take the necessary legally binding measures to counter that threat.' *Libyan Arab Jamahiriya* case (n 19) Declaration of Judge Kooijmans, 149 para 18, relying on Malcolm Shaw, 'The Security Council and the International Court of Justice: Judicial Drift and Judicial Function' in AS Muller et al (eds), *The International Court of Justice – Its Future Role After Fifty Years* (The Hague, Kluwer, 1997) 219 ff. See also Higgins (n 42) 173–74 and n 28; Sarooshi (n 23) 3 and n 4.

[81] Nigel D White, *The Law of International Organisations* (Melland Schill Studies in International Law) (Manchester, Manchester University Press, 2005) 90.

greater gravity than a 'situation' or 'dispute' under Chapter VI.[82] Some have taken the view that 'peace' under Article 39 'means the absence of organized use of force'.[83] According to this reasoning, 'threat to the peace' under Article 39 covers the same ground as 'threat of force' under Article 2(4).[84] The result of this approach would be that the Security Council's 'competence would be defined, at its limits, by Article 2(4); to go beyond that and, say, determine that a situation was a "threat to the peace" when it was not a "threat of force" would be *ultra vires*'.[85] However, this argument is not persuasive. No explicit link between Article 2(4) and Article 39 is made anywhere in the Charter.[86] Moreover, the Security Council's practice shows that it does not consider itself to be bound by such a link.[87] Nevertheless, it is essential that there is a bona fide threat.[88] As noted by the Appeals Chamber of the International Criminal Tribunal for the former Yugoslavia (ICTY) in the *Tadić* case, a 'determination that there exists [a threat to the peace under Article 39] is not a totally unfettered discretion, as it has to remain, at the very least, within the limits of the Purposes and Principles of the Charter'.[89]

In addition, the threat to the peace must normally be international in nature. Although Article 39 refers to 'threat to the peace' and not 'threat to the international peace', 'both textual and systematic interpretations favour the conclusion that the first part of the sentence of [Article] 39 does not refer to the use of force in the internal realm of States'.[90] Where,

[82] Frowein and Krisch (n 73) 723 para 17: 'The precise relationship of the notion of a threat to the peace to the concept referred to in Arts 34 and 37 is difficult to determine . . . The relationship of Chapter VI and VII indicates that, for a threat to exist, the situation must be of greater gravity, but in this regard, the judgment of the [Security Council] acquires decisive significance.'

[83] ibid, 720 para 6. See also Erika de Wet, *The Chapter VII Powers of the United Nations Security Council* (Oxford, Hart Publishing, 2004) 138–42.

[84] Nigel D White, *Keeping the Peace: The United Nations and the Maintenance of International Peace and Security*, 2nd edn (Manchester, Manchester University Press, 1997) 33–34. Advocates of this approach reason that although the injunction in Art 2(4) against the 'threat or use of force' by states is worded differently from that set out in Art 39, the two provisions deal with the same subject matter, with the 'threat of force' being tantamount to 'threat to the peace' and the 'use of force' being tantamount to 'breach of the peace' or 'act of aggression'. For more on the relationship between Arts 2(4) and 39, see White, ibid, 33–36.

[85] ibid, 34.

[86] Higgins (n 42) 173.

[87] As White (n 43) 34 noted, the Security Council has 'manifested a preference for the open system', ie one where the threat of force is not essential to a finding of a threat to the peace.

[88] Franck (n 1) 221.

[89] *Prosecutor v Tadić*, Appeal on Jurisdiction (Case IT-94-1-AR72, International Criminal Tribunal for the former Yugoslavia (Appeals Chamber), 2 October 1995), para 29. For a discussion of the purposes and principles of the Charter see section 2 above.

[90] Frowein and Krisch (n 73) 720 para 7. Cf the statement of White below, n 96. The basis of a finding by the Security Council of an 'international' aspect in relation to Art 39 has not been entirely clear. For example, in relation to ONUC, while the Security Council mentioned its deep concern at the 'threat to international peace and security' in SC Res 161 of 21 February 1961, it did not attempt to link the threat to matters outside the country. See also de Wet's discussion of the lack of an international link with the situation in Somalia (de Wet (n 83) 150–76).

as is frequently the case,[91] the matter on which the Security Council is deciding is ostensibly not 'international' in nature, the Security Council has generally made a point of linking its finding of a threat to the peace under Article 39 to the issue of regional stability.[92] For example, in February 1993, in the context of the peacekeeping operation in the former Yugoslavia (UNPROFOR), it referred to 'a threat to peace and security *in the region*'.[93] The inclusion of the last three words signals the Security Council's desire to put the threat in an international context.[94] An analysis of the resolutions in which the Security Council has explicitly invoked Chapter VII in establishing or modifying UN-led operations shows that it has rarely invoked the language of the first part of Article 39, ie 'threat to the peace', preferring instead the wording of the latter part: 'threat to international peace and security'. Thus, the Security Council appears to have read in the word 'international' before 'peace' in the phrase 'threat to the peace' in its peacekeeping practice.[95] This may stem from the desire of the Security Council not to be seen to be interfering in matters that are 'essentially within the domestic jurisdiction' of a state, as precluded (with certain exceptions) by Article 2(7).

The requirement that a threat to the peace be international in nature does not, however, imply any real limitation to the Security Council's powers for two, related reasons.[96] First, the Security Council has shown a willingness to find an international aspect in just about any threat to the peace, and states have not offered significant protest.[97] As White rightly noted, '[t]he perception is that the requirement for the threat to be against *international peace* as opposed to *internal peace* is being stretched to the break-

[91] de Wet (n 83) 175 observed that the 'vast majority of Security Council determinations in terms of Article 39 of the Charter resulted from consequences of an internal armed conflict and, in particular, from the systematic and large scale violations of human rights and humanitarian law that accompanied these conflicts'.

[92] ibid, 150–76.

[93] SC Res 807 of 17 February 1993 (emphasis added).

[94] See de Wet (n 83) 150–76, who noted that although in its various resolutions regarding the situation in the former Yugoslavia the Security Council cited its concern for the well-being of the parties concerned (including its condemnation of ethnic cleansing and the denial of humanitarian aid and medical assistance), this alone was not enough to warrant a finding of a threat to peace.

[95] The latter part of Art 39, which provides that the Security Council may 'decide what measures shall be taken in accordance with Articles 41 or 42 to maintain or restore *international* peace and security' (emphasis added), suggests a requirement that the threat under consideration be international (Frowein and Krisch (n 73) 723 para 17).

[96] White's analysis 'suggests that a finding of a "threat to the peace" is, to a large degree, a political decision on the part of the Council, and so such a finding as regards a wholly internal situation is not precluded. Generally, however, the permanent members are not going to exercise this discretion unless the situation has potential international repercussions which would affect their interests . . . Recent practice suggests that the requirement [of potential international repercussions] is something of a formality, and that the Council is in reality concerning itself with purely internal situations' (White (n 84) 36).

[97] See Frowein and Krisch (n 73) 723–24 para 18 on the Security Council's involvement in conflicts that most would consider to be primarily internal in nature.

ing point'.[98] Wellens, who carefully considered recent Security Council practice, observed that 'an enlarged notion of threats to the peace'[99] has developed over the years. He concluded:

> The broadened notion of threat, and the fact that the Security Council has resorted far more frequently than ever before to pronouncements not exactly amounting to a formal determination under article 39, have contributed to a gradual process whereby the dividing lines between chapter VI and VII became less clear and sharply-cut than perhaps the drafters of the charter had intended them to be.[100]

Second, Security Council practice indicates that it has established certain exceptions to the requirement.[101] Franck observed that such exceptions appear to 'fall into two overlapping categories: (1) those involving governments demonstrably in gross violation of fundamental norms of international law and (2) those involving especially egregious civil wars'.[102] Österdahl considered the Security Council's practice of finding humanitarian crises within a state to be threats to the peace and observed that while 'the Security Council initially went to . . . great lengths to single out every situation in which it intervened as unique or exceptional',[103] it had, more recently, moved away from that practice.[104]

3.2.1.2 Limitations on Security Council Measures under Article 39

When taking measures under Article 39 the Security Council faces two limitations. First, the measures are limited to those 'taken to restore international peace and security'.[105] The discretion of the Security Council here is wide and it appears highly unlikely that measures taken by it in relation to the establishment of a peacekeeping operation would exceed it.[106]

[98] White (n 84) 36.

[99] Karel Wellens, 'The UN Security Council and New Threats to the Peace: Back to the Future' (2003) 8(1) *Journal of Conflict and Security Law* 15, 53.

[100] ibid.

[101] Franck (n 1) 224–42.

[102] ibid, 224. See also *Tadić* (n 89) para 30 where the Appeals Chamber noted the existence of 'a common understanding, manifested by the "subsequent practice" of the membership of the United Nations at large, that the "threat to the peace" of Article 39 may include, as one of its species, internal armed conflicts'.

[103] Inger Österdahl, 'The Exception as the Rule: Lawmaking on Force and Human Rights by the UN Security Council' (2005) 10(1) *Journal of Conflict and Security Law* 1, 9.

[104] ibid, 11.

[105] The wording of Art 39 – the Security Council shall 'make recommendations, or decide what measures shall be taken in accordance with Article 41 and 42, to maintain or restore international peace and security' – leaves open the issue of whether the clause 'to maintain or restore international peace and security' was intended to modify only decisions or whether it was to modify recommendations as well. It is more reasonable to interpret the clause as modifying *both* recommendations and decisions.

[106] In the words of the Appeals Chamber in the *Tadić* case (n 89) para 39, 'Article 39 leaves the choice of means and their evaluation to the Security Council, which enjoys wide discretionary powers in this regard; and it could not have been otherwise, as such a choice involves political evaluation of highly complex and dynamic situations'.

In addition, Article 24(2) requires the Security Council, in discharging its duties in relation to the maintenance of international peace and security, to act in accordance with the purposes and principles of the UN.[107]

The measures available to the Security Council under Article 39 are limited. Article 39 does not provide a legal basis for the Security Council to *decide* on enforcement actions.[108] As is well known, an important distinction exists between 'recommendations', which, it is generally accepted, are non-binding, and 'decisions', which are generally considered to be mandatory.[109] Where the Security Council makes a *recommendation* under Article 39, it is relying on the powers bestowed upon it in that article (possibly in conjunction with other powers); where the Security Council takes a *decision*, its authority to act stems from Article 41 or 42. That is not to say that Article 39 may not provide a basis for the Security Council to *recommend* certain measures similar in nature to enforcement. However, it does not provide a legal basis for the measures; they must already be legal.[110] Where the Security Council wants to authorise activity that *would* otherwise be illegal in international law – such as the use of force other than in self-defence – it must rely on another article of the Charter.[111]

3.2.1.3 Conclusion on Article 39

In conclusion, there is no reason why a non-forceful, non-obligatory peacekeeping operation could not be established by means of a recommendation under Article 39.[112] However, there appears to be little advan-

[107] See discussion in section 2 above.

[108] cf Frowein and Krisch (n 73) 728 para 31.

[109] The mandatory nature of *decisions* taken for the maintenance of international peace and security is provided in Art 48(1). A more general agreement to 'carry out the *decisions* of the Security Council' (emphasis added) in accordance with the Charter is provided in Art 25.

[110] Frowein and Krisch (n 73) 727–28 paras 29–31 cite the 1950 recommendation of the Security Council that members of the United Nations furnish forceful assistance to South Korea and non-binding calls for Member States to enact economic sanctions as examples of Art 39 recommendations. As they note, what these types of measure have in common is that the recommended conduct is not otherwise prohibited in international law: the use of force in Korea may be said to be collective self-defence as authorised by Art 51; economic sanctions by one state against another are generally not prohibited in law.

[111] cf Vera Gowlland-Debbas, *Collective Responses to Illegal Acts under International Law: United Nations Actions in the Question of Southern Rhodesia* (Dordrecht, Martinus Nijhoff, 1990) 417–18, who suggested that the resolution authorising enforcement of sanctions against Southern Rhodesia might be attached to a recommendation under Art 39. See also JES Fawcett, 'Security Council Resolutions on Rhodesia' (1965–66) 41 *British Yearbook of International Law* 121, who suggested that a recommendation under Art 39 for the use of force 'appears to be a proper exercise' of the Security Council's Chapter VII powers; he acknowledged, however, that such a power is not express.

[112] See Georg Schwarzenberger, 'Report on Problems of a United Nations Force', International Law Association Conference, Hamburg, 1960, p 179, who cited Art 39 as a possible basis for UNEF I. It should be noted, however, that Schwarzenberger's writings on this point take the form of a report of a meeting which had cast its net rather wide – finding a potential Charter basis for interpositional peacekeeping in Arts 29, 39, 40, 41, 42, 48 and 53 as well – rather than an indication that he, himself, favoured such a conclusion. Cf Ciobanu

tage in establishing such an operation under Article 39 when it could just as easily be done under Chapter VI.[113] Higgins's observation in relation to Chapter VI, that '[u]nderstandably, and very probably also correctly, the Council has usually felt that there is little to be gained from [taking action under Chapter VI], as any recommended settlement has to be one which both parties can agree upon between themselves',[114] would apply equally to a measure taken under Article 39. As to the establishment of a militarised peacekeeping operation, there is nothing to prevent the Security Council from making a recommendation under Article 39 for such a measure so long as it is otherwise legal; however, the Article provides no legal basis for an operation relying on the use of force. Such an operation will need to find its Chapter VII basis elsewhere.[115]

3.2.2 Powers under Article 40

Article 40 of Chapter VII provides that the Security Council may 'call upon the parties concerned to comply with such provisional measures as it deems necessary or desirable' in order to 'prevent an aggravation of the situation . . . before making the recommendations or deciding upon the measures provided for in Article 39'.

3.2.2.1 Do Article 40 Measures Amount to Enforcement?

Article 40 provides that measures taken under it are to be 'without prejudice to the rights, claims, or positions of the parties concerned'. Clearly then, Article 40 measures are not in the nature of the enforcement measures authorised in, for example, the Korean action, which were intended to affect the rights of the parties.[116] In addition, the fact that Article 40 refers to measures decided upon under Article 39, which, in turn, refers to decisions in accordance with Articles 41 and 42 and makes no mention of Article 40, suggests that only Articles 41 and 42 provide for enforcement decisions.[117] In short, it is generally agreed that Article 40

(n 66) 22, who argued that Art 39 alone is not a legitimate basis as it only allows for a 'recommendation' and not 'action'. Because 'by deciding to organize peace-keeping operations the Council takes action, its decision could not, strictly speaking, be made in the exercise of its broad recommendatory power under Article 39'.

[113] See discussion of Chapter VI above, section 3.1.

[114] Higgins in the *American Journal of International Law* (n 65) 13.

[115] As discussed below, section 3.2.4, Art 42 provides for forceful measures. Some have argued that if the use of force is sufficiently limited, it might be considered to fall within the parameters of Art 41 – despite that article's specific requirement that measures taken under it do not involve the use of force. See discussion below at section 3.2.3.2. Similarly, some have argued that an authorisation to use a limited amount of force may find its basis in Art 40. See discussion below, section 3.2.2.4.

[116] For a discussion of the Korean action see chapter 2, section 2.3.3.1.

[117] *Prosecutor v Tadić* (n 89) para 33.

does not empower the Security Council to take enforcement measures.[118] Thus, Security Council measures thereunder do not fall within the enforcement exception to the Article 2(7) prohibition on intervention in matters essentially within domestic jurisdiction.[119] Nor will they trigger the enforcement-related exception in relation to Article 2(1) or (4), discussed above.

Rather than enforcement, actions under Article 40 may better be classed as 'preventive measures'.[120] Support for such an approach comes both from the *travaux préparatoires*[121] and from a systematic analysis of the Charter, which distinguishes between 'enforcement measures' and 'preventive measures'.[122]

3.2.2.2 Are Measures under Article 40 Binding?

There is some dispute as to whether Article 40 bestows a power on the Security Council to create binding obligations on states.[123] Arguments both for and against such a position based on the wording of the provision and its placement in Chapter VII are persuasive. Arguments that Article 40 does *not* create binding obligations include the following: (1) only Articles 41 and 42 are listed in Article 39 as measures that the Security Council may *decide* to take to restore international peace and security;[124] (2) Article 40 provides that the Security Council may merely 'call upon' states to comply, implying a request rather than a demand;[125] and (3) measures under the article are described as 'necessary or desirable', thereby suggesting a recommendatory nature.[126] Arguments that Article 40 *is* binding are also supported by the provision's wording,[127] the word-

[118] See eg EM Miller (pseudonym for Oscar Schachter), 'Legal Aspects of the United Nations Action in the Congo' (1961) 55 *American Journal of International Law* 1, 5–6. White (n 43) 56 n 113, 228 characterised Art 40 as a 'non-enforcement provision' – at least not in 'the full blown sense of Article 42'.

[119] Miller/Schachter, ibid, 5–6. See also Higgins (n 46) 58, who argued that the non-enforcement nature of ONUC was evident from the Security Council's operating on the basis that Art 2(7) was applicable (ie that the exception for enforcement actions did not apply). See also *Prosecutor v Tadić* (n 89) para 33.

[120] Schachter made this point when he observed that 'Article 40 refers to the objective of prevention rather than enforcement' (ibid, 5).

[121] ibid, 6 n 22.

[122] At times the Charter refers to 'enforcement or preventive' measures or actions (see Arts 2(5), 5 and 50), and at times refers only to 'enforcement measures' (see Art 2(7)).

[123] See *Prosecutor v Tadić* (n 89) para 33: 'the question of their mandatory or recommendatory character is subject to great controversy'.

[124] As noted, generally only 'decisions' are considered to be binding on states.

[125] Frowein and Krisch (n 73) 734 para 16 and n 44 observed that the words 'calls upon', while often ambiguous, are 'usually restricted to merely recommendatory measures'.

[126] ibid, 734 para 13.

[127] Arguably, the wording of the final sentence of the article, which obliges the Security Council to 'duly take account of failure to comply with such provisional measures', has a mandatory ring to it. Moreover, the words 'call upon' do not necessarily refer only to recommendatory measures as Frowein and Krisch assert in n 125 above. It may be noted that the

ing of other provisions in Chapter VII,[128] and a systematic interpretation of the Charter.[129]

Many commentators have adopted a third way. Recognising that Article 40 does not clearly fall into the category of a binding decision or a non-binding recommendation, they posit that the Security Council *may* bind states under Article 40 *only where it makes its intention to do so clear*.[130] As noted by Schachter:

> Kelsen has noted that the language used in Article 40, namely, 'call upon the parties to comply' falls between 'recommendations' (as in Chapter VI) and 'deciding on measures' (as under Articles 41 and 42); in his view, this leaves to the Council the choice as to whether the 'call' made under Article 40 is a simple recommendation or a legally binding decision. It is, of course, obvious that if the Council indicates that its resolution is a recommendation, it does not consider that resolution to be mandatory. But if the Council should characterize its call to the parties under Article 40 as obligatory (as it has done [with ONUC] by referring to Article 25), this would be within its authority.[131]

Schachter linked a finding by the Security Council that a threat to the peace, breach of the peace or act of aggression existed with it acting mandatorily under Article 40.[132] Higgins also took the view that '"host state" consent is not *necessarily* needed [to put in place a peacekeeping operation] if there is a threat to the peace, breach of the peace, or act of aggression'.[133] To

words 'call upon' are used in Art 41; there the Security Council's authority to bind is generally undisputed.

[128] Nothing in the text of Art 25 or Art 48(1), which requires states to carry out *decisions* taken by the Security Council, limits states' obligations to decisions under Art 41 or 42.

[129] As pointed out by Jochen Frowein and Nico Krisch, 'Article 40' in Simma (n 5) 729–35, 734 para 14, the systematic interpretation of the Charter supports the view that Art 40 measures may be binding: '[S]ince recommendations for non-binding ceasefires are possible already under Chapter VI, the inclusion of [Art] 40 in Chapter VII seems to be meaningful only if it confers additional powers [on] the [Security Council] and thus if it allows binding effects.'

[130] The findings of the ICJ in *LaGrand (Germany v United States of America)*, Judgment [2001] ICJ Rep 466, 734 para 14 may strengthen the argument that provisional measures under Art 40 of the UN Charter are binding when the ICJ intends them to be. There, the Court considered whether Art 41 of the Statute of the International Court of Justice, which grants the Court 'the power to indicate, if it considers that circumstances so require, any provisional measures which ought to be taken to preserve the respective rights of either party', resulted in a binding obligation on states. Based on the object and purpose of the Statute and the context of Art 41 therein, the Court ruled that enforcement measures under that Statute were binding on states.

[131] Miller/Schachter (n 118) 6.

[132] Schachter held the view that the government of the Congo was unable to call for the withdrawal of ONUC, which he considered to be an Art 40 operation of a mandatory character. While he was dealing with the question of withdrawal of consent, his reasoning implies that the host state's consent was not essential in the circumstances. He observed that since the Security Council considered that the situation in the Congo 'involved a threat to international peace and security, and since the Council adopted measures of a mandatory character pursuant to Chapter VII of the Charter, the territorial government could not by unilateral action decide that the threat was over or that measures taken by the Council should be terminated'. ibid, 15.

[133] Higgins (n 53) 5.

determine if a particular Article 40 measure is binding, one must have regard to the intention of the Security Council.[134] Given that the recent practice of the Security Council has been to specifically invoke Chapter VII when taking mandatory measures, it is arguable that a clear indication of the Security Council's intention – either through an invocation of Chapter VII or by means of an equally clear indicator – is essential; a reference to a triggering event in a resolution would not, alone, be a sufficient indicator of the Security Council's intention to act mandatorily.[135]

We know that Security Council practice has been to obtain host state consent for peacekeeping operations; that would, of course, include an operation established as a mandatory measure under Article 40. Though some might take the view that a consistent Security Council practice of obtaining host state consent for mandatory measures under Article 40 leads to the conclusion that host state consent is necessary in law, the better view is that the Security Council's practice of obtaining host state consent is in the nature of a non-legal requirement, motivated by a desire to obtain the host state's cooperation.[136] Even accepting that a measure adopted by the Security Council under Article 40 may be binding on the state(s) that is the object of the measure, it would not appear to be binding on the membership as a whole '*insofar as that Article was being suggested as a basis for* a United Nations force'.[137]

3.2.2.3 Prerequisites to Security Council Measures under Article 40

The Security Council's freedom to act under Article 40 to establish peacekeeping operations is not unlimited. Four prerequisites for Security Council

[134] See Rosalyn Higgins, 'The Advisory Opinion on Namibia: Which UN Resolutions are Binding under Article 25 of the Charter?' (1972) 21 *International and Comparative Law Quarterly* 270. See also Gill (n 20), who took the view that a determination of a threat to or breach of the peace under Art 39 meant that measures taken under Art 40 were *necessarily* binding on states (ibid, 47). See also Andreas Paulus, 'Article 29' in Simma (n 5) 539–63, 547. White (n 84) 103–04, who adopted a similar approach, spoke in terms of 'recommendations' for provisional measures and 'decisions' for provisional measures, echoing the division under Art 39.

[135] Frowein and Krisch (n 73) 727 para 27: 'Unless other factors indicate that action under Chapter VII is envisaged, . . . resolutions [where the Security Council has determined the existence of a triggering event without a specific statement that it is acting under Chapter VII] should, according to the general rule, be interpreted narrowly and should not be regarded as providing for enforcement action.'

[136] In the same way that the Security Council's practice of obtaining consent for quasi-enforcement operations, discussed in chapter 2, does not reflect a legal requirement but is considered politically desirable, obtaining consent for an Article 40 measure does not always mean that consent is required. It could be argued that the Security Council's practice of obtaining host state consent for a mandatory measure under Art 40 shows it to be acting with an abundance of caution: a 'belt and braces' approach. Paulus (n 134) 554 para 53 put it this way: 'Since the "mix" between Chapter VII authorization and consent of the parties will be different in each individual case, the basis for each force has to be analysed separately. The trend goes in the direction of both seeking the consent of the parties involved and using Chapter VII prerogatives as a sort of safety belt.'

[137] Higgins (n 53) 2–3.

action thereunder may be noted, though all would appear to be easily met. A first requirement is that it must find an Article 39 triggering event to have occurred – that is, a threat to peace, breach of the peace or act of aggression.[138] It is generally agreed that such a finding need not be express;[139] however, in practice determinations regarding an Article 39 triggering event have tended to be express 'in those cases where [the Security Council] intended to create binding effects for the parties and where it was thus undisputed that the action fell under [Article] 40 and not under chapter VI'.[140] As noted, the extent of the Security Council's discretion in making a finding of a threat to international peace is broad.[141] Second, Article 24(2) requires that the Security Council, in discharging its duties in relation to the maintenance of international peace and security, must act in accordance with the purposes and principles of the UN. The requirements (and the exceptions thereto) as discussed in section 2 of this chapter would apply. Third, the wording of Article 40 stipulates that the provisional imposition of measures under Article 40 must be in order to 'prevent an aggravation of the situation'. This requirement does not appear to affect the Security Council's freedom to act in any substantial way: it may be assumed that the Security Council would not impose provisional measures unless, in its discretion, it considered them likely to prevent matters from getting worse.[142] A fourth requirement under Article 40 is that the Security Council must deem the measures 'necessary or desirable'. Given the discretionary nature of the terms, this requirement would not serve to impede the Security Council's freedom to act under Article 40.[143]

3.2.2.4 Limitations on Security Council Measures under Article 40

Three limitations exist with regard to the type of operation the Security Council may establish under Article 40. First, measures must be 'without prejudice to the rights, claims, or position of the parties concerned'. In order to comply with the 'without prejudice' limitation, the measures called for by the Security Council under Article 40 must 'leave unaffected the legal positions of the States concerned, particularly those of any

[138] See Frowein and Krisch (n 129) 731 para 3 and n 9.

[139] In discussing the issue of the legal basis for ONUC, the Secretary-General noted that 'the Council's resolutions could be regarded as implicitly adopted under [Article] 40 and had been based on an implicit finding under [Article] 39' (*Annual Report of the Secretary-General on the Work of the Organization*, 16 June 1960–15 June 1962). Higgins (n 42) 236 observed that the 'less rigorous terms' of Art 40 meant that it was better suited to an implied determination under Art 39 than under Art 42. Cf Frowein and Krisch (n 129) 731 para 6.

[140] Frowein and Krisch (n 129) 731 para 6. See also Frowein and Krisch (n 73) 727 para 27.

[141] See discussion above, section 3.2.1.1.

[142] cf Frowein and Krisch (n 129), who argue that the wording means that the measures may only be called upon when 'an aggravation is impending' (732 para 7). Even if this approach is correct, the test would appear to be very easily met.

[143] Had only the word 'necessary' been used, there may have been an argument that this placed a limitation of proportionality on the measures. However, the inclusion of the word 'desirable' as an alternative obviates such an argument.

parties to the dispute'.[144] This language broadly equates with peacekeeping's 'fundamental principle' of impartiality.[145] Were a peacekeeping operation to favour the legal or political position of one party to a dispute over another, the operation would lose its impartiality and, as such, its claim to a constitutional basis under Article 40. It is not entirely clear whether the 'without prejudice' requirement applies only to the position of states vis-à-vis one another or whether it also applies to the relationship between the government and certain opposing groups within the state. Some have argued that the constitutional basis for ONUC, where the peacekeeping force was authorised to ensure the withdrawal of mercenaries and to prevent a region from seceding, could not have been located in Article 40 as the 'without prejudice' requirement was not adhered to.[146] While the establishment of a peacekeeping operation to oversee the maintenance of a demilitarised zone, for example, would appear to comply with the 'without prejudice' limitation, less clear would be the establishment of a peacekeeping operation charged with facilitating the restoration of the status quo ante, for example, by monitoring a demilitarised zone that corresponded with a pre-existing border.[147]

Second, the measure must be provisional in nature. To an extent, this requirement overlaps with the 'without prejudice' requirement – that is, if a measure is to be permanent, it would be difficult for it not to impact on the claims or rights of the parties. While it may rightly be noted that the duration of some peacekeeping operations suggests that they have taken on a semi-permanent character – for example, UNTSO and UNMOGIP have been in operation for over 60 years – the fact that peacekeeping mandates generally require periodic renewal speaks to their provisional nature.[148]

A third limitation on the nature of the measures the Security Council may establish based on Article 40 relates to the level of force authorised.[149] Some take the view that Article 40 may never provide the legal basis for

[144] Frowein and Krisch (n 129) 732 para 8. They continued: 'Thus under [Art] 40 the [Security Council] cannot call upon States to recognize conclusively as lawful a certain status of a territory or a border' (732 para 10).

[145] It will be recalled that Hammarskjöld observed that the impartiality requirement meant that an operation must not 'serve as a means to force settlement, in the interests of one party, of political conflicts or legal issues recognized as controversial' (United Nations, *Report of the Secretary-General on Compliance with General Assembly Resolution 1123 (XI)* (UN Doc A/3512), 24 January 1957, para 5); nor should an operation 'be used to enforce any specific political solution of pending problems or to influence the political balance decisive to such a solution' (*Summary Study* (n 57) para 167).

[146] Gazzini (n 75) 40–41.

[147] Frowein and Krisch (n 129) 733 para 10.

[148] '[P]eace-keeping operations are intended to be provisional and thus temporary measures.' United Nations, *The Blue Helmets: A Review of United Nations Peace-Keeping*, 2nd edn (New York: UN Sales No E.90.I.18, 1990) 8.

[149] Of course, a limitation on the use of force in a mandatory Art 40 measure does affect the right of participants to act in self-defence.

the establishment of mandatory forceful measures, as this would 'constitute an evasion of [Article] 42 which exclusively regulates compulsory military operations'.[150] Others, however, take the view that Article 40 *can* provide the constitutional basis for an operation authorised to use force beyond self-defence, so long as the force authorised is of a limited nature. Higgins took the view that 'minimal use of force by United Nations peacekeeping operations may be authorized by reference to Article 40 of the Charter'.[151]

White observed that '[t]o say that the Charter base of a force is Article 40 suggests Chapter VII action with its overtones of enforcement'.[152] While it is true that the final sentence of Article 40 – 'The Security Council shall duly take account of failure to comply with such provisional measures' – sounds a note which suggests the threat of follow-up, it would be reading too much into it to argue that it suggests enforcement featuring the use of force beyond self-defence – unless that force found its basis in a separate authorisation under Article 42. This is clear from the progressive structure of Chapter VII, whereby Security Council action progresses, from provisional measures under Article 40 to non-forceful sanctions under Article 41 and, ultimately, to forceful sanctions under Article 42. While there may be scope for an argument that some, limited level of force beyond self-defence may be permissible, if necessary any such use of force would need to be very limited indeed and incidental to other tasks of the operation.

3.2.2.5 Conclusions on Article 40

Among the articles of the Charter, it is Article 40 that is most frequently invoked as providing the constitutional basis for certain peacekeeping operations.[153] Experts have pointed to Article 40 as the constitutional basis for UNTSO,[154] UNMOGIP,[155] ONUC,[156] UNIPOM,[157] UNIIMOG,[158]

[150] Frowein and Krisch (n 129) 732 para 8. While it is conceivable that Art 40 may provide a basis for the Security Council to call upon a state to 'agree to the stationing of UN truce-observers and to co-operate', it could by no means be a basis for obliging a state to 'facilitate the stationing of peace-keeping forces' (ibid).

[151] Rosalyn Higgins, 'International Law and the Avoidance, Containment and Resolution of Disputes (General Course on Public International Law)' [1991] *Recueil des Cours* 230, 329.

[152] White (n 43) 185.

[153] See, generally, Hitoshi Nasu, *International Law on Peacekeeping: A Study of Article 40 of the UN Charter* (Leiden, Brill, 2009).

[154] White (n 43) 184. See also Simmonds (n 47) 22, who observed that UNTSO probably fell under Art 40.

[155] Higgins observed that SC Res 47 of 21 April 1948, establishing UNMOGIP (the United Nations Military Observer Group in India and Pakistan), 'would seem clearly to fall within the terms of Article 40 of the Charter, even though that Article was not specifically mentioned'. Rosalyn Higgins, *United Nations Peacekeeping 1946–1967: Documents and Commentary, Vol II: Asia* (Oxford, Oxford University Press, 1970) 350. See also Bowett (n 8) 63–64.

[156] See eg Miller/Schachter (n 118).

[157] White (n 43) 189 took the view that the United Nations India-Pakistan Observation Mission could at least potentially have been created under Art 40.

[158] ibid, 190–91.

UNFICYP,[159] UNEF II,[160] UNDOF,[161] UNIFIL[162] and UNTAG.[163] The Secretary-General made the following statement in relation to UNCRO in 1995, suggesting that he considered the endeavour to fall under Article 40:

> As the Council is considering the question of maintaining a UN peacekeeping presence in Croatia, it is timely for me to restate the basic principles of such a presence. A UN peacekeeping force . . . is an interim measure whose purpose is to help the parties to find a durable peace based on agreement between the parties themselves. It is not intended nor equipped to impose a solution on the parties.[164]

It must be recalled, of course, that this statement, with its focus on the non-imposition of a solution by a peacekeeping operation, was made in 1995 – a time when the second phase of militarised peacekeeping had been abandoned and the third phase has not yet been embraced.[165]

We have seen that in order for the Security Council to rely on Article 40, four prerequisites must be met. None of these would appear likely to impede Security Council action under the article. The two limitations on peacekeeping operations established under Article 40 correspond to two of the 'fundamental principles' of peacekeeping: such operations must not prejudice the positions of the parties – in effect, they must be impartial – and they must not use force beyond-self-defence. As to this latter point, there may be scope to argue that *some* level of force beyond self-defence may be permissible, so long as the use of force is incidental to the operation. However, it would be difficult to reconcile the defence-of-mandate approach to self-defence – which as noted in chapter 2 can open the door to the use of virtually any level of force depending on how the mandate is drafted – with Article 40, let alone a militarised peacekeeping operation. As to the final 'fundamental principle', we have seen that the Security Council may take binding measures under Article 40 where it expresses its intention to do so; in such circumstances, there is no legal requirement that the host state consent.

Where a host state does consent to an operation the mandate of which envisages the use of force beyond self-defence (subject to the possible

[159] ibid, 202–03.

[160] Here White noted that the Security Council's 'emphasis on consent and self-defence indicates the essentially non-enforcement nature of UNEF II' (ibid, 202–05).

[161] ibid, 205.

[162] White observed that SC Res 425 of 19 March 1978 'contained a non-mandatory call for provisional measures based on Article 40' (ibid, 205–06). The mandate of UNIFIL was modified in the summer of 2006.

[163] White described the United Nations Transitional Assistance Group (Namibia) as having been 'created as a necessary corollary to the implementation of widely drawn provisional measures'. He observed that UNTAG's mandate could have been adapted to enable it to enforce the peace if there had been a finding of a threat to the peace combined with a specific authorisation of the Security Council (ibid, 206–08).

[164] United Nations, *Report of the Secretary-General Submitted Pursuant to Security Council Resolution 994 (1995)* (UN Doc S/1995/467), 9 June 1995, 5.

[165] See discussion on this point in chapter 2, section 2.4.2.

exception of the use of incidental force) or to an operation that is not impartial, may that consent be treated as a waiver of the requirements of Article 40 in the same way that we have seen that a host state can waive the protections under the principles set forth in Article 2(1), (4) and (7)? The answer must surely be no. As regards impartiality, the wording of Article 40 explicitly requires that measures established under it are without prejudice to the rights or positions of parties; as regards the use of force that goes beyond self-defence, while it is not explicitly prohibited in Article 40, it is clear from the structure of Chapter VII that the article was not intended to provide for forceful measures. In neither case do states parties possess the authority to modify the terms of Article 40 by consenting to an operation not envisaged therein.

The question of whether militarised peacekeeping may find its constitutional basis in Article 40 will be discussed further in chapters 4, 5 and 6 below, which will consider the Security Council's militarised peacekeeping practice to date.

3.2.3 *Powers under Article 41*

Article 41 provides that the Security Council 'may decide what measures not involving the use of armed force are to be employed to give effect to its decisions, and it may call upon the Members of the United Nations to apply such measures.' The article provides a list of such measures.[166] As the ICTY Appeals Chamber in the *Tadić* case observed: 'It is evident that the measures set out in Article 41 are merely illustrative *examples* which obviously do not exclude other measures'.[167] The Security Council possesses a broad discretion regarding what type of measures to take thereunder; however, as discussed below, certain limitations do exist.

3.2.3.1 Prerequisites to Security Council Measures under Article 41

As discussed above, the Security Council must determine the existence of a triggering event under Article 39 before it may decide to take measures under Article 41.[168] In addition, as with other measures whereby the Security Council is discharging its duties in relation to the maintenance of international peace and security, it must act in accordance with the purposes and principles of the UN.[169]

[166] The article speaks of measures including 'complete or partial interruption of economic relations and of rail, sea, air, postal, telegraphic, radio, and other means of communication, and the severance of diplomatic relations'.

[167] *Prosecutor v Tadić* (n 89) para 35.

[168] The finding need not be explicit, though in practice the Security Council has tended to be; see above, nn 139–40 and accompanying text.

[169] Art 24(2). See discussion in section 3.2.1.1 above.

3.2.3.2 Limitations on Security Council Measures under Article 41

The fundamental limitation[170] on measures established under Article 41 is set out in the text of the Article: they must be 'measures not involving the use of armed force'. As such, it seems axiomatic to exclude Article 41 as a possible constitutional basis for peacekeeping where the operation is empowered to use force beyond self-defence.[171] The question has been raised, however, as to whether limited military measures could be taken in support of an operation under Article 41, without passing to Article 42. Higgins put the question this way:

> even if the Security Council did not pass to military measures *per se* under Article 42 as the chosen means to enforce the peace, could certain limited military measures be employed to ensure the efficacy of the alternative means chosen, namely economic sanctions? This question has never been addressed in these terms, but such limited actions have in fact been authorized without any sense that the Security Council was passing from Article 41 to Article 42.[172]

Similarly, some have spoken of an 'Article 41½' authority, whereby the Security Council may authorise limited force to enforce sanctions with-

[170] Also, while not included in the wording of Art 41, the reference in Art 39 to decisions 'in accordance with Articles 41 and 42, to maintain or restore international peace and security' appears to impose an additional limitation. Such a limitation would not appear to present a significant obstacle to the Security Council's freedom of action (see the *Tadić* case (n 106) para 31). It could be argued that the wording of Art 41, which speaks of a requirement that the measures taken by the Security Council 'give effect to its decisions', amounts to another limitation; however, in view of the broad discretion held by the Security Council, this would appear not to be a genuine limitation. See also Jochen Frowein and Nico Krisch, 'Article 41' in Simma (n 5) 735–49, 744 para 21, who took the view that measures taken under Art 41 must remain 'within the general framework of Chapter VII powers'.

[171] Bowett (n 8) 177 described the Secretary-General's reference to Art 41 as a basis for ONUC as 'scarcely appropriate' in view of that force's right to use armed force; see also Frowein and Krisch, ibid, 744 para 21.

[172] Higgins (n 151) 328. These remarks were not made in the context of peacekeeping, but rather in the context of sanctions-related enforcement; Higgins gave the examples of the limited authorisations to use force in the context of the sanctions in Southern Rhodesia (where the Security Council called on the UK to 'prevent, by the use of force if necessary, the arrival at Beira of vessels reasonably believed to be carrying oil destined for Southern Rhodesia', and empowered the UK to 'arrest and detain the tanker known as the *Joanna V* upon her departure from Beira in the event her oil cargo is discharged there' (SC Res 221 of 9 April 1966)) and Iraq (where the Security Council called on Member States which were cooperating with the government of Kuwait and which had maritime deployments in the area 'to use such measures commensurate to the specific circumstances as may be necessary under the authority of the Security Council to halt all inward and outward maritime shipping' (SC Res 665 of 25 August 1990)), discussed above in chapter 2. She noted the possible existence of the implication 'that force could be authorized to implement economic sanctions without that use of force being viewed as military sanctions under Article 42' (329). White (n 81) appears to be opening the door to the use of force in an Art 41 peacekeeping operation when he posits that since 'the list of non-forcible measures in Article 41 is not meant to be exhaustive, it may be possible to imply wide-ranging mandatory, non-forcible, but coercive powers' (81). The nature of White's 'coercive' powers is not entirely clear; however, if those coercive powers involve the use of armed force, they will be precluded by the plain language of Art 41.

out going so far as relying upon Article 42.[173] Given the structure of the Charter, which, as noted, envisages provisional measures under Article 40, followed, if necessary, by non-forceful sanctions under Article 41 and, again, if necessary, by forceful sanctions under Article 42, and given the fact that Article 42 is the only provision in Chapter VII authorising the use of force,[174] such an argument is difficult to make.[175]

Some commentators have gone so far as to exclude Article 41 as a basis for peacekeeping any operations because all such operations are empowered to use force in self-defence.[176] However, this view is not sound. The mere fact that a peacekeeping operation possesses the right to use force in self-defence does not make the operation forceful. As has been argued throughout, all UN operations, no matter how peaceful, must possess the inherent right to self-defence.[177] This point is eloquently made by Schwarzenberger, who takes the view that the *potential* use of force in self-defence in a peacekeeping operation does not preclude it from finding its legal basis in Article 41:

> [T]he emphasis is . . . on the primary functions of such a body which can be fulfilled without any resort to armed force. On this assumption the fact that the force may use its weapons in self-defence affects status as little as does a civilian's exercise of his right of self-defence under municipal law.[178]

While the reasoning of Schwarzenberger is undoubtedly correct, it presumes a definition of self-defence that is reasonable. Where the definition of self-defence in UN peacekeeping is adapted to include defence of the property of the mission or the protection of certain civilians, matters become far less clear. As noted by Ciobanu:

> [T]he analogy between the use of armed force in self-defense by forces carrying out peace-keeping operations and the exercise of their right of self-defense by

[173] See eg Niels Blokker, 'Is the Authorization Authorized? Powers and Practice of the UN Security Council to Authorize the Use of Force by "Coalitions of the Able and Willing"' (2000) 11(3) *European Journal of International Law* 541, 543. See also Louis B Sohn, 'The Authority of the United Nations to Establish and Maintain a Permanent United Nations Force' (1958) 52 *American Journal of International Law* 229, 230: 'It is . . . conceivable that the Council may decide that the use of a UN Force for such purposes as patrolling a frontier or occupying a disputed one would not constitute a measure "involving the use of armed force" but, on the contrary, should be considered merely as a measure designed to prevent the use of armed force by others; accordingly [the Security Council] may use its authority under Article 41 to "decide what measures not involving the use of armed force are to be employed to give effect to its decisions".'

[174] See n 150 and accompanying text. Though the quote from Frowein and Krisch in the text accompanying n 150 relates to Art 40, it would also apply to Art 41.

[175] The argument that limited force may acceptable to support Security Council measures taken under Art 40 (see nn 151–52 and accompanying text) may be somewhat easier to make: unlike Art 41, Art 40 does not explicitly provide for the exclusion of measures involving the use of armed force.

[176] Ciobanu (n 66) 18.

[177] See chapter 2, section 2.1, n 19.

[178] Schwarzenberger (n 112) 7.

> individuals under municipal law does not appear . . . entirely appropriate. The United Nations forces are authorized to use force in order to bring about their mandate should armed resistance be mounted to hinder their actions, but no authorization is given to individuals to affirm forcefully their rights in society.[179]

In short, it is clear that a peacekeeping operation authorised to use force in self-defence may find its basis in Article 41, where self-defence is defined in a traditional sense *not* including defence-of-mandate or the defence of civilians. Where an operation is authorised to use force to defend its mandate (no matter that it is styled as 'self-defence' by the UN), the nature of the force authorised and used will need to be considered on a case-by-case basis. If the primary functions of the operation can be achieved without recourse to armed force, an argument may be made that such an operation may have its constitutional basis in Article 41. Where a peacekeeping operation is authorised to use force significantly beyond self-defence, whether to defend civilians or to accomplish other tasks, the constitutional basis for the operation (or certain of the tasks assigned to it) may not be found in Article 41.

3.2.3.3 Consent Issues under Article 41

It is clear, based on the use of the word 'decide' in Article 41, coupled with the distinction drawn in Article 39 between the Security Council making recommendations and deciding on 'measures . . . in accordance with Article 41 or 42', that the drafters of the Charter envisaged Security Council decisions as being of a different order from Security Council recommendations.[180] By virtue of Articles 25 and 48, Member States agree to take action to carry out the *decisions* of the Security Council.[181] Moreover, the potential for the Security Council to take measures under Article 41 which bind all states is clear from the *travaux préparatoires*, Security Council practice and decisions of international tribunals.[182] The ICTY Appeals Chamber made the following observation regarding the Security Council's enforcement powers:

[179] Ciobanu (n 66) 18.

[180] *Prosecutor v Tadić* (n 89) para 33.

[181] However, Art 25 limits the obligation of parties to carry out the decisions of the Security Council to those which are 'in accordance with the present Charter'. The fact that no such explicit limitation is found in Art 48 may be relied upon to imply that the Security Council, when engaging in enforcement, has greater leeway. This echoes the point made above in relation to the Security Council's obligation to act in conformity with 'the principles of justice and international law' pursuant to Art 1 when engaging in enforcement action (see nn 20–22 and accompanying text). However, in the same way that it does not appear unreasonable to expect *all* decisions of the Security Council, including enforcement decisions, to be in conformity with the principles of justice and international law, it does not seem unreasonable to expect compliance with the Charter.

[182] Frowein and Krisch (n 170) 739 para 8.

> These powers are *coercive* vis-à-vis the culprit State or entity. But they are also *mandatory* vis-à-vis the other Member States, who are under an obligation to cooperate with the Organization (Article 2, paragraph 5, Articles 25, 48) and with one another (Articles 49), in the implementation of the action or measures decided by the Security Council.[183]

Enforcement measures under Article 41 were not envisaged by the drafters of the Charter as *necessarily* being binding. The Security Council would be within its rights to decide on measures but leave matters regarding compliance with the decision up to the states themselves.[184]

State consent, then, is not required for an Article 41 enforcement measure. This has led some to argue that if host state consent is present, a measure may not have its constitutional basis in Article 41. This reasoning is flawed. It is true that, generally speaking, target states do not consent to Article 41 sanctions. Clearly, if a state's interests would be harmed by the imposition of Article 41 sanctions it would not consent to them. The apartheid regime in South Africa would not, for example, consent to Article 41 sanctions designed to remove it from power. Indeed, the ICJ in the *Certain Expenses* case considered the existence of the consent of the host state to be significant in making its finding that ONUC 'did not involve "preventive or enforcement" measures against any state under Chapter VII'.[185]

However, not all Article 41 measures are taken *against* a state; they are not, in the words of Frowein and Krisch, necessarily 'taken to overcome the will of the recalcitrant State'.[186] For example, after the outbreak of the Yugoslav conflict, the Security Council enacted an arms embargo at the request of the Yugoslav government.[187] The government had signed a ceasefire the previous week and apparently viewed the embargo as not being harmful to its interests.[188] Moreover, an enforcement measure under Article 41 may be to the benefit of the target state as regards third states. As Frowein and Krisch observed, a pattern of practice has emerged whereby governments involved in internal conflicts have

> sought international enforcement measures in support of their efforts to calm down hostilities or to overcome rebel groups. In such situations, [Article] 41 is the only legal basis allowing for binding measures *vis-à-vis* third States, and these measures are often crucial to the successful maintenance of peace. Moreover, in cases such as those involving the establishment of transitional administrations, likewise effected with the consent of the host State, the use of Chapter VII endows the operations with greater legitimacy and independence.[189]

[183] *Prosecutor v Tadić* (n 89) para 31.
[184] White (n 84) 107.
[185] *Certain Expenses* (n 11) 177. See discussion of this case in chapter 4, sections 2 and 3.
[186] Frowein and Krisch (n 170) 739 para 9.
[187] ibid.
[188] SC Res 713 of 25 September 1991.
[189] Frowein and Krisch (n 170) 739 para 9.

In sum, we see that where Security Council measures are being brought *against* a state such that they are harming its interests, the consent of that state would be illogical and would be a clear contra-indicant of the action amounting to enforcement under Article 41. However, in circumstances where the consenting state does not perceive its interests to be harmed, its consent does not impact on the question of whether measures were taken under Article 41.

3.2.3.4 Conclusions on Article 41

Ciobanu observed that a 'respected body of opinion' holds that Article 41 may provide a constitutional basis for peacekeeping; however, he did not elaborate on the type of operation envisaged.[190] Some commentators consider that the Security Council's creation of peacekeeping operations functioning as territorial administrations in Eastern Slavonia (UNTAES)[191] and Kosovo (UNMIK)[192] have their bases in Article 41.[193] In the resolutions establishing each, the Security Council explicitly invoked Chapter VII and made an explicit finding of the existence of 'a threat to international peace and security'. In the words of Bothe: 'The establishment of a UN administration certainly qualifies as a "measure not involving the use of armed force" in the sense of [Article 41].'[194] While this may be the case, it is not always so. For example, the territorial administration in East Timor, UNTAET, which was authorised to use 'all necessary measures to fulfil its mandate',[195] may not be said to have its constitutional basis in Article 41.[196] Even if one accepts the argument that 'limited' force beyond self-defence (such as defence-of-mandate) may be authorised under Article 41 so long as the primary functions of the operation may be achieved without recourse to armed force,[197] it cannot reasonably be asserted that the level of force authorised by the phrase 'all necessary measures' is of a limited nature.

Where the Security Council intends that the measures it takes under Article 41 are to be binding, consent is not required. Where the consent of the affected state is forthcoming, it is not necessarily a contra-indicant to the Security Council having established a peacekeeping operation based

[190] Ciobanu (n 66) 17; this is a view with which Ciobanu disagrees. Bowett (n 8) 177 observed that Art 41 'might conceivably be used as a basis for some kinds of peace-keeping operations, and indeed it was an article cited by the Secretary-General on at least one occasion'.

[191] SC Res 1037 of 15 January 1996.

[192] SC Res 1244 of 10 June 1999.

[193] White (n 81) 81. See also Michael J Matheson, 'United Nations Governance in Postconflict Societies' (2001) 95 *American Journal of International Law* 76.

[194] Bothe (n 5) 685 para 87.

[195] SC Res 1272 of 25 October 1999.

[196] cf Bothe (n 5) 685 para 87, who considers UNTAET to be an Art 41 operation despite its authorisation to use all necessary measures.

[197] See section 3.2.3.2 above.

on its Article 41 powers; as noted, in some cases, the affected state may consider a binding Article 41 enforcement measure to be in its interests. Whether or not a peacekeeping operation is established with the host state's consent, the wording of Article 41 means that it may only provide a basis for measures not involving the use of armed force (or at least measures not requiring the use of significant force). Where a state does consent, is the limitation on the use of force lifted? While, as noted, states may opt to waive the protections afforded to them in the principles set out in Article 2(1), (4) and (7), they do not possess the ability to read out the phrase 'measures not involving the use of force' from Article 41. As such, it would appear that militarised peacekeeping cannot locate its constitutional basis in Article 41. This matter will be examined further in the context of the Security Council's militarised peacekeeping practice below in chapters 4, 5 and 6.

3.2.4 *Powers under Article 42*

Article 42 provides that the Security Council 'may take such action by air, sea, or land forces as may be necessary to maintain or restore international peace and security' if it should 'consider that measures provided for in Article 41 would be inadequate or have proved to be inadequate'. It provides a non-exhaustive list of measures which the Security Council may adopt under this Article.[198]

3.2.4.1 Prerequisites to Security Council Measures under Article 42

In addition to the prerequisites outlined in relation to Article 41 – the need for determination (perhaps explicitly) that a triggering event under Article 39 has occurred and the need to act in accordance with the purposes and principles of the UN[199] – Article 42 measures feature another prerequisite: there must be a determination by the Security Council 'that measures provided for in Article 41 would be inadequate or have proved to be inadequate'. There is nothing in the wording of Article 42 to indicate that this needs to be a formal, written determination.[200] Moreover, the wording – 'Should the Security Council consider that measures provided for in Article 41 would be inadequate or have proved to be inadequate' – makes clear that the Security Council may take action under Article 42

[198] 'Such action may include demonstrations, blockade, and other operations by air, sea, or land forces of Members of the United Nations.'

[199] See the discussion above, n 169 and accompanying text.

[200] The argument that the Security Council must make an explicit determination that non-forceful measures would be inadequate was made by states opposed to the use of force in Iraq in 1990/91. See Oscar Schachter, 'United Nations Law in the Gulf Conflict' (1991) 85 *American Journal of International Law* 452, 455–56, 462–63, where he outlined this argument (which he rejected).

even without giving Article 41 measures a chance to be successful, so long as it is thought that such measures would be inadequate.[201]

3.2.4.2 Limitations on Security Council Measures under Article 42

Certain limitations exist with regard to the nature of the measures the Security Council may take under Article 42. First, Article 42 limits action to that which is 'necessary to maintain or restore international peace and security'. As we saw above in the discussion of the Article 39 requirement that measures taken under Articles 41 and 42 must be 'to maintain or restore international peace and security', there is a large measure of discretion on the part of the Security Council in this regard.[202] However, in Article 42, unlike Article 39, the word 'necessary' appears. This, arguably, indicates that any resort to force must conform to the principle of proportionality, as recognised by international law.[203]

Second, in contradistinction to measures taken elsewhere in the Charter, measures under this provision must involve the use of force. The wording of the provision speaks of 'action by air, sea or land *forces*' (emphasis added). Moreover, it is clear from the progressive nature of Chapter VII that Article 42 necessarily envisages the use of force. If the Security Council were to rely on Article 42 to establish a non-forceful measure, it would be an indication that the measures available to it under Article 41 had not been exhausted, as required. The lack of forcefulness of UNEF I was an essential aspect of the Court's finding that it did not constitute an Article 42 enforcement action in the *Certain Expenses* case.[204]

Some have argued that the force authorised must be of a sufficient level in order for it to have its basis in Article 42.[205] For example, Schachter, writing in 1961, rejected Article 42 as a possible basis for ONUC, citing

> the expectation at San Francisco . . . that Article 42 would be resorted to for military action of an international character – that is to say, directed against the troops of a state or another governmental authority which bore respon-

[201] See Frowein and Krisch, 'Article 42' in Simma (n 5) 749–59, 753 para 7.

[202] See the *Tadić* case (n 106) para 31.

[203] Frowein and Krisch (n 201) 753 para 8. See Frowein and Krisch (n 73) 711–12 para 30.

[204] *Certain Expenses*. This case is discussed in detail in chapter 4, section 3.

[205] Based on the fact that the force authorised in the context of enforcing sanctions against Southern Rhodesia had been 'closely circumscribed' by the Security Council and the use of force was minimal, Fawcett (n 111) noted that it might be said that the force did not meet 'a certain intensity and scale', envisaged in Art 41, and applicable under Art 42. However, he offered two convincing counter-arguments: 'First, there is nothing in Art 42 to suggest that only major hostilities are contemplated; on the contrary, a blockade may be effective without a shot's being fired and "demonstrations" are in their very nature a show rather than a use of force. Second, it is obviously desirable, and closer to the purposes of the Charter, that the use of force by or through the United Nations itself should be as far as possible restricted in time and place to what is necessary to maintain or restore peace' (119).

> sibility for a breach of peace or act of aggression. Use of troops for internal security purposes at the request of the territorial state does not have this kind of international coercive character, and it is doubtful, therefore, that it should be described legally as the use of armed force within the meaning of Article 42.[206]

At the time Schachter took this view, the only example of Article 42 practice was in relation to the Security Council's authorisation to use force in the operation in the Korean Peninsula.[207] However, as discussed in chapter 2, practice has evolved considerably since then and authorisations to use force for internal security purposes at the request of the territorial state (whether in the form of militarised peacekeeping or quasi-enforcement operations) are now the norm. Moreover, as Schachter himself observed, nothing in the text of Article 42 – 'such action by air, sea or land forces as may be necessary to maintain or restore international peace and security' – requires that the action authorised thereunder must constitute 'sanctions' *against* a state or government authority.[208] Nor is there any requirement in the text for a minimum level of forcefulness.

3.2.4.3 Consent Issues under Article 42

The discussion above in relation to the binding nature of Article 41 measures is largely applicable to Article 42.[209] As discussed above,[210] the drafters of the Charter envisaged that when the Security Council needed to establish forceful measures under Article 42, it would rely on forces which had been pre-committed by states pursuant to agreements under Article 43. No such agreements have been made, with the effect that the Security Council's ability to use force under Article 42 is limited. While it may decide on enforcement measures that impact on the legal rights of Member States, it may not *compel* Member States to participate in enforcement actions.[211] Franck put it this way: 'While participation in military action has . . . been voluntary, the authority and objectives of *ad hoc* forces have usually been formulated in mandatory terms.'[212] So, for example, while the Security Council's resolution authorising the use of force ('all

[206] Miller/Schachter (n 118) 8.

[207] This operation is discussed in chapter 2, section 3.1.

[208] Miller/Schachter (n 118) 7. He noted: '[O]ne could conclude on the basis of the language alone that the military measures contemplated by the resolutions on the Congo were adopted in order to maintain international peace and therefore constitute action under Article 42' (7–8). Schachter did not accept that conclusion, however.

[209] See above, section 3.2.3.3. As with Art 41, the reference in Art 39 to a 'decision' under Art 42 and the commitment of members at Arts 25 and 48 to accept and carry out decisions of the Security Council show that Art 42 decisions were intended to be binding. See discussion above, nn 180–84 and accompanying text.

[210] See chapter 2, section 3.

[211] Higgins (n 53) 3.

[212] Franck (n 42) 27.

necessary means') under Article 42[213] against Iraq in 1990 did not create a legal obligation on any state to participate in the operation, it did make the use of force by Member States against Iraq lawful, which it might not otherwise have been.[214]

As with Article 41 enforcement, the consent of the host state can be a contra-indicant to a measure being established under Article 42. With regard to full-blown enforcement, such as in Korea or Iraq/Kuwait, the measures are taken against the recalcitrant states; it would be entirely illogical for either state to consent to the action. Indeed, if North Korea and Iraq had been in favour of Security Council measures to remove them from the area they had invaded, they would simply have adhered to the Security Council's call on them to withdraw, obviating the need for enforcement action. However, as we have seen, states do tend to consent to quasi-enforcement operations. Such consent may not be relied upon as an indicator that the Security Council is not taking measures under Article 42, merely that the measures taken are not *against* the host state as was the case with North Korea or Iraq. The government, by consenting, may simply be indicating its perception that it is to the benefit of the host state (or its government) that the military force is authorised.

Similar considerations are at play in UN-led operations. While the Security Council has never explicitly invoked Article 42 when establishing peacekeeping operations – nor, for that matter, has it ever done so in the context of enforcement operations – there is nothing to prevent it from doing so. It is necessary to study the wording of the resolution – Is there an invocation of Chapter VII? Is there a determination that there has been an Article 39 triggering event? Is there authorisation to use considerable force? – to gain insight into its intent. If the Security Council is acting under Article 42 in establishing a peacekeeping operation, host state consent is not legally required. The fact that the host state has consented does not, in itself, mean that the operation may not have its basis in Article 42. Host state consent is only an indication that an operation is not an Article 42 enforcement action *against* the state. In the *Certain Expenses* case, the ICJ cited consent of the host state as an important factor in finding ONUC not to be an enforcement action *against* that state; however, it did not rule out the possibility that the operation had its constitutional basis in Article 42.[215] Bowett, writing in 1964, well before the Security Council had developed its quasi-enforcement practice or its practice of militarised peacekeeping (beyond ONUC), was prescient in observing that neither

[213] Art 42 was not invoked in SC Res 678 of 29 November 1990; however, this is widely believed to be the constitutional basis of this operation. See discussion in chapter 2, section 3.1.

[214] Of course, in the case of Iraq's invasion of Kuwait, the use of force was also said to have been legal, based on the principle of collective self-defence.

[215] The *Certain Expenses* case is discussed in detail in chapter 4, sections 2 and 3.

Article 41 nor Article 42 'necessarily presuppose[s] that the action has to be enforcement action *against* a state'.[216]

3.2.4.4 Conclusions on Article 42

In sum, in order to determine whether the Security Council is acting under Article 42 in establishing a peacekeeping operation, regard must be had to that organ's intent. Host state consent is not required in law for mandatory measures taken under Article 42, and the Security Council's practice of generally obtaining such consent is only an indication that an operation is not an Article 42 enforcement action *against* the state. As discussed in chapter 2, the nature of Article 42 enforcement has changed over the years and nothing precludes the Security Council from establishing a forceful operation – whether UN-led (militarised peacekeeping) or state-led (quasi-enforcement) – through the invocation of its Article 42 powers. Whether militarised peacekeeping operations (or some of them) have been established by the Security Council in exercise of its powers under Article 42 will be considered in chapters 4, 5 and 6.

4. IMPLIED SECURITY COUNCIL POWERS

In addition to its explicit powers, the Security Council may possess implied powers in certain circumstances.[217] The ICJ held in the *Reparations* case that the drafters of the Charter bestowed powers on the UN to bring a claim on behalf of one of its employees 'by necessary implication as being essential to the performance of its duties'.[218] The majority of the Court did not feel it necessary to indicate an express power from which the implied power derived; instead, it linked the implied power to the UN's 'purposes and functions' in a more general sense.[219] This approach was later confirmed by the ICJ in the *Effect of Awards* case, where the Court recognised that while there was no provision in the Charter authorising any of the principal organs to adjudicate disputes with its staff, the power to establish an employment tribunal arose by 'necessary intendment'.[220] Citing 'the expressed aim of the Charter to promote freedom and justice

[216] Bowett (n 8) 176 n 34.

[217] See, generally, Jan Klabbers, *An Introduction to International Institutional Law* (Cambridge, Cambridge University Press, 2002) 69 and White (n 81).

[218] *Reparations for Injuries Suffered in the Service of the United Nations*, Advisory Opinion [1949] ICJ Rep 174, 182.

[219] ibid, 180. Famously, Judge Hackworth disagreed with the majority, calling for implied powers to 'flow from a grant of express powers' and to be '"necessary" to the exercise of powers expressly granted' (198).

[220] *Effect of Awards of Compensation Made by the UN Administrative Tribunal*, Advisory Opinion of 13 July 1954 [1954] ICJ Rep 47, 57.

for individuals' and 'the constant preoccupation of the United Nations Organization to promote this aim',[221] it found that the power to establish an employment tribunal was 'essential to ensure the efficient working of the Secretariat' and to secure high standards.[222]

In the *Certain Expenses* case,[223] the Court considered whether the General Assembly was empowered to authorise expenses of peacekeeping operations as expenses of the Organization.[224] Based on a consideration of the broad nature of the General Assembly's powers, including in relation to matters of international peace and security,[225] and the relatively narrow nature of the limitations upon the General Assembly's functioning provided in the Charter, the Court held that the General Assembly did possess the necessary power. This represented a further liberalisation of the Court's approach to implied powers; its emphasis was not on 'the implication of powers necessary to make an express provision effective as in the *Reparation* case, but on the absence of any provision in the Charter prohibiting the exercise of such a power'.[226] White characterised this approach as leading to the finding of 'inherent powers' (rather than just 'implied' ones), whereby an organ's power to act is, in effect, 'only limited by provisions in the Charter which clearly prohibit such acts'.[227] In short, there is considerable scope to argue, based on the Court's jurisprudence, that the Security Council has a broad power to impose measures to restore international peace and security, unless it is specifically prohibited from doing so elsewhere in the Charter.[228]

[221] ibid.

[222] ibid, 56–58.

[223] The *Certain Expenses* case is considered in detail in chapter 4, sections 2 and 3.

[224] As the Court observed, it was argued that expenses resulting from operations for the maintenance of international peace and security could not be 'expenses of the Organization' under Art 17(2) 'inasmuch as they fall to be dealt with exclusively by the Security Council, and more especially through agreements negotiated in accordance with Article 43 of the Charter'. This argument was based 'in part upon the view that when the maintenance of international peace and security is involved, it is only the Security Council which is authorized to decide on any action relative thereto' (*Certain Expenses* (n 11) 162).

[225] It observed that while by Art 24(1) the Members of the UN confer on the Security Council primary responsibility for the maintenance of international peace and security, '[t]he responsibility conferred is "primary", not exclusive'. ibid, 163.

[226] White (n 81) 47. He continued: 'In effect, the General Assembly's powers are only limited by provisions in the Charter which clearly prohibit such acts; in the case the restriction was that only the Security Council could order enforcement action under Chapter VII' (ibid).

[227] ibid, 48. He argued that inherent powers lend themselves to the 'creation of peacekeeping forces by the UN in that it may be difficult to argue that such forces are "necessary" or "essential" for the achievement of express powers'. For a critique of White's analysis of inherent powers, see Klabbers (n 217) 75–78.

[228] See also the *Namibia* case (n 2). The Court held that the fact that certain specific powers of the Security Council were enumerated in Art 24(2) did not 'exclude the existence of general powers to discharge the responsibilities conferred in' Art 24(1), ie, its primary responsibility for the maintenance of international peace and security. Instead, the Court endorsed a Statement of the Secretary-General, made to the Security Council on 10 January 1947, in which he observed that 'the Members of the United Nations have conferred upon the Security Council powers commensurate with its responsibility for the maintenance of

The approach of the ICJ has been criticised as being overly-liberal.[229] Franck's reference in the epigraph of this chapter to the possibility of a modest augmentation of express powers through reliance on implied powers which are necessarily incidental to the effective implementation of the enumerated ones, would appear to represent a sounder approach to treaty interpretation – even where, as with the UN Charter, the treaty is also considered by many to be a constitution. Many legal experts have been more cautious regarding implied powers, prudently attempting to link an implied peacekeeping power to an existing power held by the Security Council in a particular article of the Charter, to one of the Organization's purposes (in particular, its purpose at Article 1(1) of restoring international peace and security) or, more generally, to the powers enumerated in a Chapter of the Charter. These more cautious approaches to implied peacekeeping powers – which link implied powers to powers outside Chapter VII or under it – are considered below.

4.1 Chapter VI½ and Implied Powers

Before turning to the particular articles or Chapters of the UN Charter that have been argued over the years to provide a basis for an implied peacekeeping power, the concept of 'Chapter VI½' will be briefly addressed. As is well known, many commentators – both legal and political – have been content to rely on the imprecise concept of Chapter VI½ as the basis for peacekeeping. However, those invoking the phrase 'Chapter VI½' do not appear to be advancing a legal argument that an implied power exists. Instead, they would appear to be using the term to acknowledge that the activities carried out by peacekeeping operations frequently fall between two stools. What commentators are effectively saying when they rely on Chapter VI½ is that the functions of peacekeeping operations go further than the peaceful activity envisaged in Chapter VI, but do not go as far as Chapter VII enforcement action.

Following on from the concept of Chapter VI½ is the concept of 'Chapter VI¾' operations. Some have referred to peacekeeping operations vested with the authority to use force beyond self-defence (or significantly beyond it) as Chapter VI¾ operations. Once again, those invoking the phrase do not appear to be addressing the constitutional basis of these operations. Instead, the term is being used to provide a label for operations which are potentially even more forceful than Chapter VI½ operations, thereby coming even closer to a Chapter VII operation.[230]

peace and security. The only limitations are the fundamental principles and purposes found in Chapter I of the Charter' (ibid, 52).

[229] See eg White (n 81).

[230] As noted above, some use the term 'Chapter VII peacekeeping' – though as noted, this may mean different things to different people. See above, nn 53–55 and accompanying text.

4.2 Powers Implied Outside Chapter VII

As noted, the tendency of commentators is to link an implied peacekeeping power for the Security Council to explicit powers already provided for that organ in the Charter. Such explicit powers may fall outside Chapter VII of the Charter or within it. Turning first to the Security Council's powers outside Chapter VII, a number of implied peacekeeping powers have been suggested. First, some commentators have simply referred generally to 'Chapter VI' powers or 'Chapter VI peacekeeping'. This would appear to be less in the nature of an invocation of implied powers and more a way of underlining that measures taken under Chapter VI must not be forceful in nature and are generally agreed to be recommendatory only.[231]

Second, it has been argued that Article 1(1), which sets out the first of the Organization's purposes – to maintain international peace and security[232] – can provide a constitutional basis for peacekeeping.[233] This view is at variance with a systematic reading of the Charter, which indicates that Article 1(1) sets out a basic objective of the Organization, with the specific powers by which that objective may be achieved being left until later in that instrument.[234] As Bowett observed in the context of ONUC: '[S]imple reliance on Article 1(1) is not enough, for it divorces the question [of the operation's constitutional basis] entirely from the equally important question whether a particular organ has the power to undertake a given course of action.'[235]

Third, Schachter suggested that '"observational" peacekeeping activities such as truce supervision' may fall within the Security Council's general authority under Article 24.[236] According to Article 24(1), Member States of the UN 'confer on the Security Council primary responsibility for the maintenance of international peace and security, and agree that in carrying out its duties' the Security Council acts on their behalf. This amplifies the Organization's focus on the maintenance of international peace and security as set out in Article 1(1) and assigns the task primarily to the Security Council. The ICJ in the *South West Africa* case made it clear that Article 24(1) vested general powers in the Security Council – in addition to those specifically referred to in Article 24(2) – and cited Article 24(1)

[231] Art 34 is generally thought to be an exception to the Chapter's non-binding character; see n 62 above.

[232] For the text of Art 1(1) see above, 70.

[233] Halderman (n 15).

[234] See discussion on this point above, section 2.1.

[235] Bowett (n 8) 179. Later, however, he conceded that it was 'arguable' that the United Nations had the inherent power to establish ONUC or UNEF I based on Art 1(1)'s stated purpose of maintaining international peace and security through effective collective measures for the prevention and removal of threats to the peace, etc. He observed that this inherent power could exist 'even if the Forces designated for these tasks are of a more limited nature than those anticipated for enforcement measures under Chapter VII' (311 and n 70).

[236] Schachter (n 61) 81.

as the legal basis for the Security Council resolution which determined, inter alia, that 'the continued presence of the South African authorities in Namibia is illegal'.[237] According to Gill, '[t]hese "implied" or general powers to take measures not referred to elsewhere in the Charter have been a source of controversy and the extent of such powers is still by no means clear'.[238]

Fourth, some commentators have suggested that Article 29, which provides that '[t]he Security Council may establish subsidiary organs as it deems necessary for the performance of its functions',[239] provides a legal basis for peacekeeping operations.[240] It is uncontroversial that peacekeeping operations may be characterised as subsidiary organs;[241] however, based on the wording of Article 29 and its position within the overall structure of the Charter, it is clear that it merely provides the Security Council with the power to *establish* a subsidiary organ. The power of the subsidiary organ actually to perform the functions for which it was established must be found elsewhere in the Charter.[242] In the words of Bowett:

> [A] Resolution which contemplates a subsidiary organ with a given function has to find its constitutional basis first and foremost in the articles justifying the function – and not in an article giving a general power to establish subsidiary organs.[243]

4.3 Chapter VII Implied Powers

Given the exceptional nature of the Security Council's powers under Chapter VII – the ability to authorise force, despite the general prohibition set out in Article 2(4), and to create obligations for states without their consent, despite the focus on state sovereignty in paragraphs (1) and (7) of Article 2 – a higher level caution is warranted when arguing in favour of the existence of implied powers thereunder. While Higgins's observa-

[237] *Namibia* case (n 2) 52.

[238] Gill (n 20) 69 and the discussion at n 96 of that article.

[239] A similar power exists for the General Assembly in Art 22, and UNEF I was considered to be a subsidiary organ of the General Assembly. GIAD Draper, 'The Legal Limitations upon the Employment of Weapons by the United Nations Force in the Congo' (1963) 12 *International and Comparative Law Quarterly* 387, 391.

[240] Draper, ibid, 387. See also Schwarzenberger (n 112) 8. He referred to Art 29 as a possible basis for the establishment of UNEF.

[241] That ONUC was a subsidiary organ established under Art 29 was implied by the ICJ in *Certain Expenses* (n 11) at 177. For more on the relationship between the Security Council and peacekeeping operations as Art 29 subsidiary organs (and the parameters of that relationship), see Sarooshi (n 23) ch 3.

[242] Schwarzenberger (n 112) 8 n 20b. See also Hans Kelsen, *The Law of the United Nations: A Critical Analysis of its Fundamental Problems* (London, Stevens & Sons, 1950) 391–92. See also Alexander Orakhelashvili, 'The Legal Basis of the United Nations Peace-Keeping Operations' (2003) 43 *Virginia Journal of International Law* 485, 503.

[243] Bowett (n 8) 178.

tion that it is doubtful whether the 'grave sanctions of Article 42' can be brought into play 'casually, and via the "backdoor"' was made in another context, her characterisation of Article 42 measures as grave – as, I would submit, are Article 41 measures – supports the view that great care needs to be taken when implying enforcement powers.[244] The question as to 'whether the choice of the Security Council is limited to the measures provided for in Articles 41 and 42 of the Charter (as the language of Article 39 suggests), or whether it has even larger discretion in the form of general powers to maintain and restore international peace and security under Chapter VII at large', arose in the *Tadić* case before the ICTY.[245] While not explicitly ruling out a general power, the Appeals Chamber exercised restraint. It cited the clear language of Article 39 and its 'channelling of the very broad and exceptional powers of the Security Council under Chapter VII through Articles 41 and 42' and concluded that those two articles left the Security Council with such wide discretion as not to warrant searching for any wider powers.[246] Nevertheless, arguments have been posited that additional Chapter VII powers may be implied.

First, it might be argued that the Security Council possesses a 'general' Chapter VII power to establish certain operations. Schachter observed that 'the Council could act on a liberal construction of its authority derived from its general powers to maintain and restore international peace and security. On that approach, the reference to Chapter VII in [the relevant resolution] would call for no further specification.'[247] While this observation was made in the context of a discussion of the legal basis for the Security Council's authorisation of the use of force in the 1990/91 Gulf War, it might equally be argued to apply to the Security Council's militarised peacekeeping activities. Another commentator posited that there exists an implied power to establish an administrative peacekeeping operation (UNMIK) based on the Security Council's general obligation to preserve international peace and security under Chapter VII, and linked this to the purposes and principles set out in Articles 1 and 2.[248] Moreover, Bowett appeared to rely, in part, on a general Chapter VII power when he observed that while that ONUC was 'clearly a "Chapter VII situation," a

[244] Higgins (n 42) 236.

[245] *Prosecutor v Tadić* (n 89) para 31.

[246] ibid.

[247] Schachter (n 200) 461. As he noted, this position was taken by the then Legal Counsel to the Secretary-General of the United Nations, C-A Fleischhauer, in a panel discussion held at the American Society of International Law Annual Meeting on 19 April 1991 (ibid, n 28). The question raised by Higgins in relation to the authority to use force to ensure compliance with sanctions in Rhodesia and Iraq may have been alluding to an implied power. See n 172 and accompanying text.

[248] Epaminontas E Triantafilou, 'Matter of Law, Question of Policy: Kosovo's Current and Future Status under International Law' (2004–05) 5 *Chicago Journal of International Law* 355, 359.

situation involving a threat to international peace and security . . . no specific article of Chapter VII quite fits the Resolutions adopted – at least so far as the establishment of the Force is concerned'.[249]

However, as noted the exceptional nature of enforcement powers, mean that a particular level of caution is required before such powers may be implied. Moreover, implying enforcement powers would appear to be incompatible with the structure of Chapter VII, which makes clear the progressive nature of Security Council action thereunder: the Security Council may, if appropriate, begin with a recommendation under Article 39, before progressing to provisional measures under Article 40 and then, if necessary, to non-forceful sanctions under Article 41. It is only as a last resort, when all else has failed, that the Charter envisages that the Security Council may authorise forceful measures. An argument that the Security Council may authorise forceful measures based on an implied power – and potentially without following the progressive steps in Chapter VII – goes too far.

Second, it might be asserted that a 'general' Article 39 power provides a basis for peacekeeping. In the same way that some have cited an implied power linked to Article 39 as a basis for the Security Council's authorisation of force in relation to the Southern Rhodesian sanctions[250] and in relation to the enforcement action in the Korean situation,[251] it might be argued that such a power could be the basis for militarised peacekeeping. Bowett invoked, inter alia, 'the general powers of Article 39' as a basis for the establishment of ONUC.[252] As discussed above,[253] Article 39 does not provide a legal basis for a measure to restore international peace and security. It would be contrary to the fundamental nature of Article 39 (and its distinction between the Security Council's ability to 'make recommendations, or decide what measures shall be taken in accordance with Articles 41 and 42'), as well as the progressive nature of Chapter VII as a whole, to rely on an implied power linked to that article as a basis for a mandatory peacekeeping operation; it would be unnecessary to look to an implied power under Article 39 for a basis for a recommendatory one.

Finally, it been posited that Article 48(1), which requires states to take 'the action necessary to carry out the decisions of the Security Council for the maintenance of international peace and security', may provide

[249] Bowett (n 8) 178.

[250] For example, Gowlland-Debbas (n 111) 417–18 suggested that the resolution authorising enforcement of the sanctions against Southern Rhodesia might be attached to a recommendation under Art 39.

[251] See Burns H Weston, 'Security Council Resolution 678 and Persian Gulf Decision Making: Precarious Legitimacy' (1991) 85 *American Journal of International Law* 516, 521. In support of his assertion that Art 39 was the basis for the force used against North Korea, Weston relied on Higgins (n 42) 197–210.

[252] Bowett (n 8) 179.

[253] In this chapter, section 3.2.1.3.

the legal foundation for a peacekeeping operation.[254] However, as Bowett wrote:

> [T]he Security Council decisions for the maintenance of peace, to which this article refers, must be taken under some other authority in the Charter; and Article 48(1) merely regulates the nature and extent of the participation in the decision already taken. In other words, Article 48(1) could regulate the implementation of a decision for a United Nations Force, but not provide the actual basis for its establishment.[255]

As Bowett noted, it is 'doubtful' whether Article 48(1) might provide 'a separate constitutional basis for the establishment of a United Nations Force'.[256]

In short, despite the views of certain commentators, neither an implied power based on Chapter VII generally nor an implied power based on any of the articles therein provides a satisfactory basis for the establishment of peacekeeping operations.

4.4 Limitations on Implied Powers

In the *Certain Expenses* case, the ICJ rejected a proposal to read in a limitation on the power of the General Assembly under Article 17(2). The Court observed:

> Since no qualification is expressed in the text of the Charter, it could be read in, only if such qualification must necessarily be implied from the provisions of the Charter considered as a whole, or from some particular provision thereof which makes it unavoidable to do so in order to give effect to the Charter.[257]

This finding, coupled with the Court's finding in the same case that 'when the Organization takes action which warrants the assertion that it was appropriate for the fulfilment of one of the stated purposes of the United Nations, the presumption is that such action is not ultra vires the Organization',[258] indicates that implied limitations on the Security Council's powers will not lightly be found to exist.

Nevertheless, the explicit restrictions or limitations on the Security Council's powers contained within the Charter, and discussed above, must necessarily continue to apply even if the Security Council were

[254] Schwarzenberger (n 112) 138. See also Louise Doswald-Beck, 'The Legal Validity of Military Intervention by Invitation of the Government' (1985) 56 *British Yearbook of International Law* 189. See also Bowett (n 8) 284–85, who noted that the Soviet government took the view that the authority for the establishment ONUC could be found under Art 48(1).

[255] Bowett (n 8) 284.

[256] ibid, 284–85. See also Ciobanu (n 66) 17, who endorsed Bowett on this point.

[257] *Certain Expenses* (n 11) 168.

[258] ibid.

found to be entitled to exercise an implied power. Nothing in the purposes and principles suggests that they will govern the Organization's conduct only where it is acting pursuant to an explicit power.[259] Indeed, one of the primary factors in the Court's finding of implied powers in the *Effect of Awards* case was the need for the UN to act in accordance with the 'aim[s] of the Charter'.[260] In the *Namibia* case, while the Court observed the potential for implied powers under Article 24, it made the following qualification: 'The only limitations are the fundamental principles and purposes found in Chapter I of the Charter.'[261]

Moreover, if the Security Council was found to be able to exercise an implied power based upon, or of a similar nature to, an explicit power, the limitations or prerequisites associated with the explicit power must surely apply. An argument that because the Security Council is exercising an implied power instead of an explicit one it is somehow exempt from the limitations envisaged by the drafters would appear to have no basis in the Charter or in international law. Moreover, if accepted, it could lead to wholly unintended results: on the one hand there would be explicit powers which feature carefully drafted limitations and restrictions and, on the other, implicit powers which are limitless. Thus, it must be the case that even if an implied or general power enforcement power is found to exist, the above-discussed limitations relating to enforcement activity will continue to apply.

4.5 Conclusions on Implied Powers

In conclusion, there is little support for the view that the constitutional basis of peacekeeping operations may be found in implied powers. Where a peacekeeping operation is authorised to use force only in self-defence and may only be established with the consent of the host state, there is little need to turn to implied powers. As we have seen, certain of the articles in the Charter – including, possibly, 33(2), 34 and 36 in Chapter VI and 39 and 40 in Chapter VII – may, arguably, provide an explicit basis for this type of operation.

An implied power of the Security Council to establish a peacekeeping operation that features force beyond self-defence (or, some would argue, force significantly beyond self-defence) and/or to establish mandatory measures (whether or not the state in question consents) would amount to the equivalent of Chapter VII measures to restore international peace and

[259] Bowett (n 8) 311 observed: 'If one seeks a basis for ONUC and UNEF in the doctrine of implied powers and the principle of effectiveness, it is necessary to ask what uses of force, other than for enforcement measures under Articles 41 and 42, are inherent in the Charter and *within the purposes and principles of the Charter*' (emphasis added).

[260] Effect of Awards (n 220) 57.

[261] *Namibia* case (n 2) 52.

security. Given the exceptional nature of these powers, an argument that the Security Council may conduct measures not provided for in Chapter VII based on an implied power – whether associated with a particular article of the Chapter or based on the Chapter as a whole – is very difficult to make. Such an argument would effectively disregard the overall structure of the Charter, which places mandatory measures to restore international peace and security in carefully drafted provisions in Chapter VII, as well as the structure of Chapter VII itself, which limits the use of mandatory force to Article 42 enforcement measures and only when the Security Council considers that the measures provided for in Article 41 would be inadequate or have proved to be inadequate. Such powers ought not to be lightly implied. Even assuming that an implied power to take mandatory and/or forceful measures is considered to exist – for example based on the Security Council's explicit powers in Article 24(1) or based on Article 39 – the limitations associated therewith must surely apply.

5. OVERALL CONCLUSIONS ON THE SECURITY COUNCIL'S LEGAL POWERS/CONSTRAINTS

In section 2 above, we saw that the purposes and principles, and in particular paragraphs (1), (4) and (7) of Article 2, can impact on the Security Council's freedom of action. Moreover, we saw that two exceptions exist with regard to the restrictions associated with each of those paragraphs: (1) where the Security Council is engaging in enforcement action under Chapter VII, and (2) where the host state has consented to the Security Council's action. In section 3, we saw that, depending on the Charter provision under which the Security Council is acting in establishing measures, certain limitations or prerequisites may exist. These impact on the Security Council's ability to do one (or more) of the following: (1) authorise measures relying on force beyond self-defence (or considerably beyond self-defence), (2) authorise obligatory measures, and (3) authorise measures that are not impartial.

As a result, the following categories of peacekeeping emerge, each with its own legal requirements in relation to the three 'fundamental principles' of peacekeeping: (1) peacekeeping as an enforcement measure, (2) peacekeeping as a mandatory measure under Article 40, and (3) peacekeeping where consent is legally required. Each will be considered in turn.

5.1 Peacekeeping as an Enforcement Measure

Where the Security Council is taking binding enforcement measures under Article 41 or 42, there is no need for host state consent. There is no violation of the principles set out in Article 2(1), (4) or (7) as the host state has, in effect, given its consent in advance by virtue of its agreeing to the provisions of the UN Charter, including Article 25. With an enforcement operation against a state, that state has, '[b]y its own conduct . . . forfeited the rights to inviolability of its territory'.[262] As discussed, the fact that host state consent is not legally required for a peacekeeping operation established under Article 41 or 42 might lead some to the mistaken conclusion that if a host state *does* consent to an operation it has not been established under either of those articles. While it is true that host state consent is an indicator that the Security Council has not established an enforcement action *against* the state, host state consent may not be said to prove that the Security Council has not established an enforcement operation at all; where the host state considers an enforcement action to be in its interests, it may very well consent to it.

As to the use of force, an operation established under Article 41 has different limitations from one established under Article 42. Peacekeeping operations established under Article 42 may use force beyond self-defence – indeed, an Article 42 operation *must* be authorised to use force beyond self-defence. A peacekeeping operation established under Article 42 would not violate the principles of non-intervention or non-use of force set out in Article 2 of the Charter (purposes and principles) due to its enforcement nature.

While an Article 41 operation would not violate Article 2(4) due to its enforcement nature, the wording of Article 41 limits such an operation to measures 'not involving the use of armed force'. Nevertheless, nothing would preclude a force established under Article 41 from defending itself – as discussed, the right to self-defence is an inherent one. Some have taken the view that a force established under Article 41 *may* be able to use force beyond self-defence, so long as it is of a very limited nature. Whether or not a peacekeeping operation established under Article 41 has the consent of the host state is irrelevant regarding the operation's ability to use force; while the host state may consent to a forceful operation on its territory, it cannot, through consent, modify the terms of Article 41.

Finally, where a peacekeeping operation is established as an enforcement measure under Article 41 or 42, the 'fundamental principle' of impartiality is not applicable.

[262] Bowett (n 8) 412. While Bowett referred to an 'aggressor' state, this term would appear to be applicable to any state against which enforcement powers are being used by the Security Council – whether the situation leading to the Security Council's invocation of Art 42 has been deemed by it under Art 39 to be a 'threat to the peace', 'a breach of the peace' or an 'act or aggression'. For more on this see discussion of Art 39 above, section 3.2.1.

5.2 Peacekeeping as a Mandatory Provisional Measure under Article 40

Where the Security Council finds there to be a triggering event under Article 39 and indicates its intention to act in an obligatory manner, it may impose provisional measures pursuant to Article 40 without any need for host state consent; 'the State must accept the presence of a United Nations Force'.[263] This is so despite the non-enforcement nature of Article 40 measures. In the words of Bowett, 'it does not automatically follow that every military action short of enforcement measures decided upon by the Security Council requires the consent of the State on whose territory such action occurs'.[264]

Article 40's non-enforcement character means that an operation established under it will not fall within the enforcement exception to the Article 2(4) prohibition on the use of force; as such, the Security Council will need to limit the use of force to self-defence in such an operation – or, arguably, force of a very limited nature – unless the host state invited the forceful operation onto its territory, thereby waiving the protections provided in Article 2(4) – as well as Article 2(1) or (7). However, host state consent does not modify the nature of Article 40, which, when read with the other provisions of the Charter, does not envisage (even though it does not specifically exclude) the use of force (significantly) beyond self-defence.[265]

Finally, any peacekeeping operation established as a mandatory measure under Article 40 must be impartial. Because such operations are non-enforcement in nature, they will not fall under the enforcement exception to Article 2(7)'s prohibition on intervention into matters which are essentially within the domestic jurisdiction of a state. As such, any such operation will need to ensure that it does not interfere in matters essentially within the domestic jurisdiction of the state – unless, of course, it has host state consent.[266] However, even if the operation takes place with the consent of the host state, the wording of Article 40 still requires that the measures taken thereunder be 'without prejudice to the rights claims, or position of the parties concerned', a phrase which largely corresponds with the concept of impartiality.

[263] ibid, 414–15. Bowett observed that a convincing alternative argument may be made to the effect that the requirement of consent can only be eliminated when the action taken is in the nature of an enforcement action – an argument he rejected.

[264] ibid, (n 8) 414.

[265] As noted, some take the view that a limited amount of force may be acceptable under this article (see above, nn 149–52 and accompanying text).

[266] Schachter made this point in the context of ONUC, the constitutional basis of which he considered to be Art 40. He noted that because the operation 'did not constitute "enforcement measures", the exception to the domestic jurisdiction restriction of Article 2, paragraph 7, does not apply; that is to say, the Council action, although mandatory, must still be subject to the principle that there shall be no intervention in matters essentially within the domestic jurisdiction of any state.' Miller/Schachter (n 118) 5.

5.3 Peacekeeping where Consent is Legally Required

Where a peacekeeping operation is not established as a mandatory enforcement measure under Article 41 or 42 or a mandatory provisional measure under Article 40, the Security Council may act only with the consent of the parties. Such measures may find their constitutional basis in certain articles of Chapter VI, Article 39 or Article 40 (where the Security Council is not acting mandatorily).[267] If the host state consents to an operation that is not impartial or authorises it to use force beyond self-defence, the state waives the protection afforded to it in paragraphs (1), (4) and (7) of Article 2.[268] However, the question will remain: can the peacekeeping operation use force beyond self-defence? The answer would appear to be no, based on the fact that there is no Charter basis for consent-based, forceful peacekeeping operations.

This leads to the following question: do measures implemented by the Security Council to establish peacekeeping operations need a constitutional basis in the Charter, or can they simply be based on the consent of the host state? According to Bowett the answer is no: 'consent is not part of the constitutional basis of a United Nations Force: the constitutional basis must be found in the Charter, not in consent *per se*'.[269] However, the Separate Opinion of Judge Sir Gerald Fitzmaurice in the *Certain Expenses* case takes another approach. In that case, where the question was whether the expenses of UNEF I and ONUC were expenses of the Organization within the meaning of Article 17(2) of the Charter, Judge Fitzmaurice observed:

> Another illustration would be if, at the invitation of one or more Member States (as can happen), the Organization engaged in some activity, or assumed some function, quite outside the normal scope and framework of the Charter. Such action would not be illegal if it was carried out with the consent of all the States affected by it; nor would the resultant expenditures be invalid. But they would, ex hypothesi, not be expenditures contemplated or provided for by the Charter. Despite their 'non-invalidity' therefore, they could not rank as 'expenses of the Organization' within the meaning of Article 17, paragraph 2, to which all Member States would be obliged to contribute, irrespective of how their votes had been cast in relation to the resolutions authorizing the expenditures in question. Member States cannot, in my opinion, be bound to contribute to expenditures incurred outside the scope and framework of the Charter (even

[267] As discussed above in section 4.2, while arguments may be made that implied powers outside Chapter VII to establish non-obligatory, non-forceful peacekeeping operations exist, it is not necessary to imply those powers in view of the nature of its explicit powers.

[268] The Security Council's practice indicates that when it establishes militarised peacekeeping operations based on its Chapter VII powers, it tends to obtain the consent of the host state. However, if a host state is willing to consent to a forceful peacekeeping operation there is arguably no reason why the Security Council cannot establish such an operation without relying on its Chapter VII powers.

[269] Bowett (n 8) 422; see also 311–12.

> if these are not illegal in se), except by their specific consent given ad hoc in relation to the particular case.[270]

In order for an activity engaged in by the UN outside the scope and framework of the Charter with the agreement of all affected states to be 'non-invalid', it must not be proscribed in international law. A proscribed action could not find its legal basis in an agreement between the Organization and affected states. Given that international law does not proscribe a state from genuinely inviting an entity onto its territory and authorising it to use force,[271] the inviting state can make no claim of a violation of the principles of non-intervention or non-use of force, whether based on the purposes and principles of the Charter or on customary international law. According to the logic of Judge Fitzmaurice, therefore, there would appear to be no reason why a forceful, non-obligatory peacekeeping operation cannot have its constitutional basis in an agreement with the host state outside the parameters of the UN.

However, in practice, this has not been the basis for militarised peacekeeping operations. First, the fact that expenses associated with such an operation would not be those of the Organization – that is, Member States would not be obliged by Article 17 to pay them – would be highly problematic for the functioning of any peacekeeping operation. Moreover, even if the question of expenses were not an issue, it is clear that the Security Council considers itself to be acting under the Charter – and not some other agreement – when it authorises peacekeeping operations to use force beyond self-defence. After all, the Security Council's current practice is to invoke Chapter VII when establishing militarised peacekeeping operations or assigning certain tasks to them.[272]

In short, peacekeeping operations for which consent is required (ie, all but those established under Article 41 or 42 as enforcement or under Article 40 as mandatory provisional measures) must use force only in self-defence. Given the importance of host state consent to the legality of certain peacekeeping operations, it is important to address two issues that might emerge. First, is the consent genuine? Second, what happens if the consent is revoked by the host state?

5.3.1 *Nature and Legality of the Consent*

Where the consenting government lacks representativeness, the legality of the involvement of the peacekeeping operation in the country's internal affairs may be called into question. This issue has arisen in the context of intervention by invitation, which, as noted, is akin to a host

[270] *Certain Expenses* (n 11), Separate Opinion of Judge Fitzmaurice, 205.
[271] See this chapter, sections 2.2 and 5.3.1.
[272] See discussion of the operations in chapters 4, 5 and 6.

state's request for or consent to a peacekeeping operation.[273] One particular fear with intervention by invitation is that an inviting state might rely on foreign forces to support its cause in a civil conflict even though the inviting government lacks representativeness, thereby potentially interfering with the population's right to self-determination.[274] The circumstances in which it is necessary to consider the representativeness of the inviting government[275] and any decision in that regard will fall to the Security Council or the Secretary-General.[276] A related concern that has arisen in the context of intervention by invitation is the situation where the bona fides of the consent of the host state and/or the legitimacy of the motives of the intervening state are in question.[277] However, there would appear to be little scope for such problems with peacekeeping, assuming that one accepts that it is not realistic that the Security Council might authorise a peacekeeping operation as a ruse to intervene in a state. Another issue that might raise concern is where a host state has consented to force in the face of pressure from the international community. The consent of the government of Sudan to the presence of a hybrid AU/UN force in Darfur, for example, came about only after that government was subjected to considerable international pressure.[278] However, this situation would appear to be entirely different to a situation where the 'invitation' of the state is not bona fide. The spectre of a relatively powerless state being forced into consenting by powerful states on the Security Council may cause some discomfort; however, it would not appear to invalidate the consent in any way.[279]

[273] See this chapter, section 2.2.

[274] Doswald-Beck (n 254). See also Gray (n 6) 81, who noted the possibility of concerns relating to 'the inalienable right of every state to choose its political, economic, social, and cultural systems'.

[275] Doctrine and practice show that both de facto control and recognition are important factors. See, generally, Doswald-Beck (n 254). The potential for interference in internal affairs argues in favour of peacekeeping operations maintaining impartiality and refusing to engage in the use of offensive force on behalf of the host state government against belligerents or rebels. According to Doswald-Beck, 'peacekeeping forces which do not become involved with internal affairs' are an example of an acceptable invited operation (189).

[276] For example, in the case of the peacekeeping operation in Haiti in 1993, the Security Council was careful to emphasise that it was acting at the invitation of the government, by which it was referring to the deposed Aristide government (see SC Res 867 of 23 September 1993 referring to United Nations, *Letter Dated 26 July 1993 from the Secretary General Addressed to the President of the Security Council [Annexing a 'Letter Dated 24 July 1993 from the President of the Republic of Haiti Addressed to the Secretary-General']* (UN Doc S/26180), 28 July 1993).

[277] Gray (n 6) 84–88 noted that certain 'invitations' were suspect, including the USSR's intervention in Hungary in 1956, said to be at the request of the Prime Minister, and Iraq's claim that it had been invited into Kuwait in August 1990.

[278] See discussion of this issue in chapter 6 below. Indonesia was subjected to a similar level of international pressure before it consented to the quasi-enforcement operation in East Timor, INTERFET; see chapter 5 below.

[279] Although the consent of a state to a peacekeeping operation is unlikely, in itself, to be classified as a treaty, the treatment of coercion of states in making treaties in the Vienna Convention on the Law of Treaties 1969 (23 May 1969, entered into force 27 January 1980;

The question of whether consent might need to be renewed or reissued may also arise. For example, when the government changes, is its successor bound by the previous government's agreement, or is it incumbent on the UN to request a renewal of consent? Given that government consent is a legal requirement for certain peacekeeping operations, it might be argued that a renewal of consent is called for when the government changes. In a similar vein, is it necessary to renew consent where the Security Council plans to modify the operation's mandate? If the operation is one where consent was not originally legally required, then so long as the constitutional basis of the operation has not changed, there is no legal requirement for consent to a changed mandate. If host state consent *was* a legal prerequisite for the establishment of the operation, the Security Council will be entitled to modify its functions (or some of them) without host state consent only so long as it does so as a measure to restore international peace and security, in reliance on its mandatory powers under Article 40, 41 or 42. Issues relating to renewal of consent will presumably only arise where the host state government voices its concern at the continued presence of the operation. To an extent, therefore, these issues overlap with issues relating to withdrawal of host state consent, considered immediately below.

5.3.2 *Withdrawal of Consent*

If we are to accept that a peacekeeping operation based on consent is akin to an intervention by invitation, it is clear, based on the above-quoted passage from the Definition of Aggression[280] – which provides that if visiting forces overstay or act in contravention of the conditions set for them, the intervention by invitation turns into aggression – that host states have the right to revoke consent, at least absent an agreement to the contrary.

Most famously, the issue of withdrawal arose in the context of Secretary-General Thant's controversial decision to withdraw UNEF I from Egypt in May 1967 when requested to do so by the government there.[281] In the view of many, this withdrawal was the primary cause of the 'Six Day War', which took place in the region the following month.[282] The issue was not

UNTS vol 1155, 331) is illustrative. Art 52 of that treaty makes clear that only when a treaty's 'conclusion has been procured by the threat or use of force in violation of the fundamental principles of international law embodied in the Charter of the United Nations' is it void. This test would not appear to be met by the pressure applied to the Sudanese government.

[280] See the quotation accompanying n 36 above.

[281] At the time of withdrawal, Egypt operated as the United Arab Republic, a state representing a union formed between it and Syria in 1958. The union was to dissolve with Syria's departure in 1961.

[282] United Nations, *Report of the Secretary-General on the Withdrawal of the Emergency Force* (UN Doc A/6730/Add.3), 26 June 1967, para 32, as reproduced in Rosalyn Higgins, *United Nations Peacekeeping 1946–1967: Documents and Commentary, Vol I: The Middle East* (Oxford, Oxford University Press, 1969) 344–62.

whether Egypt's consent was necessary before UNEF I could be stationed there; this was 'clearly beyond doubt'.[283] Instead, the issue was the factual one of whether Egypt had agreed (formally or informally) not to exercise its right to withdraw consent until the operation had completed its work.[284] Hammarskjöld had taken the view that, in the circumstances, 'the "consent" principle did not give Egypt the freedom to demand UNEF's withdrawal before its task was completed'.[285] However, the issue came to a head after Hammarskjöld's death and his successor, Secretary-General Thant, took a more pragmatic approach. Citing the fact that Egypt had placed no 'limitation on its right to withdraw its consent to the continued stationing and operation of [UNEF I] on its territory'[286] and recognising that UNEF I's size and mandate were such that it could not act without the cooperation of Egypt, Thant felt that there was no choice but to withdraw the force.[287]

Some have thought it reasonable to conclude that when a state consents to a peacekeeping operation, it enters into an implied agreement not to withdraw that consent until the known mandate is fulfilled.[288] Others have proposed that 'where consent is a legal prerequisite to the presence of the Force then, *prima facie*, the Force must withdraw in reasonable time upon termination of such consent'.[289] Either way, it is clear that, where consent is a legal prerequisite to the presence of a force, renewed consent must be obtained where the mandate of the operation changes substantially – unless in changing the mandate the Security Council is taking binding measures to restore international peace and security through an exercise of its powers under Article 40, 41 or 42. Where consent is not a legal prerequisite to the establishment of an operation, the fact that the host state has consented does not, somehow, bestow on that state the ability to terminate the operation by withdrawing its consent.[290]

283 Higgins, ibid, 362–63.
284 ibid.
285 ibid.
286 *Report of the Secretary-General* (n 283) para 74.
287 ibid, para 99.
288 Higgins (n 42) 230. See also Bowett (n 31) 420–21 and the authorities cited by him at n 30.
289 Bowett (n 8) 422.
290 ibid.

Chapter 4

When Peacekeeping and Enforcement Overlap: Twentieth Century Practice

The vulnerability of lightly armed, widely dispersed peace-keepers was dramatically illustrated in Bosnia and Herzegovina, where Governments assigned to the United Nations the impossible task of serving as a peace-keeper in the midst of war.

UN, *The Blue Helmets*[1]

1. INTRODUCTION

THIS CHAPTER EXAMINES UNEF I and ONUC, operations established in 1956 and 1960 respectively. It also considers four peacekeeping operations established in the early 1990s under the stewardship of Boutros-Ghali: UNPROFOR in the former Yugoslavia, UNOSOM II in Somalia, UNMIH in Haiti, and UNAMIR in Rwanda. The operations represent but six of the some 50 operations that took place in the twentieth century;[2] however, each teaches us valuable lessons regarding the militarisation of peacekeeping in the twentieth century.[3] Moreover, these operations provide background information that is essential to understanding today's approach to militarised peacekeeping, which will be considered in detail in chapters 5 and 6.

[1] United Nations, *The Blue Helmets: A Review of United Nations Peace-Keeping*, 3rd edn (New York, UN Sales No E.96.I.14, 1996) 6.

[2] Three operations, which began in late 1999 (UNAMSIL, UNTAET and MONUC), will be considered as 21st century peacekeeping operations in chapter 5 below.

[3] As noted in chapter 2, with regard to post-ONUC peacekeeping operations – such as UNFICYP, UNEF II and UNIFIL – the UN indicated that self-defence included the right to defend the operation's mandate (see chapter 2, section 2.3). While the defence-of-mandate approach to the definition of self-defence could have resulted in the use of considerable force, commanders of these operations tended to exercise restraint. UNIFIL, more than any of the other operations during this period, relied of the use of force where necessary. See Trevor Findlay, *The Use of Force in UN Peace Operations* (Oxford, Oxford University Press for the Stockholm International Peace Research Institute (SIPRI), 2002) 108–201; Ray Murphy, *UN Peacekeeping in Lebanon, Somalia and Kosovo* (Cambridge, Cambridge University Press, 2007). These operations, and others in existence during the 20th century, where force was not authorised beyond self-defence (or defence-of-mandate), are not discussed as they reveal no new lessons.

2. UNEF I (NOVEMBER 1956–JUNE 1967)

By today's standards of peacekeeping, it is difficult to imagine an argument that a peacekeeping force with as limited a mandate as UNEF I amounted to an enforcement action. However, it must be recalled that this operation was much larger and had a considerably greater capacity to employ force than the observer missions that had preceded it. France and the Soviet Union (and its allies) refused to pay their apportioned shares of the cost of UNEF I and ONUC, believing that they lacked legitimacy.[4] This led the General Assembly, by a resolution adopted on 20 December 1961, to request an Advisory Opinion from the International Court of Justice on whether the expenses associated with UNEF and ONUC constituted 'expenses of the Organization' within the meaning of Article 17(2) of the UN Charter. The *Certain Expenses* case[5] is the sole occasion on which the ICJ has considered – in a somewhat guarded way – the dividing line between peacekeeping and enforcement.

2.1 Mandate and Functioning

On 26 June 1956, Egyptian President Nasser announced the nationalisation of the Suez Canal Company; shortly thereafter, British, French and Israeli forces invaded Egypt.[6] The Security Council could not act due to the exercise by the UK and France of their vetoes,[7] and the matter was taken up by the General Assembly.[8] On 4 November 1956, the General Assembly adopted a resolution calling upon the Secretary-General to submit a plan 'for the setting up, with the consent of the nations concerned, of an emergency international United Nations Force to secure and supervise the cessation of hostilities in accordance with all the terms of' a previously called for ceasefire.[9] The next day, the General Assembly approved a

[4] Thomas M Franck, *Recourse to Force: State Action against Threats and Armed Attacks* (Cambridge, Cambridge University Press, 2002) 38.

[5] *Certain Expenses of the United Nations (Article 17, Paragraph 2, of the Charter)*, Advisory Opinion of 20 July 1962 [1962] ICJ Rep 151.

[6] Rosalyn Higgins, *United Nations Peacekeeping 1946–1967: Documents and Commentary, Vol I: The Middle East* (Oxford, Oxford University Press, 1969) 222. See also Mona Ghali, 'United Nations Emergency Force I' in William J Durch (ed), *The Evolution of UN Peacekeeping* (New York, St Martin's Press, 1993) 104–30.

[7] Higgins, ibid, 260, referring to a draft resolution of 31 October (S/3710).

[8] See GA Res 337 (V) of 30 November 1950 (the 'Uniting for Peace' resolution), whereby a situation involving a threat to international peace and security may be sent to the General Assembly on a procedural vote where the Security Council is not able to act due to an exercise of the veto.

[9] GA Res 998 (ES-I) of 4 November 1956.

plan submitted by the Secretary-General[10] and established UNEF I[11] with Egypt's consent.[12]

While the precise nature of the tasks that UNEF I was charged with is the subject of considerable debate,[13] its functions, in general terms, were summarised as follows by the Secretary-General:

> [T]he functions of [UNEF I] would be, when a cease-fire is being established, to enter Egyptian territory with the consent of the Egyptian Government, in order to help maintain quiet during and after the withdrawal of non-Egyptian troops, and to secure compliance with the other terms established [by the General Assembly].[14]

A review of UNEF I's tasks reveals the emergence of two types of functions. On the one hand, many of them may be described as non-military in nature, including clearing minefields, overseeing exchanges of prisoners, repairing roads and running the telephone switchboard. On the other hand, several of its functions may more accurately be described as military – or at least potentially military – in nature. These included activities such as maintaining calm between the Egyptian forces and the Anglo-French forces, guarding key installations, providing protection to British and French ships, and conducting border control.[15] Any of these latter activities could potentially require an exercise of armed force going beyond self-defence. However, the amount of force actually used by UNEF I was very limited.[16] Despite some controversy as to whether it should engage in broader functions – with Israel, for example, wanting it to be involved in dispute settlement – the restrictive approach favoured by the Secretary-General prevailed.[17]

[10] *Official Records of the General Assembly, First Emergency Special Session, Annexes,* agenda item 5 (A/3289), reproduced in Higgins (n 6) 233.

[11] GA Res 1000 (ES-I) of 5 November 1956. The mission was originally referred to simply as UNEF; however, after UNEF II was established, it came to be referred to as UNEF I. I will refer to it as UNEF I throughout.

[12] Indeed, Higgins (n 6) 262 noted that it was only because of this consent that the Soviet Union abstained on, rather than voted against the Security Council resolution creating it.

[13] See Higgins (n 6) 243–55. See also Ghali (n 6) 113.

[14] United Nations, *Second and Final Report of the Secretary-General on the Plan for an Emergency International United Nations Force Requested in Resolution 998 (ES-I), Adopted by the General Assembly on 4 November 1956* (UN Doc A/3302), 6 November 1956, para 12. For a more detailed listing of the particular tasks undertaken by UNEF in its first year see United Nations, *Report of the Secretary-General* (UN Doc A/3694 and Add.1), 9 October 1957.

[15] Higgins (n 6) 241–60.

[16] *Certain Expenses* (n 5) 171.

[17] See Ghali (n 6) 113.

2.2 Evaluation

2.2.1 *Adherence to the 'Fundamental Principles'*

As discussed in chapter 2,[18] Secretary-General Hammarskjöld emphasised that UNEF I was not established 'to undertake enforcement actions'.[19] He went to great lengths to downplay the military nature of the operation, stressing that force could only be used in self-defence, and defining the concept in such a way that while peacekeepers were permitted to use reasonable force, they could do so only in reaction to force used against them; they could never initiate force. He also stressed the importance of the operation acting impartially (it was said not to have been established to influence the military or political balance) and the need for host state consent. Indeed, as discussed in chapter 2, it was in the context of UNEF I that the Secretary-General first set out the 'fundamental principles' of peacekeeping.

However, the operation was not universally viewed as being of a non-enforcement nature, and an ICJ Advisory Opinion relating to its nature was requested. It was argued before the ICJ in the *Certain Expenses* case that the expenses associated with the General Assembly-established UNEF I were not 'expenses of the Organization' within the meaning of Article 17(2), because they related to the maintenance of international peace and security, a matter that should properly, it was argued, be dealt with by the Security Council.[20] The Court considered the role of the General Assembly in relation to the maintenance of international peace and security and held that, while the Charter conferred 'primary' authority on the Security Council in this regard,[21] the General Assembly also had a role to play[22] – albeit a more limited one that did not include authorising coercive or enforcement action.[23] Thus, it was necessary for the Court to ascertain whether UNEF I was an enforcement operation and therefore ultra vires the authority of the General Assembly.

[18] See chapter 2, section 2.2.

[19] *Report of the Secretary-General* (October 1957) (n 14) para 15. Cf the earlier *Report of the Secretary-General on Compliance with General Assembly Resolution 1123 (XI)* (UN Doc A/3500), 15 January 1957, where the Secretary-General described the 'primary duty' of UNEF I as being 'to supervise and *enforce* the cease-fire to which the parties committed themselves in response to the request of the General Assembly in the resolution of 2 November' (emphasis added). UNEF was not 'established in order to compel a withdrawal of the British, French and Israeli forces' (Higgins (n 6) 262–63).

[20] *Certain Expenses* (n 5) 162.

[21] See Art 24 of the UN Charter.

[22] *Certain Expenses* (n 5) 163.

[23] The Court held that, based on Art 11(2) of the Charter, only the Security Council could order 'coercive or enforcement action' (ibid, 164). However, it limited the impact of this finding by holding that the word 'action' in Art 11(2) 'must mean such action as is solely within the province of the Security Council' as 'is indicated by the title of Chapter VII of the Charter, namely "Action with respect to threats to the peace, breaches of the peace, and acts of aggression"' (ibid, 165). For the text of the relevant part of Art 11(2) see n 34 below.

The Court engaged in an analysis of the functions that UNEF I had been authorised by the General Assembly to undertake,[24] as well as the functions it had actually undertaken. In particular, it considered whether UNEF I was of a sufficiently forceful nature to be classed as an enforcement action. In considering the issue of the force authorised, the Court voiced the concern that one of the tasks assigned to UNEF was to 'secure' the cessation of hostilities.[25] It noted that the verb 'secure' 'as applied to such matters as halting the movement of military forces and arms into the area and the conclusion of a cease-fire, might suggest measures of enforcement, *were it not that the Force was to be set up "with the consent of the nations concerned"* '.[26] Clearly then, the Court considered state consent to be a contra-indicant of an enforcement action against the state.

The Court also considered the Secretary-General's reports (as endorsed by the General Assembly)[27] outlining how the operation was to function. Here, it placed great emphasis on the Secretary-General's assurances that there was host state consent and that the endeavour featured only limited force. The Court reproduced the following passage from a report of the Secretary-General on UNEF I:

> While the General Assembly is enabled to establish the Force with the consent of those parties which contribute units to the Force, it could not request the Force to be stationed or operate on the territory of a given country without the consent of the Government of that country. This does not exclude the possibility that the Security Council could use such a Force within the wider margins provided under Chapter VII of the United Nations Charter. I would not for the present consider it necessary to elaborate this point further, since no use of the Force under Chapter VII, with the rights in relation to Member States that this would entail, has been envisaged.
>
> The point just made permits the conclusion that the setting up of the Force should not be guided by the needs which would have existed had the measure been considered as part of an enforcement action directed against a Member country. There is an obvious difference between establishing the Force in order to secure the cessation of hostilities, with a withdrawal of forces, and establishing such a Force with a view to enforcing a withdrawal of forces.[28]

[24] ibid, 170.

[25] In GA Res 998 (ES-I) of 4 November 1956, the General Assembly requested that the Secretary-General submit a plan for the setting up, with the consent of the nations concerned, of an emergency international United Nations Force to secure and supervise the cessation of hostilities in accordance with all the terms of the General Assembly's previous Resolution 997 (ES-I) of 2 November 1956.

[26] *Certain Expenses* (n 5) 170 (emphasis added).

[27] In GA Res 1001 (ES-I) of 7 November 1956, the General Assembly (without a dissenting vote) concurred 'in the definition of the functions of the Force as stated in paragraph 12 of the Secretary-General's report'.

[28] *Second and Final Report* (n 14) paras 9 and 10. Quoted in *Certain Expenses* (n 5) 170–71.

In reaching its decision that UNEF I was not an enforcement action, the Court also gave prominence to the Secretary-General's assurance that the force was

> in no way a military force temporarily controlling the territory in which it is stationed; nor, moreover, should the Force have military functions exceeding those necessary to secure peaceful conditions on the assumption that the parties to the conflict take all necessary steps for compliance with the recommendations of the General Assembly.[29]

Based on the 'description of the functions of UNEF, as outlined by the Secretary-General and concurred in by the General Assembly without a dissenting vote', the Court concluded that there was no 'evidence that the Force was to be used for purposes of enforcement'.[30] Moreover, it stressed the fact that there was no evidence of such a purpose 'in the subsequent operations of the Force, operations which did not exceed the scope of the functions ascribed to it'.[31] Because UNEF I was not an enforcement action against the state, the General Assembly was within its rights to establish it.

While the Court did not outline the parameters of enforcement beyond describing it as '[a]ction with respect to threats to the peace, breaches of the peace, and acts of aggression',[32] its reasoning makes clear that it considered enforcement actions against a state – as distinct from the UNEF I operation – to be (1) forceful and (2) non-consensual in nature.

2.2.2 *Constitutional Basis*

The *Certain Expenses* decision made it clear that the General Assembly possesses a role regarding international peace and security that is secondary to that of the Security Council, and recognised that it is able to act in ways which are not 'merely hortatory'.[33] Given the Court's finding that the operation was not an enforcement action against the state – and therefore not within the exclusive purview of the Security Council as per the second sentence of Article 11(2)[34] – it was not required to adjudicate on the constitutional basis of UNEF I. It did, however, make the following observation:

> Since the resolutions of the General Assembly in question do not mention upon which article they are based, and since the language used in most of them might

[29] *Second and Final Report* (n 14) para 12. Quoted in *Certain Expenses* (n 5) 171.
[30] *Certain Expenses* (n 5) 171.
[31] ibid, 171.
[32] ibid, 165.
[33] ibid, 163.
[34] The second sentence of Art 11(2) provides: 'Any [question relating to the maintenance of international peace and security] on which action is necessary shall be referred to the Security Council by the General Assembly either before or after discussion.'

imply reference to either Article 14 or Article 11, it cannot be excluded that they were based upon the former rather than the latter article.[35]

Elsewhere in the decision the Court made reference to the General Assembly's powers under Article 35.[36] For the purposes of this book – and given that the General Assembly no longer establishes peacekeeping operations – little turns on which article the Security Council was acting under.

3. ONUC (JULY 1960–JUNE 1964)

3.1 Mandate and Functioning

After Belgium sent troops into the Congo against the wishes of the Congolese government, the Security Council passed three resolutions in July and August 1960. First, Resolution 143 of 14 July 1960 called for the immediate withdrawal of Belgian forces and authorised the provision of such military assistance as necessary.[37] Later that month it passed Resolution 145, reiterating its call for Belgium to withdraw and calling on other states not to impede the restoration of law and order in the Congo.[38] In the same resolution, it observed that 'the complete restoration of law and order in the Republic of the Congo would effectively contribute to the maintenance of international peace and security'.[39] Third, in August, the Security Council passed Resolution 146, which again called for Belgian withdrawal and called on 'Member States, in accordance with Articles 25 and 49 of the Charter of the United Nations, to accept and carry out the decisions of the Security Council and to afford mutual assistance in carrying out measures decided upon by the Council'.[40]

As the situation in the country deteriorated, the UN authorised increasingly forceful measures. Following a constitutional crisis in the country in September 1960, the General Assembly (which, by then, had taken temporary control of the operation) called on the Secretary-General to continue to 'take vigorous action in line with the Security Council's resolutions' and to 'assist the Central Government . . . in the restoration and maintenance of law and order throughout the territory . . . and to safeguard its unity, territorial integrity and political independence in the interests of international peace and security'.[41] In February 1961, the matter again came

[35] *Certain Expenses* (n 5) 172.
[36] ibid, 154. Art 35 allows any member of the UN to bring a dispute or situation to the attention of the Security Council or the General Assembly – in conjunction with Art 11(2).
[37] SC Res 143 of 14 July 1960.
[38] SC Res 145 of 22 July 1960.
[39] ibid.
[40] SC Res 146 of 9 August 1960.
[41] GA Res 1474 (ES-IV) of 20 September 1960.

before the Security Council. With civil war looming following the death of Prime Minister Lumumba,[42] the Security Council, in Resolution 161, authorised ONUC to take '*all appropriate measures* to prevent the occurrence of civil war in the Congo, including arrangements for cease-fires, the halting of all military operations, the prevention of clashes, and the use of force, if necessary, in the last resort'.[43]

Following Secretary-General Hammarskjöld's death in September 1961,[44] 'the ground shifted somewhat'.[45] The new Secretary-General, U Thant, was less averse to the use of force[46] and more willing to take sides in internal questions, such as the prevention of Katanga's secession from the country.[47] In November of that year, the Security Council declared all secessionist activities against the Republic of Congo to be contrary to national law and Security Council decisions and authorised the Secretary-General to 'take vigorous action, including the requisite measure of force, if necessary, for the immediate apprehension, detention . . . or deportation of all foreign military and paramilitary personnel . . . and mercenaries' and '*all necessary measures*' to prevent their return.[48] The mission reached its apex of forcefulness as it began to seize control of positions in Katanga to ensure that it had free movement and to use force to ensure the removal of mercenaries.[49]

3.2 Evaluation

3.2.1 Adherence to the 'Fundamental Principles'

ONUC began as a peacekeeping operation along the lines of UNEF I, with the 'fundamental principles' of peacekeeping present: the force was

[42] Findlay (n 3) 70. Lumumba, who had been jailed by a rival government, was killed in January of that year; his death was announced on 13 February 1961 (Rosalyn Higgins, *United Nations Peacekeeping 1946–1967: Documents and Commentary, Vol III: Africa* (Oxford, Oxford University Press, 1980) 394).

[43] SC Res 161 of 21 February 1961, Part A, para 1 (emphasis added). The resolution further called for the immediate 'withdrawal of all Belgian and other foreign military and paramilitary personnel and political advisers not under the United Nations Command, and mercenaries'.

[44] On 17 September 1961, on a flight to Northern Rhodesia as part of the UN's efforts to resolve the situation in the Congo, Secretary-General Hammarskjöld's plane crashed and he was killed.

[45] Higgins (n 42) 47. The death of several Italian peacekeepers in November 1961 in a separate incident also increased the tensions surrounding the mission (ibid, 354–56).

[46] Findlay (n 3) 77.

[47] Donald W McNemar, 'The Postindependence War in the Congo' in Richard A Falk (ed), *The International Law of Civil War* (Baltimore, Johns Hopkins University Press, 1971) 292.

[48] SC Res 169 of 24 November 1961, para 4 (emphasis added).

[49] See United Nations, *The Blue Helmets: A Review of United Nations Peace-Keeping* (New York, UN Sales No E.85.I.18, 1985) 215–57. See also Higgins (n 42) 304–445 and 47; Findlay (n 3) 77–80.

established with the consent of the government (indeed at its request), it was impartial in nature, and its authorisation to use force was limited. As circumstances on the ground changed, the operation moved away from all three of these principles, arguably abandoning them altogether.

At the start of the mission, Hammarskjöld steadfastly maintained that the rules relating to the use of force as set out after UNEF I had not changed: the mission (1) must never *initiate* the use of armed force and (2) must only use force in response to an armed attack, including an attempt to make the mission withdraw from legitimately held positions.[50] However, Hammarskjöld's position was to evolve, and he eventually recognised an expanded concept of self-defence for the operation. This concept included a right to use force to respond to 'attempts to overrun or displace UN positions'[51] and to engage in the 'disarming and, if necessary, the detention of those *preparing* to attack UN troops'.[52] Later he was to indicate that conduct considered to be '[*i*]*ncitement to or preparation for* violence, including troop movements and confirmed reports of an impending attack, would warrant protective action by UN troops'.[53] Moreover, he authorised the use of 'ONUC troops in Katanga to "prevent the burning of villages and the killing of civilians by force if necessary" on the grounds that the attacks there had strong elements of genocide' – though he noted that this was 'still to be based on an interpositional strategy using force in self-defence'.[54] According to former Under-Secretary-General Sir Brian Urquhart, Hammarskjöld considered that ONUC's mandate, as it stood following Resolution 161, authorised its forces to 'arrest anyone actually leading a mob demonstration'.[55]

Instructions to the troops as to when force could be used were provided in the form of Operations Directives, written by the force commanders, deputy commanders or chiefs of staff.[56] 'Through these documents Hammarskjöld's UNEF-based guidelines and subsequent revisions were interpreted, embellished and expanded by ONUC into what would today

[50] See the comments of the Secretary-General in United Nations, *First Report of the Secretary-General on the Implementation of Security Council Resolution 143 (1960) of 14 July 1960* (UN Doc S/4389), 18 July 1960, para 15. Moreover, even SC Res 161 of 21 February 1961 was 'deemed by Hammarskjöld . . . to give no additional rights to use force' (Higgins (n 42) 47). See also *Secretary-General's Letter to Contributing States after SC Resolution 161 of 27 February 1961* (S/4752), Annex VII, reproduced in part in Higgins (n 42) 51.

[51] Higgins (n 42) 51–52. Higgins refers to Brian Urquhart, *Hammarskjöld* (London, Bodley Head, 1973) 561–62.

[52] Higgins, ibid (emphasis added), again referring to Urquhart, ibid.

[53] Higgins, ibid (emphasis added).

[54] Findlay (n 3) 69.

[55] Higgins (n 42) 51–52. Higgins refers to Urquhart (n 51) 561–62. Nevertheless, Hammarskjöld remained a voice of moderation compared to some. He was determined to emphasise the distinction between the use of force he felt strictly necessary and the all-out waging of war by the peacekeepers against separatist Katanga (Higgins (n 42) 395 et seq).

[56] Findlay (n 3) 60.

be called rules of engagement.'[57] These echo Hammarskjöld's increasing tolerance of the use of force as the operation progressed. In February 1961, Operations Directive No 8 called on ONUC to engage in civilian protection. It provided that, 'where feasible, every protection was to be afforded unarmed groups subjected by any armed party to acts of violence likely to lead to loss of life. In such cases, UN troops were to interpose themselves, using armed force if necessary, to prevent such loss of life.'[58] In March 1961, the Secretariat authorised an Operations Directive which 'envisaged the possibility of UN troops intervening in three circumstances – when civil war threatened to break out; when it had already broken out; and when an armed clash threatened to envelop ONUC forces'.[59]

Clearly, the level of force authorised was such that Hammarskjöld's 'margin of freedom'[60] regarding what constituted self-defence was stretched to breaking point. Whereas Hammarskjöld had, in the context of UNEF I, interpreted the meaning of the term 'self-defence' to include defence of a position – a valid and necessary interpretation of the term – the use of force authorised in ONUC clearly went much further, surpassing any realistic definition of self-defence. He viewed as acceptable the use of force to quell those inciting violence, to protect non-UN units and the civilian population, to expel mercenaries, and to detain those *preparing* to attack UN troops, and the use force *in advance of* an armed attack.[61] That the level of force authorised for ONUC went well beyond self-defence was accepted by most experts.[62] However, confusingly, the UN itself – in an early example of its tendency to argue that the 'fundamental principles' were being adhered to when they were not[63] – characterised the use

[57] ibid, 60.

[58] ibid, 68.

[59] ibid, 71.

[60] Hammarskjöld noted that while peacekeeping operations could 'never include combat activity', '[t]here will always remain, of course, a certain margin of freedom for judgement, as, for example, on the extent and nature of the arming of the units and of their right of self-defence' (United Nations, *Summary Study of the Experience Derived from the Establishment and Operation of the Force (Report of the Secretary-General)* (UN Doc A/3943), 9 October 1958, para 178). See discussion in chapter 2, section 2.2.

[61] Derek W Bowett, *United Nations Forces: A Legal Study of United Nations Practice* (London, Stevens & Sons, 1964) 202.

[62] See eg Bowett, ibid, 213, where he observed that ONUC 'placed considerable strain on the concept of self-defence'. See also Nigel D White, *The United Nations and the Maintenance of International Peace and Security* (Manchester, Manchester University Press, 1990) 201, who described the interpretation that ONUC was acting in self-defence as 'unacceptably wide'. Cf McNemar (n 47) 292, who described the use of force by ONUC – even at its more forceful stages when it was engaged with the Katanga gendarmerie – as 'strictly speaking, self-defence'.

[63] Adam Roberts, 'From San Francisco to Sarajevo: The UN and the Use of Force' (1995–96) 37(4) *Survival* 7, 15: '[S]ome military actions [in the Congo] were dressed up as self-defence when in fact they were essentially proactive.' See also Findlay (n 3) 51 and 85–86. Later, Schachter wrote of the tendency of the UN to stretch the meaning of self-defence 'to incredulity and beyond its usual legal meaning' (Oscar Schachter, 'Authorized Uses of Force by the United Nations and Regional Organizations' in Lori Damrosch and David Scheffer (eds), *Law and Force in the New International Order* (Boulder, Col, Westview, 1991) 84).

of force as being in self-defence.[64] A distinction must be drawn, however, between the level of force authorised and the level of force actually used. Aside from the Katanga situation,[65] the operation's commanders tended to employ offensive force only very sparingly.[66] As Findlay observed, while ONUC's potential to use considerable force in relation to the prevention of civil war was significant, 'in the event it used force minimally, reluctantly and mostly in self-defence'.[67]

ONUC also tested the impartiality principle. McNemar described ONUC as 'one of the primary actors in the civil war'.[68] Berdal observed that '[t]he effect of [the] steady expansion [of] ONUC's mandate was to ensure that the UN force became, and would remain for the duration of its deployment, a factor in the domestic politics and internal power struggles of the newly independent territory'.[69] Once again, the UN represented the operation as adhering to the 'fundamental principles'.[70] As Franck observed, the Security Council's insistence on ONUC's impartiality was

> not entirely convincing as a statement either of law or of fact . . . To some members . . . it seemed as if the UN were intervening against the secessionist side in what was essentially a civil war, even while denying it.[71]

Of course, depending on the constitutional basis of the operation, impartiality may or may not have been a legal requirement.[72] ONUC's constitutional basis will be considered below.

In addition, certain issues relating to host state consent arose with regard to ONUC. Without doubt ONUC was established pursuant to a request made by President Kasavubu and Prime Minister Lumumba, on

[64] UN publications on peacekeeping, even in the aftermath of ONUC, cited 'force only in self-defence' as a characteristic of peacekeeping. See eg United Nations, *The Blue Helmets: A Review of United Nations Peace-Keeping*, 2nd edn (New York, UN Sales No E.90.I.18, 1990) 3. Bowett observed: 'The use of force to protect the civilian population was scarcely self-defence and the Secretary-General was obliged to describe it as "on the outer margin of the mandate of the United Nations"' (201, quoting a statement of the Secretary-General addressed to the Security Council of 15 February 1961 United Nations, Official Record of the 935th Meeting of the Security Council, para 27.

[65] Rosalyn Higgins, *The Development of International Law through the Political Organs of the United Nations* (Oxford, Oxford University Press, 1963) 234; Findlay (n 3) 71–81.

[66] Higgins, ibid, 233–35.

[67] Findlay (n 3) 66.

[68] McNemar (n 47) 252.

[69] Mats Berdal, 'The Security Council and Peacekeeping' in Vaughan Lowe et al (eds), *The United Nations Security Council and War: The Evolution of Thought and Practice since 1945* (Oxford, Oxford University Press, 2008) 175–204, 182.

[70] In Resolution 146, for example, the Security Council '*reaffirm[ed]* that the United Nations Force in the Congo will not be a party to or in any way intervene in or be used to influence the outcome of any internal conflict, constitutional or otherwise' (SC Res 146 of 9 August 1960).

[71] Thomas M Franck, *Fairness in International Law and Institutions* (Oxford, Clarendon Press, 1995) 227.

[72] As discussed in chapter 3, if it was an enforcement action under Art 41 or 42, impartiality would not have been required; however, if it was established as a mandatory measure under Art 40, it would have been.

behalf of the new Congolese government.[73] However, very shortly after this request was made, discord occurred within the government and there was a split between Lumumba and Kasavubu. In addition, a third faction, the 'Collège des universitaires' led by Colonel Mobutu, was soon to emerge.[74] That such governmental discord was in evidence at a time when ONUC's mandate was being strengthened might lead us to ask whether the host state was in actual fact consenting to the revisions to the operation. A number of consent-related issues arose.

First, did the change in government place any onus on the UN to seek a renewal of the host state's consent? So long as a mandate did not legally require host state consent and continued unchanged, no such renewal would be necessary. If host state consent *was* legally required there would apper to be no onus on the UN to renew it. After all, if a new government wanted to withdraw consent for the original mandate it could presumably do so.[75]

Second, was there a need for renewed consent in light of the changes to the mandate? Host state consent to a peacekeeping operation does not extend to a substantial modification of that operation's mandate. Therefore, important questions arise regarding the initial constitutional basis of ONUC and whether the constitutional basis changed as the operation became increasingly forceful. If when ONUC was established host state consent was a legal prerequisite and the mandate was substantially changed, renewal of host consent would be necessary – *unless* the revised mandate was such that the operation became either an enforcement action (under Article 41 or 42) or a mandatory measure under Article 40. If consent was not a legal prerequisite from the outset of ONUC, then there would be no need for host state consent to a changed mandate – *unless* the mandate changed from an enforcement operation under Article 41 or 42 or a mandatory measure under Article 40 to an operation in relation to which consent *was* a legal prerequisite.[76] The constitutional basis of the operation is discussed below.

[73] By means of two cables to the Secretary-General dated 13 July 1960, the President and Prime Minster called for the immediate dispatch of UN assistance (GIAD Draper, 'The Legal Limitations upon the Employment of Weapons by the United Nations Force in the Congo' (1963) 12 *International and Comparative Law Quarterly* 387, 388–89).

[74] Bowett (n 61) 230–31.

[75] Some, however, argue that consent may not be withdrawn until the known mandate has been fulfilled. See discussion on this point in chapter 3, section 5.3.2.

[76] Schachter took the view that the Congolese government was unable to call for the withdrawal of ONUC, as he viewed ONUC as an Article 40 operation of a mandatory character. He observed: '[I]t may be reasonably maintained that, since members of the [Security Council] considered that the situation . . . involved a threat to international peace and security, and since the [Security Council] adopted measures of a mandatory character pursuant to Chapter VII of the Charter, the territorial government could not by unilateral action decide that the threat was over or that measures taken by the [Security Council] should be terminated.' Of course, similar reasoning would apply if the operation had been established as an enforcement measure under Art 41 or 42. EM Miller (pseudonym for Oscar

A third consent-related issue is this: who should the UN deal with in matters of consent where there is no clear government?[77] As noted in chapter 3, it seems right to leave this decision to the UN's judgement.[78] In the case of ONUC the Secretary-General decided to recognise President Kasavubu as Head of State and deal directly with him.[79] Of course, where a consenting government is effective but lacks representativeness issues of its legitimacy – and that of a peacekeeping operation dependent on its consent – may arise.

3.2.2 Constitutional Basis

While neither of the first two resolutions establishing ONUC (Resolution 143 of 14 July 1960 and Resolution 145 of 22 July 1960) indicated under which Chapter the Security Council was acting,[80] the Secretary-General voiced the view that each was based in Chapter VII.[81] The specific invocation of Articles 25 and 49 in Resolution 146 of 9 August 1960 made it clear that the Security Council considered that it was acting under Chapter VII; its reference back to the two previous Security Council resolutions arguably confirmed that they too were taken under Chapter VII.[82] Although it did not invoke Chapter VII when it passed Resolution 161 in February 1961,[83] there is little doubt that the Security Council was acting under that Chapter, given its characterisation of the situation as a 'threat to international peace and security' and the level of force authorised: 'all appropriate measures to prevent the occurrence of civil war in the Congo, including arrangements for cease-fires, the halting of all military operations, the

Schachter), 'Legal Aspects of the United Nations Action in the Congo' (1961) 55 *American Journal of International Law* 1, 15.

77 '[D]uring a constitutional crisis between September 1960 and September 1961 which was caused by the dismissal of Congolese Prime Minister Lumumba, Congo had no formal legal government.' Carsten Stahn, *The Law and Practice of International Territorial Administration: Versailles to Iraq and Beyond* (Cambridge Studies in International Law) (Cambridge, Cambridge University Press, 2008) 240.

78 See chapter 3, section 5.3.1.

79 Bowett (n 61) 231. The UN 'declined to deal with any other representative of a régime founded on military force as a representative of the Government', though certain interaction was inevitable. (ibid).

80 Though, arguably, the invocation by the Security Council of the 'maintenance of international peace and security' wording in SC Res 145 signals a Chapter VII authorisation.

81 See the oral statement of the Secretary-General delivered to the General Assembly on 8 August 1960 (UN Doc S/PV 884) 9–10, as reproduced in Miller/Schachter (n 76) 4. The ICJ also appeared to view SC Res 143 as being established under Chapter VII: it noted that it was 'clearly adopted with a view to maintaining international peace and security' (*Certain Expenses* (n 5) 175).

82 Miller/Schachter (n 76) 3.

83 While not explicitly designating the situation there a 'threat to the peace' under Art 39, the Security Council came close. It cited its deep concern at the 'threat to international peace and security' in the context of the killing of Congolese leaders, including Lumumba, and at the prevalence of conditions which 'threaten[ed] international peace and security' (SC Res 161 of 21 February 1961).

prevention of clashes, and the use of force, if necessary, in the last resort'.[84] For similar reasons, its resolution of November 1961 authorising ONUC to 'take vigorous action, including the requisite measure of force, if necessary, for the immediate apprehension, detention . . . or deportation of all foreign military and paramilitary personnel . . . and mercenaries' and 'all necessary measures' to prevent their entry or return,[85] clearly has its basis in Chapter VII – though, again, that Chapter was not specifically invoked. As was the case with UNEF I, the Court in *Certain Expenses* needed to address the question of whether or not ONUC was an enforcement action. Here the objection to ONUC – which was primarily an exercise of Security Council powers[86] – was different in nature to the objection to UNEF I. One argument was that the resolution establishing ONUC had

> been implemented in violation of provisions of the Charter inasmuch as under the Charter it is the Security Council that determines which States are to participate in carrying out decisions involving the maintenance of international peace and security, whereas in the case of the Congo the Secretary-General himself determined which States were to participate with their armed forces or otherwise.[87]

The Court did not find this argument persuasive. Citing 'a record of reiterated consideration, confirmation, approval and ratification by the Security Council and by the General Assembly of the actions of the Secretary-General in implementing the resolution of 14 July 1960', it found that it was 'impossible to reach the conclusion that the operations in question usurped or impinged upon the prerogatives conferred by the Charter on the Security Council'.[88] Nothing in the Charter forbade the Security Council from acting 'through instruments of its own choice'.[89] As such, the financial obligations associated with ONUC were found to 'constitute obligations of the Organization for which the General Assembly was entitled to make provision under the authority of Article 17'.[90]

The Court found that ONUC was not an enforcement action against the state. It did not find it necessary, however, to indicate the operation's constitutional basis:

[84] SC Res 161 of 21 February 1961, Part A, para. 1. The resolution further called for the immediate 'withdrawal of all Belgian and other foreign military and paramilitary personnel and political advisers not under the United Nations Command, and mercenaries'.

[85] SC Res 169 of 24 November 1961, para 4.

[86] ONUC was established by the Security Council and – with the exception of a period at the end of 1960 and the start of 1961 when the matter was transferred to the General Assembly – its mandate and the revisions thereto were under the control of the Security Council.

[87] *Certain Expenses* (n 5) 175.

[88] ibid, 176–77.

[89] ibid, 177.

[90] ibid.

> It is not necessary for the Court to express an opinion as to which article or articles of the Charter were the basis for the resolutions of the Security Council, but it can be said that the operations of ONUC did not include a use of armed force *against* a State which the Security Council, under Article 39, determined to have committed an act of aggression or to have breached the peace. The armed forces which were utilized in the Congo were not authorized to take military action *against* any State. The operation did not involve 'preventive or enforcement measures' *against* any State under Chapter VII and therefore did not constitute 'action' as that term is used in Article 11.[91]

However, its finding that Resolution 143 of July 1960, which established ONUC, was 'clearly adopted with a view to maintaining international peace and security'[92] suggests that it viewed ONUC as a Chapter VII operation.

In finding that ONUC was not an enforcement action against a state, the Court shifted its approach somewhat from that taken in relation to UNEF I. The Court did not enter into a detailed discussion of the forcefulness of ONUC – as recommended by the Secretary-General, as provided by the General Assembly or the Security Council or as actually occurred. Had the Court engaged in a review of the Security Council or General Assembly resolutions authorising the use of force by ONUC as part of its Advisory Opinion, it would have had to acknowledge that the force authorised was considerable. Similarly, had the Court considered the positions of the Secretaries-General with regard to the use of force by ONUC, as it had done with UNEF I, it would have been forced to concede that there was increasing acceptance of the use of offensive force over the course of the operation. Also absent from the Court's ruling was any discussion of what level of force was actually used, and in particular whether force was ever actually used against representatives of the state itself, such as its military.[93]

Such an omission is striking, given how essential these factors were, rightly, considered by the Court to be in its characterisation of UNEF I. Of course, the Court was not in a position to point to a lack of forcefulness in ONUC in the same way that it had been able to in relation to UNEF I. Instead, it focused on the fact that the force was not directed *against* the state. The observation that ONUC had entered the Congo with the consent of that government[94] appears to have been the primary basis for the Court's determination that the operation did not represent an enforcement action against it.[95]

[91] ibid (emphasis added).

[92] ibid, 175.

[93] In fact, the use of force beyond self-defence was relatively limited (with the exception of the situation in Katanga).

[94] *Certain Expenses* (n 5) 175.

[95] As Bowett (n 61) 180 observed: 'The existence of consent may certainly be regarded as evidence that ONUC was not in the nature of an "enforcement action" under Article 42 of the Charter, and, indeed, the ICJ in the *Expenses Case* appears to have stressed the fact of consent as evidence of this.'

It could perhaps be argued that it was unnecessary for the Court to enter into a consideration of ONUC's use of force (potential or actual) against the state. After all, the operation was present in the state with the consent of the government – indeed, at its request. This consent, it could be argued, provided something of a guarantee that ONUC would not act against the government; if it did, the government could simply withdraw its consent and the operation would end. Even accepting that the government possessed a right to withdraw its consent – which, as noted, depends on factors such as the operation's constitutional basis[96] – such an argument presumes the continued existence of a functioning government, something that was clearly not present in the Congo at all stages of the operation. Moreover, if host state consent alone were to have the effect of ensuring that force was not used *against* a government (thereby rendering the operation non-enforcement in nature), it would raise the issue of why the Court was at such pains to detail the non-forceful nature of UNEF I: it need only have pointed to Egypt's consent to that operation in order to rebut any argument that UNEF I was enforcement. In addition, an argument that Congo's consent to ONUC meant that the operation could never use force against that state would do considerable violence to the concept of impartiality: ONUC would be required to ignore actions by the Congolese government or its national forces which, if committed by spoilers, would have justified the use of forceful action.[97] Of course, where a peacekeeping operation is established under Article 41 or 42, there is no requirement that it be impartial.[98]

Given that the ICJ's reasoning as to why ONUC did not amount to enforcement action against a state was quite limited, and given that the Court did not consider it necessary to express an opinion as to which article or articles of the Charter provided the basis for the Security Council resolutions establishing or modifying ONUC, let us turn to the analyses of commentators of the day with regard to both of these questions. Most commentators writing at the time took the view that the operation was

[96] See nn 75–76 above and accompanying text.

[97] The relationship between the National Congolese Army (the ANC) and the government of the Congo was complicated. While the ANC represented the armed force of the government of Prime Minister Lumumba and President Kasavubu, the government's exercise of control over them was variable (see eg United Nations, *Official Records of the 896th Meeting of the Security Council*, 9 September 1960, para 102). According to Abi-Saab, this permitted ONUC 'to deal with these ANC elements not as part of the National Army, ie of the Congolese government, but as mere outlaws or criminals' (Georges Abi-Saab, *The United Nations Operation in the Congo 1960–1964* (Oxford, Oxford University Press, 1978) 57–58). An Operations Directive relating to the use of force by ONUC recognised that 'lawless elements in the Congo were often' troops from the ANC. It was also made clear in an Operations Directive that 'ONUC's obligations to assist in the maintenance of law and order were "in no way diminished" when the ANC was itself involved' (Findlay (n 3) 61).

[98] See chapter 3.

established under Article 40.[99] This view was influenced by the Court's finding that ONUC was not an enforcement action against a state, coupled with the desire to find a Charter provision into which the Security Council's measures could be slotted.[100]

However, in view of the requirements of Article 40, discussed in chapter 3, that article cannot provide ONUC with its constitutional basis. As noted, Article 40 does not provide for the use of force; Article 42 is the only provision in the Charter empowering the Security Council to establish a forceful operation. Even if, as some argue, a limited use of force may be attached to a provisional measure under Article 40, the level of force authorised and used in the ONUC operation can in no way be described as 'limited'. Moreover, any operation established as a mandatory measure under Article 40 is obliged to act impartially – the provisions of Article 40 require the measures taken thereunder to be without prejudice to the positions of the parties[101] – which, as noted, the operation arguably failed to do. Moreover, if ONUC was an operation established as a mandatory measure under Article 40, it would continue to be subject to the provisions of Article 2(7),[102] eg, it would be difficult to argue that the operation did not interfere with matters that were 'essentially within the domestic jurisdiction' of the state. Similarly, the robustness of the force used means that it cannot be classed as an enforcement measure 'not involving the use of armed force' under Article 41. Again, even if one accepts that the use of a limited amount of force beyond self-defence or coercion may be legitimately implied into Article 41,[103] the level of force authorised for ONUC cannot be so classified.

A number of commentators writing at the time provided their own elaboration of the Court's two bases for finding ONUC not to amount to Article 42 enforcement: (1) it was not sufficiently forceful, and (2) it occurred with the consent of the host state.[104] Turning first to the nature of the operation's

[99] Higgins (n 42) 55 and 144. See also Miller/Schachter (n 76) 4; Fouad Riad, 'The United Nations Action in the Congo and its Legal Basis' (1961) 17 *Revue Egyptienne de Droit International* 19.

[100] Bowett (n 61), who found that, in establishing ONUC, 'the Council acted under Chapter VII of the Charter so as to establish a United Nations Force for the purpose of supervising and enforcing compliance with the provisional measures ordered under Article 40 and for other purposes which were consistent with the general powers of the Council under Article 39' (180), observed that while ONUC was clearly a 'Chapter VII situation, . . . no specific article of Chapter VII quite fits the Resolutions adopted – at least so far as the establishment of the Force is concerned' (179).

[101] See discussion on this point in chapter 3, section 3.2.24.

[102] A point readily conceded by Schachter, who considered ONUC to be an Art 40 measure (Miller/Schachter (n 76) 5).

[103] See discussion in chapter 3, section 3.2.3.2.

[104] In addition they put forward a variety of further arguments as to why ONUC was not an Art 42 operation against the state, including: the lack of any formal invocation of 'a threat to peace, breach of peace or act of aggression' under Art 39 (see eg Higgins (n 42) 58); the absence of an invocation of Art 42 in the resolutions or debates leading thereto (see Miller/Schachter (n 76) 8 and Higgins (n 42) 55); the absence of renegotiations with the contributing states which,

authorisation to use force, commentators stressed the fact that the level of forcefulness authorised was relatively limited in comparison with the level of force to be authorised in operations under Article 42, as envisaged by the drafters.[105] Based on the *travaux préparatoires*,[106] they observed that ONUC 'was essentially to fulfil a function fundamentally different from the objective contemplated under Article 42'[107] and that its purposes 'were essentially different from those for which, at San Francisco, forces used under Article 42 were contemplated'.[108] Schachter put it this way:

> The kind of military action which the Council authorized in the Congo was restricted essentially to the maintenance of internal law and order, the purpose of which was to enable the Belgian troops to be speedily withdrawn. While this was a use of armed force, it was essentially of a police or 'criminal law' character, and in that sense seems fundamentally different from the type of enforcement measure which had been envisaged as the military sanctions of Article 42. Certainly expectation at San Francisco was that Article 42 would be resorted to for military action of an international character – that is to say, directed against the troops of a state or another governmental authority which bore responsibility for a breach of the peace or act of aggression. Use of troops for internal security purposes at the request of the territorial state does not have this kind of international coercive character, and it is doubtful, therefore, that it should be described legally as the use of armed force within the meaning of Article 42.[109]

Second, a number of commentators argued that the non-enforcement nature of ONUC was clear from the fact that the operation took place with host state consent.[110] As noted, this is closely linked to a belief that the target of the forceful measures was not a state.[111]

it was argued, would have had to occur if the Security Council was to turn a non-enforcement operation into an enforcement operation (Bowett (n 61) 176 and n 36); the 'ample evidence that the UN still regarded itself as bound by the domestic jurisdiction requirements' in Art 2(7) (Higgins (n 42) 58); the view of the Secretary-General that the action did not fall under Art 42 (Bowett (n 61) 176); and the view that the operation fitted more neatly under another article in Chapter VII (see Higgins (n 42) 55 and 144; Miller/Schachter (n 76) 4; Riad (n 99) 19).

[105] Bowett (n 61) 176; see also R Simmonds, *Legal Problems Arising from the United Nations Military Operations in the Congo* (Dordrecht, Martinus Nijhoff, 1968) 62.

[106] United Nations Conference on International Organization, San Francisco, 25 April–26 June 1945 (Washington, DC, US Govt Print Off Doc) 334, 580–81.

[107] Simmonds (n 105) 61 and n 12. He continued: 'Although [the later resolutions] conferred upon ONUC the power of *initiative* which went beyond the purely defensive role to which it had previously been limited, they cannot, in a real sense, be regarded as authorizing "enforcement action" or shifting the constitutional basis to Article 42' (62).

[108] Bowett (n 61) 176.

[109] Miller/Schachter (n 76) 8.

[110] Simmonds (n 105) 61 observed that it was 'doubtful whether the use of troops for internal security purposes at the request of the territorial state could ever be tantamount to an enforcement action'.

[111] McNemar (n 47) 286 stressed that an important distinction between ONUC and Art 42 enforcement was that 'ONUC was not established as a means of taking sanctions against Belgium as an aggressor but rather as an effort to maintain law and order'. Schachter maintained that the drafters intended action under Article 42 necessarily to amount to sanctions against a state or governmental authority (Miller/Schachter (n 76) 7).

Both arguments have now been overtaken by practice. As discussed in chapter 2, Security Council enforcement under Article 42 has evolved such that more quasi-enforcement operations have been established than full-blown ones. Quasi-enforcement operations possess the very characteristics that Schachter and others viewed as precluding ONUC from being an Article 42 operation. First, they are not, as Schachter felt the drafters would have required, of 'an international character' 'directed against the troops of a state or another governmental authority which bore responsibility for a breach of the peace or act of aggression'. Instead, quasi-enforcement operations are used 'for internal security purposes at the request of the territorial state' – the very thing Schachter warned was not intended by the Security Council. Second, quasi-enforcement operations are frequently established by the Security Council with the consent of the host state. Clearly, where a host state consents to a quasi-enforcement operation, it does not consider that operation to be directed *against* it.

Based on its level of forcefulness and its Chapter VII basis, it may be concluded that ONUC was an Article 42 enforcement operation. Such a conclusion was reached by various commentators of the day.[112] Moreover, since the end of the Cold War, increasing numbers of commentators have come to describe ONUC as an enforcement action: some simply label it enforcement[113] or 'collective security';[114] others, more cautiously, (perhaps out of a belief that the Court's *Certain Expenses* Advisory Opinion precludes a finding that it was enforcement) have labelled it 'de facto enforcement'[115] or 'verging on enforcement'.[116]

Contrary to the assertions of many, the conclusion that the constitutional basis of ONUC lay in Article 42 does not contradict the ICJ's findings in the *Certain Expenses* case. As Bowett observed, the Court's finding that ONUC did not 'involve "preventive or enforcement measures" against any state under Chapter VII'[117] is 'not conclusive on the non-applicability of Articles 41 and 42': 'the words used in [Articles] 41 and 42 do not necessarily pre-suppose that the action has to be enforcement action *against a*

[112] For example, Finn Seyersted, 'UN Forces: Some Legal Problems' (1961) 37 *British Yearbook of International Law* 351, 446 took the view that what began as an Art 40 operation changed into an Art 42 operation with SC Res 161 of 21 February 1961. See also Robert Jennings, 'The United Nations Force and the Congo', *The Listener*, LXVI/No 1699 (19 October 1961), 589.

[113] Findlay (n 3) 85–86 described ONUC as 'an enforcement operation – in the sense of defeating a breakaway regime and reasserting the authority of the central government'.

[114] Franck (n 4) 25. Franck's use of the term 'collective security' appears to be synonymous with the term 'enforcement action' used herein.

[115] Hilaire McCoubrey and Nigel D White, *The Blue Helmets: Legal Regulation of United Nations Military Operations* (Aldershot, Dartmouth, 1996) 53.

[116] White (n 62) 209.

[117] *Certain Expenses* (n 5) 177.

State'.[118] Rather, Article 42 can provide a constitutional basis, as it did with ONUC, for an enforcement action where the force authorised is *in aid of the state.*

It would be overstating matters to suggest that the ICJ in 1961 envisaged the type of operation that has become commonplace since the end of the Cold War – referred to herein as quasi-enforcement. However, the fact that the Court relied on the phrase 'enforcement . . . *against* any State' and the fact that it endorsed the Secretary-General's description of ONUC as not 'part of an enforcement action *directed against a Member country*',[119] may indicate that it recognised the possibility of a type of Article 42 enforcement that was not against the state.[120]

3.2.3 *Conclusion and Assessment of Success*

We see in ONUC the first militarised peacekeeping operation. Based on the level of force authorised and its lack of impartiality, the only Charter provision in which the operation may find its basis (latterly at any rate) is Article 42 – despite the fact that the host state initially consented to the operation. As noted, such a finding is not at variance with the finding of the ICJ in the *Certain Expenses* case that the operation was not an enforcement action *against a state*. This interpretation of the *Certain Expenses* case – suggested by some at the time – has become all the more persuasive since the end of the Cold War in light of the changed nature of Security Council enforcement.

On a certain level, ONUC may be said to have been something of a success:[121] the politics of the day meant that the military operation was successful in ensuring that Katangan secession was avoided.[122] However, the operation came at a great cost: in monetary terms to the Organization, to the lives of peacekeepers and to the cohesion of the Organization. Observers have described it as 'split[ing] the Security Council, almost

[118] Bowett (n 61) 176 n 34. While Bowett disregarded this possibility – finding instead that the 'Court did not feel these to be the appropriate articles' – he did not have the benefit of the substantial post-Cold War practice of the Security Council, whereby enforcement operations (eg quasi-enforcement operations) have been established under Art 42 but not *against* the state.

[119] *Second and Final Report* (n 14) para 10, quoted in *Certain Expenses* (n 5) 170–71 (emphasis added).

[120] It is true, however, that the ICJ did not always make reference to the idea that the enforcement it was speaking of was *against the state* – at one point in the decision it observed that UNEF I and ONUC were 'not enforcement actions within the compass of Chapter VII of the Charter' (*Certain Expenses* (n 5) 166).

[121] See, generally, Eric S Packham, *Success or Failure? The UN Intervention in the Congo After Independence* (Commack, NY, Nova Science Publishers, 1998).

[122] Secretary-General Thant had the backing of the 'USA (which mollified the other Western powers) and India (which took care of the non-aligned countries)' (Findlay (n 3) 86).

bankrupt[ing] the United Nations';[123] as causing the UN's 'most serious crisis of legitimacy';[124] and as amounting to the 'UN's Vietnam'.[125] In the words of Findlay, ONUC was not 'particularly helpful to the orderly development of UN peace operations doctrine. Indeed, it discredited that endeavour by demonstrating that political machinations could ultimately render Security Council resolutions and peacekeeping mandates and norms irrelevant.'[126]

ONUC revealed a UN which, despite ignoring the 'fundamental principles' of peacekeeping, wanted to maintain the pretence that the operation complied with them. Findlay observed that the UN's 'deliberate playing down of the significance of ONUC's military operations by two successive secretaries-general and their staffs was clearly designed to avoid further controversy'.[127] Of course, there are significant advantages to mischaracterising an operation such as ONUC. If states view peacekeeping operations as being non-forceful in nature, they are far more likely to contribute troops. If peacekeeping is considered a strictly impartial endeavour, a host state will be far more likely to consent to such an operation's presence – something that may or not be legally required, but which is always advantageous as regards the functioning of the operation.

4. MISSIONS IN THE MID-1990S

After the Cold War, ONUC lost its unique status. In the early 1990s, four peacekeeping operations were created, which shared many of ONUC's characteristics. These operations – in the former Yugoslavia, Somalia, Rwanda and Haiti – were established (or modified) in circumstances where security had broken down. Aspects of the operations in the former Yugoslavia (latterly)[128] and Somalia were explicitly established under Chapter VII – though no detail was given regarding the particular article of that Chapter that was being invoked. While consent of the host state was obtained in relation to the establishment and modification of two of the four operations (the exceptions being UNOSOM II in

[123] Simon Chesterman, 'The Use of Force in UN Peace Operations', August 2004, http://pbpu.unlb.org/pbps/Library/Chesterman%20External%20Paper%20(31-08-2004).pdf (accessed 1 April 2011), 8.

[124] Franck (n 71) 226.

[125] William J Durch (ed), *The Evolution of UN Peacekeeping: Case Studies and Comparative Analysis* (Washington, DC, St Martin's Press for the Henry L Stimson Center, 1993) 31.

[126] Findlay (n 3) 86.

[127] ibid, 86. He observed that the UN actually conducted an enforcement operation 'while all along denying that it was doing more than acting in self-defence and preserving its freedom of movement' (ibid, 85–86, relying on EW Lefever and W Joshua, *United Nations Peacekeeping in the Congo, 1960–1964: An Analysis of Political, Executive and Military Control* (Washington, DC, Brookings Institution for the US Arms Control and Disarmament Agency (ACDA), 1966) 139.

[128] That is to say, from mid-February 1993 onwards.

Somalia throughout and UNPROFOR in the former Yugoslavia latterly), careful analysis is required in order to determine whether or not such consent was a legal prerequisite. In section 4.1 each of the four operations will be considered briefly, and in section 4.2 they will be evaluated with particular regard to whether or not they adhered to the 'fundamental principles' of peacekeeping, what their constitutional basis was and whether the militarised operations were successful.

4.1 Mandates and Functioning

4.1.1 The Former Yugoslavia (February 1992–December 2002)[129]

Slovenia and Croatia declared their independence from the Socialist Federal Republic of Yugoslavia (SFRY) on 25 June 1991. The following day the national army was ordered by the federal government to take control of the SFRY. By late 1991, matters had begun to deteriorate rapidly and in February 1992 the United Nations Protection Force in the former Yugoslavia (UNPROFOR) was established 'to create the conditions of peace and security required for the negotiation of an overall settlement of the Yugoslav crisis'.[130] Despite concerns that the conditions for peacekeeping did not actually exist,[131] the Secretary-General advised the Security Council that the 'normal rules in United Nations peace-keeping operations for the bearing and use of arms' should apply.[132] This would have included an understanding that force was only to be used in self-defence or in defence-of-mandate. It was not long into the mission's tenure, however, before the Security Council felt compelled to make the mission more forceful.

There is scope for disagreement regarding the question of when the mission was militarised. In the view of Boutros-Ghali, 'mission creep' began with Resolution 752 of 15 May 1992, some three months after the establishment of the mission.[133] Others see Resolution 776 of 14 September 1992, authorising the enlargement of UNPROFOR's mandate and strength in Bosnia and Herzegovina in order to facilitate the delivery of humanitarian assistance, as a turning point.[134] Arguably, the mission was militarised in

[129] See Findlay (n 3), chapter 7 for a detailed discussion of this complicated mission and its offshoots.

[130] SC Res 743 of 21 February 1992, para 5.

[131] The Secretary-General concluded that 'the danger that a UN peace-keeping operation will fail because of lack of cooperation from the parties is less grievous than the danger that delay in its dispatch will lead to a breakdown of the cease-fire and to a new conflagration in Yugoslavia' (United Nations, *Further Report of the Secretary-General Pursuant to Security Council Resolution 721 (1991)* (UN Doc S/23592), 15 February 1992, 7).

[132] ibid, 6.

[133] Boutros Boutros-Ghali, *Unvanquished: A US-UN Saga* (Random House, 1999) 40.

[134] Christine Gray, *International Law and the Use of Force*, 3rd edn (Oxford, Oxford University Press, 2008) 282–83. While SC Res 776 of 14 September 1992 itself does not invoke Chapter VII, it does authorise UNPROFOR to use force to deliver humanitarian aid and makes

February 1993 when, with Resolution 807, the Security Council explicitly invoked Chapter VII in relation to the functioning of UNPROFOR, calling for its 'unimpeded freedom of movement' in order for it to carry out its functions.[135]

What is clear, however, is that by June 1993,[136] when the Security Council passed Resolution 836 determining the situation in Bosnia and Herzegovina to 'continue to be a threat to international peace and security', invoked Chapter VII and increased the scope and forcefulness of UNPROFOR's mandate such that it was charged with deterring acts against the Security Council's 'safe areas',[137] the nature of the mission had become more militarised than any previous peacekeeping mission since ONUC. The Security Council authorised it 'to take the necessary measures, including the use of force in reply to bombardments against the safe areas'[138] – despite the fact that, confusingly, the use of such force was to be 'in self-defence'.[139] In almost all resolutions subsequent to Resolution 807, Chapter VII was specifically invoked.[140] By June 1995, the operation arguably reached its height of forcefulness when the Security Council reinforced UNPROFOR by establishing a heavily-armed Rapid Reaction Force (RRF) to enable it to carry out its mandate.[141]

The fact that, early in the mission, the Security Council, acting under Chapter VII, authorised a NATO-led quasi-enforcement operation[142] to intervene militarily *concurrently* with UNPROFOR in Bosnia and Herzegovina makes an assessment of the level of forcefulness of UNPROFOR difficult.[143] Although the NATO-led operation was separate from UNPROFOR, because it was working hand-in-glove with UNPROFOR (including the use of a 'dual key' approach whereby the approval of both the UNPROFOR commander and the NATO commander was required before the NATO-led quasi-enforcement operation could use force), the quasi-enforcement operation's forcefulness and that of UNPROFOR became intermingled.[144]

reference to SC Res 770 of 13 August 1992, in which the Security Council, invoking Chapter VII, authorised Member States to use force to deliver humanitarian aid.

[135] SC Res 807 of 19 February 1993, para 4.

[136] SC Res 836 of 4 June 1993, para 5.

[137] The Security Council, acting under Chapter VII, established 'safe areas' in April and May 1993 (SC Res 819 of 16 April 1993 and SC Res 824 of 6 May 1993).

[138] SC Res 836 of 4 June 1993, para 9.

[139] ibid.

[140] Gray (n 134) 284.

[141] SC Res 998 of 16 June 1995, para 9.

[142] Known as 'Operation Sky Monitor' and, later, 'Operation Deny Flight'.

[143] See eg SC Res 770 of 13 August 1992, SC Res 781 of 9 October 1992, SC Res 816 of 31 March 1993, and SC Res 836 of 4 June 1993.

[144] At least this impression was given to those on the ground. For a discussion of the relationship between the two forces see Gray (n 134) 289–92.

It must also be borne in mind, when considering the forcefulness of UNPROFOR, that its use of force was influenced not just by its changing mandate, but also by the variable approaches of its different force and contingent commanders.[145] So, for example, when General Rose became force commander in January 1994, he announced a more 'robust' approach, whereby UNPROFOR would 'no longer request permission of the parties to traverse their territory but would simply inform them of its intentions'.[146] Findlay observed that Rose was soon to backtrack, however, when Serb forces began to resist and 'discovered the strategy of taking UN peacekeepers and others hostage to stave off military action'.[147] According to a chastened Rose: 'Patience, persistence and pressure is how you conduct a peacekeeping mission. Bombing is a last resort . . . and I'm not going to fight a war in white painted tanks.'[148]

After Croatia demanded the withdrawal of UNPROFOR from its territory in early 1995, the Security Council established the United Nations Confidence Restoration Operation in Croatia (UNCRO) to take over from UNPROFOR there.[149] In early 1996, UNCRO was replaced by two missions: the United Nations Transitional Administration for Eastern Slavonia, Baranja and Western Sirmium (UNTAES),[150] and the United Nations Mission of Observers in Prevlaka (UNMOP).[151] The Security Council explicitly invoked Chapter VII in its resolutions establishing the UNCRO and UNTAES mandates; however, in each case the mandated tasks were not forceful in nature.[152] Also in March 1995, the United

[145] Findlay (n 3) 219–27.

[146] ibid, 224. For example, in one incident, '[a]fter checking with the Danish troops, but without seeking permission from UN Headquarters, Rose ordered Danish tanks to relieve the besieged town of Tuzla' (ibid).

[147] ibid, 225.

[148] ibid, quoting Rose in a newspaper report.

[149] SC Res 981 of 31 March 1995. For a discussion of the issue of consent in relation to UNPROFOR and its offshoots, see Christine Gray, 'Host-State Consent and United Nations Peacekeeping in Yugoslavia' (1996–97) 7 *Duke Journal of Comparative and International Law* 241.

[150] SC Res 1037 of 15 January 1996. When UNTAES was wound up in January 1998, its policing functions were taken over by the United Nations Civilian Police Support Group (UNPSG), which ran until October 1998.

[151] SC Res 1038 of 15 January 1996. UNMOP was terminated in December 2002.

[152] The mandate of UNCRO was set out in SC Res 981 of 31 March 1995 at para 3, which endorsed United Nations, *Report of the Secretary-General Pursuant to Security Council Resolution 947 (1994)* (UN Doc S/1995/222 and Corr 1), 22 March 1995. The mandate included matters such as facilitating previous Security Council resolutions, facilitating the delivery of humanitarian aid, monitoring and reporting, and performing the monitoring functions envisaged in the Cease-fire Agreement of 29 March 1994 (set out in the Annex to United Nations, *Letter Dated 30 March 1994 from the Secretary-General Addressed to the President of the Security Council* (UN Doc S/1994/3677), 30 March 1994). The mandate of UNTAES, set out at paras 10 and 11 of SC Res 1037 of 15 January 1996, was also non-military in nature, consisting of such functions as monitoring, supervising and facilitating, and contributing 'by its presence to the maintenance of peace and security in the region' (ibid, para 10). Although the mandates of UNCRO and UNTAES were established under Chapter VII, based on the nature of their functions it would appear that in each case the invocation of Chapter VII was directed at the

Nations Preventive Deployment Force (UNPREDEP) was established to replace UNPROFOR in the Former Yugoslav Republic of Macedonia.[153] In late 1995, after the Dayton Peace Agreement[154] came into effect in Bosnia and Herzegovina, UNPROFOR ceased to exist entirely.[155]

4.1.2 Somalia (April 1992–March 1995)

In April 1992, the UN's activities in Somalia began with the United Nations Operation in Somalia (UNOSOM I),[156] which had the primary purpose of escorting humanitarian aid to the civilian population in post-Barré Somalia. The situation on the ground proved too dangerous for the mission to operate and it was withdrawn. In December 1992, the Security Council took up an offer of assistance from the USA and established a quasi-enforcement force,[157] the US-led Unified Taskforce (UNITAF).[158] The operation was successful in restoring calm and facilitating the distribution of food aid during its short tenure in the country.[159] However, in part because the US forces considered disarming Somali militias to be beyond the scope of the operation, the improvement to the security situation was temporary, with Somali warlords simply 'lying low' until the Taskforce departed.[160]

In March 1993, as UNITAF was preparing to withdraw, Boutros-Ghali, noting a continuing security threat,[161] requested that the Security Council mandate the returning mission – rechristened UNOSOM II – with a variety of 'military tasks'.[162] The Secretary-General observed that in light

authorisation in the same resolutions for Member States (through NATO) to provide close air support to the missions, rather than to empower the peacekeeping missions themselves to use force.

[153] SC Res 983 of 31 March 1995.

[154] General Framework Agreement for Peace in Bosnia and Herzegovina (reprinted in 35 ILM 89; an earlier version initialled in Dayton, Ohio on 21 November 1995 may be found at UN Doc A/50/790-S/1995/999), signed in Paris, France on 14 December 1995.

[155] An International Police Task Force, which came to be known as the United Nations Mission in Bosnia and Herzegovina (UNMIBH), was established there (SC Res 1035 of 21 December 1995). UNMIBH's mandate expired in December 2002. In the same resolution a NATO-led Implementation Force (IFOR), known as 'Operation Joint Endeavour', was also established, IFOR was succeeded by the Multi-national Stabilization Force (SFOR) (SC Res 1088 of 12 December 1996), which, in turn, was succeeded by an EU-led force (EUFOR) (SC Res 1575 of 22 November 2004).

[156] UNOSOM I was established by SC Res 751 of 24 April 1992. The mission was originally referred to as 'UNOSOM', but later, after UNOSOM II was established, it was retroactively renamed UNOSOM I. I will refer to the operation from April 1992 to March 1993 as UNOSOM I and thereafter as UNOSOM II.

[157] SC Res 794 of 3 December 1992, paras 7–10.

[158] Also known as 'Operation Restore Hope'.

[159] Boutros-Ghali (n 133) 60.

[160] ibid, 60.

[161] United Nations, *Further Report of the Secretary-General Submitted in Pursuance of Paragraphs 18 and 19 of Resolution 794 (1992)* (UN Doc S/25354), 3 March 1993, para 55.

[162] ibid, para 57.

of the continuing threat to peace and security in the country, the returning mission 'will not be able to implement [its] mandate unless it is endowed with *enforcement powers* under Chapter VII of the Charter'.[163] The Security Council acceded to the Secretary-General's request, and in March 1993,[164] acting under Chapter VII, established UNOSOM II, which was larger and more forceful than UNOSOM I, and which assumed many of the functions of UNITAF.[165] It was to undertake such tasks as preventing 'any resumption of violence and, if necessary [taking] appropriate action against any faction' violating the ceasefire, securing the disarmament of the factions, and maintaining security.[166] Moreover, it was empowered to take 'such forceful action as may be required to neutralize armed elements that attack or *threaten to attack*' UN personnel or property and that of its agencies, the ICRC and NGOs.[167] Neither the Secretary-General's report nor the Security Council resolution endorsing it made any mention of any obligation on the part of UNOSOM II to limit itself to the use of force in self-defence.[168]

Despite the fact that UNITAF, which had been deployed in 40 per cent of the country, initially comprised 37,000 troops, UNOSOM II was to carry out its functions in the entire country with only 28,000 troops.[169] In the words of a UN Report examining the UN's role in Somalia:

> [I]t was ironic – and ill-boding – that the Unified Task Force (UNITAF), a multinational force set up under the direction of the Security Council and given wide power, ample resources and a limited mandate, handed over operational responsibility to UNOSOM II, which was given far less authority but a much broader mandate. Moreover, UNITAF, with all its resources, covered only part of southern Somalia, while UNOSOM II, with more limited resources, was supposed to cover the entire country.[170]

UNOSOM II was described by the report as 'under-manned, under-resourced and under-funded'.[171]

It is not surprising, therefore, that the operation suffered serious setbacks almost immediately. In June 1993, 26 peacekeepers were killed in a violent

[163] ibid, para 58 (emphasis added). See also *The Blue Helmets* (n 1) 296.
[164] SC Res 814 of 26 March 1993.
[165] ibid, para 6.
[166] ibid, para 5, which approved *Further Report of the Secretary-General* (n 161).
[167] ibid, para 57 (emphasis added).
[168] Indeed the Secretary-General's approach to the rules of engagement – which were to be drafted by the force commander – provide no indication of a desire to see the amount of force limited in any way. He noted only that the actions would need to be 'judged necessary to fulfil the mandate' (ibid, para 88). As noted, this Report was approved by the Security Council in SC Res 814 of 26 March 1993.
[169] *Further Report of the Secretary-General* (n 161) paras 70–74.
[170] United Nations Best Practices Unit (DPKO), *The Comprehensive Report on Lessons Learned from United Nations Operation in Somalia (UNOSOM): April 1992–March 1995*, March 1995, www.peacekeepingbestpractices.unlb.org/PBPS/Pages/PUBLIC/ViewDocument.aspx?docid=509&cat=8&scat=18&menukey=_5_3_30 (accessed 1 April 2011), para 14.
[171] ibid, para 19.

confrontation with forces on the ground. This led to the Security Council strengthening the force's mandate. Again acting under Chapter VII, it authorised UNOSOM II to take 'all necessary measures against all those responsible for the armed attacks' on the personnel of UNOSOM II.[172]

Matters were to deteriorate further when 18 US soldiers, one UN peacekeeper and hundreds of Somalis[173] were killed in an incident that began on 3 October 1993. The US had inserted military units independent of the UN chain of command[174] and one such unit, the US Delta Force, 'in an operation planned, decided, and launched entirely without the knowledge of United Nations officials' staged a raid in South Mogadishu.[175] When the raid failed and US personnel were captured, the US looked to the UN peacekeeping troops to rescue its captured forces. It was in the process of doing so that the deaths occurred; many others were wounded. In the face of the killings, the US ordered the withdrawal of its forces.

As a result, in February 1994, UNOSOM II's mandate was redefined.[176] While it was still authorised under Chapter VII, it was no longer authorised to use 'all necessary measures' and its focus was to be on non-forceful measures, such as encouraging the parties to respect a ceasefire and to make efforts to provide humanitarian aid. The diminished operation withdrew, rather ignominiously, before completing its mission – the first United Nations ever to do so.[177]

As for UNOSOM II's *actual* use of force beyond self-defence, this was relatively limited. Findlay observed that it did, at times, use 'force in defence of its mission and in enforcing disarmament', and that '[a]fter June 1993 it used substantial military force in attempting to capture or kill General Aideed and his senior lieutenants'.[178] However, the most violent military engagements were 'initiated and conducted not by UNOSOM [II] forces but by US troops acting outside the UN chain of command'.[179]

4.1.3 *Rwanda (October 1993–March 1996)*

Another stain on the UN's reputation – according to many, the biggest to date – was the genocide in Rwanda which occurred despite the pres-

[172] SC Res 837 of 6 June 1993.

[173] Some estimates run as high as 1,000 Somali deaths. See Boutros-Ghali (n 133) 103–04.

[174] ibid, 93. The US had also had left behind nearly 4,000 troops from UNITAF 'to perform logistics and support duties while wearing blue berets and patches identifying them as under UN command'.

[175] ibid, 103–04.

[176] SC Res 897 of 4 February 1994.

[177] United Nations, *The Causes of Conflict and the Promotion of Durable Peace and Sustainable Development in Africa: Report of the Secretary-General* (UN Doc S/1998/318), 16 April 1998, para 31.

[178] Findlay (n 3) 192.

[179] ibid. For a discussion of the instances in which UNOSOM II actually used force, see ibid, 192–204.

ence of a UN peacekeeping mission. The tragic story of Rwanda in 1994 is well known.[180] The United Nations Assistance Mission for Rwanda (UNAMIR I)[181] was established in October 1993 to monitor the Arusha Peace Agreement and to contribute to 'the security of the city of Kigali'.[182] Early in the operation, the force commander sought authorisation from the DPKO to use force to pre-empt serious attacks on the Tutsis which – the mission had been reliably informed[183] – were being planned. This request was denied.[184]

After a plane carrying the presidents of Rwanda and Burundi was shot down on 6 April 1994, 'the systematic killing of Tutsis and of Hutu members of the political opposition began'.[185] When 10 Belgian peacekeepers were targeted and killed, the Belgian government withdrew its contingent[186] and the Security Council reduced the size of UNAMIR I from 2,500 to 270 personnel and downgraded its mandate such that it would 'only act as an intermediary in securing a cease-fire, help in the resumption of humanitarian assistance and monitor developments'.[187] Some saw the Security Council's near withdrawal of the mission without the immediate emplacement of a quasi-enforcement force as facilitating the genocide, which continued unabated.

In response to a public outcry, the Security Council took two measures. First, it authorised an increase in the mission's strength to 5,500 troops[188] and gave the mission – by now referred to by the Secretary-General as UNAMIR II – an expanded mandate. Indicating its concern 'that the

[180] See United Nations Department of Public Information, *The United Nations and Rwanda 1993–1996* (Blue Book Series, vol 10) (New York, UN Sales No E.96.1.20, 1996). See also Romeo (Lt-Gen) Dallaire and Brent (Maj) Beardsley, *Shake Hands with the Devil* (Toronto, Vintage Canada, 2003).

[181] Some, including the Security Council, referred to the operation as 'UNAMIR' throughout; others, such as Secretary-General Boutros-Ghali, divided the mission into 'UNAMIR I' and 'UNAMIR II'. The Secretariat uses the term UNAMIR II in some of its literature but does not list it as a separate operation on its peacekeeping website (www.un.org/en/peacekeeping/list.shtml, accessed 1 April 2011). For the purposes of this discussion, I will use the term 'UNAMIR I' for the period 5 October 1993 to 16 May 1994 and the term 'UNAMIR II' for 17 May 1994 (when the mandate was considerably strengthened) onwards.

[182] SC Res 872 of 5 October 1993.

[183] Dallaire and Beardsley (n 180) 130–31.

[184] In reply to requests by the force commander for authorisation to mount a military operation, the DPKO 'informed UNAMIR [I] headquarters that such action went beyond the UNAMIR [I] mandate' (*The United Nations and Rwanda 1993–1996* (n 180) 32). As noted by the Independent Inquiry, 'The Force Commander submitted a draft set of Rules of Engagement for UNAMIR [I] on 23 November 1993, seeking Headquarters' approval. Headquarters never responded to that request' (United Nations, *Letter Dated 15 December 1999 from the Secretary-General Addressed to the President of the Security Council [Enclosing 'the Report of the Independent Inquiry into the Actions of the United Nations During the 1994 Genocide in Rwanda', 15 December 1999]* (UN Doc S/1999/1257), 16 December 1999, 3). See also Findlay (n 3) 227.

[185] *The United Nations and Rwanda 1993–1996* (n 180) 37.

[186] ibid, 40. See also Boutros-Ghali (n 133) 134.

[187] SC Res 912 of 21 April 1994.

[188] SC Res 918 of 17 May 1994.

continuation of the situation in Rwanda constitutes a threat to peace and security in the region', the Security Council charged UNAMIR II – 'within the limits of the resources available to it' – to contribute to 'the security and protection of . . . civilians at risk in Rwanda, including through the establishment of . . . secure humanitarian areas' and to provide security for humanitarian relief operations.[189] In addition, UNAMIR II was authorised 'to take action in self-defence against persons or groups who threaten protected sites and populations, United Nations and other humanitarian personnel or the means of delivery and distribution of humanitarian relief'.[190] Second, the Security Council established a French-led quasi-enforcement operation, *Opération Turquoise*, under Chapter VII, authorising it to use 'all necessary means'[191] to create a safe area in the southwest of the country.[192] UNAMIR II was slow to emerge, with UN Member States showing extreme reluctance to volunteer troops.[193] Before UNAMIR II reached its full strength, the genocide had ended and an estimated 800,000 people had been massacred.[194]

4.1.4 Haiti (September 1993–March 2000)[195]

One final UN operation deserves brief mention. In December 1990, Jean-Bertrand Aristide was elected President of Haiti in UN-monitored elections. In 1991, however, General Raoul Cédras led a coup against the government and seized power. In 1993, the Governors Island Agreement was negotiated, providing that General Cédras would cede power to President Aristide in October of that year.[196] In September 1993, the United Nations Mission in Haiti (UNMIH) was established to assist in modernising the Haitian armed forces and to provide training to local police.[197] The military government refused to cede power and, as a result, UNMIH was unable to deploy in October 2003 as intended.

[189] ibid.

[190] ibid.

[191] *Opération Turquoise* was 'aimed at contributing, in an impartial way, to the security and protection of displaced persons, refugees and civilians at risk' (SC Res 929 of 22 June 1994).

[192] *Opération Turquoise* took place from May to August 1994. (Findlay (n 3) 282).

[193] Boutros-Ghali (n 133) 138–40 outlined the difficulty the UN had in finding the required troops: 'On August 1 [1994] I told the Security Council that the United Nations was as far from attaining the 5,500 troops authorized as it had been on May 17, the day Resolution 918 had been adopted.'

[194] *Letter Dated 15 December 1999* (n 184) 3.

[195] UNMIH was in existence between March 1993 and June 1996, when it was replaced by a series of smaller UN operations in possession of more limited mandates: the United Nation Support Mission in Haiti (UNSMIH), July 1996–July 1997; the United Nations Transition Mission in Haiti (UNTMIH), July–November 1997; and the United Nations Civilian Police Mission in Haiti (MIPONUH), December 1997–March 2000.

[196] Unattributed, 'Sanctions Expanded to Secure Compliance with 1993 Agreement – Haiti; Governors Island Agreement', *UN Chronicle*, September 1994.

[197] SC Res 867 of 23 September 1993.

On 31 July 1994,[198] the Security Council authorised a quasi-enforcement action, the Multinational Force (MNF),[199] to be led by the USA. The Security Council established the MNF under Chapter VII and authorised it to use 'all necessary means'[200] to fulfil its aims, which included facilitating the departure from Haiti of the Cédras regime. The Security Council also revised and expanded UNMIH's mandate to include, inter alia, 'sustaining the secure and stable environment [once it had been established by the MNF] and protecting international personnel and key installations'.[201] On 30 January 1995, having deemed that 'a secure and stable environment'[202] prevailed, the Security Council called for the departure of MNF and the return of UNMIH.[203]

4.2 Evaluation

4.2.1 Adherence to the 'Fundamental Principles'

4.2.1.1 Force Only in Self-Defence

It is beyond doubt that the Security Council authorised UNOSOM II to use force beyond self-defence. It found a threat to international peace and security, invoked Chapter VII, and authorised the operation to take 'such forceful action as may be required to neutralize armed elements that attack or threaten to attack' – the word 'threaten' clearly implies the use of preemptive force – and, later, to take 'all necessary measures against all those responsible for the armed attacks' on its personnel.[204]

Whether the Security Council intended to authorise the use of force beyond self-defence for the other three operations is less clear. Therefore, it is necessary to closely examine the resolutions establishing or modifying the mandates of the operations and the background leading to the adoption of these resolutions, in order to determine that organ's

198 SC Res 940 of 31 July 1994.
199 Also known as 'Operation Uphold Democracy'.
200 SC Res 940 of 31 July 1994, para 4.
201 ibid, para 9.
202 SC Res 975 of 30 January 1995, para 5.
203 ibid, para 8.
204 The UN Legal Counsel, in considering the powers of the peacekeeping mission in Liberia in 2003, stated that, where the Security Council invokes the phrase 'all necessary means' or 'to take the necessary measures', it is 'of course . . . beyond all doubt that the Security Council had made use of its powers under Chapter VII of the Charter to authorize [the use of] armed force (other than in situations of self-defence)'. United Nations, 'Note to the Under-Secretary-General of the Department of Peacekeeping Operations, United Nations' [2003] *United Nations Juridical Yearbook*, 13 October 2003, Part Two, Chapter VI, 538–40 (UN Sales No E.07.V.1) 539. For discussion of this Legal Opinion in the context of UNMIL in Liberia, see chapter 6, section 2.2.1.

intention.[205] Turning to Resolution 918, which established UNAMIR II, we see mixed signals as to whether the Security Council intended to authorise force beyond self-defence. On the one hand, the Security Council expressed concern that the continuation of the situation in Rwanda constituted a threat to peace and security in the region and it bestowed tasks on the operation, including contributing to the security and the protection of civilians at risk and providing security for humanitarian operations, that might reasonably have been expected to require force beyond self-defence. On other hand, the Security Council did not invoke Chapter VII in the resolution; nor did it authorise UNAMIR II to use 'all necessary measures' (or wording to a similar effect). Moreover, the fact that the resolution recognised that the operation 'may be required to take action *in self-defence* against persons or groups who threaten protected sites and populations, United Nations and other humanitarian personnel or the means of delivery and distribution of humanitarian aid' sends mixed signals.[206] The reference to 'action in self-defence' suggests a limitation on the operation's use of force to situations of self-defence; however, the reference to action being taken against those threatening 'protected . . . populations' suggests an authorisation to use force in circumstances beyond self-defence – at least as that term is normally defined.

Turning to the background of the drafting of Resolution 918 establishing UNAMIR II, we see that it was conceived in the knowledge that a large-scale killing campaign was taking place in Rwanda and amidst calls for the mission to be empowered to take measures 'to stop the killing of innocent civilians'.[207] Moreover, the resolution was drafted following a plea from the Secretary-General to consider authorising forceful action.[208] However, despite this, a subsequent non-paper (which formed the basis of Security Council discussions on Resolution 918) 'explicitly stated that the revised mandate would not envisage enforcement actions, would depend primarily on deterrence to carry out its tasks and would resort to *force only in self-defence*'.[209] Weighing all these factors, it is very difficult to discern the Security Council's intention; however, given the explicit statement in the non-paper, it must be concluded that the Security Council did not intend to authorise the use of force beyond self-defence.

[205] According to the UN Legal Counsel, in discerning the Security Council's intention, regard must be had to 'the interpretation of the resolution, specifically, on the ordinary and natural meaning which is to be given to its terms when they are read in the context of the resolution as a whole and in the light of its object and purpose, and against the background of the discussions leading to, and the circumstances of, its adoption, in particular the [relevant Secretary-General's reports]'. ibid, 539. See also the discussion in chapter 3 nn 2 to 4 and accompanying text.

[206] SC Res 918 of 17 May 1994, para 4 (emphasis added).

[207] *Letter Dated 15 December 1999* (n 184) 23.

[208] United Nations, *Letter Dated 29 April 1994 from the Secretary-General Addressed to the President of the Security Council* (UN Doc S/1994/518), 29 April 1994, 2.

[209] *Letter Dated 15 December 1999* (n 184) 24 (emphasis added).

By Resolution 940, the Security Council characterised the situation in Haiti as a threat to peace and security in the region and gave UNMIH new tasks that could require the use of force beyond self-defence, including sustaining the secure and stable environment established by the MNF and protecting international personnel and key installations, and increased its troop levels.[210] However, the resolution did not invoke Chapter VII in relation to the strengthened operation; nor did it authorise the use of 'all necessary measures' in relation to any of UNMIH's tasks. The strengthened mission's rules of engagement provided that 'UNMIH forces may intervene to prevent death or grievous bodily harm of innocent civilians at the hands of an armed person or group' and authorised '"search, apprehension, and disarmament" when acting in self-defence'.[211] A report of the Secretary-General, issued shortly after UNMIH's mandate was changed, made the following observation:

> UNMIH's rules of engagement will be defined in accordance with its mandate under resolution 940 (1994). In accordance with normal practice, they will authorize the use of force in exercise of the right of self-defence, including opposing forcible attempts to impede the discharge of the Mission's mandate. The concept of 'assistance' to the Government of Haiti in sustaining the secure and stable environment established during the multinational force phase may include the use of force, if no other means are adequate or available for the above purpose.[212]

Once again, the reference to self-defence appears to preclude any use of force beyond self-defence. However, once again, 'self-defence' is said to include action that would normally be considered to go beyond self-defence, including 'sustaining the secure and stable environment' established by the MNF – a force that *was* specifically established under Chapter VII and given an authorisation to use 'all necessary means' to establish and maintain a secure and stable environment – and civilian protection. Weighing all these factors, it is very difficult indeed to discern whether or not the Security Council intended to authorise the use of force beyond self-defence. The fact that it did not invoke Chapter VII or authorise it to use 'all necessary means' or to 'take the necessary means' suggests, in light of its practice in relation to UNOSOM II and UNPROFOR, that it did not.

Finally, we turn to the issue of whether or not the Security Council intended to vest UNPROFOR in its later stages with an authority to use force beyond self-defence. Here again, we see conflicting signals. For example, in Resolution 836 the Security Council determined there to

[210] SC Res 940 of 31 July 1994, para 8.

[211] Rules 6 and 8 of UNMIH's ROE as reproduced in Findlay (n 3) 275).

[212] United Nations, *Report of the Secretary-General on the Question Concerning Haiti* (UN Doc S/1995/46), 17 January 1995 para 64 (emphasis added). This Report was considered by the Security Council in SC Res 975 of 30 January 1995.

be a threat to international peace and security, indicated that it was acting under Chapter VII (in relation to the whole of the resolution), and assigned UNPROFOR tasks that were likely to require force beyond self-defence (deterring acts against safe areas, occupying key points on the ground) – all factors indicating an intention to authorise force beyond self-defence. While the Security Council specifically authorised the operation to 'take the necessary measures', it did so in terms that appear to indicate that force was limited to self-defence: '*The Security Council . . . [a]uthorises* UNPROFOR . . . in carrying out the mandate [including deterring acts against safe areas] . . . acting in self-defence, to take the necessary measures, including the use of force, in reply to bombardments against the safe areas . . . or to armed incursion into them . . .'[213] To authorise the use of 'the necessary measures' by a peacekeeping operation 'acting in self-defence' is a contradiction: 'the necessary measures' language represents an authorisation to use force *beyond* self-defence. Moreover, if the operation was merely to use force *in* self-defence, there was no need to indicate that in a resolution – the right exists for all peacekeeping operations – or to invoke Chapter VII and authorise the use of 'all necessary measures'.

Observers have suggested that the ambiguous language was necessary to facilitate consensus among Security Council members, with one describing it as a 'masterpiece of diplomatic drafting, but largely unimplementable as an operations directive'.[214] The issue of whether UNPROFOR was authorised to use force beyond self-defence was left unclear – just as the Security Council had apparently intended. Findlay put it this way:

> This was a carefully worded compromise between those who wished to use force to protect the safe areas (mostly the non-aligned members of the Security Council), on the one hand, and France, Spain and the UK, on the other hand, who were concerned for the well-being of their troops and believed that real protection was impossible. It was designed to give the impression of protecting the safe areas without actually doing so.[215]

In the words of Yasushi Akashi, formerly the Secretary-General's Special Representative for the former Yugoslavia, '[T]his routine combination of Chapter VII and the "authorization" of the use of force in self-defense has further compounded the degree of confusion, even among knowledgeable observers, over the conditions in which force can be used by UNPROFOR.'[216]

[213] SC Res 836 of 4 June 1993, para 9. See also SC Res 871 of 4 October 1993, para 9, which provided: '*The Security Council . . . Authorizes* UNPROFOR, in carrying out its mandate in the Republic of Croatia, acting in self-defence, to take the necessary measures, including the use of force, to ensure its security and its freedom of movement.'

[214] Shashi Tharoor, 'Should UN Peacekeeping Go "Back to Basics"?' (1995–96) 37(4) *Survival* 52, 60.

[215] Findlay (n 3) 265.

[216] Yasushi Akashi, 'The Use of Force in a United Nations Peace-Keeping Operation: Lessons Learnt from the Safe Areas Mandate' (1995–96) 19 *Fordham International Law Journal* 312, 317.

Similarly, the Security Council was not clear as to whether the RRF, established by Resolution 998 in June 1995, was authorised to use force beyond self-defence. Resolution 998 did not authorise the RRF to take 'the necessary measures' or invoke Chapter VII; however, the RRF was established 'in support of UNPROFOR, functioning within its existing mandate',[217] and its existing mandate, by reference to previous Security Council resolutions including Resolution 836 discussed above, did feature an invocation of Chapter VII and an authorisation to 'take the necessary measures' 'in self-defence'.[218] The size of the RRF (12,500 troops), the fact that it was backed by artillery and attack helicopters,[219] the circumstances leading to its creation,[220] the nature of the tasks assigned to it[221] and even its name[222] all suggested the potential to use force beyond self-defence. At the same time, however, the Secretary-General recognised that UNPROFOR's success depended 'to a very large extent on the readiness of the parties to cooperate with it' and indicated that the contributing governments (France, the Netherlands and the UK) intended that this remain the case.[223]

While the Security Council's intention regarding whether or not UNPROFOR could use force is unclear – apparently, deliberately so – the nature of the protection tasks assigned to it, its Chapter VII basis and its authorisation to 'take the necessary measures', suggest that UNPROFOR was authorised to use force beyond self-defence, from the period beginning June 1993.

4.2.1.2 Host State Consent

With an analysis of the 'fundamental principle' of consent, two issues arise: first, whether host state consent was obtained, and second, whether host state consent was a legal prerequisite. The first will be considered

[217] United Nations, *Letter Dated 9 June 1995 from the Secretary-General Addressed to the President of the Security Council* (UN Doc S/1995/470), 9 June 1995, 5. The Security Council established the RRF on the terms set out in this letter (SC Res 998 of 16 June 1995, paras 9 and 10).

[218] See SC Res 998 of 16 June 1995, which makes reference to UNPROFOR's mandate. UNPROFOR's mandate at the time was based on SC Res 743 of 21 February 1992 (which established UNPROFOR), as extended and modified by numerous Security Council resolutions which invoked Chapter VII.

[219] Findlay (n 3) 254.

[220] It was established in response to the continuing humiliation of UNPROFOR troops (ibid).

[221] It was to 'provide the Commander of UNPROFOR with well-armed and mobile forces with which to respond promptly to threats of United Nations personnel' (*Letter Dated 9 June 1995 from the Secretary-General* (n 217) 2).

[222] The British indicated a reluctance to refer to it as a 'rapid reaction force', noting that they 'are not there to war-fight [but to] keep the peace' (Findlay (n 3) 255, relying on public comments of the British Armed Forces Minister).

[223] *Letter Dated 9 June 1995 from the Secretary-General* (n 217) 2.

here, and the second, which depends on the constitutional basis of each operation, will be discussed below in section 4.2.2.

It is clear that Haiti consented to the strengthening of UNMIH in January 1995.[224] The situations in Rwanda, Somalia and the former Yugoslavia, however, are less clear. While there was some discussion about whether or not the consent of the parties was required for the establishment of UNAMIR II,[225] the fact that the government of Rwanda did not oppose this in its capacity as a member of the Security Council (on which it happened to be sitting at the time UNAMIR II was established) may be taken as indicating its consent. With UNOSOM II in Somalia there was no government in place to provide consent.[226] However, if there had been a government in place, given that the operation was not against the state – rather, it was targeting lawless elements of that society in order to restore security and facilitate the distribution of humanitarian aid – there is no reason to think that such consent would not have been forthcoming. In the resolution establishing UNPROFOR, the Security Council stressed the 'request by the Government of Yugoslavia of 26 November 1991 for a peace-keeping operation'.[227] As the mandate evolved, however, the Security Council no longer made reference to host state consent.

4.2.1.3 Impartiality

The impartiality principle became an indirect casualty of the move away from the self-defence principle. The more forceful the operations became, the less likely they were to appear impartial. The fact that the operation in the former Yugoslavia was linked with the NATO-led quasi-enforcement operation resulted in the perception that UNPROFOR was not impartial. When the Security Council established the RRF in June 1995, China and Russia expressed clear misgivings regarding the loss of impartiality of the force: both voiced concern that UNPROFOR would become (or

[224] The Security Council made explicit reference to the consent of the government there for the expansion of the operation. SC Res 975 of 30 January 1995, which referred to United Nations, *Letter Dated 27 January 1995 from the Permanent Representative of Haiti to the United Nations Addressed to the President of the Security Council* (UN Doc S/1995/90), 30 January 1995.

[225] While the US proposed explicitly referring to the need for the parties' consent in the resolution establishing UNAMIR II, according to the Secretariat's notes, 'a number of delegations questioned the advisability of seeking clear consent from the parties' (*Letter Dated 15 December 1999* (n 184) 24). Ultimately, there was no reference to the consent of the parties in SC Res 918 of 17 May 1994.

[226] The resolution was passed without the need for a vote. SC Res 918 of 17 May 1994; see United Nations, *Provisional Record of the 3378th Meeting of the Security Council* (UN Doc S/PV.3377), 16 May 1994. Representatives of the interim government took part in the deliberations of the Council (*Letter Dated 15 December 1999* (n 184) 23).

[227] SC Res 721 of 27 November 1991 refers to a letter of 26 November 1991 by the Permanent Representative of Yugoslavia addressed to the President of the Security Council (S/23240). Regarding the consent of the republics, see Gray (n 149) 245–48.

would be seen to be) a party to the conflict.[228] In the same resolution in which the Security Council created the RRF, adding thousands of heavily armed troops as an 'integral part' of UNPROFOR, it asserted that the status of UNPROFOR and its impartiality would be 'maintained'.[229] As Boutros-Ghali remarked, 'Alice in Wonderland would have enjoyed the resolution'.[230]

With regard to UNOSOM I, despite the fact that the Security Council had invoked Chapter VII and authorised the operation to take 'all necessary measures against all those responsible for' armed attacks against peacekeepers on 6 June 1993, the Secretary-General's Special Representative for Somalia, Admiral Howe, stated on 12 June 1993: 'UNOSOM II is impartial and takes no sides in disputes among factions or clans.'[231]

As for UNAMIR II and UNMIH, each operation took sides; however, because each was siding against illegal conduct, loss of impartiality did not appear to have been an issue.

4.2.2 *Constitutional Bases*

4.2.2.1 UNMIH and UNAMIR II

While Resolution 940, which expanded UNMIH's mandate, did determine that the situation in Haiti constituted a 'threat to peace and security in the region' – a finding that triggered its powers to act under Chapter VII – it only invoked its Chapter VII powers in relation to the paragraphs of that resolution relating to its establishment of the MNF and not those relating to UNMIH's strengthened mandate.[232] Similarly, while the resolution creating UNAMIR II indicated that 'the continuation of the situation in Rwanda constitutes a threat to peace and security in the region',[233] Chapter VII was not invoked in relation to the establishment of that peacekeeping operation.[234] Thus, neither the resolution expanding UNMIH's powers nor that creating UNAMIR II may be said to have had – expressly or impliedly – its constitutional basis in Article 40, 41 or 42; in each case the consent of the host state (which, as noted, was forthcoming) was a

[228] ibid, 263.
[229] SC Res 998 of 16 June 1995.
[230] Boutros-Ghali (n 133) 237.
[231] United Nations, 'UNOSOM II Takes "Decisive Action" to Restore Peace; Killing of 24 Peace-Keepers is Biggest Single UN Loss Ever – United Nations Operations in Somalia – United Nations Developments', *UN Chronicle*, September 1993.
[232] SC Res 940 of 31 July 1994. The paragraphs of the resolution setting out the new powers of UNMIH (paras 9 and 10) may be contrasted with the paragraph setting out the powers of the MNF (para 4); only the latter paragraph begins with the words '*Acting* under Chapter VII of the Charter of the United Nations'.
[233] SC Res 918 of 17 May 1994.
[234] Chapter VII was, however, invoked in that part of SC Res 918 which imposed an embargo against the country.

prerequisite. In neither case may the operation be classed as militarised peacekeeping.

Both were consent-based peacekeeping operations. As such, host state consent to these was legally required. In consenting, the host states signalled their waiver of protection under the principles set out at paragraphs (1), (4) and (7) of Article 2 of the Charter.

4.2.2.2 UNOSOM II and UNPROFOR

Matters were different with regard to UNOSOM II and UNPROFOR. Each operation was established (or its mandate was modified) by means of resolutions explicitly invoking Chapter VII in relation to all of the operation's functions[235] and, in each case, the situation was explicitly characterised as a threat to international peace and security. UNOSOM II at its most forceful was authorised to use 'all necessary measures' and, unlike the other operations considered in this section, the Security Council did not see fit to mention the need to act in self-defence when taking such measures. Despite the mixed signals regarding the use of force, UNPROFOR, as noted above, may be taken to have been authorised to use force beyond self-defence.

The fact that the Security Council made no reference to host state consent in many of the revisions to UNPROFOR's mandate, which authorised substantial force and invoked Chapter VII, suggests that it did not consider consent to be a legal requirement in relation to such revisions. Gray put it this way:

> Because the peacekeeping forces were authorized to go beyond limited monitoring of a ceasefire, and because they were authorized to use force to carry out their mandate, there was an obvious possibility that they would become involved in conflict with the various parties, including the host state government. Although the force was originally established on the basis of host state consent, the extension of its mandate meant that it could no longer rely on that consent to its operations.[236]

Although the Security Council did indicate that it would withdraw from Croatia when, in January 1995, that state formally gave notice of its withdrawal of consent to the deployment of UNPROFOR on its territory,[237] this would appear to have been based on the Security Council's view that the operation would not be successful in the absence of host state consent, rather than on its view that it was legally obliged to withdraw due

[235] As we will see, with later militarised operations, the Security Council's invocation of Chapter VII in relation to the functioning of peacekeeping operations does not always apply to all of the operation's functions; at times, the Security Council will invoke Chapter VII in relation to functions contained in specific paragraphs only. See eg MINUSTAH, discussed in chapter 6, section 4, and MINURCAT, discussed in chapter 6, section 7.

[236] Gray (n 149) 257.

[237] ibid, 266.

to Croatia's withdrawal of consent.[238] This appears to be the point being made by Boutros-Ghali when he welcomed the Croatian's President's subsequent announcement that he *would* accept UNCRO, a consent-based operation:[239]

> As the Council is considering the question of maintaining a UN peacekeeping presence in Croatia, it is timely for me to restate the basic principles of such a presence. A UN peacekeeping force *can operate effectively only with the consent and full cooperation of the parties*.[240]

If the Security Council viewed the withdrawal of UNPROFOR as a *legal* requirement following Croatia's withdrawal of consent, that would have amounted to a remarkable renunciation of its Chapter VII powers to bind states. Moreover, such an approach by the Security Council would be at variance with its earlier practice whereby it did not seek consent for the strengthening of UNPROFOR.

Turning to UNOSOM II, this is the most clear-cut case of a peacekeeping operation taking place without host state consent; as noted, there was no functioning government to grant such consent. While it might very well have been the case that if a functioning government had existed, it would have been in favour of the operation, this would depend, inter alia, on whether the government perceived there to be a risk that the considerable force authorised might be used against it. As discussed in chapter 3, while the existence of host state consent is not necessarily an indicator that such consent is *legally* required for the Security Council to establish an operation,[241] the *absence* of host state consent to the establishment or substantial modification of the mandate of an operation may be taken to show that the Security Council did *not* consider host state consent to be a legal prerequisite – assuming that one accepts that the Security Council would never act in a way that exceeded its powers.

In sum, both UNOSOM II and UNPROFOR at its latter stages must have been mandatory provisional measures under Article 40 or enforcement operations under Article 41 or 42. Because the Security Council

[238] Cf Gray (ibid, 266–67) who appeared to take the view that the Security Council's actions indicate its view that the continued presence of UNPROFOR in Croatia was *legally* dependent on the consent of the host state, notwithstanding the Chapter VII character of UNPROFOR.

[239] It was only once Croatia consented to a revised operation – UNCRO – that the Security Council established it – in accordance with the terms of the host state. However, UNCRO was not empowered to use 'all necessary measures' or force of a similar level and, as noted above at n 152, while the SC resolution establishing the force *did* invoke Chapter VII, that invocation appears to have been in relation to a quasi-enforcement operation established in the same resolution.

[240] United Nations, *Report of the Secretary-General Submitted Pursuant to Security Council Resolution 994 (1995)* (UN Doc S/1995/467), 9 June 1995 (emphasis added), cited in Gray (n 149) 243.

[241] As discussed, the existence of host state consent is a contra-indicant that the operation is an enforcement measure *against the consenting state*.

authorised a level of force beyond self-defence, neither operation can find its constitutional basis in Article 41 as an enforcement measure 'not involving the use of armed force'. Even if one takes the view that a limited amount of force (or coercive power) may be permissible under this Article despite its wording, the level of force authorised for both forces goes beyond 'limited force'. The level of force – when coupled with the arguable lack of impartiality – leads to the conclusion that neither operation could have its basis in Article 40.

Instead, both UNOSOM II and UNPROFOR in its later stages were established by the Security Council through the exercise of its Article 42 powers.[242] Of course, neither operation constitutes 'enforcement' in all senses of the word. The two operations were certainly not enforcement missions as originally envisaged under the Charter; this type of operation may not come into existence unless Article 43 agreements are entered into. Nor may they be classified as full-blown enforcement, along the lines of the authorisation to use force in the Korean situation in 1950 or Iraq/Kuwait in 1991. The military objectives of UNOSOM II and UNPROFOR at its most forceful were not sufficiently 'war-like'; moreover, while each operation lacked host state consent at certain stages, neither operation amounted to enforcement against the state, as discussed by the ICJ in the *Certain Expenses* case.[243] They were, however, of a similar nature to quasi-enforcement operations as discussed in chapter 2, section 3.3, though of course UNOSOM II and UNPROFOR were both UN-led.

4.2.3 Conclusion and Assessment of Success of the Militarised Peacekeeping Operations

The UN's activities in the former Yugoslavia proved in many ways to be a disaster. Despite the Chapter VII authorisation for UNPROFOR to 'take the necessary measures' in June 1993, the peacekeepers were unable to protect the 'safe areas'. While the fighting in Bosnia ultimately ceased in late 1995 after nearly four years and hundreds of thousands of deaths, this was largely brought about by the forceful actions of the NATO-led quasi-enforcement operation, an offensive against the Serbs by Moslems and Croatians, and the diplomatic intervention of the US and France which led to the Dayton

[242] Support for this conclusion may be found in Secretary-General Boutros-Ghali's characterisation of UNOSOM II as 'a country-wide enforcement operation to be carried out under United Nations command and control' (United Nations, *Letter Dated 29 November 1992 from the Secretary-General Addressed to the President of the Security Council* (UN Doc S/24868), 30 November 1992, 5). Similarly, Bothe took the view that UNOSOM II was 'undoubtedly' an example of the Security Council using its powers under Art 42 in the context of a peacekeeping operation (Michael Bothe, 'Peace-Keeping' in Bruno Simma (ed), *The Charter of the United Nations: A Commentary*, 2nd edn, vol 1 (Oxford, Oxford University Press, 2002) 648–700, 685 para 85).

[243] See discussion at section 3.2.2 above.

Agreement.[244] The UN was on the sidelines of this process. The nadir of the UN's operations in the former Yugoslavia came in July 1995 in Srebrenica, one of the 'safe areas' in Bosnia Herzegovina, when some 8,000 Muslim men and boys were massacred with UNPROFOR troops present,[245] in what was later judicially determined to be a genocide.[246]

In the words of Akashi, the Security Council entrusted UNPROFOR with a mandate 'that it knew, or should have known was not only unrealistic, but impossible to implement'.[247] The fact that 'the creation of the safe areas was a "quick fix" response to an immediate problem was evident in the Security Council's hesitation to provide UNPROFOR with the necessary resources to implement its mandate'.[248] A UN publication said the following of the operation in the former Yugoslavia:

> In the former Yugoslavia, unceasing conflict, entrenched hostility, lack of commitment and an absence of good faith among the parties characterized the crisis. The vulnerability of lightly armed, widely dispersed peace-keepers was dramatically illustrated in Bosnia and Herzegovina, where Governments assigned to the United Nations the impossible tasks of serving as a peace-keeper in the midst of war.[249]

As for UNOSOM II, no less an authority than the Secretary-General himself warned the Security Council of the Secretariat's inability to undertake an enforcement-type operation: 'The Secretariat, already overstretched in managing greatly enlarged peace-keeping commitments, does not at present have the capability to command and control an enforcement operation of the size and urgency required by the present crisis in Somalia.'[250] The Secretary-General recommended instead that forceful action be undertaken by a quasi-enforcement operation.[251] When it became clear that UNOSOM II was unable to carry out its mandate, it was withdrawn from the country, leaving the job incomplete and effectively abandoning those it was meant to be protecting. A *Lessons Learned* report on the UN's operations in Somalia put it this way:

> [T]he United Nations is not yet capable of launching a large-scale enforcement action and . . . whenever in the foreseeable future it is necessary to launch such an operation under Chapter VII, it should be done by either a single State, as occurred in Rwanda in France's Operation Turquoise, or by a coalition of States,

[244] According to one estimate, in Bosnia and Herzegovina alone some 200,000 civilians were killed. See Ruth Wedgwood, 'United Nations Peacekeeping Operations and the Use of Force' (2001) 5 *Washington University Journal of Law & Policy* 69, 74.

[245] United Nations, *Report of the Secretary-General Pursuant to General Assembly Resolution 53/35: The Fall of Srebrenica* (UN Doc A/54/549), 15 November 1999, Chapters VII and VIII.

[246] *Prosecutor vs Radislav Krstić*, Judgment (Case IT-98-33-a, International Criminal Tribunal for the former Yugoslavia (Appeals Chamber), 19 April 2004).

[247] Akashi (n 216) 315.

[248] ibid.

[249] *The Blue Helmets* (n 1) 6.

[250] *Letter Dated 29 November 1992* (n 242) 5.

[251] ibid.

> as was done early in Haiti . . . There is wide agreement that it was a mistake in Somalia for a Chapter VII operation (UNITAF) to co-exist with a Chapter VI operation (UNOSOM I). This lesson was well applied in Haiti, where a multinational force with Chapter VII powers was phased out before a Chapter VI operation, UNMIH, was deployed.[252]

The reasons for the UN's lack of capacity related largely to its lack of resources. Because the UN was – and is – continuously cash-strapped and dependent on its Member States for equipment and personnel, it will put in place operations that provide the bare minimum and operate on a most-favourable-case basis rather than 'reflect[ing] realities on the ground'.[253] The reluctance of states to contribute to such operations may reflect their unwillingness to risk the lives of their nationals, whether or not the Security Council and the Secretary-General emphasise the 'fundamental principle' of force only in self-defence. Their reluctance may also indicate that states share the Secretary-General's view that the UN lacks the capacity to lead an operation like UNOSOM II. It may be for this reason that the US assistance in Somalia featured the insertion of forces operating independently of UNOSOM II, rather than under its command. Of course, where state forces act independently of a UN-led operation there is a risk that they will act at cross-purposes or, as illustrated by the fatal US Delta Force operation in Somalia, that the independent force will imperil the UN force. Member State reluctance to volunteer troops may also illustrate their view that there is frequently a disconnect between what is being asked of a peacekeeping force and what resources are being pledged for it; nothing prevents the Security Council – perhaps in order to address intense political pressures – from establishing operations with lofty mandates but little in the way of staff or equipment to implement them. As we saw when UNOSOM II took over from UNITAF, the UN was asked to operate with far fewer resources than the US government had deemed acceptable for its own forces.

Even where an operation has the authorised personnel present, their training and professionalism will be variable. Moreover, there may be a tendency on the part of troops not to follow the orders of the UN commander. Instead, operating though their national chain of command, they may contact their government officials to express misgivings about particular orders of a commander. This can lead to the national authorities advising their troops to ignore the orders of the UN commander.[254]

[252] *Comprehensive Report on Lessons Learned* (n 170) paras 85–86.

[253] ibid, para 13.

[254] In setting out UNOSOM II as one option for the Security Council, Boutros-Ghali recognised that issue. He observed that 'Member States would . . . have to be ready to accept that the United Nations would command and control the operation and that the staff officers whom they would provide in the field and in New York would take their orders from the United Nations and not from their national authorities' (*Letter Dated 29 November 1992* (n 239) 6).

This was cited by a UN report as a factor leading to the UN's failure in Somalia.[255] The potential for different entities to have different views of whether it is appropriate for peacekeepers to use force beyond self-defence is compounded by ambiguously worded Security Council resolutions which do not make it clear whether the peacekeeping force is in the nature of enforcement or not as well as by the DPKO's tendency to stress the 'fundamental principles'. While it may be the case that such blatant ambiguity is the only way to ensure agreement among Security Council members, this is almost certainly going to lead to confusion among contributing states and by the force leadership as to the true nature of the operation and what is required of the mission participants.

When militarised UNOSOM II and UNPROFOR failed, we saw an undermining of the entire peacekeeping endeavour. The expectations of affected communities were raised – for example, those Bosnian Moslems who sought refuge in the UN's 'safe areas' in Bosnia and Herzegovina – only to be dashed. Moreover, as we saw with UNPROFOR, where the peacekeeping operation acted hand-in-glove with a quasi-enforcement operation, there was little chance that the peacekeeping operation would be perceived as impartial. Not only did this denude peacekeeping of one of its strongest assets, it also resulted in the peacekeepers being perceived as the 'enemy', leading to their being attacked and taken hostage. Regarding UNOSOM II – which he characterised as a 'peacekeeping force attempting to enforce a solution to the conflict'[256] – White observed:

> The question must be asked whether such actions are really consonant with the traditions of peacekeeping, and whether if these trends are maintained, the credibility of the United Nations as a neutral force for peace will be so seriously undermined as to confine peacekeeping to history?[257]

5. CONCLUSIONS

After UNOSOM II and UNPROFOR, it became clear that the Organization simply lacked the capacity to successfully conduct militarised peacekeeping operations. As a result, it reverted to less forceful operations. The move away from militarised peacekeeping was clear from the *volte-face* of the Secretary-General. In 1995, he published the *Supplement to an Agenda for Peace*, in which he rejected the idea that the 'fundamental principles' were optional. As he observed in that document:

> [T]he last few years have confirmed that respect for certain basic principles of peace-keeping are essential to its success. Three particularly important

[255] *Comprehensive Report on Lessons Learned* (n 170) para 45.

[256] Nigel D White, 'UN Peacekeeping – Development or Destruction?' (1994) 12(1) *International Relations* 129, 130.

[257] ibid, 130.

> principles are the consent of the parties, impartiality and the non-use of force except in self-defence. Analysis of recent successes and failures shows that in all the successes those principles were respected and in most of the less successful operations one or other of them was not.[258]

Similarly, in its 1995 *General Guidelines for Peacekeeping Operations*, the Secretariat stressed the importance of the principles of force only in self-defence, consent and impartiality – apparently suggesting that if the principles had been suspended, they had since been reinstated.[259] At paragraph 34 of these Guidelines, the Secretariat described peacekeeping as being 'incompatible with enforcement'.[260]

However, as will be discussed in the next two chapters, the lesson was soon disregarded and the UN was to embrace militarised peacekeeping, this time with a stronger commitment than ever before.

[258] United Nations, *Supplement to an Agenda for Peace: Position Paper of the Secretary-General on the Occasion of the Fiftieth Anniversary of the United Nations* (UN Doc A/50/60-S/1995/1), 3 January 1995, para 33. See the discussion of this change in position in chapter 2, section 2.4.2.

[259] See eg United Nations, *General Guidelines for Peacekeeping Operations* (United Nations (DPKO) (UN/210/TC/GG95)), on file with author.

[260] ibid.

Chapter 5

When Peacekeeping and Enforcement Overlap: Twenty-First Century Practice – The Early Operations

'If we don't want to do it properly, should we do it all? That is what the Security Council members must now ask themselves,' Mr Annan told me. The time has passed when the 15 council members can provide themselves with 'an alibi' by passing peacekeeping resolutions that cannot be implemented. 'Some of them vote for and then refuse to contribute troops to a force,' Mr Annan said.

Washington Post interview with Kofi Annan[1]

1. INTRODUCTION

THIS CHAPTER WILL consider the mandates of three peacekeeping missions that were militarised within a few months of each other at (or just before) the turn of the twenty-first century. In October 1999, the Security Council established the United Nations Transitional Administration in East Timor (UNTAET) under Chapter VII and authorised it to use 'all necessary measures to fulfil its mandate'. In February 2000, the Security Council modified the mandate of the United Nations Assistance Mission in Sierra Leone (UNAMSIL), invoking Chapter VII and authorising it to 'take the necessary action' to fulfil certain of its mandated tasks, and in the same month, it modified the mandate of the United Nations Organization Mission in the Democratic Republic of the Congo (MONUC), invoking Chapter VII and authorising 'the necessary action' to protect civilians under imminent threat of physical violence. Thus began the Security Council's third phase of militarised peacekeeping operations.[2]

[1] Jim Hoagland, 'Who Wants Peacekeeping? Put Up or Shut Up', *Washington Post*, 3 August 2000.

[2] Chapter 4 considers the first two phases: ONUC in the early 1960s and UNPROFOR and UNOSOM II in the early 1990s.

Around the same time, the Secretary-General was selecting the panel members and writing team for the Brahimi Report.[3] While the drafting process did not begin until 21 March 2000 and the Report was not presented to the Security Council and General Assembly until 21 August 2000,[4] as we shall see, the Report was influential even before its final publication.

2. SIERRA LEONE (OCTOBER 1999–DECEMBER 2005)

2.1 Mandate and Functioning

Following a coup in Sierra Leone in 1997, the Security Council established the United Nations Observer Mission in Liberia (UNOMSIL), a peacekeeping operation[5] composed of 70 observers, to work alongside a regional force, the Military Observer Group (ECOMOG), established by the Economic Community of West African States (ECOWAS).[6] In September 1999, citing an unstable security situation that had resulted in members of UNOMSIL and ECOMOG being captured and detained by rebels,[7] the Secretary-General recommended that ECOMOG and a new peacekeeping operation – the United Nations Mission in Sierra Leone (UNAMSIL) – work together in the country.

In October 1999 the Security Council passed Resolution 1270, which established UNAMSIL to replace UNOMSIL.[8] The new operation was to be larger, with up to 6,000 troops.[9] Resolution 1270 characterised the situation in Sierra Leone as continuing 'to constitute a threat to international peace and security in the region'[10] and bestowed the following civilian protection mandate on UNAMSIL:

> Acting under Chapter VII of the Charter of the United Nations . . . UNAMSIL may take the necessary action to ensure the security and freedom of movement of its personnel and, within its capabilities and areas of deployment, to afford

[3] The panel and the writing team were selected between late February and early March 2000. William J Durch, *Building a Better Peace Operation: Lessons from the Brahimi Report Process*, report prepared for the UN Foundation, 11 March 2004, www.stimson.org/images/uploads/research-pdfs/durch_building_a_better_peace_op_3-04.pdf (accessed 1 April 2011), 1.

[4] United Nations, *Identical Letters Dated 21 August 2000 from the Secretary-General to the President of the General Assembly and the President of the Security Council [Attaching Report of the Panel on UN Peacekeeping Operations (the 'Brahimi Report')]* (UN Docs A/55/305 and S/2000/809), 21 August 2000.

[5] The United Nations Observer Mission in Sierra Leone was charged with monitoring the security situation and monitoring respect for international humanitarian law in the country (SC Res 1181 of 13 July 1998). The mission is classified as peacekeeping by the DPKO; see www.un.org/en/peacekeeping/documents/operationslist.pdf (accessed 1 April 2011).

[6] SC Res 1181 of 13 June 1998.

[7] United Nations, *Eighth Report of the Secretary-General on the United Nations Observer Mission in Sierra Leone* (UN Doc S/1999/1003), 28 September 1999, paras 7 and 10–14.

[8] SC Res 1270 of 22 October 1999

[9] ibid, para 9.

[10] ibid, final preambular paragraph.

protection to civilians under imminent threat of physical violence, taking into account the responsibilities of the Government of Sierra Leone.[11]

ECOMOG was charged with maintaining security and stability and assisting UNAMSIL with any security concerns.[12]

However, just as UNAMSIL was gaining full strength in early 2000, ECOMOG announced its impending withdrawal. As a result, the Security Council considerably strengthened the mandate of UNAMSIL and increased its troop numbers to 11,000.[13] Resolution 1289 again characterised the situation as a threat to international peace and security in the region,[14] and, again invoking Chapter VII, gave UNAMSIL a number of duties previously undertaken by ECOMOG that could potentially require the use of force beyond self-defence. These duties included providing security in the disarmament process and at key locations in the country and facilitating the free flow of people and humanitarian assistance.[15] The Security Council authorised UNAMSIL 'to take the necessary action to fulfil the additional tasks'[16] and stressed the need for robust rules of engagement.[17] Indeed, such was its authorised level of forcefulness that the Secretary-General observed that the rules of engagement enabled UNAMSIL 'to use force, including deadly force, in self-defence or against any hostile attack or *intent*'.[18] Resolution 1289 also reiterated UNAMSIL's authorisation to 'take the necessary action' in relation to civilian protection.[19]

In late April/early May 2000, a series of armed attacks occurred against UNAMSIL forces, leading to the capture and detention of several hundred United Nations personnel and the destruction of disarmament and demobilisation camps.[20] On 7 May 2000, in an action known as 'Operation Palliser', UK forces were deployed at Lungi Airport and in the western part of the capital, Freetown.[21] The UK stressed that Operation Palliser

[11] ibid, para 14.

[12] A new mandate for ECOMOG (S/1999/1073, annex), adopted by ECOWAS on 25 August 1999, was approved by the Security Council (SC Res 1270, ibid, 7).

[13] SC Res 1289 of 7 February 2000.

[14] ibid, final preambular paragraph.

[15] ibid, para 10.

[16] ibid, para 10.

[17] ibid, para 9. The Security Council endorsed the views of the Secretary-General on this point as set out in United Nations, *Second Report of the Secretary-General Pursuant to Security Council Resolution 1270 (1999) on the United Nations Mission in Sierra Leone* (UN Doc S/2000/13), 11 January 2000, para 33.

[18] United Nations, *Fourth Report of the Secretary-General Pursuant to Security Council Resolution 1270 (1999) on the United Nations Mission in Sierra Leone* (UN Doc S/2000/455), 19 May 2000, para 89 (emphasis added).

[19] SC Res 1289 of 7 February 2000, para 10.

[20] *Fourth Report of the Secretary-General* (n 18) para 2. Even before this setback, there were several serious incidents, some directed against UN personnel (ibid, paras 14–24). In one incident on 30 April 2000, a Nigerian peacekeeper 'was shot and seriously wounded when he refused to surrender his weapon to a large group of armed [rebels] in the Occra Hills area' (ibid, para 19).

[21] ibid, para 69.

had been deployed in the country 'to allow for the safe evacuation of British nationals and other entitled personnel',[22] that it was entirely under UK control, and that 'UK forces will not be deployed in a combat role as part of UNAMSIL'.[23] The UK force, however, did more than evacuate UK nationals.[24] Immediately upon its arrival, it secured the airport in Lungi, assisted 'UNAMSIL in creating a security cordon around Freetown',[25] and helped to stabilise the situation on the ground.[26] The British presence, which continued long after the British nationals were evacuated,[27] was an extremely important factor in UNAMSIL's ability to gain the upper hand against the rebels. For its part, the Security Council responded to UNAMSIL's May 2000 crisis by further enlarging its personnel to 13,000.[28]

With the benefit of the support of the UK force, UNAMSIL engaged in what was described by the Secretary-General as a 'robust military operation',[29] successfully rescuing captured UN troops.[30] Several instances of the use of offensive force by UNAMSIL reportedly occurred in the period from May to July 2000. In one reported instance, UNAMSIL, with UK support, retook the town of Masiaka from the rebel forces on 4 July. On 15 July UNAMSIL launched a major operation to free a battalion of Indian peacekeepers and 11 UN observers trapped by RUF forces in the eastern town of Kailahun. The operation involved heavy losses for the RUF, including the destruction of an RUF brigade headquarters at Pendembu.[31] On July 22 'Operation Thunderbolt' – described by the Secretary-General as a 'preemptive strike'[32] – was launched by

[22] *Hansard* HC, col 23 (15 May 2000) (speech of Geoffrey Hoon, UK Secretary of State for Defence); see also *Hansard* HL col 669 (20 May 2000) (speech of Lord Burlison).

[23] *Hansard* HC, col 23 (15 May 2000) (speech of Geoffrey Hoon, UK Secretary of State for Defence).

[24] Trevor Findlay, *The Use of Force in UN Peace Operations* (Oxford, Oxford University Press for the Stockholm International Peace Research Institute (SIPRI), 2002) 301.

[25] United Nations Best Practices Unit (DPKO), *Lessons Learned from the United Nations Peacekeeping Experiences in Sierra Leone*, September 2003, 13.

[26] 'The UK intervention gave UNAMSIL breathing space to regroup, recover credibility and reassert its presence' (ibid).

[27] The Team was to remain in the country even after the departure of UNAMSIL, indicating 'its commitment to provide continued training to the Sierra Leone Armed Forces until at least 2010' (United Nations, *Twenty-Seventh Report of the Secretary-General on the United Nations Mission in Sierra Leone* (UN Doc S/2005/777), 12 December 2005, para 30).

[28] SC Res 1299 of 19 May 2000.

[29] United Nations, *Fifth Report of the Secretary-General on the United Nations Mission in Sierra Leone* (UN Doc S/2000/751), 31 July 2000, para 26.

[30] ibid, para 26. See also *Lessons Learned* (n 25) 13: 'UK military forces also conducted a rescue operation to free colleagues kidnapped by ex-SLA elements. After the intervention in May 2000, the UK promised a deterrent "over-the horizon" military option and demonstrated that commitment through highly visible "muscle flexing" military exercises that acted as a potent reminder of British capability to "spoilers"'.

[31] 46 *Keesing's Record of World Events*, July 2000, 43661.

[32] Unattributed, 'Annan Justifies UN's "Preemptive Strike" against Sierra Leone Militia', *Agence France Presse*, 25 July 2000.

UNAMSIL against rebels who had been manning illegal checkpoints on the Freetown-Masiaka road.[33]

Not all operations during this period indicated a force that was well-equipped or well-disciplined. On 8 May, UNAMSIL used gunships to attack the RUF at Masiaka; however, the UN reportedly admitted that Masiaka had fallen to the RUF after UNAMSIL troops had been forced to withdraw because they had run out of ammunition.[34] In a separate operation on 2 June 2000, Indian troops belonging to UNAMSIL used force to seize Rogberi Junction, thereby halting an RUF advance.[35] Again, UNAMSIL's success in relation to the Rogberi Junction was not unequivocal: reportedly, one of the main reasons why Rogberi Junction had fallen to the RUF in the first place was that a UNAMSIL contingent had abandoned a strategic bridge and fled to the capital, Freetown; according to the same report, the Indian troops had only been deployed in Rogberi Junction after a Nigerian detachment had refused an order by the UNAMSIL military commander to retake the town.[36]

On 4 August 2000 the Security Council passed Resolution 1313.[37] At operative paragraph 3, the Security Council

> *Expresse[d]* its intention, . . . taking into account the views of the Government of Sierra Leone, the Economic Community of West African States (ECOWAS) and the troop-contributing countries, to strengthen the mandate of UNAMSIL as established in its resolutions 1270 (1999) of 22 October 1999 and 1289 (2000) of 7 February 2000 with [certain] priority tasks.

The tasks that the Security Council called on UNAMSIL to undertake included maintaining security in particular regions, 'deter[ring] and, where necessary, *decisively counter[ing]* the threat of RUF attack by *responding robustly* to any hostile actions or threats of imminent and direct use of force', assisting the government to restore law and order, protecting civilians facing the threat of imminent physical violence, and patrolling access routes in order to 'dominate ground, ensure freedom of movement and facilitate the provision of humanitarian assistance'.[38] Reportedly, the Security Council also 'significantly stiffened the rules of engagement' of the operation.[39]

Resolution 1313 was different in a number of respects from previous resolutions regarding the mandate of UNAMSIL. First, the Security Council did not characterise the situation as posing a threat to international peace

[33] 46 *Keesing's Record of World Events*, July 2000, 43661.

[34] 46 *Keesing's Record of World Events*, May 2000, 43552.

[35] 46 *Keesing's Record of World Events*, June 2000, 43612.

[36] ibid. According to the same report, a UN assessment team was 'thought to have found tensions between the Indian Commander, Major-General Vijay Jetley and his Nigerian subordinates. Nigerian officers felt that a Nigerian should command UNAMSIL, since Nigeria provided the largest contingent of troops'.

[37] SC Res 1313 of 4 August 2000.

[38] ibid, para 3 (emphasis added).

[39] 46 *Keesing's Record of World Events*, August 2000, 43695.

and security in the region (as it had done in Resolutions 1270 and 1289). Second, it did not 'decide' to assign the additional priority tasks to the operation; rather it '[*e*]*xpresse*[*d*] its intention' to do so, 'taking into account to the views' of the host state, ECOWAS and troop-contributing states. Third, unlike the other two resolutions relating to UNAMSIL's mandate, there was no invocation of Chapter VII; nor was there any mention of the operation being authorised to 'take the necessary measures', or any language of a similar nature. The significance of this will be discussed in section 2.2 below.

Later that month, the Secretary-General – at the request of the Security Council – recommended various measures to improve the force, including a call for an increase in troop numbers to 20,500.[40] In making the recommendation, the Secretary-General made an explicit reference to the Brahimi Report, which had been released three days earlier. He described the operation in Sierra Leone as 'an important first test of our joint responsibility to implement the practical recommendations made by the Panel, with a view to making the United Nations truly credible as a force for peace'.[41] In October 2000, the Security Council sent a mission to Sierra Leone, with the UK delegate to the Security Council acting as head of mission.[42] The mission concluded, inter alia, that '[o]nly a sustained and effective military instrument, with the capability to extend its reach throughout the country and following clear political and military objectives, can maintain pressure on RUF and create incentives for dialogue and disarmament'.[43] As such, it advised that 'UNAMSIL must be strengthened in terms of numbers, effectiveness and capability'.[44] By means of a Statement by its President in November 2000, the Security Council indicated that it was 'convinced that the continuation of a credible military presence of the international community in Sierra Leone remains an indispensable element of the peace process' and reiterated its view that UNAMSIL required strengthening.[45]

Despite these conclusions and the Secretary-General's earlier request for an increase in troop numbers to 20,500 (which was repeated in October[46] and December 2000,[47] and again in March 2001),[48] the Security Council did

[40] United Nations, *Sixth Report of the Secretary-General on the United Nations Mission in Sierra Leone* (UN Doc S/2000/832), 24 August 2000, para 50.

[41] ibid, para 56.

[42] See United Nations, *Report of the Security Council Mission to Sierra Leone* (UN Doc S/2000/992), 16 October 2000.

[43] ibid, para 54(c).

[44] ibid. It also spoke of a need for 'firm, proactive peacekeeping' (ibid).

[45] United Nations, *Statement by the President of the Security Council* (UN Doc S/PRST/2000/31), 3 November 2000, 2.

[46] United Nations, *Seventh Report of the Secretary-General on the United Nations Mission in Sierra Leone* (UN Doc S/2000/1055), 31 October 2000, para 53.

[47] See also United Nations, *Eighth Report of the Secretary-General on the United Nations Mission in Sierra Leone* (UN Doc S/2000/1199), 15 December 2000, para 71.

[48] United Nations, *Ninth Report of the Secretary-General on the United Nations Mission in Sierra Leone* (UN Doc S/2001/228), 14 March 2001, para 66.

not agree to increase troop numbers until March 2001 – when it did so to the tune of just 17,500.[49] In the same resolution, it welcomed the Secretary-General's 'revised concept of operations for UNAMSIL' and his recommendation that UNAMSIL's rules of engagement allow it to 'respond robustly to any attack or threat of attack, including, if necessary, in a *pre-emptive manner*'.[50]

With the increase in UNAMSIL's size – and the continuing presence of the UK forces[51] – matters began to improve. Following peaceful elections in May 2002,[52] a gradual drawdown of troops occurred[53] and the operation was entirely withdrawn in December 2005.[54]

2.2 Evaluation

2.2.1 Adherence to the 'Fundamental Principles'

It is clear that the level of force authorised went beyond self-defence by any sensible measure. By Resolution 1270, UNAMSIL was charged with the power to 'take the necessary action' to ensure the security and freedom of movement of its personnel and to 'afford protection to civilians under imminent threat of physical violence, taking into account the responsibilities of the Government of Sierra Leone and ECOMOG'. While the use of force to ensure its own security and freedom of movement may be said to fit within the concept of self-defence as previously interpreted,[55]

[49] SC Res 1346 of 30 March 2001, para 2.

[50] *Ninth Report of the Secretary-General* (n 48) para 60 (emphasis added). The report was endorsed by the Security Council in SC Res 1346 (ibid), para 3. According to that report, the main objectives of UNAMSIL were: to assist the efforts of the government of Sierra Leone to extend its authority, restore law and order and stabilise the situation progressively throughout the entire country, and to assist in the promotion of a political process which should lead to a renewed disarmament, demobilisation and reintegration programme and the holding, in due course, of free and fair elections (*Ninth Report* para 60). The revised concept of operations was to 'take into account the Abuja Ceasefire Agreement, and the changes in the Mission's military structure and the circumstances on the ground' (para 57).

[51] By now referred to by the Secretary-General as the 'United Kingdom's short-term training team' (United Nations, *Eleventh Report of the Secretary-General on the United Nations Mission in Sierra Leone* (UN Doc S/2001/857), 7 September 2001, para 17).

[52] SC Res 1436 of 24 September 2002.

[53] United Nations, *Sixteenth Report of the Secretary-General on the United Nations Mission in Sierra Leone* (UN Doc S/2002/1417), 24 December 2002, para 2.

[54] SC Res 1620 of 31 August 2005 authorised the establishment of the UN Integrated Office in Sierra Leone (UNIOSIL) following the withdrawal of UNAMSIL at the end of 2005. UNIOSIL, charged with helping to achieve long-term stability and development in the country, is described by the DPKO as a peace-building mission (www.un.org/en/peacekeeping/pk1.htm, accessed 1 April 2011). This mission was succeeded by the United Nations Integrated Peacebuilding Office in Sierra Leone (UNIPSIL) (SC Res 1829 of 4 August 2008). UNIPSIL, originally established for one year only, has been extended twice (SC Res 1886 of 15 September 2009 and Res 1941 of 29 September 2010) and is currently scheduled to end in September 2011.

[55] See chapter 2, section 2.

an explicit Chapter VII authorisation to take the necessary action to protect civilians was virtually unprecedented.[56]

It could be argued that protecting civilians directly in one's care may amount to self-defence. It is not unheard of in national criminal law for the concept of self-defence to be extended to cover members of one's family or others in one's care.[57] However, an argument that the protection of civilians *generally* was self-defence would stretch the concept of self-defence to breaking point. Even though Resolution 1270 charged the force with civilian protection 'within its capabilities and areas of deployment' and only for 'civilians under imminent threat', given the operation's broad area of deployment, the obligation to defend civilians could extend to hundreds of thousands of people, making the type of force authorised entirely different from an obligation to defend those in one's care. In fact, the UN itself – despite its tendency to expand the concept of self-defence – does not appear to make this argument.[58] Moreover, the invocation of Chapter VII in Resolution 1270 and the authorisation to 'take all necessary measures' shows that the Security Council intended to authorise force beyond self-defence.[59] Additionally, the absence of any invocation by the Security Council of a requirement that the force be used in self-defence – as was the case with UNAMIR II and UNPROFOR for example[60] – may be

[56] It might be noted that Operations Directive No 8 from February 1961 called on ONUC to engage in civilian protection (see chapter 4, section 3.2.1). This was, of course a directive of the Secretariat and not a Security Council resolution invoking Chapter VII. Also in June 1993 UNPROFOR was charged with deterring acts against 'safe areas' (see chapter 4, section 4.1.1).

[57] See chapter 2, section 2.2.

[58] For example, the rules of engagement for MONUC, discussed in section 4 below, 'made clear that force could be used *beyond self-defence* to ensure security and freedom of movement of MONUC and to afford protection to civilians under imminent threat of physical violence' (emphasis added) (United Nations, Peacekeeping Best Practices, Military Division, *Operation Artemis: The Lessons of the Interim Emergency Multinational Force*, October 2004, www.peacekeepingbestpractices.unlb.org/PBPS/Library/Artemis.pdf (accessed 1 April 2011), 8). While this may not be said to go to the intention of the Security Council in relation to its establishment of the civilian protection mandate for UNAMSIL, it does indicate how a similarly worded civilian protection mandate was interpreted. In addition, a UN Legal Opinion, discussed in detail in chapter 6, section 2.2, considered whether the Security Council intended to authorise the peacekeeping operation in Liberia (UNMIL) to use force beyond self-defence. It cited the fact that that operation had been given a civilian protection mandate in drawing its conclusion that force beyond self-defence must have been authorised: 'UNMIL would simply not be in a position meaningfully to discharge that element of its mandate . . . if it were not able to resort to armed force, if need be' (United Nations, 'Note to the Under-Secretary-General of the Department of Peacekeeping Operations, United Nations' [2003] *United Nations Juridical Yearbook*, 13 October 2003, Part Two, Chapter VI, 538–40 (UN Sales No E.07.V.1) 359).

[59] The UN Legal Counsel offered the view that had the Security Council expressly authorised UNMIL (which was established under Chapter VII) to 'take the necessary measures' it would have been 'beyond all doubt that the Security Council had made use of its powers under Chapter VII of the Charter to authorize UNMIL to use armed force (other than in situation of self-defence)' (ibid).

[60] For example, SC Res 918 of 17 May 1994 (UNAMIR II) or SC Res 836 of 4 June 1993 (UNPROFOR). See discussion in chapter 4, section 4.2.1.1.

taken to be a further indication of the Security Council's intention to vest in UNAMSIL powers to use force beyond self-defence.

Turning to Resolution 1289, the Security Council's intention to authorise force beyond self-defence is clearer still. As noted, it characterised the situation as a threat to international peace and security in the region, it invoked Chapter VII, it authorised UNAMSIL to 'to take the necessary action to fulfil the additional tasks', and it stressed the need for robust rules of engagement.[61] Again there was no reference in the resolution to self-defence. While the Secretary-General did make reference to self-defence in his Report, the use of the word 'or' in his call for UNAMSIL 'to use force, including deadly force, in self-defence *or* against any hostile attack or intent'[62] indicates a recognition of the potential need to use force beyond self-defence in circumstances where no attack is imminent, merely intended.

It is more difficult to discern the Security Council's intention in relation to Resolution 1313. As noted, none of the traditional indicators of an authorisation of force were present.[63] The fact that the Security Council indicated that it was 'strengthen[ing] the mandate of UNAMSIL as established in its resolutions 1270 (1999) of 22 October 1999 and 1289 (2000) of 7 February 2000', and the fact that it recalled its previous resolutions,[64] might arguably be taken as evidence that it intended to bestow a Chapter VII authorisation to 'take the necessary action' on the tasks provided under Resolution 1313 based on those earlier resolutions. However, the idea that the Security Council would bestow forceful powers on an operation by means of the invocation of past resolutions is far from satisfactory; surely, such an important determination should be carried out by explicit reference to Chapter VII or 'all necessary means' (or similar language). Having said that, the nature of the additional tasks assigned to UNAMSIL, described above, indicate that use of force beyond self-defence would be required to carry them out.

As to the 'fundamental principle' of consent, it was clearly present in relation to the establishment of UNAMSIL by Resolution 1270[65] and the expansion of its mandate by Resolution 1289.[66] In passing Resolution 1313

[61] See n 59 regarding the Opinion of the UN Legal Counsel as to the significance of the use of the 'take the necessary measures' language. While he made no mention of the wording used here – ie 'take the necessary action' – it is clearly similar in nature.

[62] *Fourth Report of the Secretary-General* (n 18) para 89 (emphasis added).

[63] SC Res 1313 did not characterise the matter as a threat to international peace and security; it did not 'decide' to assign the operation the additional priority tasks but, rather, expressed its intention to do so, taking into account to the various views; there was no invocation of Chapter VII; and there was no authorisation to 'take the necessary measures' or any language of a similar nature.

[64] SC Res 1313 of 4 August 2000, first preambular paragraph.

[65] See eg United Nations, *Provisional Record of the 4054th Meeting of the Security Council* (UN Doc S/PV.4054), 22 October 1999, 6.

[66] United Nations, *Provisional Record of the 4099th Meeting of the Security Council* (UN Doc S/PV.4099), 7 February 2000, 2; United Nations (Press Release), *Security Council Expands Mandate, Numbers of Sierra Leone Force, Adopting Resolution 1289 (2000) Unanimously* (UN Doc

in August 2000, the Security Council certainly envisaged a role for the host state; however, it is not clear from its wording whether the modification of UNMIL's mandate as provided for in that resolution was subject to the host state's consent. As noted, the Security Council '[*e*]*xpresse*[*d*] its intention' to assign UNAMSIL additional priority tasks, 'taking into account the views' of the host state, ECOWAS and troop-contributing states. The intention of the Security Council is unclear. On the one hand, the wording of the resolution suggests that the Security Council did not intend the modification of the mandate to become operative until the views of the parties listed had been taken into account. On the other, the resolution does not plainly call for consent of the host state. Surely if the Security Council considered host state consent to be a prerequisite to modification of the mandate, it would have specifically called for it – as it did in 2006 in relation to the government of Sudan when attempting to modify the mandate of UNMIS.[67] It is not clear from the provisional records of the Security Council or from correspondence between the UN and Sierra Leone whether the state did consent. What is clear, however, is that the Security Council considered the mandate to have been modified by Resolution 1313, at least for a time.[68] Nor is it clear from the Security Council's provisional records whether the host state consented to the subsequent modification of the mandate when Resolution 1346 was adopted in March 2001.[69]

As to impartiality, if one adopts the broad definition of the concept as set out in the Brahimi Report – 'adherence to the principles of the Charter and to the objectives of a mandate that is rooted in those Charter principles'[70] – one might conclude that it existed throughout the operation. Certainly the Special Court for Sierra Leone found that it did on this basis.[71] But when exercising a more measured definition of the concept – such as that

SC/6801), 7 February 2000. The representative of Sierra Leone was present at a meeting of the Security Council on 11 May 2000 where SC Res 1299 was approved and endorsed the resolution (United Nations (Press Release), *Secretary-General Pleads with Council not to Fail People of Sierra Leone, Africa* (UN Doc S/6857), 11 May 2000).

[67] See chapter 6, section 6.

[68] When the Security Council renewed the mandate of UNAMSIL until 20 September 2000 (SC Res 1317 of 5 September 2000) and, again until 31 December (SC Res 1321 of 20 September 2000), it specifically invoked Resolutions 1270, 1289 *and* 1313. In extending the mandate to 31 March 2001, the Security Council, again, invoked Resolutions 1270, 1289 *and* 1313 (SC Res 1334 of 22 December 2000, para 6) and specifically recalled the objectives for UNAMSIL as set out in SC Res 1313 (ibid, para 3). However, as of March 2001, the Security Council only renewed the mandate for UNAMSIL as provided in Resolutions 1270 and 1289 (SC Res 1346 of 30 March 2001).

[69] See United Nations, *Provisional Record of the 4306th Meeting of the Security Council* (UN Doc S/PV.4306), 30 March 2001, at which SC Res 1346 of 30 March 2001 was passed.

[70] Brahimi Report (n 4) para 50.

[71] *Prosecutor v Issa Hassan Sesay, Morrison Kallon and Augustine Gbao* (Case No SCSL-04-15-T, Special Court for Sierra Leone, Trial Chamber I, 2 March 2009) paras 227 and 1907.

used by the Secretary-General in the context of UNEF I[72] – the question of UNAMSIL's impartiality is far less clear-cut. It would appear that there was a perception of partiality on the part of the RUF.[73]

2.2.2 *Constitutional Basis*

The Security Council explicitly stated that it was acting under Chapter VII in Resolution 1270, but only as regards a small part of UNAMSIL's mandate – protection of itself and civilians. Later, additional security-related tasks set out in Resolution 1289 were established through an invocation of Chapter VII in relation to the relevant paragraph.[74] As such, it would appear that certain of the operation's functions legally required host state consent, and other functions – namely those based on a mandatory decision under Chapter VII – did not.

UNAMSIL's mandate, pursuant to Resolutions 1270 and 1289, was established with the consent of the host state. As discussed in chapter 3, however, host state consent is not required for those aspects of a mandate where the Security Council relies on its mandatory Chapter VII powers – though it is required for other functions not so established. Of course, it may be noted that even where it is not legally required, host state consent is desirable for all functions, as a consenting host state is more likely to be cooperative, thereby increasing the likelihood that an operation will successfully carry out its mandate. Interestingly, the British representative on the Security Council made the following statement during the meeting at which a draft of Resolution 1289 was considered:

> UNAMSIL is not a Chapter VII peace enforcement operation, but we all recognized in formulating the mandate for the force, as set out in the draft resolution before us, that this task will require a robust and serious stance against possible threats.[75]

[72] Hammarskjold spoke of a force being 'impartial, in the sense that it does not serve as a means to force settlement, in the interests of one party, of political conflicts or legal issues recognized as controversial' (United Nations, *Report of the Secretary-General on Compliance with General Assembly Resolution 1123 (XI)* (UN Doc A/3512), 24 January 1957, para 5).

[73] Leaders of the RUF argued before the Special Court for Sierra Leone that they did not view the operation as impartial – an argument that was rejected by the Special Court as having no substance. (*Prosecutor v Issa Hassan Sesay, Morrison Kallon and Augustine Gbao* (n 71) para 1920).

[74] The Security Council's invocation of Chapter VII in relation to a particular paragraph of SC Res 1289 of 7 February 2000 (indicating that it was relying on the Chapter only in relation to the particular tasks set out in that paragraph) may be contrasted with the Security Council's practice in other resolutions of invoking Chapter VII in the final preambular paragraph (thereby signalling that the whole of the resolution fell under Chapter VII).

[75] United Nations, *Provisional Record of the 4099th Meeting of the Security Council* (UN Doc S/PV.4099), 7 February 2000, 4.

While he did not offer an explanation of how the Chapter VII functions of UNAMSIL differed from 'Chapter VII peace enforcement',[76] the basis for the British representative's comment may have been linked to the fact that the host state had consented to UNAMSIL's mandate as modified by Resolution 1289.

Whether host state consent was legally required for the modification of the mandate under Resolution 1313 (where Chapter VII was not invoked and no authorisation to use force was provided) depends on whether one accepts the argument that the Security Council, either by virtue of the nature of the functions assigned to the operation or by its recalling Resolutions 1270 and 1289, can somehow recall (or incorporate by reference) an invocation of Chapter VII. As discussed above,[77] it has traditionally been accepted that there is no formal requirement that the Security Council make an explicit finding of a triggering event, an explicit reference to an article within Chapter VII or even an explicit reference to Chapter VII. What is important is clear evidence of its intention. Given the Security Council's practice with regard to Resolutions 1270 and 1289 (where it did invoke Chapter VII and authorise UNAMSIL to take 'the necessary action'), the absence of an invocation of Chapter VII and its non-reliance on 'necessary action' language suggests that the Security Council did not intend that the forceful additional tasks bestowed under Resolution 1313 to have their basis in Chapter VII. It was perhaps for this reason that the Security Council was somewhat tentative – it did not decide to modify the mandate but only expressed an intention to do so, having taken into account the host state's views. As noted in section 2.2.1, however, the wording certainly does not make it clear that the mandate would not be modified until the host state consented.

Turning to the question of which provision under Chapter VII provides the constitutional basis for the tasks established under that Chapter, the level of force authorised must be considered. The fact that it was considerable and that significant force was, at times, used, indicates that it is not possible for the Chapter VII aspects of the operation to have their constitutional basis in Article 40 or 41. As discussed in chapter 3, neither provision provides for the use of force; Article 41 explicitly prohibits it. Even if one argues that a limited amount of force may be authorised under either article, it would be difficult to characterise the level of force authorised for UNAMSIL – and the level of force actually used – as limited. As such, the constitutional basis of the Chapter VII aspects of UNAMSIL's mandate must be found in Article 42.

[76] Secretary-General Annan made it clear that he too considered UNAMSIL to be other than 'peace-enforcement', even at a point when it had been made robust and had been authorised 'to take the necessary action to fulfil the additional tasks'. He did not, however, define peace-enforcement (see *Fourth Report of the Secretary-General* (n 18) 100).

[77] See chapter 3, section 3.2.1.

With regard to the constitutional basis of the additional, forceful tasks established by Resolution 1313, matters are less clear. Given that the Security Council did not directly rely on its mandatory Chapter VII powers in that resolution (as contrasted to its practice with Resolutions 1270 and 1289), it is difficult to find a clear intention to act under Chapter VII. Even assuming that the host state did consent – as noted, this is not clear – such consent may not provide a constitutional basis for the bestowal of forceful powers on an operation. This leaves two alternatives: to find that the Security Council was indeed acting under Chapter VII under Resolution 1313 – either by implication or by virtue of its reference to the earlier resolutions that did invoke Chapter VII in relation to certain tasks – or that the Security Council vested additional forceful tasks in UNAMSIL without a proper constitutional basis, ie it acted ultra vires its powers.

The other tasks – those not said to be based in Chapter VII – are consent-laws and would have their bases in Chapter VI or, possibly, a consent-based article in Chapter VII.

2.2.3 *Conclusion and Assessment of Success*

While the operation had many successes, the wisdom of granting it a militarised mandate requires further examination. Here, three major – and very much related – deficiencies may be observed: problems with the planning and staffing of the operation; difficulties with its command structure, as illustrated when it actually resorted to the use of force; and problems relating to the perception that UNAMSIL had lost its impartiality.

As regards the planning of the operation, it would appear that the Secretary-General was torn between acting promptly and in accordance with the wishes of the Security Council, on the one hand, and, on the other, telling 'the Security Council what it needs to know, not what it wants to hear, when recommending force and other resource levels for a new mission', as recommended by the Brahimi Report.[78] The operation was rushed into existence in the face of pressure from the Security Council and, in particular, the UK. The Secretary-General's original vision of the operation depended on ECOMOG providing security for UNAMSIL – an assumption that was unrealistic all along. Moreover, the handover of responsibilities from ECOMOG to UNAMSIL was not carefully planned or executed. In the words of a DPKO *Lessons Learned* report:

> In the first half of 2000, the UN was obliged to manage the deployment of the new UNAMSIL force, while also taking on the responsibilities of the withdrawing ECOMOG troops. There was no time for a planned and phased hand-over, resulting in considerable lack of co-operation and confusion. With ECOMOG

[78] Brahimi Report (n 4) x.

gone and UNAMSIL still not up to full strength, a security vacuum was created, which the rebels exploited.[79]

In advising the Security Council about the number of forces needed for UNAMSIL, the Secretary-General greatly underestimated the difficulty of the task; moreover, he did not appear to have due regard to the fact that members of UNAMSIL's predecessor, UNOMSIL, had been abducted by the rebel forces.[80] The Secretary-General's advice that, in the face of the departure of ECOMOG, there was 'no alternative' but to authorise a forceful UNAMSIL – indicating his assessment, presumably, that a quasi-enforcement operation was not politically possible – showed little regard for the past difficulties experienced in Somalia and the former Yugoslavia when peacekeeping operations took on enforcement-type tasks.

The Secretary-General's recommendations in relation to UNAMSIL would appear to be an example of 'cutting the suit to fit the cloth'. It appears likely that his recommendation regarding troop numbers was affected by his knowledge of how many troops states were willing to contribute. Given that it is an unfortunate truism of peacekeeping that as the mandate of an operation becomes more forceful states become less likely to volunteer troops,[81] it may be that the Secretary-General knew that 6,000 troops was all that was possible for UNAMSIL in late 1999 – and that 11,000 troops was the realistic upper limit for UNAMSIL under a militarised mandate in the political circumstances present in early 2000. If so, he would have faced the difficult choice of whether it was better to provide the Security Council with an unrealistic estimate of the number of forces required in order that the UN did *something* to try to preserve peace in Sierra Leone,[82] or to advise the Security Council that, in all the circumstances, a successful militarised peacekeeping operation was impossible.

While the latter approach might arguably have led to the establishment of a quasi-enforcement operation which was better suited to the task, it would appear that it was not politically acceptable, in light of the UK's

[79] *Lessons Learned* (n 25) 5.

[80] The Brahimi Report (n 4) observed: 'A mission such as UNAMSIL would probably not have faced the difficulties that it did in spring 2000 had it been provided with forces as strong as those currently keeping the peace as part of KFOR in Kosovo. The Panel is convinced that NATO military planners would not have agreed to deploy to Sierra Leone with only the 6,000 troops initially authorized' (106). At the same time the report recognised the fact that it was by no means clear that states would agree to provide troops for a KFOR-type force.

[81] The Brahimi Report (n 4) made a similar point when it observed that '[m]emories of peacekeepers murdered in Mogadishu and Kigali and taken hostage in Sierra Leone help to explain the difficulties Member States are having in convincing their national legislatures and public that they should support the deployment of their troops to United Nations-led operations, particularly in Africa' (105).

[82] The pressure from the Security Council, and in particular the UK, to make the force operational may also have been a factor here.

desire to see a forceful operation established as soon as possible.[83] The Secretary-General's approach would have been affected by his knowledge that, ultimately, the decision regarding the scope of the mandate rested with the Security Council. When the Secretary-General did exercise caution by not recommending a civilian protection mandate for the operation in its original form in October 1999, the Security Council showed a willingness to ignore this. The recommendation of the Brahimi Report that the Secretary-General refuse to go ahead with an operation until an adequate mandate was approved[84] is not realistic in the face of a determined Security Council.

If Annan expected the Security Council to be grateful to him for putting forward a proposal for an operation that was not of an optimal size, he would have been disappointed. When the May 2000 crisis occurred, government officials from Security Council Member States reportedly criticised Annan for encouraging the UN to begin an operation in Sierra Leone for which it lacked the military clout and had little prospect of getting a surge of support should the security situation deteriorate.[85] Presumably aware of this criticism – as well as the rebuke regarding the handling of the situation that was about to emerge from the Security Council on 4 August 2000 in its Resolution 1313[86] – the Secretary-General gave an interview to the *Washington Post*, which was published on 3 August 2000. In an opinion piece by Jim Hoagland, provocatively entitled 'Who Wants Peacekeeping? Put Up or Shut Up', Annan was quoted as offering a different perspective on the UNAMSIL's May crisis; he called on Security Council members to stop providing themselves with an alibi by passing peacekeeping resolutions that could not be implemented.[87]

[83] Indeed, among the 'lessons learned' by the DPKO in relation to UNAMSIL was the recognition 'that the pressure exercised by key members of the Security Council to speed up UNAMSIL's deployment in late 1999, early 2000 proved to be counter-productive, as the mission found itself spread thin on the ground and unable to meet emerging challenges, in particular, RUF attacks and intransigence' (*Lessons Learned* (n 25) 11). This remark would appear to be a reference to the UK, which as is illustrated by the Records of the Security Council, was pushing very hard for the operation in August and October 1999. See statements of the UK representative, eg United Nations (Press Release), *Security Council Establishes UN Mission for Sierra Leone to Aid with Implementation of Lomé Peace Agreement* (UN Doc SC/6742), 22 October 1999; United Nations (Press Release), *Security Council Expands Role of United Nations in Sierra Leone; More Military Personnel to Join Strengthened Observer Mission* (UN Doc SC/6714), 20 August 1999.

[84] Brahimi Report (n 4) para 60.

[85] Unattributed, 'West Exasperated by a Failed Intervention', *International Herald Tribune,* 16 May 2000. The report quoted a French diplomat as observing that Annan 'had considerable experience with peacekeeping in his old UN jobs and should have realized that the Security Council was risking its political credibility'. In addition, a US government official was quoted as saying, 'What may be on the point of eclipse is not just the credibility of the UN but also any prospect of humanitarian causes being a justification for international intervention'.

[86] In Res 1313, the Security Council observed that 'that the RUF offensive against UNAMSIL since May 2000 revealed serious inherent weaknesses in the mission's structure, command and control and resources' (SC Res 1313 of 4 August 2000, para 5). This statement would appear to have been directed at least in part at the Secretary-General as the architect of UNAMSIL's organisation and command structure.

[87] See the epigraph to this chapter.

By opting to recommend a force of 11,000, the Secretary-General effectively let the Security Council 'off the hook'. Instead of being in a position where it would be under pressure to authorise a quasi-enforcement force, the Security Council was able to point to the fact that it had done *something*, as recommended by the Security Council.

A second major criticism of the operation relates to its command difficulties. Its forces were unfamiliar with (or had different approaches to) the rules of engagement. In May 2000, shortly after UNAMSIL's mandate was strengthened and its troop numbers increased, hundreds of troops were taken hostage. Even when its numbers were strengthened and it began to use force against the rebels, various problems arose, including a lack of an effective command structure (with troops of certain nationality reportedly refusing to take orders) and a lack of adequate supplies. The fact that the UK sent in forces in the operation's darkest hour – and the fact that a British presence remained in Sierra Leone in different configurations throughout UNAMSIL's existence – was essential to the success of the peacekeeping operation. While the actions of that country are to be welcomed on one level, on another, the UK, due to its unwillingness to place significant numbers of its forces under UN command, undermined UNAMSIL by its apparent lack of confidence in a UN-led operation's ability to successfully carry out a militarised operation. In its *Lessons Learned* document the DPKO spoke of the possibility of differing perspectives between the UK and UNAMSIL, leading to 'unilateral action being taken . . . without coordination with the UN mission' and 'conflicting messages being sent to the Government of Sierra Leone [which] detracted from the common, coordinated international approach that was vital to the peace process'.[88] Moreover, there would appear to have been a certain amount of resentment on the part of UNAMSIL troops at the well-equipped British troops carrying out their own operations independently of UNAMSIL.[89] Despite this unwillingness to see its troops serving under UNAMSIL,[90] Britain nevertheless used its influence to hasten the establishment of the operation and to push other states to contribute troops.[91]

[88] *Lessons Learned* (n 25) 14.

[89] After 11 British soldiers were kidnapped in Sierra Leone on 25 August 2000, the deputy commander of UNAMSIL, Nigerian Brigadier-General Mohammed Garba, was critical of the British forces. He was quoted as saying that 'they had been travelling in a notoriously dangerous area without liaising with UNAMSIL. Garba said that it was not an isolated action and that the British had been carrying out "these Rambo movements" for months' (46 *Keesing's Record of World Events*, August 2000, 43695).

[90] With the exception of some seven troops (see www.un.org/en/peacekeeping/resources/statistics, accessed 1 April 2011).

[91] As reported in *The Economist* at the time: 'Britain is trying to press other countries, especially middle-ranking ones, to offer troops to Sierra Leone. But its reluctance to allow its own troops to serve under UN command undermines Britain's pleas' (unattributed, 'The UN's Frontier Force', *The Economist*, 4 November 2000, 50).

Third, the militarised nature of UNAMSIL's mandate meant it was perceived as enforcement. As noted, the RUF argued that it came to see UNAMSIL as the enemy – a force that was empowered to forcibly disarm it – and the RUF maintained that its use of force was in reaction to that perception. It considered the UN to be an opponent, rather than a neutral party. This sense that UNAMSIL was partisan appeared to extend to the entire operation, including the unarmed civilian observers attached to it. As a result, in its attacks, the RUF did not appear to make any distinction between the unarmed civilian observers attached to UNAMSIL and UNAMSIL troops authorised to act militarily.[92] Instead, the rebels appeared to take the view that once the peacekeeping operation became militarised, all peacekeepers were to be considered a threat.

3. EAST TIMOR (OCTOBER 1999–MAY 2002 AND MAY 2002–MAY 2005)

3.1 Mandate and Functioning

The United Nations Mission in East Timor (UNAMET) was established in June 1999 and was charged with conducting a popular consultation to ascertain whether the East Timorese wanted full independence or autonomy within Indonesia.[93] Responsibility for the maintenance of peace and security in relation to this consultation was to fall to the Indonesian government.[94] Following the announcement of the result of the popular consultation – 78.5 per cent rejected autonomy in favour of outright independence – pro-Indonesian forces, at times with the support of the Indonesian security forces, launched a campaign of looting and arson throughout the territory.[95] The Indonesian authorities did not respond

[92] The incident beginning on 1 May 2000 involved the RUF forces demanding that some military observers working for the mission (not troops, but unarmed observers) hand over five disarmed combatants and their weapons. 'In the course of these discussions, the RUF combatants detained three UNAMSIL military observers as well as four UNAMSIL peacekeepers of the Kenyan battalion who were providing security at that location' (*Fourth Report of the Secretary-General* (n 18) para 57).

[93] SC Res 1246 of 11 June 1999. This mission is not identified as peacekeeping by the Security Council in SC Res 1246 nor by the Secretary-General in his Report to the Security Council on which the decision to establish the mission is based (*United Nations, Question of East Timor: Report of the Secretary-General* (UN Doc S/1999/595), 22 May 1999). Nor does it appear as a peacekeeping mission on the website of the DPKO (www.un.org/en/peacekeeping/documents/operationslist.pdf, accessed 1 April 2011).

[94] SC Res 1246, ibid, paras 9 and 10. In the words of one commentator, the UN had 'meekly accepted Jakarta's assurances that an international force was unnecessary because Indonesia would provide security before and after the referendum' (Findlay (n 24) 287).

[95] Information from the DPKO website, www.un.org/peace/etimor/UntaetB.htm (accessed 1 April 2011). It continued: 'Many East Timorese were killed and as many as 500,000 were displaced from their homes, about half leaving the territory, in some cases [being required to do so] by force').

effectively to the violence and a large part of UNAMET was evacuated due to safety concerns.[96]

Although UNAMET was a small operation with a very specific purpose, its evacuation in the face of violence against the East Timorese led some to liken it to the UN's peacekeeping operations in Rwanda and the former Yugoslavia.[97] Sensitive to this criticism, the Secretary-General called for action to protect the people of East Timor.[98] At a session of the Security Council on 11 September 1999, various states called upon Indonesia to consent to the deployment of a quasi-enforcement force.[99] According to the Russian delegate, it was imperative that two conditions be met before an international force could be dispatched to East Timor: (1) the Indonesian government must consent, and (2) the force must be endorsed by the Security Council.[100] The Secretary-General implored Indonesia to consent:

> Once again I urge Indonesia to agree without further delay to the deployment of an international force. The international community is asking for Indonesia's consent to the deployment of such a force. But I hope it is clear that it does so out of deference to Indonesia's position as a respected member of the community of States.[101]

The last sentence suggests that the request for consent was made to avoid embarrassment to Indonesia, rather than owing to a belief that it was legally necessary. It may also have been considered necessary in order to ensure that certain permanent Member States of the Security Council did not use their vetoes. What is clear, however, is that there is no *legal* obligation to obtain the consent of a host state for a quasi-enforcement operation such as the one proposed. As discussed previously, by virtue of being party to the UN Charter, all states have effectively pre-consented to the Security Council establishing mandatory enforcement measures.[102]

In September 1999, having secured the consent of a reluctant Indonesia,[103] the Security Council established an Australian-led quasi-enforcement

[96] 'A small team of UNAMET staff remained in the UN Headquarters in Dili to ensure the safety of non-UN staff who had sought refuge there' (ibid).

[97] Findlay (n 24) 287. See also W Maley, 'The UN and East Timor' (2000) 12(1) *Pacific Review* 74 (referred to in Findlay (n 24)).

[98] Findlay (n 24) 287.

[99] Regardless of the legitimacy of any claim by Portugal to be entitled de jure to represent East Timor, Indonesia's de facto authority over the territory was clear.

[100] United Nations, *Provisional Record of the 4043rd Meeting of the Security Council* (UN Doc S/PV.4043), 11 September 1999, 15.

[101] ibid, 3.

[102] See discussion in chapter 3, section 3.2.4.3.

[103] The United States representative to the Security Council stressed that Indonesia must allow the international presence in East Timor, noting ominously that '[t]he Government of Indonesia must understand that, unless it followed the right course, it would suffer irreparable damage in its international relations' (United Nations (Press Release), *Security Council Hears 52 Speakers in Open Debate on Situation in East Timor* (UN Doc S/6924), 11 September 1999, summarising the statement of the US representative, Richard Holbrooke). The next day, on 12 September, the President of Indonesia made a statement 'in which he expressed

operation, the International Force for East Timor (INTERFET), 'to restore peace and security in East Timor, to protect and support UNAMET in carrying out its tasks and, within force capabilities, to facilitate humanitarian assistance operations'.[104] The Security Council determined that the situation in East Timor constituted a threat to peace and security and, acting under Chapter VII, authorised INTERFET to 'take all necessary measures' to fulfil its mandate.[105]

INTERFET began deployment on 20 September 1999[106] and, as of 30 September, it numbered 4,300 troops, of whom 3,300 were Australians.[107] By November it had grown to 9,300 troops, over half of whom were from Australia.[108] An agreement was entered into whereby the Indonesian Armed Forces agreed to cooperate with INTERFET.[109] After the arrival of INTERFET, the Indonesian army reduced its strength greatly, such that there were only some 1,200 personnel, limited to the Dili area, and military and police personnel withdrew entirely from the rest of the territory.[110] Aside from a few incidents,[111] INTERFET was not required to use substantial force; no INTERFET troops were killed in military action.[112] In the words of the Secretary-General writing in January 2000, '[i]nternal security has greatly improved, owing to the activities of [INTERFET]'.[113]

the readiness of Indonesia to accept an international peacekeeping force through the United Nations in East Timor' (SC Res 1264 of 15 September 1999). According to Findlay, the threat was even more overt: 'In a classic case of "coerced consent", the USA told Indonesia that if it did not permit the deployment of a peace operation it would lose all financial support from the World Bank and the International Monetary Fund' (Findlay (n 24) 288, relying on J Martinkus, *A Dirty Little War: An Eyewitness Account of East Timor's Descent into Hell, 1997–2000* (Sydney, Random House Australia, 2001) 349).

[104] SC Res 1264 of 15 September 1999.

[105] ibid, para 3.

[106] United Nations, *Question of East Timor: Progress Report of the Secretary-General [to the General Assembly]* (UN Doc A/54/654), 13 December 1999, para 13.

[107] Australian Department of Defence (Defence Public Affairs Organisation) (Press Release), *Operations Update East Timor*, 30 September 1999, http://pandora.nla.gov.au/parchive/2000/S2000-Nov-7/easttimor.defence.gov.au/Galleries/templates/templates/6294086dc.html (accessed 1 April 2011).

[108] Australian Department of Defence (Defence Public Affairs Organisation) (Press Release), *Operations Update East Timor*, 4 November 1999, http://pandora.nla.gov.au/parchive/2000/S2000-Nov-7/easttimor.defence.gov.au/Galleries/templates/templates/62940cc22.html (accessed 1 April 2011).

[109] The cooperation was to take place through a 'Joint Consultative Security Group' (United Nations, *Report of the Secretary-General on the Situation in East Timor* (UN Doc S/1999/1024), 4 October 1999, para 8).

[110] United Nations, *Report of the Secretary-General on the United Nations Transitional Administration in East Timor* (UN Doc S/2000/53), 26 January 2000, paras 35 and 36.

[111] Included here was a gun battle on 6 October 1999 in which two Australian soldiers were wounded and two militiamen were killed, and several incidents along the border with East Timor, including one on 17 October where Australian soldiers shot and killed three militiamen after the soldiers were ambushed (see Findlay (n 24) 289–91).

[112] ibid, 291.

[113] *Report of the Secretary-General* (n 110) para 2.

At the same time as it established INTERFET, the Security Council resolved that a United Nations peacekeeping operation should be established to take over from INTERFET 'as soon as possible'[114] and invited the Secretary-General to make prompt recommendations in this regard.[115] In October 1999, the Secretary-General recommended the establishment of a transitional operation, the UN Transitional Administration in East Timor (UNTAET), and recommended that it be given a 'robust mandate' and be charged with, inter alia, providing security, maintaining law and order, and providing interim law enforcement services.[116] The United Nations force was to have security-related tasks, including disarmament,[117] and the Secretary-General recommended 'robust rules of engagement and a rapid reaction capability'.[118]

On 25 October 1999, UNTAET was established by the Security Council 'in accordance with the Report of the Secretary-General'.[119] Though less forceful than INTERFET, aspects of UNTAET's mandate were still were of such a nature that considerable force might be required.[120] UNTAET was to feature a 'governance and public administration component, including an international police element with a strength of up to 1,640 officers; a humanitarian assistance and emergency rehabilitation component; and a military component, with up to 8,950 troops and up to 200 military observers.[121]

Resolution 1272 characterised the continuing situation in East Timor as 'a threat to peace and security'[122] and the Security Council invoked Chapter VII in relation to the whole of the resolution, not just certain para-

[114] SC Res 1264 of 15 September 1999, para 10. According to Findlay (n 24) 294, 'The Australians, conscious of the financial and political costs . . . of being the lead nation for INTERFET had pressed for a UN follow-on peacekeeping force'.

[115] SC Res 1264, ibid, para 11. The Security Council also called on the Secretary-General to 'plan and prepare for a United Nations transitional administration in East Timor, incorporating a United Nations peacekeeping operation' (ibid). The question of where the envisaged 'transitional administration' ends and the 'peacekeeping operation' begins was not entirely clear.

[116] *Report of the Secretary-General* (n 109) paras 28 and 57–58.

[117] 'The tasks of the United Nations force would be to maintain a secure environment throughout the territory of East Timor, to provide direct security for United Nations personnel and property, to monitor the prompt and complete withdrawal of any remaining Indonesian military and security personnel, to take measures to disarm and demobilize armed groups and to assist humanitarian activities as appropriate, including the safe return of refugees and internally displaced persons.' ibid, para 75.

[118] ibid, paras 76–77.

[119] SC Res 1272 of 25 October 1999. UNTAET took over from INTERFET on 28 February 2000 (Findlay (n 24) 295). Its was to comprise over 10,000 personnel, including a military component of 8,950 troops (SC Res 1272, para 4).

[120] The Secretary-General indicated that the military capability of UNTAET was to 'be close to that of INTERFET' and UNTAET would 'adopt a firm posture in maintaining security throughout the Territory' (*Report of the Secretary-General* (n 110) para 27).

[121] United Nations Press Release, *Security Council Establishes UN Transitional Administration in East Timor for Initial Period until 31 January 2001* (UN Doc SC/6745), 25 October 1999, www.un.org/News/Press/docs/1999/19991025.sc6745.doc.html (accessed 1 April 2011).

[122] SC Res 1272 of 25 October 1999, penultimate preambular paragraph. The significance of its use of the phrase 'threat to peace and security' instead of the usual 'threat to international peace and security' is unclear.

graphs.[123] Similarly, the resolution authorised UNTAET to 'take all necessary measures' to fulfil the entirety of its mandate; it did not limit this authority to particular tasks or to the military component of the force.[124] UNTAET's military component was charged with, inter alia, providing security and maintaining law and order in the territory, ensuring delivery of humanitarian assistance, providing security for UN personnel and property, and disarming and demobilising armed groups.[125] As to civilian protection, the Security Council called upon 'all parties to cooperate with humanitarian and human rights organizations so as to ensure their safety [and] the protection of civilians'.[126] Subsequently, by Resolution 1319, the Security Council authorised UNTAET to 'respond robustly to the militia threat in East Timor'.[127]

The handover of security matters from INTERFET to UNTAET took place in stages during February 2000,[128] with some 70 per cent of troops being re-hatted from INTERFET to UNTAET.[129] UNTAET inherited a territory with security largely restored.[130] This fact, along with the fact that UNTAET's largest contributor, Australia,[131] had shown itself not to be shy of using considerable force where warranted in its capacity as INTERFET's largest contributor, would appear to account in large part for UNTAET's success in maintaining security. Additionally, changes in the Indonesian government meant that relations between East Timor and Indonesia had improved dramatically by the time UNTAET began functioning. Where there were security breaches, they were generally limited in nature and there was little call for the use of force by UNTAET.[132] By mid-2000, the security situation was sufficiently improved[133] that the Secretary-General

[123] ibid, final preambular paragraph.

[124] SC Res 1272 of 25 October 1999, para 4.

[125] SC Res 1272 ibid, para 2. See also *Report of the Secretary-General* (n 109). This report was noted by the Security Council in SC Res 1272, ibid, preamble.

[126] SC Res 1272, ibid, para 10.

[127] SC Res 1319 of 20 September 2000, para 6. This phrasing was used in a subsequent resolution extending the mission to 31 January 2002 (SC Res 1338 of 31 January 2001, para 7).

[128] United Nations, *Report of the Secretary-General on the United Nations Transitional Administration in East Timor (for the Period 27 January–26 July 2000)* (UN Doc S/2000/738), 26 July 2000, para 51.

[129] Australian Department of Defence (Defence Public Affairs Organisation) (Press Release), *East Timor Transition Begins*, 7 November 2000, http://pandora.nla.gov.au/parchive/2000/S2000-Nov-7/easttimor.defence.gov.au/Galleries/templates/templates/747294db.html (accessed 1 April 2011).

[130] Findlay (n 24) 295.

[131] As of July 2000, Australia provided 1,542 of the 8,032 troops involved in the mission (*Report of the Secretary-General* (n 128) para 55).

[132] However, such incidents resulted in the deaths of two peacekeepers in July and August 2000 (United Nations, *Report of the Secretary-General on the United Nations Transitional Administration in East Timor (for the Period 27 July 2000–16 January 2001)* (UN Doc S/2001/42), 16 January 2001, para 10).

[133] 'Since mid-2000 the security situation has improved dramatically, border incursions from the West have to all intents and purposes ended, and there have been no major uses of force' (Findlay (n 24) 296).

implied that the aim of making UNTAET 'sufficiently robust so as not to invite challenges after it took over from INTERFET'[134] had been met and indicated that a reduction in troops would be appropriate if the security situation remained stable.[135] In November 2001, UNTAET began to reduce its military component.[136]

In May 2002, corresponding with the declaration of independence of East Timor,[137] the Security Council passed Resolution 1410 establishing the United Nations Mission of Support in East Timor (UNMISET) to replace UNTAET.[138] Resolution 1410 contained no explicit finding of a threat to peace and security. Instead it noted

> the existence of challenges to the short and long-term security and stability of an independent East Timor and determin[ed] that ensuring the security of the boundaries of East Timor and preserving its internal and external stability is necessary for the maintenance of peace and security in the region.[139]

In Resolution 1410 the Security Council did not invoke Chapter VII in a preambular paragraph (as it had in Resolution 1272), thereby placing the whole of the resolution under its Chapter VII authority. Instead it invoked Chapter VII in one paragraph only: the same paragraph in which it authorised the use of force. It authorised UNMISET 'under Chapter VII of the Charter of the United Nations, to take the necessary actions, for the duration of its mandate, to fulfil its mandate'.[140] Its mandated tasks included providing interim law enforcement and public security and contributing to the maintenance of the external and internal security of the country.[141] Aside from its general security obligations, the resolution did not include a civilian protection mandate.

With up to 5,000 troops authorised,[142] UNMISET's military component was smaller than that of UNTAET. Once again Australia was the largest

[134] *Report of the Secretary-General* (n 128) para 56.

[135] ibid. Certain, relatively minor, setbacks prevented this from occurring immediately (*Report of the Secretary-General* (n 132) paras 10–11).

[136] United Nations, *Report of the Secretary-General on the United Nations Transitional Administration in East Timor (for the Period 16 October 2001–18 January 2002)* (UN Doc S/2002/80), 17 January 2002, para 70.

[137] From this point forward the country is referred to in UN documents as 'Timor Leste' and it was under that name that the country was granted membership in the UN on 27 September 2002. To avoid confusion, the country will be referred to as 'East Timor' throughout.

[138] SC Res 1410 of 17 May 2002.

[139] ibid, final preambular paragraph.

[140] ibid, para 6.

[141] ibid, para 2. While the Security Council invoked Chapter VII only in relation to paragraph 6 – instead of invoking it in the preamble such that it would apply to the whole of the mandate as it had done with UNTAET – the impact of this change in approach would appear very limited. After all, the wording of para 6 makes it clear that the Chapter VII authorisation therein applies to the whole of the mandate (as detailed elsewhere in the resolution), for its entire duration.

[142] ibid, para 3.

contributor of troops (1,300), followed by Portugal (733), Japan (690) and New Zealand (658) – all states with sophisticated militaries.[143] The operation was envisaged as being of short duration, with the Security Council expressing its view that downsizing was to proceed 'as quickly as possible' once certain targets had been met, in the same resolution in which it established the operation.[144] The full complement of 5,000 troops was put in place immediately.[145] Despite a series of security-related incidents in late 2002/early 2003, UNMISET only occasionally relied on force and, as far as can be ascertained, never used offensive force.

In April 2005 UNMISET was succeeded by the United Nations Office in Timor-Leste (UNOTIL), a 'one-year, follow-on special political mission'.[146] This operation, which was not characterised as peacekeeping by the DPKO,[147] did not have a security function and was not established under Chapter VII.[148] As UNOTIL was winding down in May 2006, 'a political, humanitarian and security crisis of major dimensions'[149] developed. In a letter to the Secretary-General dated 24 May 2006, the government of East Timor cited a 'deterioration of the internal security conditions' and advised the Secretary-General that it had requested 'as a matter of urgency' assistance from the governments of Portugal, Australia, New Zealand and Malaysia in order to re-establish security.[150] The Secretary-General welcomed the force[151] and engaged in bilateral conversations with the Prime Ministers of the four countries, each of whom indicated his or her intention to send forces. This force, which came to be referred to as the 'Combined Task Force'[152] or the 'International Stabilisation Force'

[143] DPKO website, www.un.org/en/peacekeeping/contributors/2002/May2002_3.pdf (accessed 1 April 2011).

[144] SC Res 1410 of 17 May 2002, para 7.

[145] Indeed there were 5,082 troops as of 31 May 2002, according to the DPKO website; see www.un.org/en/peacekeeping/contributors/2002/May2002_4.pdf (accessed 1 April 2011).

[146] SC Res 1599 of 28 April 2005, para 1. The Security Council was to extend UNOTIL's mandate for a few months beyond its original one-year existence (see SC Res 1677 of 12 May 2006, para 1; SC Res 1690 of 20 June 2006, para 1; and SC Res 1703 of 18 August 2006, para 1).

[147] United Nations (DPKO), peacekeeping website, www.un.org/en/peacekeeping (accessed 1 April 2011).

[148] In establishing the operation the Security Council did not characterise the situation in East Timor as a threat to international peace and security.

[149] From the DPKO website, www.un.org/en/peacekeeping/missions/unmit/background.shtml (accessed 1 April 2011).

[150] United Nations, *Letter Dated 24 May 2006 from the Secretary-General Addressed to the President of the Security Council [Including, as Annex 1, 'Letter Dated 24 May 2006 from the President, Prime Minister and Speaker of the National Parliament of Timor-Leste Addressed to the Secretary-General']* (UN Doc S/2006/319), 24 May 2006.

[151] United Nations, *Letter Dated 26 May 2006 from the Secretary-General Addressed to the President of the Security Council* (UN Doc S/2006/338), 26 May 2006.

[152] The Secretary-General referred to the force in this manner in United Nations, *Report of the Secretary-General on Timor-Leste Pursuant to UN Security Council Resolution 1690 (2006)* (UN Doc S/2006/628), 8 August 2006, para 117.

(ISF),[153] arrived on 26 May 2006 and began securing key installations in the country.[154] The Security Council expressed its 'appreciation and full support' for the ISF.[155]

In August 2006 the Security Council established the United Nations Integrated Mission in Timor-Leste (UNMIT) as a 'follow-on mission' to UNOTIL.[156] Despite the recommendation of the Secretary-General that UNMIT have a security section, including a military component of approximately 350 armed and unarmed troops,[157] and the request of the government of East Timor that military operations take place under UN command,[158] UNMIT was not established as a militarised peacekeeping operation.[159] Instead, military functions were to continue to be entrusted to the ISF,[160] reportedly because Australia refused to allow its forces (which made up the bulk of the ISF) to serve under UN command.[161] Since August 2006, UNMIT's mandate has been renewed annually.[162]

The security situation in the country has been fragile, with outbreaks of violence in February and August 2007[163] and attacks against the President and Prime Minister on 11 February 2008.[164] In February 2009, the Security Council cited 'improvements in the political and security situation in Timor-Leste, which has recovered from the 2006 crisis and the events of 11 February 2008' but noted that the 'political and security situation, although generally calm, remains fragile'.[165] In February 2010, the Security Council noted the 'general stability through further improvements in the political and security situation' in the country.[166] As of February 2010,

[153] See Australian Government, Department of Foreign Affairs and Trade website, www.dfat.gov.au/geo/east_timor/east_timor_brief.html (accessed 1 April 2011).

[154] *Report of the Secretary-General* (n 152) para 10.

[155] SC Res 1690 of 20 June 2006, para 2.

[156] Unlike UNOTIL, UNMIT *is* classified as 'peacekeeping' by the DPKO (www.un.org/en/peacekeeping/missions/unmit/background.shtml, accessed 1 April 2011).

[157] United Nations, *Report of the Secretary-General on Timor-Leste Pursuant to UN Security Council Resolution 1690 (2006)* (UN Doc S/2006/628), 8 August 2006, para 118.

[158] ibid.

[159] It was, however, granted up to 1,608 police personnel and up to 34 military liaison and staff officers and charged with supporting the government and ensuring the restoration of pubic security (SC Res 1704 of 25 August 2006).

[160] ibid, para 5.

[161] La'o Hamutuk, *Submission to the Parliament of Australia Joint Standing Committee on Foreign Affairs, Defence and Trade, Inquiry into Human Rights Mechanisms and the Asia-Pacific*, November 2008, www.laohamutuk.org/Justice/08LHSubOz.pdf (accessed 1 April 2011), 2.

[162] SC Res 1802 of 25 February 2008; SC Res 1867 of 26 February 2009; SC Res 1912 of 26 February 2010; SC Res 1969 of 24 February 2011 (renewing UNMIT's mandate until 26 February 2012).

[163] United Nations, *Report of the Secretary-General on the United Nations Integrated Mission in Timor-Leste (for the Period from 27 January to 20 August 2007)* (UN Doc S/2007/513), 28 August 2007, para 16. See also UN News Centre, 'New Unrest Flares in Timor-Leste, UN Police Reports', 23 August 2007.

[164] SC Res 1802 of 25 February 2008.

[165] SC Res 1867 of 26 February 2009.

[166] SC Res 1912 of 26 February 2010.

ISF forces deployed by the governments of Australia and New Zealand remained in East Timor; however, in view of the improvements in the security situation there, their numbers were reduced in 2009 and reduced further in 2010.[167]

3.2 Evaluation

3.2.1 Adherence to the 'Fundamental Principles'

The whole of UNTAET was established under Chapter VII, and it was authorised to use 'all necessary measures' to fulfil its entire mandate. With UNMISET, however, the Security Council did not invoke Chapter VII in respect of the whole of Resolution 1410; rather it invoked the Chapter selectively, in relation to a single paragraph. That paragraph was the same one in which UNMISET was authorised to 'take the necessary actions, for the duration of its mandate, to fulfil its mandate'. Despite the Security Council's different approaches to the two operations, their level of entitlement to use force was the same: each was authorised to take 'all necessary measures' (UNTAET) or 'the necessary actions' (UNMISET) in relation to the entirety of its mandate, and for each Chapter VII was invoked in relation to all mandated tasks. In short, both operations were authorised to use force beyond self-defence in carrying out all of their mandated tasks.

As to host state consent, neither UNTAET nor UNMISET, both of which featured an invocation of Chapter VII for all mandated tasks, required it. Normally, in an operation such as UNMISET, where Chapter VII was invoked selectively, host state consent is legally required for those aspects of the mandate where the Security has *not* acted under Chapter VII. However, given that, with UNMISET, the single-paragraph invocation of Chapter VII in Resolution 1410 applied to the whole of the mandate, for its entire duration, the effect was the same as if the whole mandate had been established under Chapter VII: host state consent was not legally required for the entire mandate. While consent was forthcoming for both operations, in neither case was its existence in the circumstances a decisive indicator that it was legally required. In the same way that the Security Council's call for Indonesia to consent to INTERFET would appear to have been motivated by non-legal reasons, the Security Council's emphasis on Indonesia's consent to UNTAET[168] and the fact that the newly

[167] United Nations, *Report of the Secretary-General on the United Nations Integrated Mission in Timor-Leste (for the Period from 24 September 2009 to 20 January 2010)* (UN Doc S/2010/85), 12 February 2010, para 19.

[168] SC Res 1272 refers to SC Res 1264, which, in turn, welcomes 'the statement by the President of Indonesia on 12 September 1999 in which he expressed the readiness of Indonesia to accept an international peacekeeping force through the United Nations in East Timor' (SC Res 1264 of 15 September 1999).

independent East Timor had consented to UNMISET would appear to have been motivated by a variety of reasons, unrelated to legal need. These reasons might include a desire to pay due deference to the host state (put another way, to help it to avoid embarrassment) and/or a desire to ensure state cooperation. On the question of the impartiality of UNTAET and UNMISET, there is nothing to indicate that either operation was anything but impartial.

3.2.2 *Constitutional Basis*

Given the differing approaches of the Security Council to the invocation of Chapter VII in the resolutions establishing UNTAET and UNMISET, the two operations are, prime facie, different in nature. Ralph Zacklin, the UN's Assistant Secretary-General for Legal Affairs from 1998 to 2005, described UNTAET as having been 'established under Chapter VII', whereas he wrote of UNMISET: '[I]ts mandate was not adopted under Chapter VII; however, the Security Council authorized it "under Chapter VII . . . to take the necessary actions, for the duration of its mandate, to fulfil its mandate".'[169] In short, he distinguished between peacekeeping operations with a Chapter VII mandate and peacekeeping operations without such a mandate but charged with Chapter VII tasks. As we shall see when we come to consider subsequent militarised peacekeeping operations, the Security Council's decision to selectively invoke Chapter VII and/or selectively (ie only in relation to one or more paragraphs in a resolution) authorise the use of 'the necessary action' or 'all necessary measures' can be significant. However, with UNTAET and UNMISET, little turns on the Security Council having taken distinct approaches: while it invoked Chapter VII and authorised the use of force beyond self-defence in one paragraph only, the fact that that paragraph affected the whole mandate, for its duration, puts the operation, to all intents and purposes, in the same position it would have been in if the Security Council had invoked Chapter VII and authorised 'the necessary action' for the entire mandate. The question arises, then, as to which article of Chapter VII formed the basis for the establishment of UNTAET and for UNAMSIL's authorisation to 'take the necessary action'.

One scholar has voiced the view that Article 41 provides the constitutional basis for UNTAET, given its functioning as a territorial administration in East Timor.[170] However, the fact that it was authorised to use

[169] Ralph Zacklin, 'The Use of Force in Peacekeeping Operations' in Niels Blokker and Nico Schrijver (eds), *The Security Council and the Use of Force: Theory and Reality – A Need for Change?* (Dordrecht, Martinus Nijhoff, 2005) 91–106, 97.

[170] Michael Bothe, 'Peace-Keeping' in Bruno Simma (ed), *The Charter of the United Nations: A Commentary*, 2nd edn, vol 1 (Oxford, Oxford University Press, 2002) 648–700, 685 para 87, who considers UNTAET to be an Art 41 operation despite its authorisation to use all necessary measures.

'all necessary measures' to fulfil its mandate means that neither it nor UNMISET ('the necessary actions') may be said to comport with the wording of Article 41, which calls for 'measures not involving the use of armed force'. Even if one wishes to take the view that an authorisation to use some limited or incidental level of force beyond self-defence could comport with the wording of that article,[171] the fact that the operations were authorised to use 'all necessary measures' or to take 'the necessary actions' means that such an argument impossible to make. Nor, given the level of force authorised for both operations, can either be said to be an Article 40 operation. Again, an argument that Article 40 can provide the basis for a limited use of force has been made by some; however, in neither case is the force authorised limited.

The only remaining article that can provide the constitutional basis for UNTAET and UNMISET is Article 42.

3.2.3 Conclusion and Assessment of Success

The use of force by the militarised peacekeeping operations in East Timor was limited in nature, and their role in preserving security was largely successful.[172] This was due to a variety of factors unique to these particular operations, including the relatively small size of East Timor; the willingness of Australia – a militarily sophisticated country with interests in the region – to lead a related quasi-enforcement operation in a forceful way and then to allow its troops to be re-hatted as UN peacekeepers;[173] the fact that the two peacekeeping operations were fully staffed almost immediately; the fact that the relevant governments cooperated with the missions; and the fact that, in both cases, the security threats were of a relatively limited nature.[174]

Nevertheless, as we have seen, even with all these favourable factors in place, there were difficulties. UNMISET's departure needed to be delayed, with the Secretary-General conceding over-optimism in making recommendations regarding the number of troops necessary for the mission. The situation in East Timor continues to be problematic. Currently we see a return to non-militarised peacekeeping in East Timor, with UNMIT operating alongside a forceful government-led action force, the ISF. The Australian government's unwillingness to allow its forces to serve in a militarised peacekeeping operation, after having done so earlier with

[171] See discussion in chapter 3, section 3.2.3.2.

[172] The success is mitigated somewhat by the resumption of violence in May 2006; however, this would appear to be more in the nature of post-conflict difficulties, rather than an all-out deterioration of peace.

[173] Findlay (n 24) 292.

[174] ibid, 293.

UNTAET and UNMISET, may provide an insight into Australia's view of the suitability of militarised peacekeeping.[175]

4. DEMOCRATIC REPUBLIC OF THE CONGO (NOVEMBER 1999–30 JUNE 2010 AND JULY 1 2010–PRESENT)

4.1 Mandate and Functioning

In May 1997 the government of the Democratic Republic of the Congo was overthrown by Laurent Kabila, with the aid of forces from Uganda and Rwanda. These two states, however, were to turn against Kabila, leading him to seek help from Zimbabwe, Namibia and Angola, which sent forces to support him in August 1998, making the conflict trans-regional in nature.[176] Such was its scope that the conflict in the DRC was described by some as 'Africa's First World War'.[177] On 10 July 1999 the DRC and various neighbouring states (Angola, Namibia, Rwanda, Uganda and Zimbabwe) signed the Lusaka Ceasefire Agreement (LCA) which, inter alia, provided for all foreign forces to withdraw from the DRC.[178] The Security Council welcomed the LCA on 6 August and authorised the deployment of up to 90 UN military liaison personnel to the DRC and the other signatory states to liaise with parties and provide assistance.[179]

In November 1999, the Security Council transformed the military liaison team into the United Nations Organization Mission in the Democratic Republic of the Congo (MONUC).[180] Initially MONUC's functions were similar to those of the liaison team.[181] However, in February 2000 the Security Council passed Resolution 1291,[182] which characterised the situation in the DRC as a threat to international peace and security in the region,[183] increased MONUC's size to up to 5,537 military personnel, and

[175] Australian Foreign Minister Alexander Downer expressed that country's preference that its troops 'remain under our command and . . . that we have that sort of control over them'. He did not, however, cite reasons for the position. Unattributed, 'Australian Troops Independent of UN in Timor', *Sydney Morning Herald*, 26 August 2006.

[176] Christine Gray, *International Law and the Use of Force*, 3rd edn (Oxford, Oxford University Press, 2008) 69.

[177] See eg United Nations, *Thirty-First Report of the Secretary-General on the United Nations Organization Mission in the Democratic Republic of the Congo* (UN Doc S/2010/164), 30 March 2010, para 112.

[178] Lusaka Ceasefire Agreement of 10 July 1999 (UN Doc S/1999/815).

[179] SC Res 1258 of 6 August 1999, paras 1 and 8.

[180] SC Res 1279 of 30 November 1999, para 4. The acronym reflects the operation's French title: Mission de l'Organisation de Nations Unies en République Démocratique du Congo.

[181] ibid, para 5. In the resolution establishing MONUC, the Security Council requested that the Secretary-General submit recommendations on a further deployment (ibid, para 8).

[182] SC Res 1291 of 24 February 2000.

[183] ibid, final preambular paragraph.

expanded its mandate.[184] The Security Council authorised MONUC under Chapter VII to take such 'necessary action . . . as it deems within its capabilities' to protect civilians under imminent threat of physical violence.[185] Its rules of engagement 'made clear that force could be used beyond self-defence to ensure security and freedom of movement of MONUC and to afford protection to civilians under imminent threat of physical violence'.[186] From the outset, concern was expressed as to whether the force could realistically be expected to achieve its mandate given its limited resources. In the words of the Canadian delegate to the Security Council: 'Our main concern about this draft resolution, expressed repeatedly during the negotiations leading to its final form, is that the draft resolution does not match the Mission's mandate with the resources needed to guarantee its success.'[187] His candid assessment was that 'factors, such as cost aversion and outside political realities, [had] influenced the Council's decision-making in this instance'.[188]

The Security Council's decision to grant the operation a civilian protection mandate in the circumstances proved to be nothing more than a paper exercise, an empty gesture. The profound incongruity of MONUC being tasked with civilian protection was highlighted by the fact that it was itself dependent on the parties to the LCA to provide its personnel with security.[189] During the first year of MONUC's existence, misgivings that the resources given to the operation would not match its mandate were confirmed. MONUC took virtually no action in relation to civilian protection. States were extremely reluctant to contribute to the operation[190] – a

[184] ibid, para 4. The Security Council relied upon the Secretary-General's recommendations that it authorise a further deployment and an increased mandate, including functions such as liaising, assisting, monitoring and reporting on the situation and, in particular, on the implementation of the LCA (United Nations, *Report of the Secretary-General on the United Nations Organization Mission in the Democratic Republic of the Congo* (UN Doc S/2000/30), 17 January 2000, para 65). The recommendations were based on several favourable presumptions, including that the parties would respect and uphold the LCA and relevant Security Council resolutions (ibid, para 60).

[185] It was authorised, in the areas of its deployment and as it deemed within its capabilities, to 'protect United Nations and co-located JMC [Joint Military Commission] personnel, facilities, installations and equipment, ensure the security and freedom of movement of its personnel, and protect civilians under imminent threat of physical violence' (SC Res 1291, ibid, para 8).

[186] *Operation Artemis: The Lessons of the Interim Emergency Force* (n 58) 8.

[187] United Nations, *Provisional Record of the 4104th Meeting of the Security Council* (UN Doc S/PV.4104), 24 February 2000, 7.

[188] ibid, 7.

[189] See *Report of the Secretary-General* (n 184) para 62. The Secretary-General observed in February 2001 that in Bunia the Ugandan People's Defence Force (UPDF) was responsible for protecting MONUC premises (United Nations, *Sixth Report of the Secretary-General on the United Nations Organization Mission in the Democratic Republic of the Congo* (UN Doc S/2001/128), 12 February 2001, para 40).

[190] As late as June 2002 – some two-and-a-half years after SC Res 1291 – the Security Council continued to call upon Member States to 'contribute personnel to enable MONUC to reach its authorized strength of 5,537' (SC Res 1417 of 14 June 2002, para 2).

factor that one observer attributed to the potentially forceful civilian protection mandate.[191] Indeed, a full year after the Security Council passed Resolution 1291, MONUC consisted of only 203 of the 5,537 personnel authorised, of whom only 78 were troops.[192]

In mid-May 2002, Congolese officers mutinied against their commanding officers and local authorities in Kisangani, the DRC's third largest city. When reinforcements arrived, soldiers entered a populated area, killing dozens of civilians, committing numerous rapes, and engaging in systematic looting. Congolese military and police personnel suspected of involvement in the mutiny were arrested, and many were summarily executed on the nights of 14 and 15 May.[193] Estimates as to the number of deaths vary, with a MONUC investigation placing the figure at at least 50,[194] Human Rights Watch placing it at more than 80,[195] and the UN Special Rapporteur on Extrajudicial, Summary or Arbitrary Executions estimating that 160 people had been killed.[196] According to a Political Affairs Officer working for MONUC, 'on May 14, at the time killings were still taking place, the deputy force commander of MONUC, Brigadier-General Roberto Martinelli and local commanders decided not to deploy military observers to . . . affected areas, apparently concerned about MONUC casualties'.[197] In his report to the Security Council following the Kisingani massacre, the Secretary-General made it clear to the Security Council that, as constituted, MONUC had been in no position to aid civilians in the circumstances.[198] At the time of the Kisingani massacre, MONUC consisted of just 3,719 of the 5,537 authorised personnel[199] – forces that were described by one commentator as mostly 'lightly armed and modestly trained'.[200]

While the wording of the civilian protection mandate in Resolution 1291 – 'MONUC *may* take the necessary action, in the areas of deployment of its infantry battalions and *as it deems it within its capabilities*' (emphasis added) – arguably absolved MONUC from civilian protection responsibilities in the circumstances, many observers and civilians saw matters

[191] Katarina Månsson, 'Use of Force and Civilian Protection: Peace Operations in the Congo' (2005) 12(4) *International Peacekeeping* 503, 506–07.

[192] *Sixth Report of the Secretary-General* (n 189) para 38.

[193] Human Rights Watch, *Democratic Republic of Congo – War Crimes in Kisangani: The Response of Rwandan-Backed Rebels to the May 2002 Mutiny*, Human Rights Watch document, vol 14 No 6 (A), August 2002, www.defence.gov.au/opEx/global/opastute/info/general.htm (accessed 1 April 2011), 2.

[194] ibid, 24.

[195] ibid.

[196] ibid.

[197] ibid.

[198] United Nations, *Eleventh Report of the Secretary-General on the United Nations Organization Mission in the Democratic Republic of the Congo* (UN Doc S/2002/621), 5 June 2002, para 71.

[199] www.un.org/en/peacekeeping/contributors/2002/May2002_4.pdf (accessed 1 April 2011).

[200] James Traub, *The Best Intentions: Kofi Annan and the UN in the Era of American World Power* (London, Bloomsbury, 2006) 340.

differently. To them, the fact that MONUC had been mandated to protect civilians meant that it should do just that.[201] Several demonstrations took place in front of MONUC's headquarters, with the demonstrators 'accusing MONUC and the Security Council of not doing enough to prevent the killings in Kisangani'.[202] In the words of a report of the UN High Commissioner for Human Rights: '[M]embers of civil society were outraged at MONUC. They expected MONUC to intervene physically to protect people from the excesses and abuses.'[203]

The response of the Security Council was to condemn the massacre (several times),[204] to specifically 'recall' MONUC's civilian protection mandate as provided for in Resolution 1291[205] (seemingly implying that MONUC had not done enough in this regard), and to invite the Secretary-General to consider whether a temporary strengthening of MONUC in Kisangani, '*within the current authorized troop level*, may contribute to easing tensions'.[206] The Secretary-General – whose earlier request for additional troops had gone unheeded by the Security Council[207] – advised that if MONUC was to effectively protect civilians, it would be 'necessary for the Security Council to consider adjusting the strength of MONUC with a view to reconfiguring and re-equipping contingents considerably to permit them to intervene more actively'.[208] In particular, he requested 400 additional troops.[209] The Security Council merely took note of this request, expressing the 'intention to consider authorizing it as soon as further progress has been achieved', including the total withdrawal of foreign troops.[210]

Violence continued in the DRC, with some of the worst atrocities occurring in the second half of 2002. Flashpoints included the northeast of the country, bordering Uganda (the town of Bunia and the Ituri region more generally),[211] as well as the provinces of North and South Kivu,

[201] See eg Human Rights Watch (n 193) 2.

[202] *Eleventh Report of the Secretary-General* (n 198) para 12.

[203] United Nations, *Note by the President of the Security Council [Attaching 'Report of the United Nations High Commissioner for Human Rights on the Events that Occurred in Kisangani, Democratic Republic of the Congo, on 14 and 15 May 2002']* (UN Doc S/2002/764), 15 July 2002, 10.

[204] See United Nations, *Statement by the President of the Security Council* (UN Doc S/PRST/2002/17), 24 May 2002. The Security Council also condemned it in *Statement by the President of the Security Council* (UN Doc S/PRST/2002/19), 5 June 2002. Further, it was condemned in SC Res 1417 of 14 June 2002, para 4.

[205] SC Res 1417 of 14 June 2002, para 7.

[206] *Statement by the President of the Security Council* of June 2002 (n 204) (emphasis added).

[207] In February 2002 the Secretary-General had requested an additional 850 troops (United Nations, *Tenth Report of the Secretary-General on the United Nations Organization Mission in the Democratic Republic of the Congo* (UN Doc S/2002/169), 15 February 2002, para 28).

[208] *Eleventh Report of the Secretary-General* (n 198) para 172.

[209] ibid, para 28.

[210] SC Res 1417 of 14 June 2002, para 3 which referred to the Security Council's demands in para 12 of SC Res 1376 of 9 November 2001 for the withdrawal of foreign troops.

[211] United Nations, *Twelfth Report of the Secretary-General on the United Nations Organization Mission in the Democratic Republic of the Congo* (UN Doc S/2002/1180), 12 October 2002, paras 15–17. The conflict in the Ituri region was between Lendu-based and Hema-based militias.

bordering Rwanda.[212] A Human Rights Watch Report described an August 2002 attack on Bunia in the following terms:

> According to MONUC, 110 people died in the violence in and around Bunia, but local sources estimated the dead as at least 150. The victims included both Hema and Lendu civilians many of whom had been targeted only on the basis of their ethnicity. Several mass graves were subsequently discovered including one with twenty-six bodies of mostly women and children, many with bullet wounds in their backs.[213]

During that period, MONUC's focus was on investigation and reporting 'as soon as security conditions allowed',[214] rather than protecting civilians.[215]

Matters were to get worse. When the withdrawal of foreign forces from the DRC began in earnest in the second half of 2002, the Secretary-General proposed a revised concept of operations, such that MONUC would deal primarily with disarmament, demobilisation and repatriation of foreign armed groups.[216] In December 2002 the Security Council passed Resolution 1445 by which it endorsed the Secretary-General's new concept of operations, including his request for a doubling of troops.[217] (At the time, however, MONUC was still over 1,000 troops shy of the 5,537 troops authorised in February 2000, almost three years earlier.)[218] In order to carry out the revised concept of operations the Secretary-General observed that:

> MONUC will need to be significantly strengthened by creating a forward force. The forward force will comprise two robust task forces, based in Kindu and Kisangani, as well as one reserve battalion, riverine units and specialized enabling units to enhance the Mission's military logistics capacity.[219]

[212] ibid, paras 18–19.

[213] *Democratic Republic of Congo: Ituri: 'Covered in Blood' Ethnically Targeted Violence in Northeastern DR Congo*, Human Rights Watch document, vol 15 No 11 (A), July 2003, www.un.org/en/peacekeeping/contributors/2002/May2002_4.pdf (accessed 1 April 2011), 20–21.

[214] United Nations, *Thirteenth Report of the Secretary-General on the United Nations Organization Mission in the Democratic Republic of the Congo* (UN Doc S/2003/211), 21 February 2003, para 8.

[215] In October 2002, MONUC troops were being used to protect 'MONUC sector headquarters, logistic bases and coordination centres' (*Twelfth Report of the Secretary-General* (n 211) para 22). The *Lessons Learned* report suggested that blame for the Bunia massacres was linked to the Security Council's denial of the Secretary-General's request for MONUC to play a limited role in supporting the Lubanga Agreement (*Operation Artemis: The Lessons of the Interim Emergency Force* (n 58) 6).

[216] *Twelfth Report of the Secretary-General* (n 211) paras 8–12.

[217] SC Res 1445 of 4 December 2002. The Secretary-General's report is endorsed by the Security Council in para 10 of Resolution 1445 (United Nations, *Special Report of the Secretary-General on the United Nations Organization Mission in the Democratic Republic of the Congo* (UN Doc S/2002/1005), 10 September 2002).

[218] www.un.org/en/peacekeeping/contributors/2002/November2002_4.pdf (accessed 1 April 2011).

[219] *Special Report of the Secretary-General* (n 217) para 48.

He also indicated that there was a need for, inter alia, support by 'integral utility (transport) aviation with a lift capability of 120 personnel' and an armed helicopter unit.[220] While Resolution 1445 reiterated that the 'situation in the Democratic Republic of the Congo continues to pose a threat to international peace and security in the region',[221] that resolution did not explicitly invoke Chapter VII, nor did it authorise 'all necessary means' or language of a similar nature. The Security Council did, however, recall 'its previous resolutions and statements by its President regarding' regarding the DRC.[222]

Despite MONUC's increase in size, serious violence continued to occur in the country in 2003, in particular in the Ituri region, where Bunia is located.[223] A series of incidents occurred between January and March 2003, including the killing of hundreds and the internal displacement of 500,000–600,000 persons.[224] The Secretary-General described 'hundreds of civilians being murdered in a series of well-coordinated summary executions near the [Drodro] parish [in the Ituri region] and 16 neighbouring locations. Twenty mass graves have been identified by MONUC.'[225] He recognised 'the immense gap' between MONUC's capabilities and the 'high expectations of the population'.[226] A *New York Times* report described the situation in Bunia as leaving MONUC 'overwhelmed and humiliated'.[227] The report stated that 'a small detachment of Uruguayan guards, who had been sent to protect the UN mission in the midst of a savage battle between rival militias, remained inside the UN compound while hundreds of civilians were murdered'.[228]

The DPKO, in its analysis of the incidents, concluded that:

> Although approximately 420 bodies were recovered and many atrocities were committed, MONUC's actions directly saved around 10,000 persons at the airport and another 6,000 at headquarters in town, if not many more, who probably would have been killed had the town been abandoned by the UN.[229]

The DPKO's assessment of the conduct of the Uruguayan battalion (URUBATT) in Bunia sent mixed messages: it defended URUBATT's non-action, noting that it lacked capacity; at the same time, it underlined that URUBATT had misunderstood its authorisation to use force. It observed:

[220] ibid, para 49.
[221] SC Res 1445 (n 217) final preambular paragraph.
[222] ibid, first preambular paragraph.
[223] *Thirteenth Report of the Secretary-General* (n 214) paras 12 and 55. The North and South Kivu regions were also affected by violence during this period (United Nations, *Second Special Report of the Secretary-General on the United Nations Organization Mission in the Democratic Republic of the Congo* (UN Doc S/2003/566), 27 May 2003, paras 18–19).
[224] *Second Special Report of the Secretary-General*, ibid, para 10.
[225] ibid, para 9.
[226] ibid, para 97.
[227] James Traub, 'The Congo Case', *New York Times*, 3 July 2005.
[228] ibid.
[229] *Operation Artemis: The Lessons of the Interim Emergency Force* (n 58) 7.

> Given that URUBATT had been deployed to Bunia on the understanding that its tasks would be limited to protecting UN personnel and that it clearly lacked the capacity to do much more, the decision not to take the initiative appears justified. However, the contingent itself argued that it was constrained on principle from a more active use of force by MONUC's mandate. The contingent reportedly maintained that since MONUC's mandate was authorized under Chapter VI of the UN Charter, force could not be used except in self-defence. In fact, taking into account the specific provisions of resolution 1291 (2000) regarding the protection of civilians, and under MONUC's rules of engagement, the Uruguayan battalion could undertake pre-emptive self-defence against an anticipated attack when supported by compelling evidence that hostile units or persons were committed to an immediate attack.[230]

On 15 May 2003, the Secretary-General, citing his deep concern at the 'rapidly deteriorating situation in and around Bunia', requested that the Security Council consider deploying a quasi-enforcement force to Bunia:

> under the lead of a Member State, to provide security at the airport as well as to other vital installations in the town and to protect the civilian population. The force would be deployed for a limited period until a considerably reinforced United Nations presence could be deployed.[231]

On 30 May 2003, the Security Council authorised the deployment of an Interim Emergency Multinational Force in Bunia to work in close coordination with MONUC.[232] This force, known as IEMF or 'Operation Artemis', was authorised to 'take all necessary measures to fulfil its mandate'.[233] It was to be EU-led, with France as the main contributor. The Security Council stressed that this quasi-enforcement operation would exist 'on a strictly temporary basis' and set 1 September 2003 (3 months after its establishment) as its termination date. The force was described by one non-governmental organisation as having been 'conceived only as a stopgap, to hold the line until additional MONUC troops [were] deployed'.[234] Operation Artemis deployed in Bunia in June 2003 and withdrew in September of that same year.[235]

In the same month that he requested a quasi-enforcement operation for the DRC, the Secretary-General requested an additional 3,800 personnel

[230] ibid, 9.

[231] United Nations, *Letter Dated 15 May 2003 from the Secretary-General Addressed to the President of the Security Council* (UN Doc S/2002/574), 28 May 2003.

[232] SC Res 1484 of 30 May 2003. This force was authorised 'to contribute to the stabilization of the security conditions and the improvement of the humanitarian situation in Bunia, to ensure the protection of the airport, the internally displaced persons in the camps in Bunia and, if the situation requires it, to contribute to the safety of the civilian population, United Nations personnel and the humanitarian presence in the town' (ibid).

[233] SC Res 1484, ibid, para 4.

[234] International Crisis Group, *Congo Crisis: Military Intervention in Ituri*, Crisis Group Africa Report No 64, 13 June 2003, www.crisisgroup.org/en/regions/africa/central-africa/dr-congo/064-congo-crisis-military-intervention-in-ituri.aspx (accessed 1 April 2011), ii.

[235] ibid, 3.

for MONUC '[i]n order to provide protection to United Nations personnel and assets in various locations in Ituri and to establish a framework of security in support of the ongoing political process'.[236] Under-Secretary-General for Peacekeeping Operations, Jean-Marie Guéhenno, called for MONUC to be given a mandate that was of a similar level of robustness to that held by IEMF.[237]

In July 2003 the Security Council passed Resolution 1493, increasing MONUC's troop levels to 10,800.[238] Resolution 1493 reiterated that the situation in the DRC constituted a threat to international peace and security in the region,[239] and invoked Chapter VII in relation to the whole of the resolution.[240] In relation to two paragraphs only, the Security Council went even further: it authorised MONUC 'to take the necessary measures in the areas of deployment of its armed units, and as it deems it within its capabilities' to protect its personnel and freedom of movement, 'to protect civilians and humanitarian workers under imminent threat of physical violence', and to 'contribute to the improvement of the security conditions in which humanitarian assistance is provided'.[241] In addition, it authorised MONUC to 'use all necessary means to fulfil its mandate in the Ituri district and, as it deems it within its capabilities, in North and South Kivu'.[242] The Security Council also imposed a mandatory embargo against the importation of arms into the DRC.[243] All parties were required by the Security Council to 'provide full access to MONUC military observers, including in ports, airports, airfields, military bases and border crossings'.[244]

When the IEMF withdrew, it handed over its remaining tasks in Bunia to the strengthened MONUC.[245] While IEMF was, according to the Secretary-General, successful in restoring 'a measure of security to the town',[246] the

[236] *Second Special Report of the Secretary-General* (n 223) para 48.

[237] United Nations (Press Release), *European Union's Response to Appeal for Emergency Force Is Welcomed* (UN Doc SC/7820), 18 July 2003.

[238] SC Res 1493 of 28 July 2003, para 3. Troop numbers were increased in order to protect UN personnel and assets and establish a framework of security, as well as providing limited support to some humanitarian operations (*Second Special Report of the Secretary-General* (n 223) para 48).

[239] SC Res 1493, ibid, penultimate preambular para.

[240] ibid, final preambular para.

[241] ibid, para 25.

[242] ibid, para 26.

[243] SC Res 1493 of 28 July 2003, para 20. The measures applied 'to all foreign and Congolese armed groups and militias operating in the territory of North and South Kivu and of Ituri, and to groups not party to the Global and All-inclusive agreement, in the Democratic Republic of the Congo'. An exception was made for supplies to MONUC, IEMF and the integrated Congolese national army and police force (ibid, para 21).

[244] ibid, para 19.

[245] *Operation Artemis: The Lessons of the Interim Emergency Force* (n 58) 4.

[246] United Nations, *Fourteenth Report of the Secretary-General on the United Nations Organization Mission in the Democratic Republic of the Congo* (UN Doc S/2003/1098), 17 November 2003, para 6.

situation remained volatile. Although its proactive use of force restored order to Bunia, it did little in relation to the larger Ituri region – let alone the DRC as a whole.[247] The Secretary-General noted, with considerable understatement, that the 'interpretation of Security Council resolution 1493 (2003) has been a major challenge for MONUC'.[248] He observed that the invocation of Chapter VII in relation to part of MONUC's mandate had 'raised expectations that the Mission [would] enforce the peace throughout the country' but noted the 'wide gap between such expectations and the Mission's capacity to fulfil them'.[249]

In late May and early June 2004 there was a struggle for the control of Bukavu, the capital of South Kivu.[250] MONUC, which had some 450 troops in the area at the time, deployed an additional 554 troops to the area.[251] The MONUC military contingent in Bukavu was nevertheless overstretched.[252] According to Traub, it was at about this time that the Uruguayan soldiers were 'ordered to take up blocking positions at the airport north of the town'.[253] Traub continued:

> According to a senior DPKO official in New York, the [Uruguayan] force commander called his superiors in Montevideo and complained that he was being asked to exceed his mandate. With backing from his capital, he refused to implement the order – an act of gross insubordination in a normal military setting. On June 2, peacekeepers surrendered the airport to the rebels who poured into Bukavu, where they engaged in a four-day orgy of rape, pillage and murder.[254]

The International Crisis Group reported that '[s]everal hundred people, both civilians and fighters, were killed in Bukavu and in Kamanyola further south, and more than 30,000 Congolese . . . fled into Burundi and Rwanda'.[255] In August 2004, there was a massacre of Congolese Banyamulenge refugees in Gatumba, Burundi.[256]

[247] Some commentators have suggested that the operation may have 'skewed the military balance in Ituri and may indirectly have caused harm elsewhere' (Ståle Ulriksen, Catriona Gourlayk and Catriona Mace, 'Operation *Artemis*: The Shape of Things to Come?' (2004) 11(3) *International Peacekeeping* 522).

[248] United Nations, *Third Special Report of the Secretary-General on the United Nations Organization Mission in the Democratic Republic of the Congo* (UN Doc S/2004/650), 13 August 2004, para 58.

[249] ibid, para 59.

[250] International Crisis Group, *Pulling Back from the Brink in the Congo*, ICG Africa Briefing No 18, 7 July 2004, www.crisisgroup.org/library/documents/africa/central_africa/070704_congo_brink___modified.pdf (accessed 1 April 2011), 1.

[251] *Third Special Report of the Secretary-General* (n 248) paras 35–36.

[252] ibid, para 37.

[253] Traub (n 200) 341.

[254] ibid, 341–42.

[255] International Crisis Group (n 250) 5.

[256] *Third Special Report of the Secretary-General* (n 248) paras 37, 39 and 45. See also *Letter Dated 3 September 2004 from the Secretary-General Addressed to the President of the Security Council* (UN Doc S/2004/715), 7 September 2004. See chapter 6, section 5 for discussion of the impact of this massacre on ONUB in Burundi.

The Secretary-General put a favourable gloss on MONUC's contribution, noting that, despite its limitations, it had been 'able to protect some 4,000 internally displaced persons at its premises in Bukavu and to extract individual citizens at risk to places of safety' as well as organising several special rescue missions elsewhere in the country.[257] However, even he admitted that its contributions were not considered favourably by the people on the ground: 'MONUC was blamed by several high-level Transitional Government officials for not using its mandate under Chapter VII of the Charter of the United Nations to prevent the capture of Bukavu by dissident elements.'[258] The citizenry of the country were gravely disillusioned by MONUC's actions, pitting them against the peacekeeping operation. Violent demonstrations against MONUC resulted in 'the destruction of over $1 million worth of equipment and property . . . United Nations personnel were harassed, physically attacked and their private residences looted.'[259] Reportedly the 'people of South Kivu loathed the [Uruguayan contingent of MONUC], and thus the UN itself. When UN vehicles drove around Bukavu, local people glared at them and drew fingers across their throats'.[260] One citizen of Bukavu made the following statement to a journalist: 'The Uruguayans didn't come for peacekeeping, . . . [t]hey came for tourism.'[261]

In response to the massacres in Bukavu, the Security Council passed Resolution 1565 in October 2004, raising MONUC's troop numbers – this time by an additional 5,900, bringing the total to 16,700.[262] However, this figure was still significantly shy of the 23,900 troops the Secretary-General had recommended.[263] Resolution 1565 again characterised the situation as a threat to international peace and security in the region[264] and, once again, invoked Chapter VII in relation to all paragraphs of the resolution.[265] In Resolution 1565 the Security Council set out a revised mandate for MONUC. The tasks fell into three categories: first were tasks not requiring the use of force, such as assisting in the promotion of human rights and observing troop movements; second, the civilian protection mandate was reiterated; and third were tasks that seemed likely to require the use of considerable offensive force, including the seizure and disposal of arms in violation of the arms embargo imposed by Resolution 1493 and monitoring compliance with the embargo 'in cooperation with ONUB and, as appropriate, with the Governments concerned . . . by inspecting, as it deems it necessary and

[257] ibid, para 37.
[258] ibid, para 39.
[259] ibid, para 39.
[260] Traub (n 227).
[261] ibid.
[262] SC Res 1565 of 1 October 2004.
[263] *Third Special Report of the Secretary-General* (n 248) para 201.
[264] SC Res 1565 (n 262) penultimate preambular para.
[265] ibid, final preambular para.

without notice, the cargo of aircraft and of any transport vehicle using the ports, airports, airfields, military bases and border crossings in North and South Kivu and in Ituri'.[266] In order to carry out the tasks in the second and third categories, MONUC was authorised to use 'all necessary means, within its capacity and in the areas where its armed units are deployed'.[267]

In May 2005, in the face of continued violence[268] in the lead up to scheduled elections, the Secretary-General recommended that the Security Council consider increasing the military strength of MONUC by some 2,590 to a total of 19,290 personnel[269] and providing increased air mobility assets, including nine aircraft and 13 helicopters.[270] Despite the Secretary-General repeating his request for an increase in personnel several times,[271] the Security Council authorised only a further 841 personnel in September 2005[272] and an additional 300 personnel October 2005.[273] At about this time, Ugandan President Museveni criticised MONUC for not 'doing much' and gave the DRC government two months to disarm the Lord's Resistance Army (LRA) rebels in eastern Congo; if it did not, he said, his army would do so.[274]

In December 2005, the Under-Secretary-General for Peacekeeping contacted the President of the EU, asking that the EU 'consider the possibility of making available a deterrent force that, if necessary, could be deployed to the Democratic Republic of the Congo during the electoral process'.[275] In its March 2006 reply, the EU acceded to the request, so long as a Security Council resolution was passed under Chapter VII giving a robust mandate to the deterrent force.[276] The resolution authorising this

[266] ibid, para 4(f).

[267] SC Res 1565 (n 262) para 6.

[268] Marc Lacey, 'UN Forces Using Tougher Tactics to Secure Peace', *New York Times*, 23 May 2005.

[269] United Nations, *Special Report of the Secretary-General on Elections in the Democratic Republic of the Congo* (UN Doc S/2005/320), 26 May 2005, para 70.

[270] ibid, para 52.

[271] See United Nations, *Eighteenth Report of the Secretary-General on the United Nations Organization Mission in the Democratic Republic of the Congo* (UN Doc S/2005/506), 2 August 2005, para 86. See also United Nations, *Nineteenth Report of the Secretary-General on the United Nations Organization Mission in the Democratic Republic of the Congo* (UN Doc S/2005/603), 26 September 2005, para 72.

[272] SC Res 1621 of 6 September 2005.

[273] SC Res 1635 of 28 October 2005. This was a temporary increase of 300 personnel 'to allow for the deployment of an infantry battalion in Katanga'.

[274] United Nations Office for the Coordination of Humanitarian Affairs (IRIN), *DRC-Uganda: Disarm LRA Rebels or We Invade, Museveni Tells Kinshasa, MONUC*, 30 September 2005, www.irinnews.org/report.aspx?reportid=56540 (accessed 1 April 2011).

[275] United Nations, *Letter Dated 12 April 2006 from the Secretary-General Addressed to the President of the Security Council [Attaching as Annex I a Letter Dated 27 December 2005 from the under-Secretary-General for Peacekeeping Operations to the Presidency of the European Union and Attaching as Annex II a Response by the Minister of Foreign Affairs of the Republic of Austria Dated 28 March 2006, on Behalf of the Council of the European Union]* (UN Doc S/2006/219), 13 April 2006, Annex I.

[276] ibid, Annex II.

quasi-enforcement operation made specific reference to the fact that the DRC supported the operation's establishment.[277] The Security Council also called for the redeployment of troops from the United Nations Observer Mission in Burundi (ONUB) to the DRC on a temporary basis.[278] Two days after the Security Council resolution was passed, the Council of the European Union approved an EU military operation.[279] During the period of deployment of the EU military force, the first democratic and transparent Congolese elections in more than 40 years were successfully concluded.[280] The EU military operation ended on 30 November 2006.[281]

In April 2005, an agreement had been reached among representatives of the DRC, Rwanda and Uganda to support the efforts of the Armed Forces of the Democratic Republic of the Congo (FARDC) to disarm and repatriate to Rwanda the combatants of the Forces démocratiques de libération du Rwanda (FDLR), with the support of MONUC.[282] Initially this alliance led to various successful FARDC/MONUC operations in Ituri/Bunia in October and November 2005.[283] However, such operations were not without cost. After 25 civilians were killed in an apparent reprisal by the FDLR,[284] protests took place against MONUC among the local population, who feared reprisals if MONUC and the FARDC continued to carry out military operations against the force.[285]

On 21 April 2006, a joint FARDC/MONUC operation took place in the hamlet of Kazana in the Ituri district. According to an eyewitness report, civilians found themselves fleeing mortars, machine-gun fire and

[277] SC Res 1671 of 25 April 2006, para 1. See also United Nations, *Letter Dated 30 March 2006 from the Permanent Representative of the Democratic Republic of the Congo to the United Nations Addressed to the President of the Security Council [Attaching a Press Communiqué of the Congolese Supreme Defence Council Dated 20 March 2006 Endorsing an EU Force]* (UN Doc S/2006/203), 30 March 2006.

[278] SC Res 1669 of 7 April 2006. This redeployment was extended by SC Res 1692 of 30 June 2006 and SC Res 1711 of 29 September 2006. In December 2006, a further increase of 916 military personnel was authorised (SC Res 1736 of 22 December 2006).

[279] United Nations, *Letter Dated 8 February 2007 from the Secretary-General Addressed to the President of the Security Council [Annexing a Letter Dated 22 January 2007 from the Secretary-General and High Representative for the Common Foreign and Security Policy of the European Union to the Secretary-General of the United Nation, Which Enclosed 'Report of the Secretary-General and High Representative for the Common Foreign and Security Policy of the European Union on the European Union Operation in the Democratic Republic of the Congo']* (UN Doc S/2007/70), 9 February 2007, para 3.

[280] ibid, para 4. On 27 November the Supreme Court confirmed the results of the elections, leading to the inauguration of President Kabila on 6 December 2006.

[281] ibid, para 12. However, an EU Police mission in Kinshasa, which had run concurrently with the military operation, was extended by the Council of the European Union until June 2007 (ibid, paras 14–15).

[282] *Eighteenth Report of the Secretary-General* (n 271) para 18.

[283] United Nations, *Twentieth Report of the Secretary-General on the United Nations Organization Mission in the Democratic Republic of the Congo* (UN Doc S/2005/823), 28 December 2005, paras 21 and 22.

[284] ibid, para 27.

[285] ibid, para 28.

rocket-propelled grenades fired by the joint forces.[286] The same eyewitness attested that 'after the fighting stopped, as the peacekeepers stood idly by, Congolese troops set every house on fire'.[287] Several civilian deaths were reported;[288] however, this was denied by the UN, whose spokesman cited a thorough investigation into the matter.[289] Several months after this statement was made, and after engaging in a subsequent investigation, the UN reiterated its denial of any civilian casualties.[290] While conceding that the FARDC had caused property damage, MONUC's press release downplayed the significance of this, describing it as the burning of 'temporary huts that had been occupied by militia' or the destruction of 'individual huts . . . during the fighting and by retreating militia'.[291]

In late January/early February 2007 the Secretary-General reported serious incidents in Bas-Congo (the DRC's westernmost province), resulting in more than 100 deaths, mainly of civilians.[292] Additional violence occurred from 22 to 25 March 2007 in Kinshasa. A MONUC investigation into these killings noted 'the Government's limited law enforcement capacity and the poor discipline of some Congolese national police and FARDC personnel, who responded to the unrest with a disproportionate use of force and, in some cases, with summary executions'.[293] MONUC refused to condemn the Bas-Congo killings outright.[294] *The Economist* summarised MONUC's quandary as follows: 'It is supposed to protect Congo's civilian population, while helping to build up and train the revamped security forces. But the new army is widely viewed as Congo's main human-rights abuser.'[295] An opinion piece from the *New York Times* described the FARDC as the 'worst abuser of human rights in the country today' and noted that the 'United Nations excuses its cooperation

[286] Aidan Hartley, 'Congo's Election, the UN's Massacre', *New York Times*, 28 July 2006.

[287] ibid.

[288] ibid.

[289] United Nations, *Highlights of the Noon Briefing by Marie Okabe, Deputy Spokesman for the Secretary-General, with Amad Fawzi, Director of the News and Media Division, UN Headquarters, New York*, 28 July 2006, www.un.org/News/ossg/hilites/hilites_arch_view.asp?HighID=630 (accessed 1 April 2011).

[290] United Nations (MONUC Press Release), *DR Congo: MONUC Response to the Media on MONUC/FARDC 21 Apr, 2006 Joint Operation in Kazanga, Ituri*, 6 October 2006, http://reliefweb.int/node/215513 (accessed 1 April 2011).

[291] ibid.

[292] United Nations, *Twenty-Third Report of the Secretary-General on the United Nations Organization Mission in the Democratic Republic of the Congo* (UN Doc S/2007/156), 20 March 2007, para 14.

[293] ibid, para 15. The Secretary-General described the FARDC in the following, rather unflattering terms: 'FARDC remains fragile because of weak command and control; high levels of corruption; poor operational planning and tactical skills; poor administrative and logistical capacity to oversee the deployment, payment, sustenance and equipping of troops; very limited training capacity; and questionable loyalty on the part of some troops' (para 29).

[294] Unattributed, 'Congo: Keep the United Nations Engaged', *The Economist*, 10 February 2007.

[295] ibid.

with this ragtag force of co-opted former militiamen by saying it wants to change their behaviour by working with them rather than withholding aid'.[296] It described MONUC as 'an ill-equipped third-world army, with Vietnam-era American armor and Soviet aircraft'.[297]

The mandate of MONUC was altered by Resolution 1756 in May 2007.[298] Once again, the resolution stated that the situation in the DRC constituted a continuing threat to international peace and security[299] and, once again, the resolution invoked Chapter VII in relation to all of its paragraphs.[300] The Security Council modified MONUC's mandate, bestowing upon it a variety of tasks as provided under the following categories: first, protection of civilians and UN personnel; second, the DRC's territorial security; third, disarmament and demobilisation of foreign and Congolese armed groups; fourth, security sector reform; and fifth, support for the strengthening of democratic institutions and the rule of law in the DRC.[301] In addition, Resolution 1756 authorised MONUC to use 'all necessary means, within the limits of its capacity and in the areas where its units are deployed', to carry out all of its tasks in the first category, two of its tasks in the second category (monitoring the arms embargo imposed by Resolution 1493, including by inspecting, without notice if necessary, the cargo of aircraft and any transport vehicle using the ports, airports, airfields, military bases and border crossings in North and South Kivu and Ituri and seizing and disposing of any arms in violation of the measures imposed by Resolution 1493), most of its tasks in the third category, and the task, in the fifth category, of assisting 'in the establishment of a secure and peaceful environment for the holding of free and transparent elections'.[302]

Despite its knowledge of the FARDC's propensity to violate human rights, the Security Council was nevertheless committed to MONUC working alongside the FARDC. This was clear from Resolution 1756, where the Security Council admonished the FARDC for its part in 'persistence of violations of human rights and international humanitarian law in the Democratic Republic of the Congo'[303] but, nevertheless, called for MONUC to 'use all necessary means' to provide military support for certain FARDC operations.[304] Similarly, in Resolution 1794, in December

[296] Hartley (n 286).
[297] ibid.
[298] SC Res 1756 of 15 May 2007.
[299] ibid, penultimate preambular para.
[300] ibid, final preambular para.
[301] ibid, paras 2 and 3. All of MONUC's tasks in the first four categories were said to be 'to assist the Government of the Democratic Republic of the Congo in establishing a stable security environment in the country' (para 2(1) *chapeau*).
[302] ibid, para 4.
[303] ibid, preambular para 10.
[304] ibid, para 4.

2007, when the Security Council extended MONUC's mandate, it directed MONUC to

> use all necessary means, within the limits of its capacity and in the areas where its units are deployed, to support the FARDC integrated brigades with a view to disarming the recalcitrant foreign and Congolese armed groups, in particular the FDLR, ex-FAR/Interahamwe and the dissident militia of Laurent Nkunda, in order to ensure their participation in the disarmament, demobilization, repatriation, resettlement and reintegration processes, as appropriate.[305]

In the same resolution, it deplored 'the persistence of violations of human rights and international humanitarian law' carried out by elements of the FARDC and the Congolese National Police (PNC).[306] The paradox of vesting MONUC with a significant militarised mandate to support the FARDC in the very same resolutions in which it deplores its conduct would appear to have been lost on the Security Council.[307]

In October 2008, citing, inter alia, the resumption of conflict in Ituri and in Haute-Uele and a crisis emanating from the FARDC's offensive against one of the rebel forces, the *Congrès National pour la Défense du Peuple* (CNDP), the Secretary-General advised the Security Council that the resources available to MONUC 'were not commensurate with the security challenges on the ground'.[308] As such, he requested a further increase in the size of MONUC. In November 2008, the Security Council granted 'a temporary increase of MONUC's authorized military strength by up to 2,785 military personnel, and the strength of its formed police unit by up to 300 personnel'.[309] According to the Secretary-General, this would provide 'a reserve force and special forces that [would] enable the Mission, if requested by the Government, to redeploy rapidly to . . . support FARDC should the need arise'.[310]

In December 2008, the Security Council passed Resolution 1856, modifying the mandate of MONUC from that day forward. As with previous resolutions, 1856 reiterated that the situation in the DRC posed a threat to international peace and security in the region and invoked Chapter VII in relation to the whole resolution. Once again, the Security Council set out a large number of tasks for MONUC of a very similar nature to those provided in Resolution 1794 and grouped them in order of

[305] SC Res 1794 of 21 December 2007, para 5.

[306] ibid, 13th preambular paragraph.

[307] Some have suggested that the Security Council's willingness to see MONUC and the FARDC work together – despite the latter's obvious flaws – was a concession to the DRC government, which it wanted to keep 'on-side'.

[308] United Nations, *Letter Dated 31 October 2008 from the Secretary-General to the President of the Security Council* (UN Doc S/2008/703), 12 November 2008, Annex, para 2.

[309] SC Res 1843 of 20 November 2008, para 1.

[310] *Thirty-First Report of the Secretary-General* (n 177) para 115.

priority.[311] As regards certain of these tasks – relating to civilian protection, disarmament, ensuring adherence to sanctions imposed, and supporting the FARDC – it authorised MONUC to 'use all necessary means, within the limits of its capacity and in the areas where its units are deployed'.[312] The Security Council underscored 'the importance of MONUC implementing the mandate described in this resolution in full, including through robust rules of engagement', and requested that 'the Secretary-General . . . ensure that MONUC's concept of operation and rules of engagement are updated by 31 January 2009 to bring them fully in line with the provisions of this resolution'.[313]

In early 2009, the CNDP ousted its leader, ended its rebellion, and agreed to integrate into the FARDC if the Congolese government agreed to launch joint military operations with the Rwandan army against the FDLR.[314] The government agreed and the planning of the operation began. MONUC was not given any role in this and was not even informed of the plan's existence.[315] Only after protests were six MONUC military officers permitted to join in the planning of the operations, with the objective of ensuring that civilian protection formed part of the military operations. MONUC's role was limited, with one MONUC military official telling Human Rights Watch, 'We were kept in the dark'.[316] A Human Rights Watch report outlined the difficulties MONUC had in attempting to ensure that the Congolese forces it was fighting alongside would not violate international law.

> In September 2009, several months into its joint operations with the Congolese army, MONUC developed a draft policy note on conditionality [ie that it would fight alongside FARDC only so long as FARDC did not commit grave human rights violations], which it presented to the Congolese government for comment. It sought to present the proposed new conditions as helping the government implement its own policy of 'zero tolerance'. The draft policy stated that MONUC would 'seek to suspend its support to battalions who committed grave violations of human rights and who, after notification from MONUC, took no action and continued to commit such violations'. The policy note added, however, that 'such targeted measures would have no effect on the global envelope of support from MONUC to the FARDC' and that the support taken from the abusive battalion would be 'redirected' toward another battalion whose behaviour was more exemplary.[317]

[311] SC Res 1856 of 22 December 2008, paras 3 and 4.
[312] ibid, para 5.
[313] ibid, para 8.
[314] Human Rights Watch, *'You Will Be Punished' Attacks on Civilians in Eastern Congo*, 13 December 2009, www.hrw.org/node/87151 (accessed 1 April 2011), 135.
[315] ibid, 136.
[316] ibid, 136.
[317] ibid, 140.

For obvious reasons, this policy was not judged to be acceptable by the UN Office of Legal Affairs, which advised MONUC that if it had reason to believe that such violations were continuing despite intervention to stop them, it must cease participating in the operations completely.[318] Human Rights Watch reported that in an internal document dated November 2009, 'MONUC said that it was doing its best to incorporate the legal advice in very challenging circumstances' and observed that it had 'not had the luxury of devising an airtight policy and then implementing it under controlled conditions'; it was required 'to take action to deal with a rapidly evolving situation on the ground'.[319]

In mid-2009, President Joseph Kabila requested that the United Nations submit a plan for the progressive drawdown of MONUC troops by June 2010.[320] In December 2009 the Security Council passed Resolution 1906, extending MONUC's mandate, but just until 31 May 2010.[321] The resolution set out MONUC's mandate in a manner similar to that adopted in relation to many previous resolutions providing for MONUC's mandate: it determined that the situation in the DRC continued to pose a threat to international peace and security,[322] it invoked Chapter VII in relation to all of its paragraphs,[323] it modified MONUC's tasks and priorities, and it authorised the operation to 'use all necessary means, within the limits of its capacity and in the areas where its units are deployed', in relation to certain tasks only.[324] The wording of the resolution featured a mix of the mandatory and the recommendatory: the Security Council used the word '[D]*ecides*' in the paragraph modifying MONUC's mandate,[325] it used '[A]*uthorises*' in relation to the resort to 'all necessary means', and, when setting out specifics regarding the particular tasks, its wording was sometimes mandatory and sometimes recommendatory only.[326]

[318] ibid, 139, relying on confidential legal advice from the Office of Legal Affairs sent from DPKO to MONUC on 2 April 2009, which Human Rights Watch had obtained.

[319] ibid.

[320] United Nations, *Letter Dated 21 May 2010 from the Chair of the Security Council Committee Established Pursuant to Resolution 1533 (2004) Concerning the Democratic Republic of the Congo Addressed to the President of the Security Council* (UN Doc S/2010/252), 25 May 2010, para 22.

[321] SC Res 1906 of 23 December 2009, para 1.

[322] ibid, penultimate preambular para.

[323] ibid, final preambular para.

[324] ibid, para 6, which refers to the tasks set out in para 3(a)–(e) of SC Res 1856 of 22 December 2008 and paras 9, 20, 21 and 24 of SC Res 1906 (ibid).

[325] ibid, para 5: '*Decides* that, from the adoption of this resolution, MONUC, working in close cooperation with the Government of the Democratic Republic of the Congo, shall have the following mandate, in order of priority . . .' It then groups the various tasks that are elaborated upon later in the resolution.

[326] ibid, para 20: 'MONUC shall deter any attempt at the use of force to threaten the Goma and Nairobi processes from any armed group, particularly in the eastern part of the Democratic Republic of the Congo, and undertake all necessary operations to prevent attacks on civilians and disrupt the military capability of armed groups that continue to use violence in that area.' ibid, para 21: '*Requests* MONUC, working in close cooperation with the Government of the Democratic Republic of the Congo, to continue its coordination of

In addition, the Security Council, in Resolution 1906, requested that the Secretary-General undertake a strategic review of the situation in the DRC and MONUC's progress.[327] In the requested report to the Security Council the Secretary-General observed that, despite significant achievements in MONUC's first 10 years of operation,[328] many serious problems remained.[329] The report cited the conclusion of a UN technical assessment mission that the 'continued significant presence' of MONUC was essential to address security challenges in the Kivus and Orientale provinces and beneficial in the other eight provinces.[330] It suggested that it might be realistic for MONUC to withdraw if this took place over a period of three years and if the security situation continued to improve.[331] However, President Kabila, citing the sovereignty of the DRC and a desire to see the country 'fly with its own wings', called for a withdrawal to begin in June 2010 and be completed by 30 June 2011.[332] The prospect of MONUC being required to leave the country despite the fact that civilians continued to be vulnerable was criticised by UN officials[333] and NGOs.[334]

A mission of the Security Council visited the DRC in mid-May 2010. Its terms of reference were, inter alia, to 'reaffirm the commitment of the Security Council to MONUC and to discuss the future reconfiguration of MONUC, in particular the critical tasks that need to be accomplished before MONUC can envisage its drawdown without triggering a relapse into instability'.[335] Shortly upon the mission's return, the Security Council passed

operations with the FARDC brigades . . .' MONUC was vested with the authority to use 'all necessary means' in relation to the tasks in both paras 20 and 21.

327 ibid, paras 1 and 2.

328 *Thirty-First Report of the Secretary-General* (n 177) paras 22–25.

329 He cited the lack of security caused by the presence of foreign and Congolese armed groups in the Eastern DRC, the general instability in the Kivus and parts of the Orientale province, the FDLR's continuing reprisal attacks against civilians, the fact that elements of the national security institutions continued to be responsible for serious human rights violations and continuing attacks by the LRA against civilians in the Uélé districts in the Orientale province (ibid, para 2).

330 ibid, para 91.

331 ibid.

332 ibid, para 100. Though he later changed the date by which forces must withdraw to August 2010 (para 106).

333 John Holmes, Under-Secretary-General for Humanitarian Affairs and Emergency Relief Coordinator, is quoted as saying: 'We are worried by the prospect of a rapid or premature withdrawal of MONUC because MONUC is very important for our activities in the sense of providing stability, providing security for humanitarians.' Thomas Hubert, 'UN says Congo Pull-Out Would Undermine Aid Work', *Reuters*, 1 May 2010, www.reuters.com/article/2010/05/01/us-congo-democratic-monuc-idUSTRE6400VX20100501 (accessed 1 April 2011).

334 See eg Fabienne Hara, Vice President for Multilateral Affairs, International Crisis Group, 'Time to Pull Out UN Troops in Congo? Not So Fast', *Christian Science Monitor*, 14 May 2010, www.csmonitor.com/Commentary/Opinion/2010/0514/Time-to-pull-out-UN-troops-in-Congo-Not-so-fast (accessed 1 April 2011).

335 United Nations, *Letter Dated 14 April 2010 from the President of the Security Council Addressed to the Secretary-General (Security Council Mission to Africa – Democratic Republic of the Congo)* (UN Doc S/2010/187) 14 April 2010, Annex, 2.

Resolution 1925, which extended MONUC to 30 June 2010 and, as of 1 July 2010, changed its name to the United Nations Organization Stabilisation Mission in the Democratic Republic of the Congo (MONUSCO).[336] The change in the name of the operation was said by the Security Council to reflect the fact that 'a new phase has been reached' in the country.[337]

MONUSCO, which was initially authorised only until 30 June 2011, would involve up to 2,000 fewer military personnel, who would withdraw 'from areas where the security situation permits'.[338] Resolution 1925 was very similar in nature to the various resolutions modifying the mandate of MONUC, in that it determined that the situation in the DRC continued to pose a threat to international peace and security[339] and it invoked Chapter VII in relation to all of its paragraphs.[340] It modified MONUC's tasks and divided them into two categories. The first, under the heading 'protection of civilians', included more than the title would suggest. In addition to tasks involving protecting civilians and protecting the UN mission, the mandate called for MONUSCO to assist the FARDC in prosecution persons it arrested and to support the government in 'bring[ing] the ongoing military operations against the FDLR, the Lord's Resistance Army (LRA) and other armed groups, to a completion', as well as assisting with matters relating to disarmament. A second category, entitled 'stabilization and peace consolidation', featured tasks such as strengthening and supporting the DRC's judicial institutions, supporting reform of the police and providing assistance with elections. Finally, MONUSCO was charged under this heading with seizing and disposing of any arms whose presence in the DRC violated the measures imposed by paragraph 1 of Resolution 1896. The Security Council authorised MONUC to 'use all necessary means, within the limits of its capacity and in the areas where its units are deployed' in carrying out all of the activities under the heading 'protection of civilians' and with certain of its tasks under the heading 'stabilization and peace consolidation', including seizing and disposing of any arms prohibited by the embargo.[341] The resolution made no reference the consent of the DRC government.

It was shortly after MONUSCO was established – from 30 July to 2 August 2010 – that the rapes occurred in Luvngi, as discussed in chapter 1.

[336] SC Res 1925 of 28 May 2010, para 1.
[337] ibid.
[338] ibid, para 3.
[339] ibid, penultimate preambular para.
[340] ibid, final preambular para.
[341] ibid, para 11.

4.2 Evaluation

4.2.1 Adherence to the 'Fundamental Principles'

Turning first to the 'fundamental principle' of force only in self-defence, we see that MONUC's initial mandate as set out in Resolution 1279 did not authorise force beyond self-defence. This was to change in a gradual way. With Resolution 1291 in February 2000, the Security Council, citing a 'threat to international peace and security in the region', authorised MONUC under Chapter VII to 'take the necessary action' to protect itself and to protect civilians. The invocation of Chapter VII was contained in a single paragraph and the authorisation to use force beyond self-defence was for a limited purpose.[342] According to the DPKO, the rules of engagement provided that '*force could be used beyond self-defence* to ensure security and freedom of movement of MONUC and to afford protection to civilians under imminent threat of physical violence'.[343] In short, we see the Security Council authorising the use of force beyond self-defence for limited purposes only.

The Security Council's intention regarding the use of force beyond self-defence when it passed Resolution 1445 in December 2000 is more difficult to ascertain. While the resolution did characterise the situation in the DRC as continuing to pose a threat to international peace and security in the region, it did not invoke Chapter VII at any point in the resolution, nor did it did authorise 'all necessary means' or language of a similar nature. At the same time, however, it called for a doubling of troops and endorsed a revised concept of operations proposed by the Secretary-General, calling for MONUC to be significantly strengthened through the creation of a forward force comprised of two robust taskforces and an armed helicopter unit and other significant military assets. Its use of the word 'endorse' instead of 'decide' as regards the Secretary-General's revised concept of operations and its lack of an explicit invocation of Chapter VII or an explicit bestowal on MONUC to 'take necessary measures' in carrying out its duties, leads to the conclusion that this was not an authorisation to use force beyond self-defence. The fact that the Security Council invoked its previous resolutions and presidential statements in Resolution 1445 would appear to have no impact on the Security Council's intention with regard to this resolution, given that its previous authorisation of the use of force beyond self-defence was limited to civilian protection and did not impact on the mandate as a whole.

[342] As noted, some may argue that the use of force to protect civilians is tantamount to self-defence; while such a position may have some merit where the civilians in question are in the direct care of the operation, it is not at all convincing where, as here, the mandate is to protect civilians generally. See nn 57–60, above.

[343] *Operation Artemis: The Lessons of the Interim Emergency Force* (n 58) 8 (emphasis added).

The adoption of Resolution 1493 in July 2003 marked a change in the Security Council's approach to the authorisation of force beyond self-defence. Instead of invoking Chapter VII in a particular paragraph only, the resolution provided in its final preambular paragraph that it was '*Acting* under Chapter VII of the Charter of the United Nations', thereby affecting the whole of the content of the resolution. Moreover, in addition to repeating its authorisation to use 'the necessary measures' in protecting civilians, it went further and authorised the use of 'all necessary means' to fulfil the entirety of MONUC's mandate, but only in relation to certain geographical areas: the Ituri district and North and South Kivu.[344] From this point onwards, modifications to MONUC's mandate took this form: reiteration of the existence of a threat to international peace and security in the preamble; invocation of Chapter VII in the final paragraph of the preamble; bestowal of a number of additional functions, many of which appear to require the use of substantial offensive force; and authorisation to employ 'all necessary means' in relation to certain tasks of the operation but not others.[345] A similar approach was taken when the operation was converted to MONUSCO.[346] In short, the extent of MONUC's authorisation to use force beyond self-defence steadily increased from Resolution 1291, when it was authorised to use 'the necessary measures' to carry out its civilian protection mandate, through to Resolution 1493, when the authorisation to use force applied to all of its tasks, but only in relation to a certain geographical part of the DRC, until, beginning with Resolution 1565, the Security Council authorised the use of 'all necessary means', and therefore the use of force beyond self-defence, in relation to all geographical parts but for certain tasks only.

Regarding the 'fundamental principle' of consent, matters are somewhat unclear. The Security Council did not specifically make reference to the consent of the host state when it established MONUC by means of Resolution 1279; instead it made reference to the Lusaka Ceasefire Agreement in which the parties, including the DRC, agreed to a 'UN force [which] shall include peacekeeping and peace enforcement operations'.[347] As the mandate was modified, Security Council resolutions tended not to make specific reference to the consent of the host state, instead tending to reaffirm 'the sovereignty, territorial integrity and political independence of the Democratic Republic of the Congo'. This reaffirmation may be a reflection of the Security Council's awareness that the host state was in a

[344] See discussion in chapter 7, section 3 on the import, if any, of the Security Council's reliance on the different phrases authorising force.

[345] eg SC Res 1565 of 1 October 2004; SC Res 1756 of 15 May 2007; SC Res 1794 of 21 December 2007; SC Res 1843 of 20 November 2008; SC Res 1856 of 22 December 2008; SC Res 1906 of 23 December 2009.

[346] SC Res 1925 of 28 May 2010.

[347] Lusaka Ceasefire Agreement (n 178) s 8.2.

position to reject any changes to the mandate that did not have their bases in a mandatory provision of Chapter VII.

It is even less clear that the host state consented to MONUC's role as enforcer of the arms embargo and other sanctions affecting the DRC. From July 2003, the Security Council imposed a mandatory arms embargo against the DRC and demanded that 'all parties provide full access to MONUC military observers, including in ports, airports, airfields, military bases and border crossings' for the purpose of ensuring that the embargo was observed.[348] While it is not clear that MONUC consented to the arms embargo, there is nothing to indicate it did not; as we saw in chapter 3, a state which is the target of the sanctions may consent if it perceives them to be in its interests.[349] Here that may very well have been the case at the outset; after all, DRC's army and police were exempt from the impact of the arms embargo.[350] However, as the Security Council extended the scope of the arms embargo, imposed targeted sanctions (assets freeze and travel ban)[351] and broadened the criteria under which individuals and entities could be designated as subject to the sanctions such that the DRC was also affected,[352] it becomes less clear that the DRC would have considered it to be in its best interests to consent to such measures.

If the DRC did not consent to these sanctions, it is very unlikely that it would have consented to the change in MONUC's mandate, whereby it was tasked with enforcing the sanctions – including 'inspecting, as it deems it necessary and without notice, the cargo of aircraft and of any transport vehicle using the ports, airports, airfields, military bases and border crossings in North Kivu, in South Kivu and in Ituri' and to seize or collect arms and dispose of them.[353]

When President Kabila made clear his desire that the forces should leave the DRC in 2009, the Security Council took this very seriously,

[348] SC Res 1493 of 28 July, para 19.

[349] See discussion in chapter 3, section 3.2.3.3, of the Yugoslav government's consent to the arms embargo put in place in that country.

[350] The Security Council excluded MONUC, IEMF and 'the integrated Congolese national army and police forces' from the embargo (SC Res 1493, para 21).

[351] SC Res 1596 of 18 April 2005, paras 13 and 15 respectively.

[352] For example, by April 2005, instead of an exemption from the arms embargo for the 'integrated Congolese army and national police forces' (as had been the case under SC Res 1493), the exemption applied to 'units of the army and police of the Democratic Republic of the Congo, *provided that the said units*: – have completed the process of their integration, or – operate under the command, respectively, of the état-major intégré of the Armed Forces or of the National Police of the Democratic Republic of the Congo, or – are in the process of their integration, in the territory of the Democratic Republic of the Congo outside the provinces of North and South Kivu and the Ituri district'. SC Res 1596, ibid, para 2 (emphasis added). However, in March 2008 the Security Council decided that the arms embargo (established by Res 1493 para 20 and Res 1596 para 1) would 'no longer apply to the supply, sale or transfer of arms and related materiel, and the provision of any assistance, advice or training related to military activities to the Government of the Democratic Republic of the Congo'. SC Res 1807 of 31 March 2008.

[353] SC Res 1565 of 1 October 2004, para 4(f) and (g).

sending a mission to the host state and agreeing to concessions, including the re-naming of the operation and the withdrawal of 2,000 troops. Despite these concessions, it is not clear from the provisional record or from the wording of the resolution extending (and renaming) MONUC in 2010[354] that host state consent was forthcoming.

Rarely has the Secretariat acknowledged that the 'fundamental principle' of host state consent can ever be absent from a peacekeeping operation.[355] However, in 2009 the Under-Secretary-General for Peacekeeping made the following remarks to the Special Committee on Peacekeeping Operations:

> UN peacekeeping . . . faces new risks. It is increasingly used in situations where the scale of hostilities threatens to overwhelm peacekeepers' capacities to respond. As we saw recently in the Eastern DRC, we have limited reserve capacities to call on when faced with extreme hostilities. Eight of our missions are mandated to protect civilians. Three missions operate in an environment of an ongoing conflict. We have increasingly found ourselves operating in non-permissive environments and *even under conditions of withdrawal of consent*.[356]

While this statement does not specify which operations have had to operate under conditions of withdrawal of consent – nor does it indicate whether the consent that has been withdrawn is that of the host state or that of a party – MONUC would appear to be one such operation.

An argument that the 'fundamental principle' of impartiality was present throughout these operations is a very difficult one to make in light of the fact that the Security Council, time and time again, invoked Chapter VII and specifically authorised MONUC to use 'all necessary means' when assisting the government of the DRC in its battles against the rebels. In effect, MONUC became a party to the conflict, fighting alongside the DRC's FARDC. In the words of the Secretary-General, writing in October 2008:

> In view of the near total disintegration of the FARDC in the face of advancing CNDP troops, MONUC has become the only organized force in Goma and has been compelled to step in to substitute for the role of the national security forces.[357]

Where a peacekeeping force fights alongside government forces – indeed fights *in place of* them – it can scarcely be said to be acting impartially, even if that term is defined as sweepingly as it was in the Brahimi Report – ie

[354] SC Res 1925 of 28 May 2010.

[355] As noted in chapter 2, section 4.3, the Capstone Doctrine provides that where consent is absent, an operation is not peacekeeping but peace-enforcement. United Nations DPKO and Department of Field Operations, *United Nations Peacekeeping Operations: Principles and Guidelines* ('Capstone Doctrine'), 2008, http://pbpu.unlb.org/pbps/Library/Capstone_Doctrine_ENG.pdf (accessed 1 April 2011), endnote 20 at 43.

[356] United Nations, *Remarks of the Under Secretary-General for Peacekeeping Operations, Mr Alain Le Roy, to the Special Committee on Peacekeeping Operations* 23 February 2009, www.un.org/en/peacekeeping/articles/article230209.htm (accessed 1 April 2011) (emphasis added).

[357] United Nations, *Letter Dated 31 October 2008 from the Secretary-General to the President of the Security Council* (UN Doc S/2008/703), 12 November 2008, Annex, para 4.

'adherence to the principles of the Charter and to the objectives of a mandate that is rooted in those Charter principles'.[358] Kjeksrud suggested that MONUC was impartial 'to the *mandate*' since the Security Council gave the UN force the task of supporting the FARDC,[359] but this seems tautologous. A mandate that is not impartial can hardly be said to be upheld impartially. And even Kjeksrud conceded that 'MONUC is hardly perceived to be impartial'.[360] If one relies on a definition of impartiality more in keeping with common usage, such as that posited by Hammarskjöld – ie that the force must be 'impartial, in the sense that it does not serve as a means to force settlement, in the interests of one party, of political conflicts or legal issues recognized as controversial'[361] – it becomes clear that the forces were not impartial.

4.2.2 Constitutional Basis

When MONUC was established in November 1999,[362] it was not a Chapter VII operation. That Chapter was not invoked, no mention was made of a need to restore international peace and security, and MONUC's functions were non-military in nature. By February 2000, however, the Security Council had passed Resolution 1291, which characterised the situation in the DRC as a threat to international peace and security in the region, and, in paragraph 8, invoked Chapter VII and authorised 'the necessary action' in relation to a civilian protection mandate. As such, at this stage MONUC was a peacekeeping operation with only some tasks authorised under Chapter VII; consent of the host state was legally required in relation to all other aspects of the mandate.

By July 2003, the Security Council had broadened MONUC's mandate such that its invocation of Chapter VII impacted on the whole resolution; however, only in relation to certain of its tasks was it vested with the authority to use 'the necessary measures' or 'all necessary means'.[363] It repeated this practice in subsequent resolutions and took a similar approach with MONUSCO. Thus, from July 2003 MONUC/MONUSCO was a Chapter VII operation.

In relation to MONUC's civilian protection mandate from February 2002 onwards and in relation to the tasks for which the Security Council

[358] Brahimi Report (n 4) para 50.

[359] Stian Kjeksrud, 'Matching Robust Ambitions with Robust Action in UN Peace Operations – Towards a Conceptual Overstretch?', Robust Peacekeeping Seminar, Paris (hosted by the French Ministry of Defense and the Research Network on Peacekeeping Operations (ROP) of the University of Montreal), 12–13 April 2010, www.operationspaix.net/IMG/pdf/RPK_Stian_Kjeksrud-1.pdf (accessed 1 April 2011), 5.

[360] ibid.

[361] United Nations, *Report of the Secretary-General on Compliance with General Assembly Resolution 1123 (XI)* (UN Doc A/3512), 24 January 1957, para 5.

[362] SC Res 1279 of 30 November 1999.

[363] SC Res 1493 of 28 July 2003.

authorised MONUC/MONUSCO to use 'all necessary measures' from July 2003 onwards, the Security Council relied on its Article 42 powers. As discussed, only Article 42 can provide a constitutional basis for authorisations of force of this level. As to the tasks bestowed upon MONUC or MONUSCO under Chapter VII, but for which they were not authorised to use 'all necessary means', one could argue that the Security Council nevertheless intended to enable MONUC/MONUSCO to use force beyond self-defence. As we will see in the discussion of the peacekeeping operation in Liberia (UNMIL), an authorisation to use 'all necessary means' (or similar) is not essential to a Security Council authorising a peacekeeping operation to use force beyond self-defence, so long as it so intends.[364] However, where the Security Council bestows such an authorisation on some tasks and not on others, as it did here (and did not do with UNMIL, where no tasks were given an authorisation to use 'all necessary means') its intention to exclude the authorisation to use forced beyond self-defence would appear clear.

The tasks bestowed upon MONUC/MONUSCO that are not accompanied by an authorisation to use force beyond self-defence clearly still fall under Chapter VII (as noted, that Chapter was invoked in a general way in the resolutions establishing or modifying their mandates). As such, they would have their constitutional bases in Article 41, Article 40 or a provision of Chapter VII where host state consent is required. Given that the operations appeared to lack impartiality at certain times, they would not fit under Article 40, with its requirement that measures taken thereunder 'shall be without prejudice to the rights, claims or position of the parties concerned', thereby leaving Article 41 or a consent-based article.

4.2.3 Conclusion and Assessment of Success

From the start, MONUC's civilian protection mandate was unrealistic, leading states to express their concern at its unworkable nature. Initially, it served only to create unrealistic expectations on the part of the population – expectations that were promptly dashed by the operation's inability to undertake its civilian protection mandate, especially during its first two years.[365]

It was only with the establishment of Operation Artemis in 2003 that matters began to improve. In many ways the EU's participation in that quasi-enforcement operation was reminiscent of the UK's intervention to help a beleaguered UNAMSIL in Sierra Leone by sending in Operation Palliser in May 2000.[366] As was the case with UNAMSIL, developed states with their highly trained and equipped military were willing to step in – but only when the level of atrocity was particularly high and only on their

[364] See discussion of UNMIL in chapter 6, section 2.2.1.
[365] Månsson (n 191) 508.
[366] See discussion in section 2.1 above.

own terms. As with the British in Sierra Leone, the EU forces in the DRC acted independently of the UN rather than serving as part of it. Indeed, when a newly fortified MONUC took over the functions of Operation Artemis in September 2003, *none* of the participants in IEMF were willing to re-hat with MONUC.[367] Not only did this mean that 'MONUC lacked the Special Forces' intelligence and overflight capabilities that were crucial to the IEMF's success',[368] it had another important effect. The unwillingness of developed states to volunteer troops to serve as a part of a UN-led militarised operation suggests a lack of confidence in such operations. The fact that two of the main contributors to Operation Artemis, France and the UK, were permanent members of the Security Council, which bestowed the militarised mandate on MONUC, made their unwillingness to volunteer troops for MONUC particularly regrettable.[369]

When the operation was given a militarised mandate for Bunia/Ituri and the Kivus in July 2003 and, later, in October 2004 for certain tasks throughout the country, expectations were heightened. When these expectations were not met – as almost invariably they were not – the result was further criticism of MONUC (and the UN generally) by politicians, international NGOs and those under MONUC's protection. Some Congolese referred to MONUC peacekeepers as 'tourists'; others referred to them as 'butterflies' – 'pretty to look at, but otherwise useless'.[370]

Finally, the relationship between MONUC and the FARDC was highly problematic. While the decisions of the Security Council in this regard may well have been animated by a desire to ensure the continued cooperation of the DRC government, such a role drives a coach and horses through any principle of impartiality. When the force with which the UN is aligning itself is a notorious human rights violator and an entity that engages in the very acts that a peacekeeping operation is charged with preventing, that operation is necessarily tarnished. For the first time we see the spectre of a UN peacekeeping operation finding itself in a position whereby it apparently considered it necessary to explain away the conduct of government soldiers, with whom it worked but over whom it had no control.

[367] *Operation Artemis: The Lessons of the Interim Emergency Force* (n 58) 14.

[368] ibid. A request by the DPKO that the IEMF make occasional visits was turned down by the EU.

[369] France and the UK's contribution to MONUC, while not non-existent, generally involved the contribution of fewer than 10 troops by each country. This did not change after the strengthening of MONUC in September 2003. By the end of October 2005, both the UK and France had completely ceased to contribute troops to the operation. China, which at times contributed only a single soldier to the force, contributed approximately 220 troops in the period from April 2003. Russia's contribution to MONUC was extremely limited throughout; where it contributed troops at all, it generally amounted to one or two soldiers. The contribution of the US was zero (www.un.org/en/peacekeeping/resources/statistics, accessed 1 April 2011).

[370] Unattributed, 'Democratic Republic of Congo: The UN Gets Tougher', *The Economist*, 12 March 2005.

Chapter 6

When Peacekeeping and Enforcement Overlap: Twenty-First Century Practice – The Later Operations

You can anticipate being let down by everyone on whom you depend for support, be that troops, funding, logistics or political engagement. Only by shining a spotlight on those failures in every possible way can you mobilise the attention necessary to get the action you need. Bear in mind that whoever fails you will, in the end, be the most active in blaming you for whatever goes wrong.

Open letter from the former force commander of UNAMIR, Lieutenant-General Roméo Dallaire, to the new UNAMID force commander designate, General Martin Agwai[1]

1. INTRODUCTION

THIS CHAPTER WILL consider a second group of militarised peacekeeping missions established in the twenty-first century. These six operations took place (or are continuing to take place) in Liberia, Côte D'Ivoire, Haiti, Burundi, Sudan, and the Central African Republic and Chad. Apart from the operations in Burundi and in the Central African Republic and Chad, all are still functioning at the time of writing. As we shall see, the operations in all six countries or regions are/were militarised to a greater or lesser extent.

[1] www.guardian.co.uk/commentisfree/2007/sep/17/adauntingmandate (accessed 1 April 2011).

2. LIBERIA (SEPTEMBER 2003–PRESENT)

2.1 The Mission

After a rebel force led by Charles Taylor attempted a coup against Liberia's President Samuel Doe in 1989, control of the country was split. In June 1990, President Doe asked ECOWAS to send a peacekeeping force to help him re-establish control.[2] ECOWAS established the ECOWAS Cease-Fire Monitoring Group (ECOMOG) to enforce a truce, by force if necessary.[3] A ceasefire that had been agreed in November 1990 broke down, leading to renewed fighting in mid-1992. ECOMOG became a principal combatant, with some 600 of its troops being taken hostage by Charles Taylor's forces.[4] At the request of ECOWAS states, the Security Council designated the situation in Liberia a threat to international peace and security, invoked Chapter VII and imposed a complete embargo on all military shipments, except for supplies for ECOMOG.[5] In September 1993 the Security Council established the UN Observer Mission in Liberia (UNOMIL) to monitor compliance with a Peace Agreement signed by the three Liberian parties on 25 July 1993, to observe and verify an election process and to coordinate with ECOMOG 'without participation in enforcement operations'.[6] The mandate of UNOMIL[7] was terminated on 30 September 1997, after elections were held.[8] The last contingent of ECOMOG withdrew from Liberia in November 1999.[9]

The election, which was won by Charles Taylor, did little to quell the tensions between the government and opposition party leaders, and the civil war resumed. By early May 2003, the two rebel movements had gained control of nearly two-thirds of the country and were threatening to seize the capital.[10] An ECOWAS-brokered ceasefire agreement, signed

[2] Thomas M Franck, *Recourse to Force: State Action Against Threats and Armed Attacks* (Cambridge, Cambridge University Press, 2002) 156.

[3] ibid.

[4] ibid, 157.

[5] ibid; SC Res 778 of 19 November 1992.

[6] SC Res 866 of 22 September 1993, para 3. According to the DPKO, 'UNOMIL was the first United Nations peacekeeping mission undertaken in cooperation with a peacekeeping operation already established by another organization' (www.un.org/en/peacekeeping/missions/unmil/background.shtml, accessed 1 April 2011).

[7] Characterised by the DPKO as peacekeeping; see the list of peacekeeping missions at www.un.org/en/peacekeeping/documents/operationslist.pdf (accessed 1 April 2011).

[8] In November 1997 the Secretary-General established the United Nations Peace-Building Support Office in Liberia (UNOL) to assist the government in consolidating peace following the elections. This latter mission has been classified by the UN Secretariat as a 'peace-building mission or political office'.

[9] United Nations, *Report of the Secretary-General to the Security Council on Liberia* (UN Doc S/2003/875), 11 September 2003, para 3.

[10] ibid, para 9.

on 17 June 2003, was almost immediately breached.[11] In a letter of 28 June 2003 to the Security Council – citing the deaths of hundreds of civilians in fighting in and around Monrovia, the wanton destruction of property, widespread looting, food shortages and cholera outbreaks – the Secretary-General warned the Security Council of 'a major humanitarian catastrophe' in the making.[12] He recommended that the Security Council

> take urgent action to authorize the deployment to Liberia of a highly trained and well-equipped multinational force, under the lead of a Member State, to prevent a major humanitarian tragedy and to stabilize the situation in that country. Such a force would be authorized under Chapter VII of the Charter of the United Nations.[13]

What was missing, however, was a suitably powerful Member State to take the lead in the proposed quasi-enforcement operation. Some observers,[14] and the Secretary-General himself,[15] voiced the opinion that the United States was the most appropriate country to lead the quasi-enforcement operation in light of its historical ties to Liberia.[16] Commentators cited the UK's role in Sierra Leone[17] and Australia's action in East Timor[18] as models for US leadership. In the words of an International Crisis Group Report: 'The missing link is the United States.'[19] The US, however, was reluctant to assume a significant role, citing the nature of the operation,[20] its commitments in Afghanistan and Iraq, and its ongoing 'war on terror'.[21] When US President George W Bush sent 35 American troops to the country in June 2003, he explained that they were 'solely for the purposes of protecting American citizens and property'.[22] He linked any further US involvement in the country to President Taylor's stepping down.[23]

[11] United Nations, *Letter Dated 18 June 2003 from the Secretary-General Addressed to the President of the Security Council* (UN Doc S/2003/659), 19 June 2003.

[12] United Nations, *Letter Dated 28 June 2003 from the Secretary-General Addressed to the President of the Security Council* (UN Doc S/2003/678), 28 June 2003.

[13] ibid.

[14] Unattributed, 'Why Liberia is Not Somalia', *The Economist,* 19 July 2003. See Fareed Zakaria, 'Take the Lead in Liberia', *Newsweek,* 18 August 2003.

[15] The Secretary-General asked the United States to 'consider spearheading the deployment of that force' (*Report of the Secretary-General* (n 9) para 10).

[16] Liberia was colonised by freed American slaves who declared an independent republic in 1847. Unattributed, 'Goodbye to All That?', *The Economist,* 16 August 2003.

[17] 'Why Liberia is Not Somalia' (n 14). See also Peter Beinart, 'Ugly Stepfather', *The New Republic,* 23 June 2003.

[18] Zakaria (n 14).

[19] Beinart (n 17).

[20] 'Pentagon officials balked at the use of American troops, arguing that such a mission would be difficult and ill defined' (Zakaria (n 14)).

[21] Stephen Dinan, '"Strong Case" Sought for US role in Liberia', *The Washington Times,* 9 July 2003.

[22] Beinart (n 17).

[23] Zakaria (n 14).

In August 2003, by Resolution 1497, the Security Council authorised the establishment of an ECOWAS-led quasi-enforcement operation in Liberia under Chapter VII, authorising it to 'take all necessary measures to fulfil its mandate',[24] in support of the implementation of the 2003 ceasefire agreement.[25] Three days later, the force – known as the ECOWAS Mission in Liberia (ECOMIL) or simply 'the Multinational Force' – began to deploy. The Multinational Force was made up of African states with the support of troops from the United Nations Mission in Sierra Leone.[26] In early August, some 2,300 US marines were positioned off the Liberian coast on three gunships.[27] Taylor left the country on 11 August, seeking sanctuary in Nigeria.[28] However, the US remained reluctant to become more involved. While the Bush administration did send some 200 marines into Monrovia in late August,[29] the role of the US was more limited than many had hoped.[30] The last US troops vacated the country in early October, just over a month after their arrival.[31] The security situation in the country, while improved, remained 'highly unstable'.[32]

Also by Resolution 1497, the Security Council called for the establishment of a peacekeeping force to follow on from the ECOWAS-led force; it was to deploy by 1 October 2003.[33] In September 2003, by Resolution 1509, the Security Council established the United Nations Mission in Liberia (UNMIL) and requested that the Secretary-General transfer authority from ECOMIL to UNMIL on 1 October 2003.[34] UNMIL was charged with supporting a Comprehensive Peace Agreement reached on 18 August 2003[35] and was to consist of up to 15,000 UN military personnel.[36] The Security Council determined that the situation in Liberia 'continue[d] to

[24] SC Res 1497 of 1 August 2003, para 5.

[25] ibid.

[26] ibid.

[27] Daniel Eisenburg et al, 'Who will Stop the Killing?' *Time South Pacific*, 4 August 2003, 38; Simon Robinson and Stephen Faris, 'Better Late than Never: African Peacekeepers Finally Begin to Deploy in War-Ravaged Liberia. But Will the Americans Ever Come Ashore?', *Time South Pacific*, 11 August 2003, 48.

[28] 'Goodbye to All That?' (n 16).

[29] Tom Masland and Jonathan Clayton, 'Liberia: "Thank You, George Bush"', *Newsweek*, 25 August 2003, 8.

[30] In the words of the Secretary-General, the role of the US was 'limited in time and scope' (*Report of the Secretary-General* (n 9) para 10).

[31] Unattributed, 'US Out, UN In', *West Central Africa Monitor*, November 2004, 5.

[32] *Report of the Secretary-General* (n 9) para 22.

[33] Referred to by the Security Council as a 'United Nations stabilization force' (SC Res 1497 of 1 August 2003, para 2). The Secretary-General was requested to submit recommendations regarding the size, structure and mandate of the force.

[34] See SC Res 1509 of 19 September 2003. The Security Council based its resolution on the *Report of the Secretary-General* (n 9).

[35] SC Res 1509, ibid. The Secretary-General terminated UNOL in September 2003 (see *Letter Dated 16 September 2003 from the Secretary-General to the President of the Security Council* (UN Doc S/2003/899), 17 September 2003, and its responsibilities were transferred to UNMIL (see *Report of the Secretary-General* (n 9) para 114).

[36] SC Res 1509 (n 34).

constitute a threat to international peace and security in the region, to stability in the West Africa subregion, and to the peace process for Liberia'[37] and established the whole of Resolution 1509 under Chapter VII.[38] UNMIL was given a wide variety of tasks, several of which – such as providing security at key government installations and helping to establish security conditions for humanitarian assistance – were of a potentially forceful nature.[39] Additionally, it was charged with protecting civilians under imminent threat of physical violence, within its capabilities and without prejudice to the efforts of the government.[40] Despite the fact that UNMIL was to assume many of the functions of the Multinational Force[41] – from which it received many of its 're-hatted' troops – the Security Council did not authorise UNMIL to 'take all necessary measures' (or language of similar effect) to fulfil its mandate – as it had for the Multinational Force.

It will come as no surprise that the Secretary-General had a very difficult time establishing the operation. After all, he was left with 12 days to establish a force that was ultimately to number 15,000 troops – the largest peacekeeping force at the time.[42] The Secretary-General, with considerable understatement, described the process of generating troops for UNMIL as 'not . . . completely satisfactory'.[43] As of 31 October 2003, the end of the first operational month of UNMIL, only 4,481 of the authorised 15,000 troops were on the ground.[44] Of these, a mere nine were contributed by permanent Member States of the Security Council; the US contributed a single soldier.[45] As for the non-permanent members of the Security Council, with the exception of Pakistan's contribution of three soldiers, none chose to volunteer troops.[46]

[37] ibid, penultimate preambular para.

[38] ibid, final preambular para.

[39] ibid, para 3.

[40] ibid.

[41] The resolution asks the Secretary-General to 'transfer authority from the ECOWAS-led forces to UNMIL on 1 October 2003' (SC Res 1509, para 1).

[42] UNAMSIL, for which 17,500 troops had been authorised in March 2001, had already begun its drawdown process. MONUC's troop numbers in late 2003 were lower than the 15,000 authorised in Liberia and were not increased to 16,700 until October 2004.

[43] United Nations, *First Progress Report of the Secretary-General on the United Nations Mission in Liberia* (UN Doc S/2003/1175), 15 December 2003, para 7.

[44] www.un.org/en/peacekeeping/contributors/2003/October2003_4.pdf (accessed 1 April 2011).

[45] www.un.org/en/peacekeeping/contributors/2003/October2003_5.pdf (accessed 1 April 2011). The contributions from the permanent members of the Security Council were as follows: China (4); France (1); Russia (0); UK (3); US (1). A year later, in October 2004, the contributions of the permanent members had improved somewhat due to a significant increase in troops by China. At that point their contribution amounted to 577 of the 14,337 troops who were present at that time (www.un.org/en/peacekeeping/contributors/2004/October2004_4.pdf, accessed 1 April 2011), with all but 10 of those coming from China (www.un.org/en/peacekeeping/contributors/2004/October2004_5.pdf, accessed 1 April 2011).

[46] In addition to Pakistan, the non-permanent members of the Security Council at the time were Angola, Bulgaria, Cameroon, Chile, Germany, Guinea, Mexico, Spain and Syria (www.un.org/en/peacekeeping/contributors/2003/October2003_5.pdf, accessed 1 April 2011).

UNMIL began the process of disarmament on 7 December 2003,[47] despite the fact that it was operating at only one-third of its authorised capacity.[48] The reason for the push for disarmament (despite recommendations by the military that troop numbers were inadequate for this task)[49] is unclear. While some diplomats and officials in Liberia indicated that the Special Representative of the Secretary-General in Liberia, Jacques Paul Klein – a US national – was doing the bidding of the US, this was denied by the US government.[50] As the fighters came to realise that they were not to be financially compensated in return for surrendering their weapons, riots broke out and several people were killed.[51] UNMIL suspended disarmament on 17 December 2003.[52] It resumed in February 2004 and was completed on 31 October 2004.[53]

The fact that the operation was not at full capacity impacted on UNMIL's ability to protect civilians throughout the country.[54] However, even when UNMIL eventually had its full complement of troops in mid-2004,[55] its ability to protect civilians was limited. As of September 2004, most border crossings remained under rebel control.[56] On 29 October 2004 riots occurred in Monrovia which left 16 dead.[57] A *Lessons Learned* report described UNMIL forces as being 'thin on the ground', a factor which 'had implications for the safety and protection of civilians'.[58] The Report

[47] International Crisis Group, *Rebuilding Liberia: Prospects and Perils*, Crisis Group Africa Report No 75, 30 January 2004, www.crisisgroup.org/~/media/Files/africa/west-africa/liberia/Rebuilding%20Liberia%20Prospects%20and%20Perils.pdf (accessed 1 April 2011), 4.

[48] As of 30 November 2003, only 5,455 of the 15,000 troops authorised for UNMIL were in place (www.un.org/en/peacekeeping/contributors/2003/November2003_4.pdf, accessed 1 April 2011). As of 12 December 2003, the operation consisted of only 5,848 of the 15,000 troops authorised. Aside from 66 troops contributed by China, no permanent member contributed troops by this stage; Ireland (300) and the Netherlands (270) were the only countries from outside Africa and Asia to contribute troops (*First Progress Report of the Secretary-General* (n 43) Annex).

[49] *Rebuilding Liberia* (n 47), 4.

[50] ibid.

[51] ibid, 5.

[52] ibid.

[53] United Nations, *Letter Dated 6 December 2004 from the Chairman of the Security Council Committee Established Pursuant to Resolution 1521 (2003) Concerning Liberia Addressed to the President of the Security Council [enclosing the November 2004 Report of the Panel of Experts on Liberia]* (UN Doc S/2004/955), 6 December 2004, para 63.

[54] For further detail regarding attacks against civilians during this period, see *First Progress Report of the Secretary-General* (n 43) paras 9–16 and 53–58.

[55] As of 31 May the operation consisted of 14,649 of the 15,000 authorised troops (www.un.org/en/peacekeeping/contributors/2004/May2004_4.pdf, accessed 1 April 2011).

[56] United Nations, *Letter Dated 23 September 2004 from the Chairman of the Security Council Committee Established Pursuant to Resolution 1521 (2003) Concerning Liberia Addressed to the President of the Security Council [enclosing the September 2004 Report of the Panel of Experts on Liberia]* (UN Doc S/2004/752), 24 September 2004, para 8.

[57] *Panel of Experts Report* (n 53).

[58] Festus Aboagye and Alhaji Bah, 'Liberia at a Crossroads: A Preliminary Look at the United Nations Mission in Liberia (UNMIL) and the Protection of Civilians' (Institute for Security Studies, Paper 95), November 2004, www.apsta-africa.org/pdf/paper95.pdf (accessed 1 April 2011), 7.

further noted that 'even where UNMIL was present, the inaction of troops arising from the narrow interpretation of UNMIL's mandate regarding the use of force for the protection of civilians, compromised the readiness and willingness of the force to do so'.[59] Moreover, the Report concluded that, as at it was written in November 2004, '[i]n spite of its robust mandate, UNMIL is yet to use force to achieve its mandate and may not have the occasion to, except for a couple of incidents to dismantle unauthorised checkpoints by armed elements'.[60]

By 2005, the security situation in Liberia had become 'relatively calm'[61] and, in Resolution 1626, the Security Council requested that the Secretary-General make recommendations for a drawdown plan.[62] In the same resolution, it charged UNMIL with providing security for the Special Court for Sierra Leone and authorised the provision of an additional 250 military personnel.[63] In Resolution 1626, the Security Council again found that the situation posed a threat to international peace and security in the region,[64] and again invoked Chapter VII in relation to the entire resolution.[65]

The drawdown process has been slow.[66] Three stages of drawdown were completed in September 2008, March 2009 and May 2010, reducing UNMIL's troop numbers to 8,102 as at August 2010.[67] Security concerns and 2011 elections have meant that the Security Council has judged the presence of the force to continue to be necessary.[68] UNMIL's mandate was most recently renewed up to 30 September 2011 by Resolution 1938.[69] Again a threat international peace and security was found to exist, and again Chapter VII was invoked in relation to the whole resolution.[70] UNMIL was further charged with assisting the Liberian government with 2011 general presidential and legislative elections.[71]

[59] ibid, 16.

[60] ibid, 7. Nevertheless, the report concluded that the civilian protection mandate was 'having a significant impact on the civilian population'.

[61] Unattributed, 'Global Law vs Local Warlord', *The Economist*, 14 May 2005.

[62] SC Res 1626 of 19 September 2005, para 13.

[63] ibid, para 5.

[64] ibid, penultimate preambular para.

[65] ibid, final preambular para.

[66] In July 2006, the Security Council reconfigured the operation slightly by decreasing the military component of the force by 125 and increasing the civilian police component by the same number (SC Res 1694 of 13 July 2006).

[67] United Nations, *Twenty-First Progress Report of the Secretary-General on the United Nations Mission in Liberia* (UN Doc S/2010/429), 11 August 2010, para 61. This figure includes the additional troops deployed to provide security for the Special Court for Sierra Leone. In SC Res 1971 of 3 March 2011, the Security Council authorised the withdrawal of those military personnel.

[68] The Secretary-General described the security situation in the country as 'stable, but fragile' (*Twenty-First Progress Report of the Secretary-General*, ibid, para 10).

[69] SC Res 1938 of 15 September 2010. The Security Council noted its concern that progress of the drawdown was slow.

[70] ibid, penultimate and final preambular paras.

[71] ibid, para 2.

2.2 Evaluation

2.2.1 *Adherence to the 'Fundamental Principles'*

The issue of whether UNMIL was required to adhere to the 'fundamental principle' of force only in self-defence was a matter on which no less an authority than the UN Legal Counsel himself voiced a view in an October 2003 opinion.[72] The question was raised by the Under-Secretary-General for Peacekeeping, Jean-Marie Guéhenno, who had been asked by the Permanent Representative of an unidentified state to confirm that the Security Council had indeed authorised UNMIL to use armed force for purposes or in situations other than self-defence when it established the operation in Security Council Resolution 1509. The fact that, in Resolution 1509, the Security Council had invoked Chapter VII but had not authorised the force to use 'all necessary means', left the requesting state uncertain about UNMIL's ability to use force beyond self-defence.

Citing the Security Council's determination that the situation in Liberia constituted a threat to international peace and security and the Security Council's statement that it was acting under Chapter VII, the Legal Counsel opined that '[t]he Security Council has therefore determined that the situation in Liberia falls within the scope of Chapter VII of the Charter and has decided, in resolution 1509 (2003), to exercise its powers under that Chapter'.[73] He continued:

> The powers of the Security Council under Chapter VII of the Charter include the power to establish a United Nations operation. They also include the power to authorize that operation to use armed force for purposes or in situations other than self-defence. Whether the Security Council has in fact exercised that power and granted such authorization depends on the content of the resolution that it has adopted.[74]

He observed that Security Council Resolution 1509 did not 'expressly' authorise UNMIL to use 'all necessary means' or to 'take the necessary measures' to fulfil any of its functions, noting that:

> [h]ad such express wording appeared in the resolution, it would, of course, have been beyond all doubt that the Security Council had made use of its powers under Chapter VII of the Charter to authorize UNMIL to use armed force (other than in situations of self-defence).[75]

[72] United Nations, 'Note to the Under-Secretary-General of the Department of Peacekeeping Operations, United Nations' [2003] *United Nations Juridical Yearbook*, Part Two, Chapter VI, 538–40 (UN Sales No E.07.V.1). Hans Corell served as Under-Secretary-General for Legal Affairs and Legal Counsel of the United Nations from March 1994 to March 2004.

[73] ibid, 539.

[74] ibid.

[75] ibid.

He stated that it did not, however, follow 'from the fact that no such express wording appears in the resolution that the Security Council has not exercised that power and granted such authorization'.[76] Instead, he opined, one must consider the intention of the Security Council.

> Whether it has [granted an authorisation to use force beyond self-defence] depends upon the interpretation of the resolution, specifically, on the ordinary and natural meaning which is to be given to its terms when they are read in the context of the resolution as a whole and in the light of its object and purpose, and against the background of the discussions leading to, and the circumstances of, its adoption, in particular the report that the Secretary-General submitted pursuant to resolution 1497 (2003).
>
> Applying these tests, it is evident that the Security Council fully intended, in adopting Resolution 1509 (2003), to authorize UNMIL to use armed force, otherwise than in self defence.
>
> This is clear from the wording of the resolution itself. So, for example, UNMIL would simply not be in a position meaningfully to discharge that element of its mandate which is set out in operative paragraph 3 *(j)* of the resolution [ie 'to protect United Nations personnel, facilities, installations and equipment, ensure the security and freedom of movement of its personnel and, without prejudice to the efforts of the government, to protect civilians under imminent threat of physical violence, within its capabilities'] if it were not able to resort to armed force, if need be.
>
> It is also clear from the history and circumstances of the adoption of the resolution. Thus, the Secretary-General, in the report that he submitted pursuant to resolution 1497 (2003), proposed a concept of operations for UNMIL that was explicitly structured on the assumption that it should have 'a robust mandate' which would enable it to take 'a robust approach' and pre-empt potentially destabilizing events (S/2003/875, paragraph 57). The Security Council, in the eighteenth preambular paragraph of its resolution 1509 (2003), *'[w]elcom[ed]* the Secretary-General's report . . . and its recommendation'. Moreover, article IV of the Comprehensive Peace Agreement sets out the request of the parties to the United Nations to 'deploy a United Nations Chapter VII force' in Liberia to support the transitional Government and assist in the implementation of the Agreement. Resolution 1509 (2003), establishing UNMIL, represents the United Nations' response to that request.
>
> This being so, we would advise that you write back to the Permanent Representative of [State] confirming that it is the considered view of the Secretariat that the Security Council, by its resolution 1509 (2003) of 19 September 2003, has authorized UNMIL to use armed force for purposes or in situations other than self-defence.[77]

Resolution 1509 did not specifically indicate that the Security Council had obtained (or was relying upon) the consent of the host state. It did, however, make reference to the August 2003 Comprehensive Peace Agreement.

[76] ibid.
[77] ibid.

The parties to that Agreement, including the government of Liberia, had requested that the UN 'deploy a United Nations Chapter VII force in the Republic of Liberia to support the transitional government and to assist in the implementation of this Agreement'.[78] However, general consent to a 'Chapter VII force' in a peace agreement is different from a host state consenting to a specific mandate, where, as here, the mandate authorises the use of force beyond self-defence. As is clear from the Legal Opinion above, even where a Security Council establishes a Chapter VII operation, the question remains as to whether it authorised force beyond self-defence.

On the issue of the 'fundamental principle' of impartiality, there is little to suggest that UNMIL functioned in a partial way – either when impartiality is defined in the over-broad way as proposed by the Brahimi Report or when it is defined in a more traditional way.

2.2.2 *Constitutional Basis*

It is clear from the wording of Resolution 1509 that UNMIL was established by the Security Council by exercise of its Chapter VII powers. This was emphasised by the Opinion of the UN Legal Counsel. However, that fact alone does not provide a full answer regarding the constitutional basis of the force. As noted by the UN Legal Counsel, the Security Council possesses various powers under that Chapter, including the power to authorise the use of force beyond self-defence. As the UN Legal Counsel pointed out, where the Security Council invokes Chapter VII and authorises 'all necessary measures' it is 'beyond all doubt' that force beyond self-defence has been authorised. Where, as here, there is no authorisation to use 'all necessary measures', we must look to the Security Council's intention as indicated, inter alia, by the content of the resolution that it has adopted and the background to it. As discussed, with UNMIL it appears that the Security Council authorised the use of force beyond self-defence.

As discussed in chapter 3, only one article of the UN Charter empowers the Security Council to authorise the use of offensive force under Chapter VII: Article 42. As such, the forceful tasks of the operation would appear to have their constitutional basis in that article. It has been argued by some scholars that an 'incidental' or 'limited' use of force may, nevertheless fall under Article 40[79] or Article 41.[80] Given that, for UNMIL, the Security Council did not invoke the 'all necessary measures' language and given the relatively limited force used in the operation, this may be the type of operation that those scholars had in mind. Nevertheless, an argument

[78] 'Comprehensive Peace Agreement Between the Government of Liberia and the Liberians United for Reconciliation and Democracy (LURD) and the Movement for Democracy in Liberia (MODEL) and Political Parties', Accra, 18 August 2003, para 1.

[79] Chapter 3, section 3.2.2.4.

[80] Chapter 3, section 3.2.3.2.

relying on Article 40 or 41 for the establishment of a forceful operation remains very difficult to make in any circumstances;[81] it is even more difficult to make in relation to UNMIL, if one accepts the view of the Legal Counsel that the operation may use 'armed force, otherwise than in self-defence' without finding the existence of any qualification or limitation.

The non-forceful aspects of the operation were also explicitly established by means of the Security Council acting under Chapter VII. The mandatory language used by the Security Council in relation to UNMIL – '[*d*]*ecides* to establish . . .UNMIL', '[*d*]ecides that UNMIL shall have the following mandate' – suggests that it was making a binding decision. If so, the non-forceful tasks would fall under Article 40 or 41.

2.2.3 *Conclusion and Assessment of Success*

The circumstances of this operation highlight the disconnect between what the Security Council is prepared to demand of a militarised peacekeeping operation and what its members are willing to contribute to ensure the success of such an operation. It was only following considerable pressure that the US participated in the quasi-enforcement force – and then only in a very limited way. With the transition from quasi-enforcement to militarised peacekeeping, what had been very limited participation on the part of Security Council Member States became, to all intents and purposes, non-existent.

Moreover, the Security Council's move from quasi-enforcement to militarised peacekeeping was so hurried as to be unseemly. Requiring UNMIL to take over from ECOMIL only two months after ECOMIL was established – and a mere 12 days after UNMIL itself was established – meant that UNMIL was destined to encounter significant problems. The Liberian example shows that the 90-day timeframe for fully deploying a militarised peacekeeping operation, as recommended by the Brahimi Report,[82] was unrealistic. This has been acknowledged by the DPKO itself.[83]

By the end of UNMIL's first month of operation, re-hatted ECOMIL troops made up some 80 per cent of its troops. While such troops had the obvious advantage that they were immediately available, there were difficulties associated with these forces. We see the converse of the situation in East Timor as regards the parties' perception of the re-hatted troops.

[81] It is a particularly difficult argument to make in relation to Art 41, which specifically speaks of 'measures not involving the use of armed force'.

[82] United Nations, *Identical Letters Dated 21 August 2000 from the Secretary-General to the President of the General Assembly and the President of the Security Council [attaching Report of the Panel on UN Peacekeeping Operations (the 'Brahimi Report')]* (UN Docs A/55/305 and S/2000/809), 21 August 2000, para 88.

[83] United Nations Best Practices Unit (DPKO), *Lessons Learned Study on the Start-up Phase of the United Nations Mission in Liberia*, April 2004, www.peacekeepingbestpractices.unlb.org/PBPS/Library/Liberia%20Lessons%20Learned%20(Final).pdf (accessed 1 April 2011), 1.

When Australian troops were re-hatted from the quasi-enforcement operation INTERFET in East Timor to the militarised peacekeeping operation UNTAET, the parties on the ground were fully aware of the military might of Australia and its willingness to use it and acted accordingly. Here, as a DPKO report observed: 'It was known that [the re-hatted] troops would not be sufficiently equipped and would fall below UN operational and logistical requirements.'[84] As a result:

> UNMIL civilian support staff, who were already in high demand due to staffing shortages . . . had to be taken away from other tasks to address the support needs of the ex-ECOMIL troops, and some UN owned equipment . . . intended for other mission needs had to be diverted to the re-hatted troops.[85]

The speed at which the operation was established clearly added to the difficulties in finding states willing to volunteer troops. Moreover, the decision of the Special Representative in Liberia to begin the disarmament process despite only one-third of the forces authorised for UNMIL having been deployed, was described by the International Crisis Group as 'a dangerous miscalculation'.[86] Its report continued:

> UNMIL was not ready. It did not have enough troops on the ground, and coordination with UN agencies was poor. Failure to have all appropriate mechanisms in place led to days of chaos, the deaths of nine people (suspected members of armed factions) and the wounding of one peacekeeper.[87]

Another problem encountered by UNMIL, directly linked to the speed with which it was required to function and the quantity and quality of the troops on which it relied, was that of disappointed public perception. As the DPKO *Lessons Learned* report observed:

> Overall, there is a positive public perception of UNMIL in Liberia, particularly due to the dramatic improvement in security in the capital and the fact that the political process is on course. However, the perception that deployment had been slow had begun to erode some of the good will by early 2004. Until 27 December 2003, for example, no troops had been deployed outside the capital, which was puzzling and frustrating to the population, particularly since more than 7,500 troops had already arrived in the country by 30 November 2003.[88]

Finally, because UNMIL had been given many of ECOMIL's tasks without ECOMIL's 'all necessary measures' authorisation,[89] confusion abounded on the part of the Member States contributing to UNMIL as to whether or not its peacekeepers were empowered to use force beyond

[84] ibid, 6.
[85] ibid.
[86] International Crisis Group (n 47) i.
[87] ibid.
[88] *Lessons Learned* (n 83) 14–15.
[89] It was, however, established by the Security Council under Chapter VII.

self-defence.[90] This confusion cannot have been ameliorated by the UN Secretariat's consistent tendency to emphasise the 'fundamental principle' of force only in self-defence or in defence-of-mandate for UN peacekeeping operations.

3. CÔTE D'IVOIRE (APRIL 2004–PRESENT)

3.1 The Mission

In October 2000, a highly contested presidential election was held in Côte d'Ivoire. Laurent Gbagbo was declared to have won in a controversial decision by the Supreme Court,[91] and unrest followed.[92] In September 2002, after a group of military officers attempted to oust President Gbagbo, outright civil war ensued.[93] Upon the outbreak of the conflict, French troops, present at the request of Gbagbo,[94] helped to evacuate Westerners;[95] however, the French government insisted that its troops would not 'play an active role in any military conflict'.[96] On 29 September 2002, ECOWAS recommended that immediate arrangements be made to deploy ECOWAS troops to Côte d'Ivoire.[97]

On 23 January 2003, the conflict officially ended with the signing of the Linas-Marcoussis Agreement, which provided that a new Government of National Reconciliation would be formed. It would seek assistance from ECOWAS, France and the United Nations in guaranteeing the reform and restructuring of the defence and security forces.[98]

In February 2003, the Security Council welcomed the deployment of an ECOWAS force – referred to as 'ECOFORCE' or 'ECOMICI' – and the involvement of the French troops.[99] It characterised the situation in the

[90] See discussion of the October 2003 Legal Opinion in section 2.2.1.

[91] United Nations, *Report of the Secretary-General on Côte d'Ivoire* (UN Doc S/2003/374), 26 March 2003, para 4.

[92] According to a Human Rights Watch report, his presidency was viewed as illegitimate because 14 of the 19 presidential candidates who ran alongside him had been excluded (Human Rights Watch, *'Because they have the guns . . . I'm left with nothing.' The Price of Continuing Impunity in Côte d'Ivoire*, Human Rights Watch document, vol 18 No 4 (A), May 2006, www.hrw.org/legacy/english/docs/2005/05/03/cotedi10567.htm (accessed 1 April 2011), 4.

[93] Jeremy Kahn, 'No Way Out', *The New Republic*, 24 November 2003.

[94] *Report of the Secretary-General* (n 91) para 13. French forces were already based in Côte d'Ivoire under longstanding bilateral defence arrangements (ibid).

[95] Kahn (n 93) 17.

[96] Unattributed, 'Cracks in the Ivory', *The Economist*, 14 October 2002.

[97] *Report of the Secretary-General* (n 91) para 11. The force's mandate 'included monitoring a proposed ceasefire, ensuring the disengagement of the insurgents from the areas that had fallen under their control, and disarming the rebel groups' (ibid).

[98] ibid, para 21.

[99] SC Res 1464 of 4 February 2003, para 8.

country as constituting a threat to international peace and security in the region and, in relation to one paragraph of the resolution only, invoked Chapter VII and authorised the ECOWAS force and the French forces to 'take the necessary steps' in relation to civilian protection.[100] As of March 2003, there were some 3,900 French forces in Côte d'Ivoire playing what was described by the Secretary-General as a 'robust interposition role'.[101] As for the ECOWAS force, it was still in the process of deploying troops in March;[102] however, even at this early stage there were reports of shortfalls in equipment and funding.[103] In May 2003, the Security Council established the United Nations Mission in Côte D'Ivoire (MINUCI) – described by the DPKO as a 'political mission' rather than a peacekeeping operation[104] – to facilitate implementation of the Linas-Marcoussis Agreement.[105]

The non-implementation of the Linas-Marcoussis Agreement,[106] coupled with the serious troop and logistical shortfalls of the ECOWAS force, led ECOWAS to propose the transformation of the force 'into a reinforced United Nations peacekeeping force'.[107] In February 2004, the Security Council, determining that the situation continued to pose a threat to peace and security in the region and acting under Chapter VII – now invoking that Chapter in relation to the entire resolution, rather than in relation to one paragraph only – decided to establish the United Nations Operation in Côte d'Ivoire, or UNOCI,[108] from 4 April 2004, to assume the functions of the ECOWAS force and MINUCI.[109] UNOCI was authorised 'to use all necessary means to carry out its mandate within its capabilities and its areas of deployment' in relation to all of its tasks.[110] Among its tasks were monitoring a 3 May 2003 ceasefire agreement, assisting with disarmament and providing civilian protection.[111] It was to be composed of up to 6,240 troops and was to act 'in coordination with'[112] the 4,000-strong

[100] The ECOWAS forces, 'together with the French forces supporting them[, are authorised] to take the necessary steps to guarantee the security and freedom of movement of their personnel and to ensure, without prejudice to the responsibilities of the Government of National Reconciliation, the protection of civilians immediately threatened with physical violence within their zones of operation, using the means available to them' (ibid, para 9).

[101] *Report of the Secretary-General* (n 91) paras 39 and 72.

[102] An initial deployment had taken place in January 2003 (ibid, para 42).

[103] ibid, paras 40–43.

[104] See www.un.org/en/peacekeeping (accessed 1 April 2011).

[105] SC Res 1479 of 13 May 2003.

[106] Gilles Yabi, 'Côte D'Ivoire' in Blanca Antonini (ed), *Security Council Resolutions under Chapter VII: Design, Implementation and Accountabilities* (Madrid, Fundación para las Relaciones Internacionales y el Diálogo Exterior (FRIDE), 2009) 75–115, 77.

[107] United Nations, *Report of the Secretary-General on the United Nations Mission in Côte d'Ivoire Submitted Pursuant to Security Council Resolution 1514 (2003) of 13 November 2003* (UN Doc S/2004/3), 6 January 2004, para 52.

[108] Also sometimes referred to in UN documents by its French acronym, ONUCI.

[109] SC Res 1528 of 27 February 2004, para 1.

[110] ibid, para 8.

[111] ibid, para 6.

[112] ibid.

French force,[113] which the Security Council authorised to use 'all necessary means in order to support UNOCI'.[114] The French force, referred to as *Opération Licorne* or just *Licorne*, had as its primary functions the monitoring of compliance with the ceasefire and maintaining security in a demilitarised 'zone of confidence' between the combatants. The French government made clear that *Licorne* was to be limited in the tasks it would undertake.[115]

Days before the planned 4 April 2004 takeover by UNOCI from the ECOWAS force and MINUCI, the situation worsened. On 25 and 26 March 2004, demonstrations took place which led to violent confrontations between the Ivorian security force and demonstrators, resulting in the deaths of some 120 protesters.[116] *Licorne* did little to stop the events of 25 and 26 March.[117] On 4 November 2004, the Ivorian armed forces, loyal to Gbagbo, launched a series of air raids on the rebel-held north.[118] Reportedly, French and UNOCI forces ignored these attacks, which left at least 55 civilians dead.[119]

However, this laissez-faire posture on the part of France was to change abruptly when, on 6 November, a base of the French *Licorne* force was bombed by Ivorian government fighter aircraft, resulting in the deaths of nine French soldiers and one American citizen, and the wounding of 38 French soldiers.[120] According to news reports, France hit back immediately, first destroying the Ivorians' two Sukhoi-25 aircraft that had carried out the raids and then attacking the rest of the Ivorian air force, seizing the international airport in Abidjan and the commercial capital in the south and flying in reinforcements.[121]

[113] *Report of the Secretary-General* (n 107) para 52. As of 31 May, France had also contributed 171 troops to serve as part of UNOCI (United Nations, *First Report of the Secretary-General on the United Nations Operation in Côte d'Ivoire* (UN Doc S/2004/443), 2 June 2004, Annex).

[114] SC Res 1528 of 27 February 2004, para 16. In particular, the French force was authorised to 'intervene at the request of UNOCI in support of its elements whose security may be threatened', and to 'intervene against belligerent actions, if the security conditions so require, outside the areas directly controlled by UNOCI' (ibid, para 16).

[115] United Nations, *Report of the Secretary-General on the United Nations Mission in Côte d'Ivoire Submitted Pursuant to Security Council Resolution 1514 (2003) of 13 November 2003* (UN Doc S/2004/3), 6 January 2004, para 55.

[116] *First Report of the Secretary-General* (n 113) para 10. An International Commission of Inquiry concluded that the killings were part of a pre-planned operation implemented by the security forces, rather than a response to violence or threats arising from the demonstrations (ibid, paras 12 and 13).

[117] ibid, para 34.

[118] Unattributed, 'A Bloody Mess: What Next in a Former French Colony Ravaged Once Again by War?', *The Economist*, 13 November 2004.

[119] Human Rights Watch, *Country on a Precipice: The Precarious State of Human Rights and Civilian Protection in Côte d'Ivoire*, Human Rights Watch document, vol 17 No 6 (A), May 2005, http://hrw.org/reports/2005/cdi0505/cdi0505.pdf (accessed 1 April 2011), 11 and 22.

[120] United Nations, *Third Progress Report of the Secretary-General on the United Nations Operation in Côte d'Ivoire* (UN Doc S/2004/962), 9 December 2004, para 17.

[121] 'A Bloody Mess' (n 118); see also *Third Progress Report of the Secretary-General*, ibid.

In response to criticism that its actions had been heavy-handed, the French government stressed that before acting it had received unanimous approval from the UN Security Council to take 'all necessary means' to restore order.[122] This was, presumably, a reference to a Statement of the President of the Security Council of 6 November 2004, the day the French base was bombed, condemning the attack against French forces and stating that 'French forces and UNOCI are authorized to use all necessary means to carry out fully their mandate in accordance with its resolution 1528 (2004) of 27 February 2004'.[123] The attack by France was denounced by the Gbagbo government[124] and led to heightened tensions,[125] including attacks against the French community in the country.[126] Some 600 additional French troops were sent into the country, bringing *Licorne's* total to 4,600.[127] On 10 November, an evacuation of foreign nationals began and several diplomatic missions were temporarily closed.[128]

The Statement of the President of the Security Council of 6 November 2004 was followed later that month by Resolution 1572, whereby the Security Council again condemned the government airstrikes, reiterating its 'full support for the action undertaken by UNOCI and French forces in accordance with their mandate'.[129] The resolution was similar in format to Resolution 1528, in that it too found a threat to international peace and security, invoked Chapter VII in relation to the entire resolution and authorised 'all necessary means' for UNOCI and the French forces. In addition, the Security Council authorised a mandatory arms embargo against the country,[130] as well as a mandatory travel embargo and an assets freeze for individuals to be determined by a Committee,[131] and authorised all states to take 'the necessary measures to prevent the direct or indirect supply, sale or transfer to Côte d'Ivoire' of arms.[132]

[122] 'A Bloody Mess' (n 118).

[123] United Nations, *Statement by the President of the Security Council* (UN Doc S/PRST/2004/42), 6 November 2004. The statement added that the Security Council 'confirms also that UNOCI, within its capabilities and areas of deployment, is authorized to prevent any hostile action, in particular within the Zone of Confidence'.

[124] The Ivorian authorities accused the *Licorne* force of a disproportionate use of force in response to a 'mistake' caused by the Ivorian security and defence forces (*Third Progress Report of the Secretary-General* (n 120) para 18). 'Furthermore, the authorities have asked for an international inquiry into "violations of the sovereignty and territorial integrity" of the country by the French military in Côte d'Ivoire. The French Minister of Defence has explained the actions of the French forces as legitimate self-defence. She has indicated that France could not but respond to the attack.'

[125] ibid, para 19.

[126] 'A Bloody Mess' (n 118).

[127] ibid.

[128] *Third Progress Report of the Secretary-General* (n 120) para 22.

[129] SC Res 1572 of 15 November 2004.

[130] ibid, para 7.

[131] ibid, paras 9 and 11. To take effect on 15 December 2004, unless the Security Council found that the signatories of the Linas-Marcoussis and Accra III Agreements had implemented all their commitments under the Accra III Agreement.

[132] ibid, para 7.

Although the Secretary-General praised UNOCI's functioning in general,[133] it was clear that even he took the view that it had underperformed during the November 2004 crisis. He observed that the crisis had 'strained to the limit UNOCI's capacity to implement its mandate'.[134] He continued:

> [T]he recent crisis has brought into focus UNOCI's responsibilities regarding the protection of civilians, both in Abidjan and more widely in the country. At the same time the crisis has highlighted the limitations of the Mission when faced with massive unrest and attacks against certain groups of civilians that are clearly orchestrated, organized and undertaken in a climate of impunity. The question arises of how protection can best be provided for civilians, both Ivorian and foreign nationals, in such circumstances.[135]

The Secretary-General called for a strengthening of the mission, including the deployment of an additional 1,226 military personnel to bring its authorised strength to 7,466.[136] This recommendation was not immediately accepted by the Security Council, reportedly due to US opposition on 'budgetary grounds'.[137]

In the aftermath of the November crisis, the Secretary-General also commented upon UNOCI's relationship with *Licorne*. He implied that the *Licorne* force, when tested, had not provided the support to UNOCI he had envisaged. He observed:

> UNOCI's structure was predicated on the ability of the Licorne force to provide quick reaction capacity when needed. However, the recent events have illustrated the complexities of the balance between the two forces and how difficult it can be to reconcile the emergency requirements of each when both are severely stretched.[138]

While the Secretary-General's language was constrained by diplomacy, a Human Rights Watch report was subject to no such limitations:

> The French forces concentrated primarily on protecting their own and other foreign civilians who were coming under attack by pro-government militias. This robbed UNOCI of heavy weapons and a rapid reaction force which would have been needed to intervene if fighting broke out in several locations simultaneously and to extract civilians from areas of conflict. 'November showed that [Licorne] were not our rapid reaction force. They redeployed to protect French

[133] See eg *Third Progress Report of the Secretary-General* (n 120) paras 23 and 33.
[134] ibid, para 64.
[135] ibid, para 78.
[136] ibid, paras 65–67.
[137] Human Rights Watch (Human Rights News), 'Cote d'Ivoire: Militias Pose Threat to Civilians – UN Security Council Must Boost Civilian Protection', 3 May 2005, www.hrw.org/legacy/english/docs/2005/05/03/cotedi10567.htm (accessed 1 April 2011).
[138] *Third Progress Report of the Secretary-General* (n 120) para 65.

> and other foreign nationals in Abidjan', observed UNOCI force commander Major-General Abdoulaye Fall.[139]

In the words of another senior UN official, '[t]he French are here to look after mainly the French'.[140] Without the expected French support, UNOCI was compelled to pull 600 troops out of the conflict zone to protect its offices in Abidjan, further impeding UNOCI's ability to perform its civilian protection responsibilities.[141]

Resolution 1584, in February 2005, gave additional tasks to UNOCI and the French forces. Once again, the Security Council found the situation to be a threat to international peace and security in the region[142] and stated that it was acting under Chapter VII as regards the whole of the resolution.[143] UNOCI and the French forces were charged with monitoring the arms embargo and collecting and disposing of any arms brought into the country in violation of that embargo.[144] They were authorised to inspect cargo of 'aircraft and of any transport vehicle using the ports, airports, airfields, military bases and border crossings of Côte d'Ivoire' without notice.[145] Neither UNOCI nor the French forces were authorised to use 'all necessary means' in undertaking these tasks, as they had been with Resolution 1528. The assignment of these new tasks was to be 'without prejudice to'[146] their original mandates set out in Resolution 1528 or paragraph 3 of Resolution 1584, which charged the French forces with providing security assistance to UNOCI in accomplishing its inspection tasks.[147] The Security Council demanded that the government of Côte d'Ivoire and the rebel forces (*'les Forces nouvelle'* or 'FN') provide UNOCI and the French forces with 'unhindered access to equipment, sites and installations'.[148]

The security situation in the country remained very tense in the first months of 2005.[149] On 28 February a serious attack in the village of Logouale took place, leading to the deaths of as many as 50 people, according to some estimates.[150] UNOCI reacted forcefully, regaining control of the town

[139] Human Rights Watch (n 119) 23–24. The quotation from Fall (within the larger quotation) is from a Human Rights Watch interview, Abidjan, 1 March 2005.
[140] ibid, 24.
[141] ibid.
[142] SC Res 1584 of 1 February 2005, penultimate preambular para.
[143] ibid, final preambular para
[144] ibid, para 2.
[145] ibid.
[146] ibid.
[147] ibid, para 3.
[148] ibid, para 5.
[149] United Nations, *Fourth Progress Report of the Secretary-General on the United Nations Operation in Côte d'Ivoire* (UN Doc S/2005/186), 18 March 2005, para 20.
[150] Human Rights Watch (n 119) 24, placed the number of deaths at 50 and the French estimated the number of deaths at between 40 and 50; the UN put the death toll at 28.

and apprehending and disarming some 87 armed youths.[151] Despite this apparent success, at least 16 people were reportedly killed during communal clashes in the four weeks following the Logouale attack, leading to criticism of UNOCI for being ineffectual.[152]

In UNOCI's defence, UN officials pointed out that the mission was understaffed relative to Côte d'Ivoire's population of 16 million, with one observing in an interview in March 2005 that '[i]n Sierra Leone, which is one third the size of Ivory Coast in terms of population, we had three times the number of troops'.[153] Another observed: 'We were put here as a light force while the peace agreement was to be implemented but none of [the terms of the Linas-Marcoussis Agreement have been adhered to]. The objective of the mission has changed radically.'[154] In a March 2005 report to the Security Council, the Secretary-General observed that '[m]aintaining stability in the increasingly fragile security environment has remained a major challenge for the Mission'.[155] He reiterated his recommendation that additional troops be deployed,[156] in view of the deteriorating security situation[157] and the severe strain on UNOCI resulting from its new responsibilities in relation to the arms embargo.[158] A draft resolution, reportedly submitted to the Security Council by France in February 2005, calling for 1,226 additional peacekeepers – to include an 850-strong infantry battalion, backed by a fleet of eight attack helicopters – was reportedly met with resistance.[159]

After considerable delay, the Security Council increased the size of the operation with Resolution 1609 in June 2005.[160] Finding a continuing threat to international peace and security and acting under Chapter VII in relation to the whole of the resolution, the Security Council increased the size of UNOCI, temporarily granting it an additional 850 military personnel – substantially fewer than the Secretary-General had requested.[161] It also called on the force to undertake additional tasks – many of which required (at least potentially) a high degree of forcefulness, including preventing, 'within its capabilities and its areas of deployment, any hostile

[151] *Fourth Progress Report of the Secretary-General* (n 149) para 21. The force commander pointed to the halting of the militia incursion in Logouale as an example of the application of the Security Council's revised concept of operations as set out in SC Res 1572 (ibid).

[152] Human Rights Watch (n 119) 25 and 30.

[153] ibid, 30.

[154] ibid.

[155] *Fourth Progress Report of the Secretary-General* (n 149) para 25.

[156] The force numbered 6,017 of the authorised strength of 6,240 by March 2005. Its lack of a helicopter unit impeded its functioning and its ability to undertake medical evacuation of its personnel (ibid, para 24).

[157] ibid, para 25.

[158] ibid, para 85.

[159] Human Rights Watch (n 119) 29.

[160] SC Res 1609 of 24 June 2005.

[161] ibid, para 3. It also authorised an additional 750 civilian police personnel.

action', observing and monitoring the disarmament process and assisting with security measures.[162] It was also charged, once again, with monitoring the arms embargo. The Security Council authorised UNOCI 'to use all necessary means to carry out its mandate, within its capabilities and its areas of deployment'[163] in relation to all of its tasks, and reiterated the authority of the French force 'to use all necessary means in order to support UNOCI'.[164]

In December 2005 the Security Council passed Resolution 1643, renewing the arms embargo and reaffirming its readiness to impose a travel ban or an assets freeze on anyone blocking the peace process. It again characterised the situation as a threat to international peace and invoked Chapter VII in relation to the entire resolution.[165] It decided that:

> [A]ny serious obstacle to the freedom of movement of UNOCI and of the French forces which support it, or any attack or obstruction to the action of UNOCI, of the French forces, of the High Representative for the elections and of the International Working Group constitutes a threat to the peace and national reconciliation process for purposes of paragraphs 9 and 11 of resolution 1572 (2004) [which provide for a travel ban and assets freeze, respectively].[166]

The Security Council also asked the Secretary-General and the French government to report the names of anyone who presented any serious obstacle to UNOCI or the French forces.[167] In effect, this meant that non-cooperation with UNOCI – whether by the Côte d'Ivoire government or by rebel forces – could lead to a travel ban or an assets freeze.

After the Gbagbo government cancelled the elections scheduled for October 2005, the AU called for a one-year extension of Gbagbo's term of office and the appointment of a new prime minister.[168] On 4 December 2005, Charles Konan Banny was appointed transitional Prime Minister. His first months in office were characterised by civil and political unrest.[169] On 2 January 2006, unidentified assailants attacked Camp Akouédo, a military base in the Abidjan region.[170] Government security forces engaged in retaliatory attacks, primarily against West African immigrants and northern Ivorians, including, according to Human Rights Watch, arbitrary arrests, unlawful detention, torture and summary execution.[171] In mid-January, the UNOCI office in Guiglo was targeted. UNOCI used

[162] ibid, para 3.
[163] ibid, para 8.
[164] ibid, para 12.
[165] SC Res 1643 of 15 December 2005, penultimate and final paras.
[166] ibid, para 4.
[167] ibid, para 5.
[168] Human Rights Watch (n 92) 4–5. This arrangement was endorsed by the Security Council (Res 1633 of 21 October 2005).
[169] Human Rights Watch, ibid, 5.
[170] ibid, 7.
[171] ibid.

robust force in reply and five deaths resulted, including those of two children aged 14 and 16,[172] leading to questions as to whether the response of the peacekeepers was proportionate and appropriate.[173] The violence led UN and humanitarian personnel to retreat from the region; they remained absent for several months,[174] during which time the local civilians reportedly feared for their safety.[175]

In February 2006, citing its concern regarding the persistence of the crisis in Côte d'Ivoire, the Security Council authorised the immediate temporary redeployment of an infantry company from UNMIL in Liberia to UNOCI.[176] By June 2006, matters had not improved and the Security Council authorised a temporary increase in the strength of UNOCI of up to 1,500 additional personnel, including a maximum of 1,025 military personnel and 475 civilian police.[177]

UNOCI's mandate was extended once again by Resolution 1739, in January 2007.[178] This resolution was similar in nature to the previous ones (with a finding of a threat to international peace and security and a general invocation of Chapter VII). Once again UNOCI was given a variety of additional tasks, several of which were military in nature, such as the disarming of militia and the collection and disposal of material brought into the country in violation of the arms embargo.[179] And once again, UNOCI was authorised to 'use all necessary means to carry out its mandate, within its capabilities and its areas of deployment', and the French forces were authorised to use 'all necessary means' to support UNOCI.[180]

On 4 March 2007 the Ouagadougou Political Agreement was signed between Gbagbo and the leader of the FN, Guillaume Soro.[181] The Agreement, inter alia, created a new transitional government, which included Soro as Prime Minister, and called for disarmament and the holding of presidential elections. In addition, it called for the arms embargo to

[172] ibid. The killing of the children was confirmed by the Secretary-General (United Nations, *Report of the Secretary-General on Children and Armed Conflict in Côte d'Ivoire* (UN Doc S/2006/835), 25 October 2006, para 5). An Amnesty International research team which visited the region of Guiglo in April 2006 obtained versions of events from both sides. It was, however, unable to clarify which version was accurate and called for 'an independent and impartial inquiry [into the killings], with all necessary resources, including forensic expertise' (Amnesty International, *Côte d'Ivoire: Clashes between Peacekeeping Forces and Civilians: Lessons for the Future* (AI Index: AFR 31/005/2006), 19 September 2006).

[173] Human Rights Watch (n 92) 10.

[174] ibid, 11.

[175] ibid, 13.

[176] SC Res 1657 of 6 February 2006.

[177] SC Res 1682 of 2 June 2006 para 2.

[178] SC Res 1739 of 10 January 2007.

[179] ibid, para 2.

[180] ibid, paras 5 and 8 respectively.

[181] United Nations, *Letter Dated 13 March 2007 from the Secretary-General Addressed to the President of the Security Council* (UN Doc S/2007/144) 13 March 2007, Annex. On 28 November 2007, certain 'Supplementary Agreements' were also signed (see SC Res 1795 of 15 January 2008, which welcomes Supplementary Agreements 2 and 3).

be lifted[182] and for the Security Council to 'immediately lift the individual sanctions against some stakeholders of the Ivorian crisis'.[183] On 15 July 2007, by Resolution 1765, the Security Council – finding a threat to international peace and security and invoking Chapter VII in relation to the entire resolution – renewed the mandates of UNOCI and of the French forces and adapted UNOCI's mandate to deal with the new situation presented by the signing of the Ouagadougou Agreement.[184] The Security Council called on UNOCI to support the Ouagadougou Agreement in a number of ways, including through facilitating the electoral process. No mention was made of any authority to 'use all necessary means' in relation to the additional tasks.

In June 2010 the Security Council passed Resolution 1933; as usual it found a threat to international peace and security and invoked Chapter VII as regards the entire resolution.[185] Citing its concern at the delayed presidential elections, the Security Council again modified UNOCI's mandate so that it could better support the parties in implementing the Ouagadougou Agreement.[186] The operation was given a wide variety of tasks, including supporting the electoral process, providing civilian protection and monitoring the arms embargo.[187] The Security Council authorised UNOCI to 'use all necessary means' to carry out its entire mandate[188] and extended this authorisation to empower the French forces to provide UNOCI with support.[189] The Security Council maintained the strength of UNOCI at 8,650 (including 7,200 troops)[190] but indicated its intention to consider enlarging the force.[191] In 2010, in the lead up to presidential elections in the country, the Security Council decided to increase UNOCI's authorised military and police personnel by 500, from 8,650 to 9,150.[192]

The first round of the elections was finally held on 31 October 2010. Between the first round and the second round, which was held on 28 November 2010, the Security Council called for the redeployment from UNMIL to UNOCI of a maximum of three infantry companies and one

[182] See section 6.1 of the Ouagadougou Political Agreement, www.ucd.ie/ibis/filestore/The%20Ouagadougou%20Agreement%20.pdf (accessed 1 April 2011).

[183] ibid, section 6.4. On 5 June 2006 the Security Council Committee Concerning Côte d'Ivoire had put three individuals on its List of Individuals subject to the Measures imposed by paras 9 (travel ban) and 11 (assets freeze) of SC Res 1572 of 15 November 2004 (UN Press Release, *Security Council Committee Concerning Côte d'Ivoire Updates List of Individuals Subject to Measures Imposed by Resolutions 1572 (2004) and 1643 (2005)* (UN Doc Security Council/8739), 5 June 2006.

[184] SC Res 1765 of 15 July 2007.

[185] SC Res 1933 of 30 June 2010, penultimate and final preambular paras.

[186] SC Res 1933 of 30 June 2010, para 16.

[187] ibid.

[188] ibid, para 17.

[189] ibid, para 24.

[190] ibid, para 19.

[191] ibid, para 20.

[192] SC Res 1942 of 29 September 2010, para 1.

aviation unit comprised of two military utility helicopters.[193] In early December, the country's top election official declared the opposition candidate, Mr Alassane Ouattara, the winner with 54 per cent of the vote to Gbagbo's 45 per cent.[194] Despite the results – and despite their being recognised by the international community[195] – Gbagbo made clear his intention not to accept them and arranged to be sworn in as President on 4 December 2010.[196]

In December, the Security Council rejected a demand by Gbagbo that UNOCI leave the country[197] and renewed its mandate to the end of June 2011.[198] The Security Council called upon Ivorians to 'respect the will of the people and the outcome of the election in view of ECOWAS and African Union's recognition of Alassane Dramane Ouattara as President-elect of Côte d'Ivoire'.[199] In addition, the Security Council decided to maintain UNOCI's strength at 8,650,[200] to extend the temporary deployment of the 500 additional troops[201] and to extend by up to four weeks the temporary redeployment from UNMIL to UNOCI.[202] Moreover, it indicated its intention to redeploy further troops from UNMIL to UNOCI on a temporary basis.[203] In January 2011, citing the security situation, the Security Council authorised the deployment of an additional 2,000 military personnel to UNOCI,[204] and decided to re-extend the stay of the 500 additional forces temporarily assigned to the operation.[205] In February, it decided to extend the temporary redeployment of forces from UNMIL to UNOCI by up to three months.[206] At the time of writing, the security situation in Côte d'Ivoire remains fragile, and a civil war between Gbagbo's supporters and Ouattara's supporters seems imminent.

[193] SC Res 1951 of 24 November 2010.

[194] Adam Nossiter, 'Election Results Challenged in Ivory Coast', *New York Times*, 2 December 2010.

[195] Including ECOWAS, the African Union and the Security Council itself (SC Res 1962 of 20 December 2010, preamble and para 1).

[196] Adam Nossiter, '2 Oaths Taken in the Ivory Coast', *New York Times*, 4 December 2010. Ouattara also swore himself in on the same day. His oath reportedly took the form of a handwritten letter on a plain sheet of paper to the Constitutional Council (ibid).

[197] United Nations (News Centre), 'UN Agency Starts Moving Ivorian Refugees in Liberia to New Camp', 18 February 2011, www.un.org/apps/news/story.asp?NewsID=37565&Cr=Ivoire&Cr1= (accessed 1 April 2011).

[198] SC Res 1962 of 20 December 2010.

[199] ibid, para 1.

[200] ibid, para 4.

[201] ibid, para 5.

[202] ibid, para 6.

[203] ibid, para 7.

[204] SC Res 1967 of 19 January 2011, para 1.

[205] ibid, para 2.

[206] SC Res 1968 of 16 February 2011.

3.2 Evaluation

3.2.1 Adherence to the 'Fundamental Principles'

The fact that the Security Council almost invariably invoked Chapter VII, and that it almost invariably authorised UNOCI to use 'all necessary means' to carry out all of its tasks, makes it clear that the 'fundamental principle' of force only in self-defence was inapplicable to most aspects of the mandate. In the words of the UN Legal Opinion regarding the powers of UNMIL, it is 'of course . . . beyond all doubt that the Security Council had made use of its powers under Chapter VII of the Charter to authorize UNMIL to use armed force (other than in situations of self-defence)' when it authorised 'all necessary means'.[207]

The Security Council appears to have bestowed tasks upon UNOCI without an attendant authorisation to use 'all necessary means' on only two occasions. First, under Resolution 1584 on 25 February 2005, UNOCI and the French forces were assigned additional tasks without a corresponding authorisation to use 'all necessary means'. The tasks, which involved monitoring the arms embargo and collecting and disposing of any arms brought into the country in violation of that embargo, were of such a nature that they might potentially have required the use of force beyond self-defence. Two arguments might be made in favour of UNOCI being able, nonetheless, to use force beyond self-defence in relation to these tasks. First, it could be argued that the fact that Resolution 1584 specifically provided that the new tasks were 'without prejudice to their mandate set out in 1528' served to incorporate the Security Council's authorisation to use 'all necessary means' as provided in Resolution 1528. Any argument that a stipulation that certain assigned tasks are 'without prejudice' to previously assigned tasks somehow extends an earlier authorisation to use force beyond self-defence is hardly convincing. Surely, where the Security Council intends to authorise something as important as the use of all necessary measures, it must do so explicitly. Second, based on the approach taken in the Legal Opinion regarding UNMIL's capacity to use force, it may be argued that the Security Council intended to authorise the use of force beyond self-defence notwithstanding the absence of a phrase like 'all necessary means' in a Chapter VII resolution.[208] To understand the Security Council's intention, regard would need to be had to the nature of the tasks, reports of the Secretary-General and the background to the resolution. The nature of the tasks – inspecting

[207] 'Note to the Under-Secretary-General' (n 72) 539.

[208] See discussion at section 2.2.1 above, where the UN Legal Counsel considered how to discern the Security Council's intention in circumstances where it did not invoke the 'all necessary means' language.

with notice for weapons and confiscating and destroying them – would appear to be such that force beyond self-defence would be required. On the other hand, the Security Council's previous willingness to authorise 'all necessary means' in relation to other tasks entrusted to UNOCI would also be relevant to its intention. A convincing argument could be made that the Security Council's decision *not* to explicitly authorise the use of 'all necessary means' in Resolution 1584, in distinction to its practice with regard to virtually all other UNOCI-related resolutions, reveals its intention that the tasks assigned it by Resolution 1584 were not to involve the use of force beyond self-defence.

In addition, no authority was given to either UNOCI or the French forces to use 'all necessary means' in July 2007, under Resolution 1765, when they were assigned additional tasks relating to the Ouagadougou Peace Agreement; however, given that these functions were not of a military nature, relating as they did to the organisation of elections, it would appear that no such authorisation was contemplated by the Security Council.

At to the 'fundamental principle' of host state consent, this existed at the outset. In Resolution 1528, which established UNOCI, the Security Council was at pains to highlight the fact that the host state had requested the operation, referring to a 10 November 2003 letter from the President of the Republic of Côte d'Ivoire 'in which he requested the transformation of the United Nations Mission in Côte d'Ivoire (MINUCI) into a peacekeeping operation'.[209] However, in subsequent Chapter VII resolutions the Security Council was decidedly less focused on providing assurances that it was acting in conformity with the wishes of the government as represented by Gbagbo. This change in emphasis would appear to date from the Security Council's endorsement of the French forces bombing the government of Côte d'Ivoire's air force in November 2004.[210] It is self-evident that Côte d'Ivoire would not have consented to the actions taken by the French forces against its air force – indeed, as noted, the government protested strenuously.[211] While it does not appear that UNOCI participated in that action, given the fact that UNOCI received an authorisation to use force that was virtually identical to that given to the French forces, there would appear to have been nothing to prevent its participation.

In addition, it was after the attack by the French forces that the Security Council began the process of imposing a mandatory arms embargo against the country.[212] There is nothing to indicate that such an embargo was –

[209] SC Res 1528 of 27 February 2004, preamble.

[210] United Nations, *Statement by the President of the Security Council* (UN Doc S/PRST/2004/42), 6 November 2004; SC Res 1572 of 15 November 2004.

[211] See n 124 above and accompanying text.

[212] SC Res 1572, ibid.

or logically could have been – at the request of the host state;[213] indeed, both Gbagbo and the leader of the FN, Soro, called for the arms embargo and other targeted sanctions to be lifted in the Ouagadougou Political Agreement. Moreover, it is unimaginable that the Security Council was acting with the host state's consent when, in February 2005, it charged UNOCI with the tasks of monitoring the arms embargo 'by inspecting, as they deem it necessary and as appropriate without notice, the cargo of aircraft and of any transport vehicle using the ports, airports, airfields, military bases and border crossings of Côte d'Ivoire' and collecting and disposing of any arms brought into the country in violation of that embargo.[214] In short, based on the information available, there is little to indicate that the Gbagbo government consented to the modifications to UNOCI's mandate after November 2004.

Two counter-arguments may be made. First, it may be argued that there was no legitimate government from which the Security Council could obtain consent. Gbagbo's legitimacy may be challenged by arguing that from January 2003, when the Linas-Marcoussis Agreement was signed, calling for the establishment of a Government of National Reconciliation, Gbagbo was not in a position to represent the state alone. For his decisions as President to be legitimate, he would need to have acted as part of the envisaged Government of National Reconciliation.[215] Similarly, it may be argued that because Gbagbo did not hold elections when his term of office was scheduled to expire in October 2005, his governance beyond that point – or, perhaps, beyond the point to which the Security Council approved a one-year extension[216] – was illegitimate. It was certainly considered to be so after the second round of presidential elections in November 2010. As discussed above, there may be circumstances in which it is appropriate to consider the legitimacy or representativeness of a government and not simply its effectiveness at controlling the territory.[217] An argument might also be made that Gbagbo could not meet an effective control test as he did not, at times, control the whole country.[218] If an argument that Gbagbo lacked the authority to represent the government (and that no other leader filled this role) is accepted, the scenario might be likened to that in Somalia

[213] As noted in chapter 3, section 3.2.3.3, the Yugoslav government consented to an Art 41 arms embargo against it in 1991; thus it is not necessarily the case that a state must be against sanctions. However, a government must consider the sanctions to be in its best interests. In respect of Côte d'Ivoire, this does not appear to be the case. Here the Security Council used the threat of sanctions (and, once implemented, the promise to remove them) as a means of encouraging the government of Côte d'Ivoire to modify its behaviour.

[214] SC Res 1584 of 1 February 2005, para 2.

[215] A similar argument might also be made as regards the Ouagadougou Political Agreement, which also called for the establishment of a transitional government.

[216] SC Res 1633 of 21 October 2005.

[217] See chapter 3, section 5.3.1.

[218] At times, he controlled only the southern part of the territory, with the FN forces controlling the north. Yabi (n 106) 77.

in 1993 when UNOSOM II was established in the absence of a functioning government. For such an argument to be successful, one would need to accept that the 'fundamental principle' of host state consent only applies where there is a functioning government in place to provide such consent.

A second argument that the host state in fact consented to the operation and the modifications of its mandate may be based on provisions of the peace treaties entered into by the Gbagbo government. The Linas-Marcoussis Agreement specifically provided that '[t]he Government of National Reconciliation will seek the help of ECOWAS, France and the United Nations to arrange for their forces to guarantee' the various operations.[219] A related document provided as follows: 'The Conference recommends that the Secretary-General of the United Nations submit to the Security Council recommendations for the deployment of civilian and military observers who will help to supervise the implementation of the Agreement throughout Côte d'Ivoire.'[220] In a similar vein, the Ouagadougou Political Agreement reaffirmed the commitment of Gbagbo and Soro to 'all the UN Resolutions on Côte d'Ivoire, particularly the Resolutions 1633 (2005) and 1721 (2006) of the UN Security Council'.[221] It might, therefore, be argued that, in making such commitments, the government of Côte d'Ivoire effectively consented to UNOCI, no matter what tasks the Security Council might decide were appropriate for it to carry out. This argument is not convincing: a general endorsement of the role of the United Nations, or even a reaffirmation of Security Council resolutions, is not the same as a host state consenting to a specific mandate or modification thereof. It may be noted, however, that the Special Court for Sierra Leone found that UNAMSIL was 'deployed with the consent of the warring factions in accordance with Article XVI of the Lomé Agreement', despite the fact that that Agreement did not include the specific mandate of UNAMSIL.[222]

As to impartiality, this 'fundamental principle' would appear generally to have been adhered to in the operation. It might be argued that the endorsement by the Security Council of Ouattara as President in Resolution 1962 favoured one party to the dispute; however, given that the election was won pursuant to a UN-monitored election, such an argument would be misguided. The Security Council, even once it had

[219] Linas-Marcoussis Agreement, 23 January 2003 (UN Doc S/2003/99, Annex I), section 3(h).

[220] See *Conclusions of the Conference of Heads of State on Côte d'Ivoire* (Paris, 25 and 26 January 2003 (UN Doc S/2003/99, Annex II), para 15.

[221] Ouagadougou Peace Agreement, 4 March 2007, p 2.

[222] *Prosecutor v Issa Hassan Sesay, Morrison Kallon and Augustine Gbao* (Case No SCSL-04-15-T, Special Court for Sierra Leone, Trial Chamber I, 2 March 2009), para 1907. In the view of the author, the reasoning of the Special Court in this regard was not convincing. See James Sloan, 'Peacekeepers under Fire: Prosecuting the RUF for Attacks against the UN Assistance Mission in Sierra Leone' (2010) 9 *Law and Practice of International Courts and Tribunals* 242, 280–81.

expanded the forceful role of UNOCI, appeared to give little preference to the government of the host state over the FN; rather, it facilitated elections so that the nationals could themselves decide which party they preferred.

3.2.2 *Constitutional Basis*

From its very beginnings, UNOCI was established entirely under Chapter VII and authorised to use force beyond self-defence with regard to virtually all of its tasks.[223] While the Security Council established the operation with the consent of the host state, such consent does not appear to have been a legal requirement. That the Security Council did not consider it to be so became apparent when, in later resolutions, it stated its full support for the measures taken against the host state's air force, imposed an embargo against the host state, and charged the peacekeeping operation with monitoring that embargo.

Virtually the entire operation was established under Article 42. There appear to be only two exceptions to this. First, the election-related functions under Resolution 1765: given that they are non-forceful (but assigned pursuant to the Security Council's Chapter VII powers), they would appear to have their basis in Article 41 or 40 or in a non-binding provision of Chapter VII. Second, the arms embargo inspection functions under Resolution 1584 (also assigned under Chapter VII): here, as noted in section 3.2.1 above, an argument may be made that the Security Council intended to authorise the operation to use force beyond self-defence. If it did, then the activity would be based in Article 42; otherwise, it would be based in Article 41 or 40 or in a non-binding provision of Chapter VII.

It might also be noted that the fact that a task has been established under Chapter VII and the Security Council has authorised the use of 'all necessary means' in relation to it, does not mean that the execution of that task necessarily requires the use of force beyond self-defence. So, for example, when the Security Council, in Resolution 1528, invokes Chapter VII and authorises 'all necessary means' in relation to the task of promoting 'understanding of the peace process and the role of UNOCI among local communities and the parties, through an effective public information capacity, including the establishment as necessary of a United Nations radio broadcasting capability', there is clearly no need for an authorisation to use force beyond self-defence. What would appear to be happening with the resolution passed in relation to UNOCI is the opposite of what we saw with certain other militarised peacekeeping operations: instead of being very careful to narrowly tailor their authorisation – as, for example, they did with UNAMSIL and MONUC – with UNOCI, the

[223] The imposition of the sanctions regime – as distinct from the decision to mandate UNOCI and the French forces to monitor it – would appear to be an exercise of the Security Council's Art 41 powers.

Security Council opted to authorise the use of force beyond self-defence in a very liberal way.

3.2.3 Conclusion and Assessment of Success

The situation in Côte d'Ivoire is similar in many respects to that in Sierra Leone. In both cases a former colonial power that sits permanently on the Security Council took a special interest in a country, providing well-trained and well-equipped troops and, importantly, an influential voice calling on the Security Council to act. As was the case with the UK in Sierra Leone, France established its own force alongside the militarised peacekeeping mission rather than serving as a part of it.[224] France's approach – like that of the UK in Sierra Leone – shows that the fact that a Security Council Member State is committed to establishing a militarised peacekeeping operation does not necessarily mean that it possess sufficient faith in the concept of militarised peacekeeping to allow its forces to serve under such an operation.

While the support of France has benefited UNOCI, the concerns of France have proven to be different from those of UNOCI. It is clear from the November 2004 crisis that in times of difficulty, UNOCI cannot rely unconditionally on the French troops for support. The fact that the French forces are well equipped and may be reinforced almost immediately risks creating a perception amongst the spoilers that only the French forces present a credible threat, thereby undermining UNOCI. According to one report, '[o]bservers doubt that the UN force could keep order on its own'.[225] The same report quotes a diplomat in Abidjan as observing: 'It is obvious that all sides are only scared of the French.'[226]

For the most part, civilians lack protection. A commitment on the part of the Security Council to protect civilians is laudable only if such a commitment is realisable. When the Security Council bestowed a Chapter VII civilian protection mandate upon UNOCI, expectations were raised – arguably, unfairly in view of the above-discussed limitations – that the operation would make a difference in protecting vulnerable people. However, it is clear that, in all the circumstances, UNOCI is not sufficiently large to undertake that task effectively. An additional complication arises by virtue of the nature of the civilian protection mandate. As is common, it calls for UNOCI to act 'without prejudice to the responsibility of the Government'.[227] This presumes a certain level of cooperation between UNOCI and the govern-

[224] While the French did contribute troops to UNOCI, it contribution was relatively limited, representing between 182 and 188 of the over 6,000 troops composing the mission (www.un.org/en/peacekeeping/resources/statistics, accessed 1 April 2011).

[225] Unattributed, 'On the Brink: If the French Pull Out, All-Out War Looms', *The Economist*, 19 March 2005.

[226] ibid.

[227] SC Res 1528 of 27 February 2004.

ment of Côte d'Ivoire – perhaps even something amounting to deference on the part of the former toward the latter. However, given that the government itself has been linked to many of the attacks against civilians – and, indeed, against UNOCI itself – any such relationship is likely to be fraught with problems.[228]

Finally, when UNOCI did use significant force when it came under attack in January 2006, issues arose regarding the proportionality of its actions. While UNOCI's actions (which resulted in five deaths, including two children) may well represent an exercise of necessary and proportionate self-defence,[229] it is clear that where peacekeeping forces use the robust force authorised in their Chapter VII mandates proactively or offensively, there is a real possibility that breaches of international humanitarian law will occur. The impact that such breaches – or even allegations of such breaches – will have on the perception that a peacekeeping operation is impartial will be considerable.

4. HAITI (APRIL 2004–PRESENT)

4.1 The Mission

After a decade of relative calm in Haiti following Aristide's reinstatement as President in 1994,[230] serious armed conflict broke out in early February 2004 and insurgents took control of part of the country. On 29 February, President Aristide resigned and left the country. Within hours, Boniface Alexandre, the President of the Supreme Court, was sworn in as interim President.[231] Pursuant to the request of interim President Alexandre later that day, the Security Council authorised a US-led quasi-enforcement operation, the Multinational Interim Force (MIF),[232] and granted it the authority to use 'all necessary measures to fulfil its mandate'.[233] Like the quasi-enforcement operation in Liberia, MIF had its end-date built into the resolution authorising it; it was to be established 'for a period of not more than three months'.[234]

At the time the Security Council established MIF, it also declared its readiness to establish a follow-on UN stabilisation force.[235] On 30 April,

[228] For a discussion of the links between militia groups and the government see Human Rights Watch (n 119) 16–18.

[229] The results of a UN investigation do not appear to have been made public. Amnesty International (n 172).

[230] See discussion of the peacekeeping operation in Haiti in the 1990s in chapter 5, section 4.1.4.

[231] United Nations, *Report of the Secretary-General on Haiti* (UN Doc S/2004/300), 16 April 2004, para 9.

[232] SC Res 1529 of 29 February 2004.

[233] ibid, para 6.

[234] ibid, para 2.

[235] ibid.

by Resolution 1542, the Security Council established the United Nations Stabilisation Mission in Haiti (MINUSTAH), to consist of up to 6,700 troops, and requested that authority be transferred from MIF to MINUSTAH on 1 June 2004.[236] In that resolution it determined the situation in Haiti to constitute a threat to international peace and security in the region[237] and it invoked Chapter VII, but only in relation to certain mandated tasks as set out in a single section of a single paragraph.[238] That part of its mandate for which Chapter VII was applicable related to assisting the Haitian government in maintaining peace and security, improving policing, carrying out disarmament programmes and improving adherence to the rule of law. In addition MINUSTAH was given a civilian protection function. While it was clear that some of its functions – such as disarmament and the restoration and maintenance of public safety and public order – might be of a potentially forceful nature, MINUSTAH, unlike MIF, was not granted the authority to use 'all necessary means'. MINUSTAH formally took over authority from MIF on 1 June 2004 (though MIF remained in place until the end of that month).[239]

During the initial months of its existence, MINUSTAH did little to restore security to the area. In a November 2004 report, the Secretary-General noted the deteriorating security situation, particularly in Port-au-Prince.[240] MINUSTAH was criticised by civil society and the Haitian government for not intervening in a sufficiently robust way.[241] An article in *The Economist* described a rising death toll, estimated to be more than 120 by mid-December 2004, and observed that the peacekeepers had become the butt of jokes calling into question their bravery and commitment.[242] MINUSTAH's initial reluctance to use force would appear to be attributable to two main factors. First, there was a considerable delay between MINUSTAH assuming its duties and gaining a full complement of troops, leading to a 'security vacuum that has had disastrous consequences'.[243] Second, there appeared to be reluctance on the part of MINUSTAH's

[236] SC Res 1542 of 30 April 2004, para 1.

[237] ibid, final preambular para.

[238] ibid, para 7. It invoked Chapter VII in relation to only the tasks listed under section I of para 7, entitled 'secure and stable environment'; not those under section II entitled 'political process' or section III entitled 'human rights'.

[239] United Nations, *Interim Report of the Secretary-General on the United Nations Stabilization Mission in Haiti* (UN Doc S/2004/698), 30 August 2004, para 3.

[240] United Nations, *Report of the Secretary-General on the United Nations Stabilization Mission in Haiti* (UN Doc S/2004/908), 18 November 2004, para 6. Violent incidents in October led to the deaths of more than 60 people, including 13 Haiti National Police (para 14).

[241] International Crisis Group, *A New Chance for Haiti?*, Crisis Group Latin America/Caribbean Report No 10, 18 November 2004, www.crisisgroup.org/~/media/Files/latin-america/haiti/10-a-new-chance-for-haiti.pdf (accessed 1 April 2011), 18.

[242] Unattributed, 'Peacekeeping in Haiti: Operation Deep Pockets', *The Economist*, 18 December 2004.

[243] International Crisis Group (n 241) ii.

Brazilian commander[244] and the Brazilian government[245] to engage in disarmament or other activities potentially requiring the use of force beyond self-defence. According to press reports, the Brazilian general in charge of the peacekeepers, Augusto Heleno Ribeiro, noted in December 2004 that he was 'under extreme pressure from the international community to use violence' but stressed that he was commanding a 'peacekeeping force, not an occupation force'.[246] According to an International Crisis Group report:

> Brazil is under real domestic constraints. This is the first time it is leading a complex peacekeeping operation. Public opinion is not fully behind it, and when the media occasionally pays attention, it is mostly to underline that the mission is impossible.[247]

By the end of 2004, with some 6,000 of its 6,700 troops on the ground,[248] MINUSTAH grew more confrontational, frequently engaging in joint operations with the much-criticised Haitian National Police (HNP).[249] On 14 December MINUSTAH and the HNP launched a major operation to restore law and order in the shanty-town of Cité Soleil in Port-au-Prince.[250] On 17 December, a joint MINUSTAH-HNP operation disarmed 43 individuals (mostly soldiers) who had been illegally occupying the abandoned residence of former President Aristide.[251] As noted by the Secretary-General, 'the Mission's determination to take action against gang members and former soldiers . . . increased the risk of retaliation against MINUSTAH and other United Nations personnel'.[252] On 20 March 2005, MINUSTAH engaged in the forcible recovery of an illegally occupied police station;[253] on 31 March, it launched an operation in Cité Soleil to restrict the movements

[244] ibid, 17–18. See also International Crisis Group, *Haiti's Transition: Hanging in the Balance*, Crisis Group Latin America/Caribbean Briefing No 7, 8 February 2005, www.crisisgroup.org/~/media/Files/latin-america/haiti/b07_haiti_transition_hanging_in_the_balance.pdf (accessed 1 April 2011), 7.

[245] In a statement of December 2004, 'the Brazilian foreign minister said that his country was not leading a repressive force and threatened to withdraw Brazilian troops if the international community did not promptly address the pressing social and economic changes Haiti needs' (International Crisis Group, ibid, 7).

[246] *The Economist* (n 242).

[247] International Crisis Group (n 243) 7–8.

[248] www.un.org/en/peacekeeping/contributors/2004/December2004_5.pdf (accessed 1 April 2011).

[249] According to the Secretary-General, 'MINUSTAH received credible reports of elements of the Haitian National Police having been involved in a number of summary executions' (United Nations, *Report of the Secretary-General on the United Nations Stabilization Mission in Haiti* (UN Doc S/2005/631), 6 October 2005, para 43). See also United Nations, *Report of the Secretary-General on the United Nations Stabilization Mission in Haiti* (UN Doc S/2005/124), 25 February 2005, para 58, where the Secretary-General expressed his concern at 'allegations of human rights abuses attributed to HNP officers'.

[250] *Report of the Secretary-General* of 25 February 2005, ibid, para 5.

[251] ibid, para 9.

[252] ibid, para 11. The Secretary-General wrote of an attack on 11 off-duty MINUSTAH military personnel wearing civilian clothing.

[253] United Nations, *Report of the Secretary-General on the United Nations Stabilization Mission in Haiti* (UN Doc S/2005/313), 13 May 2005, para 14.

of gang members and the circulation of their weapons and ammunition;[254] and, on 9 and 10 April, MINUSTAH engaged in an operation with the HNP to apprehend criminals and gang members.[255]

Although these operations were viewed favourably,[256] there appeared to be a sense among some observers that it was too little too late. The continued violence in Haiti was seen by some as a shortcoming of MINUSTAH. A March 2005 report by a Harvard Law Student group made the following observations:

> Even now, staffed in full, the peacekeeping force continues to interpret its mandate complacently and with a narrowness unfit for the situation on the ground. After eight months under MINUSTAH's watch, Haiti is as insecure as ever. MINUSTAH has failed even to begin to implement a comprehensive program for disarmament, leaving large pockets of the country effectively ruled by illegal groups with guns and other weapons. Civilian casualties remain common in Port-au-Prince's slums, where gangs wage daily, low-level urban warfare. Large swaths of the poor countryside remain under the control of the former military, historically the major domestic force behind coups d'états [*sic*] and among the foremost violators of human rights.[257]

The Harvard report made little allowance for the operation's limited size or the longstanding existence of violence in certain parts of the country.[258] An International Crisis Group report issued in May 2005 was more measured. Nevertheless, it observed that '[t]he results of MINUSTAH's military operations, especially in Cité Soleil, have not met the expectations of either Haitian society or the international community, including MINUSTAH itself'.[259] According to news reports, the phrase 'they are here on vacation' was frequently uttered by Haitians when referring to the MINUSTAH forces.[260]

The use of force by MINUSTAH was not without problems. According to the Secretary-General, an operation conducted by MINUSTAH on 6 July 2005 in Cité Soleil aimed at apprehending and bringing to justice a prominent gang leader was said to have led to civilian casualties.[261] While the Secretary-General provided no detail regarding the incident, accord-

[254] ibid, para 15.

[255] ibid, para 16.

[256] International Crisis Group (n 244) 7.

[257] Harvard Law Student Advocates for Human Rights and Centro de Justiça Global, 'Keeping the Peace in Haiti? An Assessment of the United Nations Stabilization Mission in Haiti using Compliance with its Prescribed Mandate as a Barometer for Success', March 2005, www.fidh.org/IMG/pdf/KeepingthepeaceJusticiaGlobal-4.pdf (accessed 1 April 2011), 1.

[258] ibid, 19.

[259] International Crisis Group, *Spoiling Security in Haiti*, Crisis Group Latin America/Caribbean Report No 13, 31 May 2005, www.crisisgroup.org/~/media/Files/latin-america/haiti/13_spoiling_security_in_haiti.pdf (accessed 1 April 2011), 8.

[260] Michael Kamber, 'A Troubled Haiti Struggles to Gain its Political Balance', *New York Times*, 5 January 2005.

[261] *Report of the Secretary-General* of 6 October 2005 (n 249) para 25.

ing to newspaper reports there was mounting evidence that 'United Nations peacekeepers shot and killed unarmed civilians, including children' during the raid.[262] A statement issued by MINUSTAH said that it 'did not target civilians in the operation on 6 July, but the nature of such missions in densely populated urban areas is such that there is always a risk of civilian casualties. MINUSTAH deeply regrets any injuries or loss of life during its operation.'[263] A spokesman for the Brazilian forces, Colonel Jorge Smicelato, stated: 'Those killed were armed bandits who shot at our troops . . . No one from the civilian population was killed.'[264] Later, after an internal inquiry into the matter indicating that a number of people may have been caught in the crossfire between UN peacekeepers and armed gang members was obtained by a newspaper, the UN 'admitted that a number of innocent civilians may have become "collateral victims" and killed'.[265] It would appear to have been this incident that prompted the Under-Secretary-General for Peacekeeping to acknowledge publicly the shortcomings of MINUSTAH troops, noting: 'I have to acknowledge the forces we have do not have the kind of very specialised capacity . . . that makes absolutely sure that there will be zero civilian casualties in a densely populated environment.'[266]

Instances of civilian casualties continued. According to news reports, incidents involving MINUSTAH between 22 December 2006 and 9 February 2007 resulted in 58 injuries and six fatalities.[267] Reportedly, among the dead were women aged 18 and 20, and the wounded included six women and two children under the age of 12.[268] The level of force used in the operations remains in dispute. The Head of Mission, Edmond Mulet, denied allegations that 'UN peacekeepers had fired from helicopters, hindered Red Cross volunteers or used "heavy munitions" in the raids on December 22, December 28 and January 5'.[269] Nevertheless, he conceded that there had been 'collateral damage'.[270] According to the Haiti head of mission of the

[262] Andrew Buncombe, 'Peacekeepers Accused after Killings in Haiti', *The Independent*, 29 July 2005, http://news.independent.co.uk/world/americas/article302259.ece (accessed 1 April 2011).

[263] United Nations (MINUSTAH), *MINUSTAH Statement relating to the Operation Conducted on 06 July at Cite Soleil*, 22 July 2005, www.un.org/en/peacekeeping/missions/minustah/index.shtml (accessed 1 April 2011).

[264] Unattributed, 'UN Troops Kill Six in Haiti', *BBC News*, 30 July 2005, www.bbc.co.uk/caribbean/news/story/2005/06/050630_haitikilled.shtml (accessed 1 April 2011).

[265] Andrew Buncombe, 'UN Admits Civilians May have Died in Haiti Peacekeeping Raid', *The Independent*, 10 January 2006, http://news.independent.co.uk/world/americas/article337553.ece (accessed 1 April 2011).

[266] Buncombe (n 262) quoting Jean-Marie Guehenno.

[267] Patrick Jackson, 'When the Gloves of Peace Come Off', *BBC News*, 18 April 2007, http://news.bbc.co.uk/1/hi/in_depth/6542399.stm (accessed 1 April 2011).

[268] ibid.

[269] Andrew Buncombe, 'Civilians Caught in Crossfire during Port-au-Prince Raids', *The Independent*, 2 February 2007.

[270] ibid.

NGO *Médecins sans Frontières*, such raids 'routinely result in innocent people being killed'.[271] Others have questioned MINUSTAH's strategy of setting up roadblocks around Cité Soleil, likening it to collective punishment.[272]

As MINUSTAH became increasingly prepared to use force, gang activity in the country decreased and security increased. In the first six months of 2007, more than 500 alleged gang members were reportedly arrested by MINUSTAH forces and hundreds more were detained by the HNP.[273] According to *The Economist*:

> The majority of alleged gang leaders are thought to be among those either arrested or killed while resisting arrest. Earlier in the year, the Minustah and [HNP] made a concerted effort to break up the larger gangs based in the sprawling Cité Soleil slum to the north of the capital, and the area has remained relatively free of serious crime, confounding expectations that gang activity would resume once the spotlight shifted elsewhere.[274]

When the Security Council extended MINUSTAH's mandate for a further one-year period in October 2009, it charged MINUSTAH with supporting the 2010 elections.[275] The UN reported that by 2010, the 'violence had largely been removed from politics, and public security mostly restored with crime reduced. The media was operating freely and the economy was growing, despite the world economic crisis. Positive constitutional amendments promised sustained economic growth in years to come.'[276]

On 12 January 2010, an earthquake with a magnitude of 7.0 hit the country, causing unimaginable devastation. It is estimated that more than 220,000 people were killed and 1.5 million were rendered homeless. Among the dead were 102 UN personnel, including the Special Representative and his principal Deputy. Elections, which were scheduled for February 2010, had to be postponed. In January 2010, the Security Council increased the size of MINUSTAH to support the immediate recovery, reconstruction and stability efforts.[277] It was to consist of a military component of up to 8,940 troops of all ranks and a police component of up to 3,711 officers.[278] In a report issued in April 2010, the Secretary-General provided his recommendations regarding the future role of the peacekeeping force:

[271] ibid.

[272] Comments by Brian Concannon, head of the US-based Institute for Justice and Democracy in Haiti (ibid).

[273] Unattributed, 'Taking On the Gangs: Security in Haiti Starts to Improve', *The Economist*, 29 August 2007.

[274] ibid.

[275] SC Res 1892 of 13 October 2009.

[276] DPKO, 'Background to MINUSTAH', www.un.org/en/peacekeeping/missions/minustah/background.shtml (accessed 1 April 2011).

[277] SC Res 1908 of 19 January 2010, para 1.

[278] ibid, para 2.

> Whereas before the earthquake, the Mission was entering a period of consolidation, a surge effort is now needed for the next 18 months to two years, in which the Mission will help the Government preserve the gains of stabilization to date and enable a smooth transition to long-term reconstruction.[279]

Although he held the view that much of this surge could be achieved by scaling up activities within the current mandate, in some areas he called for greater technical, operational and logistical assistance to government and state institutions.[280]

In June 2010, the Security Council authorised the temporary deployment of an additional 680 police, increasing the contingent to 4,391 alongside the 8,940 military troops.[281] Among other things, MINUSTAH was charged with continuing to provide support in the preparation for and conducting of Haiti's elections.[282] In October 2010, the Security Council extended MINUSTAH's mandate until 15 October 2011 and expressed its intention to renew it further.[283]

4.2 Evaluation

4.2.1 Adherence to the 'Fundamental Principles'

In the resolution establishing MINUSTAH, the Security Council characterised the situation in Haiti as a threat to international peace and security in the region and invoked Chapter VII in relation to certain of its functions. Although MINUSTAH was established by the Security Council as a stabilisation force to follow on from a quasi-enforcement force (MIF) which was authorised to use 'all necessary measures to fulfil its mandate', MINUSTAH was not given a similar authorisation. The question then arises – as it did with UNMIL discussed above – as to whether a peacekeeping operation which is said to be (at least in part) an exercise of the Security Council's Chapter VII powers, but in relation to which the Security Council does not authorise the use of 'all necessary means', may use force beyond self-defence.

As was made clear by the UN Legal Counsel in his consideration of UNMIL, the answer to this question lies in the Security Council's intention.[284] There the Legal Counsel advised that the Security Council's intention could be discerned through an interpretation of the relevant

[279] United Nations, *Report of the Secretary-General on the United Nations Stabilization Mission in Haiti* (UN Doc S/2010/200), 22 February 2010, paras 43 and 53.
[280] ibid.
[281] SC Res 1927 of 4 June 2010, paras 1 and 2.
[282] ibid, para 9.
[283] SC Res 1944 of 14 October 2010, para 1.
[284] See discussion of the Opinion of the UN Legal Counsel at nn 73–78 and accompanying text.

resolution, focusing on 'the ordinary and natural meaning which is to be given to its terms when they are read in the context of the resolution as a whole and in the light of its object and purpose, and against the background of the discussions leading to, and the circumstances of, its adoption'.[285] In addition, the Legal Counsel looked to the nature of the tasks assigned to that operation in order to determine whether it would be able to discharge these without resorting to armed force.

Applying the Legal Counsel's reasoning to MINUSTAH, we see an operation possessed of tasks that potentially require force beyond self-defence. These include assisting with the maintenance and restoration of the rule of law, assisting with disarmament, 'protect[ing] United Nations personnel, facilities, installations and equipment and . . . ensur[ing] the security and freedom of movement of its personnel . . .', and 'protect[ing] civilians under imminent threat of physical violence, within its capability and areas of deployment, without prejudice to the responsibility of the Transitional Government and of police authorities'.[286] It is noteworthy that the Legal Counsel, in his Opinion finding that the Security Council intended to authorise UNMIL to use force beyond self-defence (despite the absence of an authorisation for that operation to use 'all necessary means'), cited UNMIL's task of protecting the UN and civilians – set out in virtually identical terms to MINUSTAH's mandated task – as an element of its mandate that 'UNMIL would simply not be in a position to meaningfully discharge . . . if it were not able to resort to armed force'.[287]

In adopting Resolution 1542 of 30 April 2004 establishing MINUSTAH, the Security Council welcomed the 16 April 2004 report of the Secretary-General and supported its recommendations. In that report, the Secretary-General voiced his view that in order to fulfil its mandate MINUSTAH required 'United Nations civilian police, backed up by a robust United Nations military force'.[288] In addition, the report called for MINUSTAH to

> operate under robust rules of engagement with sufficient capacity to be able to deal with threats to the implementation of its mandate. The military component would assist in the maintenance of a secure and stable environment throughout the country. It would provide security in all key town and surroundings; secure key sites and installations; provide security along major roads; deter armed groups from engaging in violence; protect access to humanitarian infrastructure; undertake disarmament tasks in conjunction with the HNP and the international civilian police; assist HNP and international police in the event of riots and organized violence, as needed; monitor major crossing points along the border; and provide protection for national and key United Nations and humanitarian assets in the country. The military component would also ensure the security and free-

[285] 'Note to the Under-Secretary-General' (n 72).
[286] SC Res 1542 of 30 April 2004, para 7(I).
[287] 'Note to the Under-Secretary-General' (n 72) 539.
[288] *Report of the Secretary-General* (n 231) para 73.

dom of movement of United Nations and associated personnel and protect, to the fullest extent possible, civilians facing imminent threat of physical violence.[289]

In order to achieve these tasks, the Secretary-General called for – and the Security Council authorised – a military component of up to 6,700 troops.[290] In view of the nature of the functions bestowed upon MINUSTAH, the number of troops authorised and the fact that the tasks overlapped to a considerable degree with tasks assigned to MIF (which was explicitly empowered to use 'all necessary measures'), it would appear that the intention of the Security Council was to bestow on MINUSTAH the right to use force beyond self-defence if necessary in relation to the tasks set out in section I, paragraph 7 of Resolution 1542.

On the issue of the 'fundamental principle' of consent, it is clear that host state consent was present from the outset.[291] At the October 2010 meeting of the Security Council at which the most recent renewal of the mandate was agreed to, the representative from Haiti addressed the meeting and endorsed the renewal.[292] The issue of whether consent was required will be addressed in section 4.2.2 below.

Finally, as regards the 'fundamental principle' of impartiality, we see an operation working closely with the government of Haiti; however, given that this relationship was forged to work chiefly against criminal behaviour, rather than, say, a succession movement, there does not appear to be a strong argument to be made that MINUSTAH's ties with the HNP are tantamount to a breach of its impartiality. However, given HNP's reputation as a frequent violator of human rights and given that MINUSTAH engages in operations with it, perception problems may, nonetheless, exist.

4.2.2 Constitutional Basis

The Security Council was explicitly acting under Chapter VII in relation to the tasks set out in section I, paragraph 7 of Resolution 1542. A reading of the resolution as a whole leaves the clear impression that those tasks not contained in section I of paragraph 7 do not appear to have their basis in Chapter VII.

We have seen that the level of force authorised for MINUSTAH was arguably intended to go beyond self-defence in relation to certain of its

[289] ibid, para 105.

[290] ibid, para 106.

[291] During the Security Council meeting at which SC Res 1542 of 30 April 2004 was passed, the President of the Security Council drew the attention of the members of the Security Council to a letter from Haiti's permanent representative authorising UN security forces to enter and operate on the territory of Haiti (United Nations, *Provisional Record of the 4919th Meeting of the Security Council* (UN Doc S/PV.4919), 21 February 2004, 2, referring to United Nations, *Letter Dated 29 February 2004 from the Permanent Representative of Haiti to the United Nations addressed to the President of the Security Council* (UN Doc S/2004/163), 29 February 2004.

[292] *Provisional Record*, ibid, 2.

tasks (despite the Security Council not authorising 'all necessary means'). Moreover, the level of force used by MINUSTAH appears, in at least some instances – eg rounding up gang leaders – to go beyond self-defence. Nevertheless, the nature of the force used has been relatively limited; it has been in the nature of protecting civilians from criminal behaviour rather than taking sides against rebel forces. As such, those who accept that Article 41 or 40 may be relied upon as the constitutional basis for forceful tasks if the use of force is sufficiently limited, may consider the Chapter VII tasks in this operation to be based therein. Otherwise, the operation's Chapter VII tasks would fall under Article 42. Whether the constitutional basis of the forceful tasks is Article 40, 41 or 42, the consent of the host state was not legally required.

As to the rest of the tasks making up MINUSTAH's mandate, they are based upon consent of the host state; host state consent is a legal requirement in relation to these tasks. The particular article authorising these tasks would be a non-mandatory article of Chapter VI.

4.2.3 Conclusion and Assessment of Success

The operation in Haiti provides a good illustration of the inflated expectations that can accompany a (somewhat) militarised peacekeeping force – and of the tendency to use the operation as a whipping boy when such expectations are not met. An expectation that a UN force with a maximum strength of 7,500 can restore law and order in a country the size of Haiti in the short time it has been there is not realistic. While it is to be expected that Haitian citizens (and perhaps even NGOs) may have unrealistically high expectations of MINUSTAH, and may be critical of it for not using what they consider to be a sufficient degree of force, it is more difficult to accept such criticism when it comes from powerful states which have contributed virtually no troops. For example, the US Secretary of State Colin Powell's criticism of MINUSTAH's reluctance to use force[293] would have had more legitimacy if that country had contributed more than three troops to the operation.[294]

The operation also illustrates the difficulties of using force in confined areas where civilians are present. While, in certain circumstances, it is legitimate to balance the risk to civilian life against legitimate military objectives, the UN acknowledged that MINUSTAH's forces were insufficiently trained to undertake this task effectively. Moreover, where civilian casualties do occur, the perception of MINUSTAH as a UN peacekeeping operation standing impartially above the fray will be seriously damaged – perhaps irreparably. MINUSTAH appears to lack the ability to deal effec-

[293] See Kamber (n 260).

[294] www.un.org/en/peacekeeping/contributors/2005/January2005_5.pdf (accessed 1 April 2011).

tively with the media; we saw an initial attempt to deny civilian deaths and, later, when forced to admit the deaths due to a leaked document, an effort to downplay the harm caused through use of the term 'collateral damage' – for many, a highly offensive term.

5. BURUNDI (JUNE 2004–DECEMBER 2006)

5.1 The Mission

The assassination of Burundian President Ndadaye in 1993 led to periods of instability in the country for much of the rest of that decade.[295] The signing of the 28 August 2000 Arusha Peace and Reconciliation Agreement for Burundi, which provided for a period of power-sharing, to be followed by elections no later than October 2004,[296] represented an important opportunity as regards the resumption of stability. Troublingly, however, not all of the factions were party to this agreement.[297] An AU operation, the African Union Mission in Burundi (AMIB), was deployed in the country in April 2003 in order to 'oversee the implementation of ceasefire agreements, support demobilisation, disarmament and re-integration (DDR), prepare the ground for a fuller UN peacekeeping operation and promote political and economic stability'.[298]

Between 1993 and 2004, the UN's involvement in Burundi 'was limited largely to attempts at quiet diplomacy – to mixed effect – through its political office, the United Nations Office in Burundi (UNOB)'.[299] When AMIB ran into financial difficulties in 2004, however, it turned to the UN for assistance.[300] This led to the Security Council establishing the United Nations Operation in Burundi (ONUB), by Resolution 1545, in May 2004, to become operational on 1 June.[301] The Security Council characterised the situation in Burundi as posing a threat to international peace and security in the region[302] and invoked Chapter VII in relation to the whole

[295] Stephen Jackson, *The United Nations Operation in Burundi (ONUB) – Political and Strategic Lessons Learned*, July 2006, www.peacekeepingbestpractices.unlb.org/PBPS/Library/ONUB%20Lessons%20Learned.pdf (accessed 30 June), 5–6. While the report is available on the DPKO's website, it was stressed that it reflected the personal views of the author and not necessarily those of the UN.

[296] SC Res 1545 of 21 May 2004.

[297] ibid.

[298] ibid. This despite the fact that the Arusha Agreement called for a UN peacekeeping force (under Art 8 of Protocol V). This decision may be attributable to antipathy towards the UN on the part of some of the parties in Burundi as well as the 'Security Council's ambivalence towards the prospect of a UN peace operation' (Jackson (n 295) 7–8).

[299] ibid, 3.

[300] United Nations, *Report of the Secretary-General on Burundi* (UN Doc S/2004/210), 16 March 2004, paras 58 and 100.

[301] SC Res 1545 of 21 May 2004.

[302] ibid, penultimate preambular para.

resolution.[303] ONUB was charged with assisting in the restoration of peace and the establishment of national reconciliation, as called for under the Arusha Agreement,[304] and was authorised to use 'all necessary means' within its capacity to carry out certain aspects of its mandate only, as set out in paragraph 5. These included ensuring respect for ceasefire agreements, providing security for the Burundian forces' disarmament operations, carrying out disarmament, monitoring disarmament, and contributing to the creation of necessary security conditions for the provision of humanitarian assistance.[305] The 'all necessary means' language was also applied to the civilian protection mandate that the operation was called upon to carry out.[306] ONUB was to consist of a maximum of 5,650 military personnel, 'as well as the appropriate civilian personnel',[307] and was initially composed of re-hatted AMIB troops.[308] Citing the tenuous security situation on the ground (one group remained outside the peace agreement and the fighting continued), the Secretary-General had advised the Security Council to deploy ONUB 'under robust rules of engagement' and, moreover, called for an 'over-the-horizon' force.[309] While the report was endorsed by the Security Council, Resolution 1545 made no mention of the establishment of an over-the-horizon force.

Member States were slow to contribute troops to ONUB.[310] In August 2004, some three months after ONUB was established and before it reached its full strength, an incident occurred which led to the deaths of 152 Congolese Banyamulenge refugees at a UNHCR transit camp in Gatumba, Burundi.[311] Despite its militarised mandate, ONUB did nothing to prevent the massacre. In fact, it was not even aware that the atrocity had taken place until it was notified the next day by a MONUC official in neighbouring DRC.[312] It might be argued that it would be expecting

[303] ibid, final preambular para.

[304] ibid. For a discussion of the process leading to the Arusha Agreement, see Jackson (n 295) 6–7.

[305] SC Res 1545 (n 301) para 5.

[306] ibid.

[307] ibid, para 4.

[308] ibid, para 3; United Nations, *First Report of the Secretary-General on the United Nations Operation in Burundi* (UN Doc S/2004/682), 25 August 2004, para 37.

[309] *Report of the Secretary-General* (n 300) para 72.

[310] 'Force generation for ONUB has met with delays, as Member States have been slow to respond to requests for specialized units and some troop contributors have requested delays in previously agreed deployment timelines, while others have deployed troops without the necessary equipment. Moreover, no troop contributor has as yet indicated interest in providing a maritime unit or in pursuing the idea of the "over-the-horizon" force envisaged in my last report.' *First Report of the Secretary-General* (n 308) para 38.

[311] ibid, para 13. The attack, which was described as 'well-planned and executed' by the Secretary-General, specifically targeted Banyamulenge refugees, while refugees of other ethnic groups and repatriated Burundians were left unharmed (ibid). The figure of 160 deaths given in that report was subsequently adjusted downwards to 152.

[312] United Nations, *Letter Dated 15 October 2004 from the Secretary-General Addressed to the President of the Security Council [conveying the Joint report of the United Nations Organization Mission in the Democratic Republic of the Congo, the United Nations Operation in Burundi and the*

far too much of such a small force, still at close to half its strength,[313] to protect civilians in a remote part of the country. However, the perception of the people on the ground was that because they had been sent a militarised UN force, they were entitled to expect that it would come to their aid when needed. As the DPKO's Independent External Study observed:

> [S]ignificant violence continued at times under ONUB's watch – most notoriously the Gatumba massacre of August 2004 . . . and the [rebel group *Forces nationales de liberation* (FNL)], in particular, continued to act with apparent impunity, questioning how much 'a dissuasive mission' (as many of those involved described it) was really dissuasive. From the perspective of the Burundian population the gap between what 5,000 highly visible peacekeepers (with an apparently strong Chapter VII mandate) seemed to promise and continued insecurity has been a source of some criticism.[314]

The response of the Security Council was to condemn the massacre 'with the utmost firmness' and to call for a joint ONUB/MONUC investigation into the matter.[315] The investigation was, however, unable to identify conclusively who was behind the massacre.[316] While other instances of violence occurred during ONUB's mandate, nothing of the magnitude of the Gatumba massacre was to recur.[317]

On 26 August 2005, President Pierre Nkurunziza was sworn in as Burundi's first democratically elected leader in more than a decade.[318] In November 2005, the Secretary-General reported that the transitional process had been successfully completed. Moreover, he advised the Security Council that discussions with members of the government revealed that '[i]t was their general view that security had been restored in most areas of the country'.[319] The Secretary-General called for the drawdown of troops to begin in December 2005[320] and, upon the expiry of ONUB's

Office of the United Nations High Commissioner for Human Rights into the Gatumba massacre of 5 October 2004] (UN Doc S/2004/821), 18 October 2004, para 41.

313 By the end of August 2004 the force consisted of only 3,183 troops (www.un.org/en/peacekeeping/contributors/2004/August2004_4.pdf (accessed 1 April 2011).

314 Jackson (n 295) 14.

315 United Nations, *Statement by the President of the Security Council* (UN Doc S/PRST/2004/30), 15 August 2004.

316 *Letter Dated 15 October 2004* (n 312) para 7 of the Joint Report.

317 The Secretary-General's reports generally stressed that, despite some minor incidents, the situation in the country generally appeared to be stable. See eg United Nations, *Third Report of the Secretary-General on the United Nations Operation in Burundi* (UN Doc S/2005/149), 8 March 2005 para 25. See also United Nations, *Fourth Report of the Secretary-General on the United Nations Operation in Burundi* (UN Doc S/2005/328), 19 May 2005, para 15.

318 *Fourth Report of the Secretary-General*, ibid, 3.

319 United Nations, *Fifth Report of the Secretary-General on the United Nations Operation in Burundi* (UN Doc S/2005/728), 21 November 2005, para 55.

320 ibid, para 58. Indeed the new government was somewhat hostile to the UN and wanted ONUB to withdraw as soon as possible. See United Nations, *Letter Dated 23 November 2005 from the Chargé d'affaires a.i. of the Permanent Mission of Burundi to the United Nations addressed to the President of the Security Council* (UN Doc S/2005/736), 23 November 2005. See also Jackson (n 295) 25.

mandate on 31 December 2006,[321] the United Nations Integrated Office in Burundi (BINUB)[322] came into existence.[323] The AU established a Special Task Force to 'assume the responsibilities that were allocated to ONUB under the ceasefire agreement', including providing protection to designated assembly areas for FNL combatants and demobilisation centres and the disarmament of combatants.[324]

5.2 Evaluation

5.2.1 Adherence to the 'Fundamental Principles'

It is, to use the words of the UN Legal Adviser, 'beyond all doubt' that ONUB was authorised to use armed force other than in situations of self-defence regarding those tasks in relation to which it was authorised to use 'all necessary means'.[325] As for those aspects of its mandate where it was not authorised to use 'all necessary means', it might be argued – along the lines of the argument employed in relation to UNMIL, discussed above – that the Security Council could, nonetheless, have intended that it be authorised to use force beyond self-defence, and its intention must be considered. However, given that the Security Council here – unlike in respect of UNMIL – specifically authorised the use of 'all necessary means' with regard to certain tasks and not others, it is submitted that its intention on this point was clear. In practice, UNOB largely complied with the 'fundamental principle' of force only in self-defence, rarely using force at all.

As to the 'fundamental principle' of host state consent, this would appear to have been present: Burundi was present at the Security Council meeting in May 2004 when the mandate of ONUB was agreed and it voiced no objection.[326]

Furthermore, there is nothing to indicate that the operation – which was in essence charged with overseeing a peace agreement – acted in a way that was not impartial.

[321] The operation received its final extension to 31 December 2006 in SC Res 1692 of 30 June 2006.

[322] In French, Bureau Intégré des Nations Unies au Burundi.

[323] SC Res 1719 of 25 October 2006.

[324] United Nations, *Ninth Report of the Secretary-General on the United Nations Operation in Burundi* (UN Doc S/2006/994), 18 December 2006, paras 6–8.

[325] 'Note to the Under-Secretary-General' (n 72); see discussion of UNMIL at section 2.2.1 above.

[326] United Nations, *Provisional Record of the 4975th Meeting of the Security Council* (UN Doc S/PV.4975), 21 May 2004. The fact that Burundi was a signatory to the Arusha Agreement, which called for a UN presence, may, for some, amount to consent to the peacekeeping operation; however, it is submitted that consent to a UN presence is different from consent to the mandate of a particular peacekeeping operation. See nn 219–222 and accompanying text on this point and on the alternate view held by the Special Court for Sierra Leone.

5.2.2 Constitutional Basis

It is clear that the Security Council established ONUB as a Chapter VII measure. Despite the fact that it did not – and in most respects did not *need to* – use force beyond self-defence, it is clear that it was vested with the authority to do so when carrying out certain of its tasks. The basis for these tasks would be Article 42. Of course, to those who accept that a limited use of force beyond self-defence may find its basis in either Article 40 or 41, either of those articles might be suggested as bases, given the limited force actually used. At the same time, however, it is difficult to reconcile an authorisation to use 'all necessary means' with the Security Council's Article 40 or 41 powers.

As to its other tasks, because these were established under Chapter VII and because of the mandatory nature of the assignment of such tasks – '[*d*]*ecides* that ONUB shall . . .' – their constitutional basis would appear to be either Article 40 or Article 41 of the Charter.

5.2.3 Conclusion and Assessment of Success

ONUB was a success on many levels: tragedy on the scale of Rwanda was avoided, democratic elections were held, and a general sense of stability returned to Burundi in a relatively short time.[327] While there appear to be no instances of the operation resorting to offensive force, the very fact that it was empowered to do so may have strengthened its ability to carry out its security-related tasks, such as disarmament, border monitoring and provision of military escorts.[328]

The DPKO's Independent External Study considered ONUB to have underperformed in the area of security, citing three reasons for this. First, it noted that the wording of the civilian protection mandate – ONUB should act 'without prejudice to the responsibility of the transitional Government of Burundi, to protect civilians under imminent threat of physical violence' – presumed that ONUB would 'operate alongside Burundian armed forces controlled by a sovereign government [the transitional government] who retained the primary responsibility to protect the civilian population'.[329] This presumed an exchange of information by ONUB with the transitional government and its forces – something which

[327] An assessment of whether the improvement in the situation there was attributable to the peacekeeping operation or to other factors is difficult indeed. As noted by Jackson (n 295) 14: 'Both the UN's own reporting and that of independent actors . . . confirm that 2004 saw a considerable improvement in the human rights situation across the country. But this may have had as much to do with the fact that by the end of 2003, [two rebel factions] had finally enacted a meaningful ceasefire, dramatically decreasing the overall level of violence, as it had to do with UN peacekeeping *per se*.'

[328] See eg *Ninth Report of the Secretary-General* (n 324) paras 64–71.

[329] Jackson (n 295) 14.

would have been highly problematic given that one of the factions associated the transitional government, the *Forces de Nationales Défense* (FDN), was itself responsible for attacks against civilians.[330] A second reason for ONUB's underperformance in relation to the maintenance of security according to the Independent External Study was the fact that AMIB, which ONUB succeeded and from which ONUB drew many of its troops, 'had set the pattern for a less assertive foreign troop presence'.[331] Finally, ONUB lacked military intelligence. As the Independent External Study observed, in order for ONUB to have 'protect[ed] civilians under imminent threat of physical violence' as the mandate specified, it would have 'require[d] effective and immediate intelligence concerning where attacks were likely to take place. But from the beginning, ONUB's intelligence capacity remained under-developed.'[332]

The fact that only 5,500 troops were authorised also had an impact on ONUB's underperformance in relation to security. According to the Independent External Study, while ONUB was permitted 'in principle [to use] deadly force to protect Burundians in imminent danger', in practice it 'interpreted the Chapter VII dimension as mainly a psychological rather than an actual deterrent'.[333] The Study suggested that in light of ONUB's size, it was unlikely that it could have been any more proactive:

> Overall, ONUB interpreted its security mandate correctly (in legal terms) and prudently (in operational ones). With only 5,500 troops, even with a very much more muscular stance on the ground, it seems unlikely that ONUB could have guaranteed security for the population across the country.[334]

ONUB simply was not in a position to carry out the mandate set for it, not only because of its size, but also because it did not feature a single soldier from any of the well-trained forces of the permanent members of the Security Council. Indeed, with the odd exception, all troops were from African or Asian states.

6. SUDAN (MARCH 2005–PRESENT)

6.1 The Mission

For more than two decades, the government of Sudan, based in Khartoum in the northern part of the country, was engaged in a conflict with the Sudan People's Liberation Movement/Army (SPLM/A), a rebel move-

[330] ibid.
[331] ibid, 15.
[332] ibid.
[333] ibid, 14.
[334] ibid.

ment in the south.[335] In addition to the north-south civil war, a separate conflict emerged in the Darfur region in 2003, involving attacks on government targets by the SPLM/A and the Justice and Equality Movement (JEM), which led to the government responding by mobilising its national armed forces and relying on local militia.[336] In June 2004, amid signs that the north-south conflict might have come to an end, the Security Council established the United Nations Advance Mission in Sudan (UNAMIS), to prepare for a 'peace support operation' to support a north-south peace.[337] Meanwhile, in Darfur, the situation worsened, resulting in a major humanitarian disaster.

On 9 January 2005[338] a Comprehensive Peace Agreement (CPA) was reached in relation to the north-south conflict and, in March 2005, by Resolution 1590, the Security Council established the United Nations Mission in Sudan (UNMIS).[339] UNMIS was to consist of up to 10,000 military personnel. In the preamble to Resolution 1590, the Security Council determined that the situation in Sudan constituted a threat to international peace and security; however, Chapter VII was not invoked in a general way, to cover all paragraphs of the resolution. The functions of UNMIS centred on assisting in the implementation of the CPA (thorough monitoring, liaising, etc) but were not said to have their constitutional basis in Chapter VII; no authorisation to use 'all necessary means' to carry out these tasks was granted by the Security Council. In relation to a single paragraph only, Chapter VII was invoked:

> Acting under Chapter VII of the United Nations Charter [the Security Council] [d]ecides that UNMIS is authorised to take the necessary action, in the areas of deployment of its forces and as it deems within its capabilities, to protect United Nations personnel, facilities, installations, and equipment, ensure the security and freedom of movement of United Nations personnel, humanitarian workers, joint assessment mechanism and assessment and evaluation commission personnel, and, without prejudice to the responsibility of the Government of Sudan, to protect civilians under imminent threat of physical violence.[340]

Although the focus of UNMIS was on the CPA (which dealt with the north-south conflict rather than the crisis in the Darfur region), the

[335] The nature of the dispute involved resources, power, the role of religion in the state and self-determination (see www.un.org/en/peacekeeping/missions/unmis/background.shtml (accessed 1 April 2011)).

[336] ibid.

[337] SC Res 1547 of 11 June 2004. In November 2004 the Security Council increased UNAMIS's staffing levels and extended its mandate (SC Res 1574 of 19 November 2004). For a discussion of the work of UNAMIS, see United Nations, *Report of the Secretary-General on the Sudan* (UN Doc S/2005/57), 31 January 2005, paras 5–10.

[338] SC Res 1590 of 24 March 2005. The Agreement incorporated the former rebel group, the Sudan People's Liberation Movement/Army (SPLM/A), into a Government of National Unity.

[339] ibid.

[340] ibid, para 16.

operation was asked to coordinate[341] with a Security Council-endorsed[342] AU force that had been deployed in Darfur in April 2004.[343] The force, known as the African Union Mission in Sudan (AMIS), had begun as a 'contingent primarily of unarmed military observers' but its armed contingent and its mandate were enhanced in October 2004, such that it became 'a major operation that included armed force protectors, unarmed civilian police, and support teams'.[344] Despite this – and further enhancements in July 2005[345] – the operation was overstretched and had considerable difficulties fulfilling its mandate in Darfur.[346] Meanwhile, UNMIS began to deploy in April 2005; however, there were substantial delays before it acquired its full complement of troops.[347]

By January 2006, the AU indicated that it favoured a transition from an AU-led to a UN-led operation in Darfur.[348] When, on 5 May 2006, the Darfur Peace Agreement (DPA) was signed, the AU called for 'concrete steps . . . to effect the transition from AMIS to a United Nations operation'.[349] This was endorsed by the Security Council, which requested that the Secretary-General make preparations for such an operation.[350] In a report of July 2006, the Secretary-General set out his recommendations for a UN force in Darfur. He envisaged a military force which was to be 'large, agile and robust', and which would include a 'robust military capa-

[341] ibid, para 6. See also para 5, where the Security Council asked the Secretary-General to report on options for reinforcing the effort to foster peace in Darfur.

[342] This force, described at para 3 of SC Res 1556 of 30 July 2004 as a 'protection force', was given a Chapter VII endorsement by the Security Council. Subsequently, the Security Council endorsed the AU's decision to 'enhance and augment' the operation and to engage in 'proactive monitoring' (SC Res 1564 of 18 September 2004, para 2).

[343] On 8 April 2004, the Sudanese government and two Darfur rebel groups signed a ceasefire agreement in which the AU was mandated to send military observers to monitor and report on the ceasefire (Human Rights Watch, *Imperatives for Immediate Change: The African Union Mission in Sudan*, Human Rights Watch document, vol 18 No 1 (A), January 2006, www.un.org/en/peacekeeping/missions/unmis/background.shtml (accessed 1 April 2011), 3).

[344] ibid, 4. This change in AMIS's mandate and increase in its troop levels – by now some were referring to the operation as AMIS II – was endorsed by the Security Council in Res 1574 of 19 November 2004, para 13.

[345] Human Rights Watch (n 343) 3.

[346] ibid. See also International Crisis Group, *To Save Darfur*, Crisis Group Africa Report No 105, 17 March 2006, www.crisisgroup.org/~/media/Files/africa/horn-of-africa/sudan/To%20Save%20Darfur.pdf (accessed 1 April 2011).

[347] United Nations, *Report of the Secretary-General on the Sudan* (UN Doc S/2005/411), 23 June 2005, paras 25–29. As of 4 March 2006, the strength of the military contingent stood at 7,697 personnel, or 78 per cent (para 30). Indeed, it was not until April 2007 that it (almost) reached its full military strength (United Nations, *Report of the Secretary-General on the Sudan* (UN Doc S/2007/213), 17 April 2007, para 33).

[348] United Nations, *Report of the Secretary-General on the Sudan* (UN Doc S/2006/160), 14 March 2006, para 23. The Security Council took note of this and asked the Secretary-General to begin contingency planning for this immediately (United Nations, *Statement by the President of the Security Council* (UN Doc S/PRST/2006/5), 3 February 2006).

[349] SC Res 1679 of 16 May 2006, para 3.

[350] ibid, paras 3 and 5.

bility to deter and defeat spoilers'.[351] He put forward three options for the Security Council, one calling for 17,300 troops, one for 18,600 troops, and one for 15,300 troops.[352] According to the Secretary-General:

> [T]he operation's primary purpose . . . should be to establish a stable and secure environment to protect civilians and support the implementation of the Darfur Peace Agreement. Initially, the focus of the security operations would be the provision of security to the vulnerable population.[353]

The Secretary-General's vision for the UN operation in Darfur was not, however, shared by the government of Sudan. The government made clear its view that 'the restoration of stability and the protection of civilians are central to the responsibilities of the Government of the Sudan'.[354] Nevertheless, in August 2006, the Security Council, in Resolution 1706, decided that the mandate of UNMIS should 'be expanded . . . [such] that it shall deploy to Darfur' and undertake a variety of militarised tasks, and sought 'the consent of the Government of National Unity for this deployment'.[355] Resolution 1706 characterised the situation as a threat to international peace and security but did not invoke Chapter VII in relation to the entire resolution. The Security Council called upon UNMIS to undertake a variety of tasks, including monitoring implementation and investigating violations of the DPA,[356] contributing to the protection of human rights and assisting in addressing regional security issues.[357] At paragraph 12, acting under Chapter VII, the Security Council authorised the use of 'all necessary means, in the areas of deployment of its forces and as it deems within its capabilities' to protect UN personnel and facilities, 'to prevent disruption of the implementation of the Darfur Peace Agreement by armed groups, without prejudice to the responsibility of the Government of the Sudan, [and] to protect civilians under threat of physical violence'.[358] It was also authorised, under Chapter VII, to 'use all

[351] United Nations, *Report of the Secretary-General on Darfur* (UN Doc S/2006/591), 28 July 2006, para 83.

[352] ibid, paras 84–87.

[353] ibid, para 71.

[354] United Nations, *Letter Dated 17 August 2006 from the Secretary-General Addressed to the President of the Security Council* (UN Doc S/2006/266), 17 August 2006, Annex (containing a 2 August 2006 letter from President Al-Bashir to Secretary-General Annan, transmitting a 'Plan of the government of the Sudan for the restoration of stability and protection of civilians in Darfur'). 'The Sudanese government had been for months publicly dismissing the idea of a Chapter VII UN force in Darfur prior to the adoption of SC Res 1706. Special Envoy Brahimi heard a firm "No" from President Bashir in person during his visit to Khartoum in late May . . . Members of the Security Council heard the same "No" directly from Bashir during their visit to Khartoum two weeks later.' David Ross Black and Paul Williams, *The International Politics of Mass Atrocities: The Case of Darfur* (New York, Routledge, 2010) 95–96 n 21.

[355] SC Res 1706 of 31 August 2006, para 1. China, Russia and Qatar abstaining.

[356] ibid, para 9.

[357] ibid, para 10.

[358] ibid, para 12.

necessary means' 'to support early and effective implementation of the Darfur Peace Agreement, to prevent attacks and threats against civilians', and to seize and dispose of arms in violation of agreements and measures imposed by Resolution 1556.[359]

The wording of the resolution left room for debate as to whether the subsequent consent of the host state was a *sine qua non* of the changed mandate coming into effect. Some argued that it was not.[360] After all, the wording suggests that the Security Council was making a resolution which was binding upon Sudan: the Security Council '*decide[d]* that UNMIS' mandate *shall* be expanded' (emphasis added). Such a view may be supported by the Security Council's reliance on Chapter VII and the invocation of the phrase 'all necessary means' in relation to performance of the mandate. The Security Council certainly does not require the consent of the host state when engaging in enforcement. Moreover, the fact that the Security Council, in the resolution's preamble, specifically made reference to its endorsement of the paragraphs of the World Summit document dealing with the responsibility to protect[361] (the first country-specific resolution of the Security Council to invoke the doctrine) suggests the possibility that the Security Council was at least contemplating taking action to protect civilians even if consent was not forthcoming.[362]

On the other hand, the Security Council had explicitly '*invite[d]*' the government of Sudan to consent to the mandate. Moreover, the essential nature of the host state's consent was emphasised in statements made by a number of Security Council Member States at the time the draft resolution was passed. Russia, China and Qatar, each of which abstained from voting on Resolution 1706, made public statements stressing the essential nature of the consent of the government of Sudan to the modification of UNMIS's mandate.[363] China – which was most strongly opposed to a reso-

[359] ibid.

[360] Black and Williams (n 354) 80.

[361] The Security Council recalls '1674 (2006) on the protection of civilians in armed conflict, which reaffirms inter alia the provisions of paragraphs 138 and 139 of the 2005 United Nations World Summit outcome document' (ibid, second preambular para). The Outcome Document (discussed in chapter 2, section 2.4.3) recognised the need to 'take collective action, in a timely and decisive manner, through the Security Council, in accordance with the Charter, including Chapter VII, on a case-by-case basis and in cooperation with relevant regional organizations as appropriate, should peaceful means be inadequate and national authorities are manifestly failing to protect their populations from genocide, war crimes, ethnic cleansing and crimes against humanity' (United Nations, *2005 World Summit Outcome Document [Resolution of the General Assembly]* (UN Doc A/RES/60/1), 24 October 2005, para 139).

[362] This was how the International Crisis Group appeared to view the resolution (see International Crisis Group, *Getting the UN into Darfur*, Crisis Group Africa Briefing No 43, 12 October 2006, www.crisisgroup.org/~/media/Files/africa/horn-of-africa/sudan/B043%20Getting%20the%20UN%20into%20Darfur.pdf (accessed 1 April 2011), 2).

[363] The Russian representative stressed that it was 'of fundamental importance that the resolution clearly states the overriding need for the consent of the Government of National Unity of the Sudan for the deployment of a United Nations peacekeeping mission in Darfur' (United Nations, *Provisional Record of the 5519th Meeting of the Security Council* (UN Doc S/

lution that would interfere with Sudan's sovereignty[364] – indicated that it had 'consistently urged the sponsors to clearly include "with the consent of the Government of National Unity" in the text of the resolution, which is a fixed and standardized phrase utilized by the Council when deploying United Nations missions'.[365] Qatar appeared to view the approach of passing the resolution without obtaining host state consent as something of a strong-arm technique against Sudan, noting, that insufficient 'efforts [had been] made to engage the Sudan instead of pressuring it into approving the resolution that the Council has now adopted'.[366] Even for some of the states sponsoring the draft resolution, host state consent was said to be essential in order for the operation to deploy.[367] The US, for its part, did not address the issue of consent; instead it called upon the government of Sudan to comply with the terms of the resolution and noted its expectation of 'full and unconditional cooperation and support for the new United Nations peacekeeping force'.[368]

The government of Sudan quickly voiced its view that Resolution 1706 was 'illegal',[369] with the Sudanese President Al-Bashir describing it as a 'comprehensive conspiracy for confiscating [Sudan's] sovereignty'.[370] The government launched a successful effort to discourage any possible troop-contributing countries from committing forces to a mission which was against Sudan's wishes.[371] 'This, in turn, raised a host of concerns, either of principle (state sovereignty) or practice for potential [troop contributing countries] who would be rightfully leery of sending soldiers to Sudan without the [government's] consent.'[372] Despite the use of diplomacy and arm-twisting by the international community – including a threat of 'confrontation' by the US[373] – the Sudanese government refused to

PV.5519), 31 August 2006, 8–9). The representative of China observed that '[s]uch a transition [from AMIS to a fortified UNMIS] can be possible and the mission can be deployed only when the consent of the Government of National Unity is obtained' (ibid, 5).

364 Black and Williams (n 354) 95 n 22, relying on John Boulton, *Surrender is Not an Option* (New York, Threshold Editions, 2007) 356.

365 *Provisional Record* (n 363) 5.

366 ibid, 7.

367 In the words of the representative of the UK: 'That does not mean that we do not attach importance to the consent and agreement of the Government of the Sudan. It remains the case that the United Nations cannot deploy in Darfur until we have that agreement; that is not in dispute' (ibid, 3).

368 ibid, 2.

369 Black and Williams (n 354) 80.

370 52 *Keesing's Record of World Events*, September 2006, 47444.

371 Black and Williams (n 354) 80.

372 ibid, 80.

373 According to a Reuters report of 27 September 2006, US Secretary of State Condoleezza Rice described Sudan's choice as being 'between cooperation and confrontation' (International Crisis Group (n 362) 5). Furthermore, considerable pressure was applied to China, a major trading partner with Sudan, including threats to dub the 2008 Olympic Games in Beijing the 'Genocide Olympics' (unattributed, 'Too Few, Too Late? Even if UN Forces are At Last Let into Darfur, Will they be Able to Save it?', *The Economist*, 21 April 2007).

consent. As such, the new operation did not get beyond the planning stages.[374]

On 16 November 2006, at a meeting in Addis Ababa, Ethiopia, the Secretary-General proposed a 'hybrid' UN-AU force for Darfur as a compromise.[375] The conclusions of the Addis Ababa meeting were endorsed by the Security Council in December 2006.[376] On 12 June 2007 Sudanese government officials announced the country's acceptance of the hybrid force[377] and, on 31 July 2007, the Security Council established an AU/UN Hybrid operation in Darfur (UNAMID) to begin implementing its tasks no later than 31 December 2007.[378] The force was to consist of up to 19,555 military personnel and was given a wide variety of tasks relating to the restoration of security in the region.[379] Although the Security Council characterised the situation in Darfur as a threat to international peace and security, it did not specifically invoke Chapter VII in relation to most of its functions. At paragraph 15, however, it indicated that it was acting under Chapter VII and decided that UNAMID was authorised to 'take the necessary action, in the areas of deployment of its forces and as it deems within its capabilities' to:

(i) protect its personnel, facilities, installations and equipment, and to ensure the security and freedom of movement of its own personnel and humanitarian workers, and
(ii) support early and effective implementation of the Darfur Peace Agreement, prevent the disruption of its implementation and armed attacks, and protect civilians, without prejudice to the responsibility of the Government of Sudan.

Member States were slow to volunteer troops and equipment for the newly established force. In an August 2007 report, the Secretary-General

374 International Crisis Group (n 362) 5.

375 Black and Williams (n 354) 80.

376 United Nations, *Statement by the President of the Security Council* (UN Doc S/PRST/2006/55), 19 December 2006. The Addis Ababa agreement also called for the 'immediate deployment of the United Nations Light and Heavy Support Packages to the African Union Mission in the Sudan' (ibid). The Secretary-General made plans in late 2006 and early 2007 for a transfer of equipment and personnel, including a 'light support package' involving the transfer of 105 military staff officers (*Report of the Secretary-General* of 17 April 2007 (n 347) para 23). Subsequently, a 'heavy support package' (comprising 3,000 well-equipped military police and aviation and logistic support) was agreed to by Sudan (Warren Hoge, 'Sudan Drops Objections to UN Aid in Darfur', *New York Times*, 17 April 2007).

377 United Nations (News Centre), 'Sudan Accepts Hybrid United Nations-African Union Peacekeeping Force in Darfur', 12 June 2007, www.un.org/apps/news/story.asp?NewsID=22881 (accessed 1 April 2011).

378 SC Res 1769 of 31 July 2007.

379 The mandate, which was established by the Security Council by reference to a report of the Secretary-General and the Chairperson of the African Union Commission, is very lengthy, running some three pages (United Nations, *Letter Dated 5 June 2007 from the Secretary-General to the President of the Security Council [attaching the Report of the Secretary-General and the Chairperson of the African Union Commission on the hybrid operation in Darfur]* (UN Doc S/2007/307/Rev.1), 5 June 2007, paras 54–55).

cited difficulties in finding offers to supply the necessary troops and indicated that critical military capabilities were lacking.[380] His call for Member States to 'urgently provide the outstanding military contributions that are critical for UNAMID to fulfil its challenging mandate'[381] appeared to go unheeded. As of 31 January 2008, UNAMID consisted of just 7,476 of the 19,555 military personnel authorised[382] and the operation was severely under-equipped.[383] While Russia pledged several desert mobile helicopters in March 2008, UNAMID 'sorely lacked the number of helicopters needed to carry out the mission in an effective manner'.[384]

In the first three months of the mission's existence, violence continued unabated in some regions. The Secretary-General characterised the security situation between January and March 2008 as 'extremely volatile'[385] and observed that approximately 115 fatalities had been reported to the UN.[386] He continued:

> UNAMID was challenged almost immediately following the transfer of authority from the African Union Mission in the Sudan (AMIS) on 31 December, when, on 7 January, the Sudanese Armed Forces fired on the first UNAMID resupply convoy, 2 km from Tine in Northern Darfur. A civilian driver was wounded when the fuel tanker he was driving was hit by a rocket-propelled grenade.[387]

Attacks against the civilian population and against UNAMID itself were to continue. In July 2008, in the most serious attack against UNAMID personnel since the start of the mission, seven peacekeepers were killed and 22 others wounded.[388] Later that month a commanding officer was shot and killed by unidentified armed men.[389] On 4 December 2009, a UNAMID escort patrol was attacked, leading to the deaths of three UNAMID peace-

[380] United Nations, *Report of the Secretary-General on the Deployment of the African Union-United Nations Hybrid Operation in Darfur* (UN Doc S/2007/517), 30 August 2007, para 9. An incident in late September 2007 involving the killing of some 10 AMIS forces in Darfur may well have had an impact on the Secretary-General's ability to secure sufficient troops (Jeffrey Gettleman, 'Darfur Rebels Kill 10 in Peace Force', *New York Times*, 1 October 2007). The report spoke of a 'concern that the spiraling violence could scare away countries that have been considering contributing troops to the long-awaited United Nations-African Union peacekeeping mission' (ibid).

[381] *Report of the Secretary-General*, ibid, para 17.

[382] United Nations, *Report of the Secretary-General on the Deployment of the African Union-United Nations Hybrid Operation in Darfur* (UN Doc S/2008/98), 30 August 2007, para 11.

[383] Samuel Totten, *An Oral and Documentary History of the Darfur Genocide* (Santa Barbara, ABC-CLIO, 2011) 26.

[384] ibid, 27.

[385] United Nations, *Report of the Secretary-General on the Deployment of the African Union-United Nations Hybrid Operation in Darfur* (UN Doc S/2008/249), 14 April 2008, para 1.

[386] ibid, para 3.

[387] ibid, para 6.

[388] United Nations, *Report of the Secretary-General on the Deployment of the African Union-United Nations Hybrid Operation in Darfur* (UN Doc S/2008/558), 18 August 2008, para 4.

[389] ibid, para 5.

keepers and the serious injury of two others.[390] In a separate incident on 5 December 2009, two UNAMID peacekeepers were killed and another was injured.[391]

Almost from the start, UNAMID was criticised for not meeting its civilian protection mandate. In July 2008, the Darfur Consortium (a group of NGOs and aid agencies) reported:

> The civilian population now looks to the first United Nations-African Union 'hybrid' mission to help improve security. But six months after initial deployment, UNAMID has failed to provide adequate protection. The force lacks critical resources, leaving the people of Darfur, humanitarian agencies and even its own peacekeepers vulnerable to ongoing attacks and extreme violence.[392]

Such criticism led the force commander, General Martin Luther Agwai, to point out the force's limitations:

> For anybody to expect that 8,000 troops and under 2,000 policemen would police an area as big as France, that person [is] daydreaming . . . With no roads, no means of communication and you expect UNAMID forces to be everywhere, I think [it] is too much of an expectation.[393]

A UNAMID spokesman reportedly characterised the situation as 'unsatisfactory' and stressed UNAMID's lack of resources.[394]

In July 2009, two years after the establishment of UNAMID, the Security Council continued to call on Member States 'to pledge and contribute the remaining helicopter, aerial reconnaissance, ground transport, medical and logistical units and other force enablers required'.[395] It expressed its concern at 'the continued seriousness of the security situation and deterioration of the humanitarian situation in Darfur, and at the recurring attacks on the civilian population'.[396] In what would appear to be something of a reproach to the force, it underlined the 'need for UNAMID to make full use of its mandate and capabilities, particularly with regard to (a) the protection of civilians across Darfur, and (b) ensuring safe, timely and unhindered humanitarian access, the safety and security of humanitarian personnel and the protection of humanitarian convoys'.[397] The Security Council did not indicate how these tasks might be accomplished given the force's limited resources as compared with the magnitude of the man-

[390] United Nations, *Report of the Secretary-General on the Deployment of the African Union-United Nations Hybrid Operation in Darfur* (UN Doc S/2010/50), 29 January 2010, para 31.

[391] ibid.

[392] Darfur Consortium, 'Putting People First: The Protection Challenge Facing UNAMID in Darfur', 28 July 2008, www.darfurconsortium.org/darfur_consortium_actions/reports/2008/Putting%20People%20First%20UNAMID%20report.pdf (accessed 1 April 2011).

[393] Totten (n 383) 27, relying on an interview with ABC News, 28 July 2008.

[394] ibid.

[395] SC Res 1881 of 30 July 2009.

[396] ibid, preamble.

[397] ibid, para 2.

date. In July 2010, UNAMID was extended for another year, until 31 July 2011.[398] Once again, the Security Council appeared to reproach UNAMID for not doing enough, again underlining the importance of making 'full use of its mandate and capabilities' and to give priority to civilian protection and humanitarian access.[399]

While the most recent UN statistics reveal that the operation has nearly the full complement of troops authorised by the Security Council – as of March 2011 there were 17,682 UNAMID troops[400] – serious problems remain. Lack of equipment continues to impede the operation's effectiveness,[401] the Sudanese government continues to obstruct the operation's freedom of movement,[402] and UNAMID peacekeepers continue to be targeted. Between July 2009 and July 2010, UNAMID peacekeepers were attacked on 28 occasions, leaving 10 dead and 26 injured, and on two occasions UNAMID personnel were kidnapped.[403] Sadly, the overall security situation does not appear to be improving. Citing more than 400 conflict-related fatalities, the Secretary-General characterised May 2010 as 'the deadliest month in Darfur since UNAMID took over from the African Union Mission in the Sudan on 31 December 2007'.[404] In July 2010, the Security Council expressed its

> deep concern at the deterioration in the security situation in Darfur, including ceasefire violations, attacks by rebel groups, aerial bombardment by the Government of Sudan, increased inter-tribal fighting, and attacks on humanitarian personnel and peacekeepers, which have restricted humanitarian access to conflict areas where vulnerable civilian populations reside.[405]

6.2 Evaluation

6.2.1 Adherence to the 'Fundamental Principles'

The 'fundamental principle' of the non-use of force except in self-defence was clearly inapplicable to the certain aspects of UNMIS's mandate – ie tasks in a single paragraph of Resolution 1590. When the Security Council attempted to expand UNMIS's mandate so that it could take over from

[398] SC Res 1935 of 30 July 2010, para 1.
[399] ibid, para 2.
[400] Figures available at www.un.org/en/peacekeeping/contributors/2011/mar11_4.pdf (accessed 1 April 2011).
[401] United Nations, *Report of the Secretary-General on the African Union-United Nations Hybrid Operation in Darfur* (UN Doc S/2010/382), 14 July 2010, para 63.
[402] See United Nations, *Report of the Secretary-General on the African Union-United Nations Hybrid Operation in Darfur* (UN Doc S/2011/222), 18 January 2011, para 35, where the report noted that UNAMID's freedom of movement was obstructed on 123 occasions during 2010.
[403] *Report of the Secretary-General* (n 401) para 29.
[404] ibid, para 22.
[405] SC Res 1935 of 30 July 2010, preamble.

AMIS in Darfur, it also limited the invocation of Chapter VII to one paragraph; however, this time, it authorised the use of 'all necessary means' (rather than 'the necessary action')[406] in relation to more tasks. This expansion of the authorisation to use force beyond self-defence may have been a bridge too far when it came to gaining the support of the Security Council; while it is not clear from the record, this may have contributed to some Security Council Member States – China being most prominent among them – insisting that the resolution be subject to host state consent. It seems likely, moreover, that it also contributed to the host state's unwillingness to consent.

With Resolution 1769, in which it established the hybrid UNAMID, the Security Council followed a similar approach to that taken with Resolution 1590 establishing UNMIS. It invoked Chapter VII only in relation to one paragraph and authorised UNAMID to 'take the necessary action' only in relation to certain tasks. However, it went further than it had with UNMIS: in addition to authorising 'the necessary action' for civilian protection and to protect the peacekeeping operation, it also authorised such action to support the implementation of the DPA, to prevent disruption of the implementation of the DPA and to prevent armed attacks.[407] These additional areas would appear to give UNAMID significantly more scope to use force beyond self-defence than is the case with UNMIS.

As to the 'fundamental principle' of host state consent, this was clearly present upon the establishment of UNMIS. In Resolution 1590 the Security Council reaffirmed its commitment to the sovereignty of Sudan and took note of the request of the parties to the CPA for the establishment of a peace support mission.[408] At the meeting at which the draft resolution was passed, the representative of Sudan spoke of his government's firm commitment to the establishment of the peacekeeping operation.[409] The attempt to modify the mandate of UNMIS so that that operation could take over from AMIS was much more complicated and is discussed above. In short, host state consent was seen as an essential element in the expansion of the mandate, and this was made clear in the minutes of the meeting at which the mandate was modified, in the wording of the modified mandate itself, and in the fact that, in the absence of host state consent, the resolution was, in effect, abandoned. Whether consent was legally required is another matter and will be discussed in the section immediately below.

[406] The reason for this change in wording is unclear. There does not appear to exist any pattern based on Security Council practice such that 'all necessary means' may be said to authorise any greater (or lesser) level of forcefulness than 'the necessary action'.

[407] SC Res 1765 of 15 July 2007, para 15.

[408] SC Res 1590 of 24 March 2005.

[409] United Nations *Provisional Records of the 5151st Meeting of the Security Council* (UN Doc 5/PV.5151), 24 March 2005, 4.

With the establishment of UNAMID, the Security Council was at pains to stress that it was acting with the consent of the government. It reaffirmed its 'strong commitment' to the sovereignty of Sudan, expressed its 'determination to work with the Government of Sudan, in full respect of its sovereignty', and commended 'the agreement of Sudan that the Hybrid operation shall be deployed in Darfur'.[410]

As to the 'fundamental principle' of impartiality, the Security Council was careful to attempt to be neutral; however, given the numerous restrictions imposed by the government of Sudan regarding the formation and implementation of the mandates (especially that of UNAMID), the government was able to ensure that it was not, itself, the object of the use of force by either mission – despite the fact that it was that government that was frequently among the worst offenders as regards attacks against civilians. As such, it is difficult to imagine that the operations would be perceived as impartial.

6.2.2 Constitutional Basis

The tasks assigned to UNMIS and UNAMID that are based in Chapter VII involve the use of force beyond self-defence. As such, the applicable article of the Charter providing the constitutional basis of these tasks is Article 42.[411] As such, while host state consent was present, it was not legally required for these tasks. However, all other aspects of the mandates appear to be consent-based and, in establishing them, the Security Council did not indicate that it was acting under Chapter VII. Given that it did indicate this much in relation to certain of the tasks, it seems reasonable to assume that these other tasks fall outside Chapter VII (presumably under a suitable article of Chapter VI), or at least outside the Security Council's mandatory powers thereunder.

What does fact that the Security Council was unable to successfully modify UNMIS to bestow upon it tasks relating to Darfur say about the need for consent? Clearly no host state consent was required in relation to those aspects of Resolution 1706 where the Security Council relied upon Chapter VII (ie those tasks set out in paragraph 12). It was, however, necessary for everything else. If the Security Council had been able to agree to act under Chapter VII in establishing the whole of Resolution 1706 and its intention to bind Sudan had been clear, consent would not have been a legal issue.

410 SC Res 1769 of 31 July 2007, preamble.

411 As noted elsewhere, while it may be argued that the authorisation to use force beyond self-defence in each could find its constitutional basis in Art 40 or 41, this argument is difficult to make for the reasons given in chapter 3, sections 3.2.2.4 and 3.2.3.2. It is especially difficult when an operation is explicitly authorised to use 'all necessary measures' or similar.

6.2.3 Conclusion and Assessment of Success

With both mandates in Sudan, the task of civilian protection is an enormous one. From the start, the Secretary-General made his position on UNMIS's ability to protect civilians clear:

> It is not possible for the United Nations to protect all Sudanese civilians under threat; this is the obligation of the relevant authorities. The United Nations and partners are focusing their attention on vulnerable groups, such as returning populations and those in volatile areas.[412]

The atrocities that were taking place against civilians in the early days of UNMIS[413] would appear to have been largely attributable to the enormous scope of UNMIS's mandate relative to its size.[414] It was also late to achieve its full complement of troops – something that has now been rectified. More recently, reports of attacks against civilians have decreased substantially, and a referendum on the independence of South Sudan, held in January 2011, saw relatively little violence.[415]

The success of UNAMID in carrying out the military tasks assigned to it has been quite limited. The reasons for the problems in this regard are many. First, it was very slow to deploy. Few states with sophisticated militaries have contributed troops and, of the five permanent Member States of the Security Council, only China has contributed personnel. The UK, whose representative proclaimed at the meeting at which UNAMID was established that '[t]here is no higher foreign policy priority for my Government', does not participate in UNAMID.[416] Second, states have been slow to provide essential equipment, and this continues to be an impediment to UNAMID's functioning. Such is the difficulty of obtaining the necessary equipment that some re-hatted AMIS forces reportedly do not even have new hats: they have to resort to placing blue plastic bags over their green AMIS helmets to show that they are part of the UN force.[417] Third, the effective protection of civilians is impossible to achieve in view of the size of the territory relative to the size of UNAMID. Even as matters relating to troop numbers and equipment improve, this is unlikely to change. Fourth, the government's reluctance to accept the force has posed considerable problems from the start. It delayed its approval of troop contributors and rejected troops from certain states, was slow to

[412] *Report of the Secretary-General* of 23 June 2005 (n 347) para 42.

[413] *Report of the Secretary-General* of 17 April 2007 (n 347) paras 54–55.

[414] ibid, para 78.

[415] Unattributed, 'Low-Key Referendum in North Sudan, Violence in Abyei, Calm in Darfur', *Sudan Tribune*, 10 January 2011.

[416] United Nations, *Provisional Record of the 5727th Meeting of the Security Council* (UN Doc S/PV.5727), 31 July 2007, 3.

[417] Ayesha Kajee, 'The Darfur Conflict and the Responsibility to Protect: Towards a Sustainable Peace' in Hany Besada (ed), *Crafting an African Security Architecture: Addressing Regional Peace and Conflict in the 21st Century* (Aldershot, Ashgate, 2010) 159–78, 171.

allocate land for bases, attempted to require UNAMID to disable its communications network when the government engaged in security operations, called for UNAMID to give the government advance notification of all movements, refused to grant it permission to fly at night, and imposed curfews on peacekeepers in certain areas.[418] While matters appear to be improving, the Security Council continued to express its 'deep concern at continuing restrictions placed upon UNAMID movement and operations' and called for 'the removal of all obstacles to the use of UNAMID aerial assets' as recently as mid-2010.[419] The fact that the force is required to undertake civilian protection 'without prejudice to the responsibility of the Government' would complicate matters at the best of times; but given the widely held view that the government is allied with the Janjaweed, UNAMID is placed in an impossible position.

7. CENTRAL AFRICAN REPUBLIC AND CHAD (SEPTEMBER 2007–DECEMBER 2010)

7.1 Mandate and Functioning

According to UN estimates, the violence in the Darfur region of Sudan resulted in more than 240,000 Sudanese fleeing into Eastern Chad. There they joined some 45,000 people seeking refuge from the violence in the Central African Republic (CAR). The presence of these groups, when added to the estimated 180,000 Chadians who were internally displaced by the civil war there, led to considerable tensions in the area.[420]

In August 2006 the Security Council charged UNMIS with the task of assisting in security matters along the borders between Sudan and Chad and between Sudan and the CAR, 'including through the establishment of a multidimensional presence'.[421] In a report to the Security Council in December of that year, the Secretary-General recommended that in view of the 'interdependence of the situation in the two countries', a single, new mission could cover both countries.[422] He put forward two conceptions of the proposed new operation: (a) a mission to simply monitor and liaise,

[418] See Darfur Consortium, 'UNAMID Deployment on the Brink: The Road to Security in Darfur Blocked by Government Obstructions', December 2007, www.darfurconsortium.org/darfur_consortium_actions/reports/2007/unamid1207web[1].pdf (accessed 1 April 2011), 1–2. See also Totten (n 383) 29; Kajee (n 417) 171.

[419] SC Res 1935 of 30 July 2010, para 7.

[420] www.un.org/en/peacekeeping/missions/minurcat/background.shtml (accessed 1 April 2011).

[421] SC Res 1706 of 31 August 2006, para 9(d).

[422] United Nations, *Report of the Secretary-General on Chad and the Central African Republic Pursuant to Paragraphs 9 (D) and 13 of Security Council Resolution 1706 (2006)* (UN Doc S/2006/1019), 22 December 2006, para 60.

or (b) a mission to monitor and liaise, as well as improving security and providing civilian protection.[423]

In September 2007, by Resolution 1778, the Security Council established the United Nations Mission in the Central African Republic and Chad (MINURCAT) to 'help create the security conditions conducive to a voluntary, secure and sustainable return of refugees and displaced persons'.[424] It was to consist of a maximum of 300 police and 50 military liaison officers and 'an appropriate number of civilian personnel'.[425] It was charged with a number of functions, including civilian protection and the promotion of human rights. However, MINURCAT was not established under Chapter VII and that Chapter was not invoked in relation to any of its functions, including its security protection functions. Nor was it authorised to use 'all necessary means' or to 'take all necessary measures' in relation to any of its functions.

Resolution 1778 also authorised the deployment, for one year, of a European Union-led operation to support MINURCAT. The EU-led operation, which came to be known as 'EUFOR' or 'EUFOR Chad/CAR', was established and authorised under Chapter VII to take 'all necessary measures', within its capabilities and within its area of operation.[426] Its functions included contributing to the protection of civilians in danger, facilitating the delivery of humanitarian aid and free movement of humanitarian personnel by helping to improve security, and contributing to the protection of UN and associated personnel.[427] It became operational on 15 March 2008 and ran until 15 March 2009.[428] It was comprised of some 3,300 troops.[429]

In Resolution 1778 the Security Council asked the Secretary-General to report on a follow-up force, to come into existence six months after the EU declared the 'initial operating capability' of EUFOR Chad/CAR.[430] The Secretary-General recommended an enhanced mandate for MINURCAT such that it would be authorised under Chapter VII to provide security.[431] He recommended a military force of up to 6,000 troops and 'logistic enablers' to take over from EUFOR Chad/CAR.[432] He observed:

> In order to achieve the required effect, the force should be led by high-quality commanders and provided the necessary capabilities, selected by the United

[423] ibid, para 62.
[424] SC Res 1778 of 25 September 2007, para 1.
[425] ibid, para 3.
[426] ibid, para 6.
[427] ibid.
[428] SC Res 1834 of 24 September 2008.
[429] United Nations, *Report of the Secretary-General on the United Nations Mission in the Central African Republic and Chad* (UN Doc S/2008/601), 12 September 2008, para 48.
[430] SC Res 1778 of 25 September 2007, para 10.
[431] *Report of the Secretary-General* (n 429) paras 65 and 95.
[432] ibid, para 95.

Nations. In this regard, and in accordance with the Brahimi report (S/2000/809), it would be recommended that the Security Council consider leaving in draft form the resolution authorizing the deployment of the force until such time as the Secretariat has firm commitments of troops and other critical mission support elements from Member States.[433]

The recommendation that the strengthened mandate remain in draft form until the required forces were committed was ignored by the Security Council and, in September 2008, it passed Resolution 1834 stating its intention to add a UN military component to MINURCAT, such that it could 'follow up' EUFOR Chad/CAR, and asked the Secretary-General to plan for such a component.[434]

In January 2009 the Security Council passed Resolution 1861 establishing a military component of MINURCAT to take over from EUFOR Chad/CAR on 15 March 2009.[435] In addition to its previous functions, MINURCAT was given new tasks, specifically authorised under Chapter VII and in relation to which it could take 'all necessary measures'. These varied depending on the country in which MINURCAT was acting. In Chad, MINURCAT was authorised to take 'all necessary measures' to contribute to protecting civilians in danger, 'facilitate the delivery of humanitarian aid and free movement of humanitarian personnel by helping to improve security', and protect UN and associated personnel.[436] In the CAR, MINURCAT was authorised to take all necessary measures to 'contribute to the creation of a more secure environment', 'execute operations of a limited character in order to extract civilians and humanitarian workers in danger', and protect UN and associated personnel.[437] The Security Council authorised a maximum of 5,200 military personnel.[438]

That transfer of military duties from EUFOR Chad/CAR to MINURCAT took place as scheduled; however, the force was slow reach its full complement: by the end of 2009, fewer than 3,000 troops were on the ground.[439] In addition, the Chadian government – always somewhat reluctant to embrace the strengthened operation[440] – was wavering. In January 2010, the government of Chad informed the Secretary-General that it did not want MINURCAT to be renewed and wanted it to withdraw from Chad when its mandate expired on 15 March 2010.[441]

[433] ibid, para 74.
[434] SC Res 1834 of 24 September 2008, paras 4 and 5.
[435] SC Res 1861 of 14 January 2009, para 3.
[436] ibid, para 7(a).
[437] ibid, para 7(b).
[438] ibid, para 4.
[439] http://assets.opencrs.com/rpts/RS22798_20100701.pdf (accessed 1 April 2011), 6.
[440] United Nations, *Letter Dated 28 October 2008 from the Permanent Representative of Chad to the United Nations Addressed to the President of the Security Council* (UN Doc S/2008/679), 30 October 2008.
[441] SC Res 1861 of 14 January 2009, para 2.

Reportedly Chad's President, Idriss Deby, was disturbed by the mission's slowness to deploy and considered it to have failed in its civilian protection duties.[442] In March 2009, the Security Council extended the mandate of MINURCAT by two months, pending discussions with Chad and the CAR on the future of the operation.[443]

Following consultations between the government of Chad and the United Nations Secretariat, the Chadian government reconsidered its request[444] and, in May 2010, in Resolution 1923, the mandate of MINURCAT was extended to 31 December 2010.[445] However, a condition of the continuation of MINURCAT was its quick withdrawal: it was to be reduced to 2,200 military personnel (1,900 in Chad and 300 in the CAR) by 15 October 2010, with all peacekeepers – civilian and military – withdrawn by 31 December 2010.[446] Resolution 1923 also modified MINURCAT's mandate such that Chapter VII was no longer invoked and the operation was no longer authorised to 'take all necessary measures' in relation to any of its functions. It was, however, given certain limited security functions, such as providing security for UN personnel and facilities and executing operations to extract UN personnel and humanitarian workers in danger, until 15 October,[447] but it was only authorised to use force in response to 'imminent threats of violence to civilians in its immediate vicinity' 'within its means and capabilities and where possible in consultation with the Government of Chad'.[448]

The hasty drawdown of MINURCAT was a cause for concern for UN officials and NGOs.[449] John Holmes, Under-Secretary-General for Humanitarian Affairs and Emergency Relief Coordinator, stated: 'We want MINURCAT to stay and we want it to stay with its full complement . . . We think they're very important for the safety and security of the people in the camps, the civilians in general and for the humanitarian operation . . . We really fear the consequences if the force were withdrawn.'[450]

[442] George Fominyen, 'Withdrawal of Chad Force Threatens Humanitarian Access', *The Independent*, 27 May 2010.

[443] SC Res 1913 of 12 March 2010.

[444] ibid. See *Letter from the Permanent Representative of Chad to the President of the Security Council 3 March 2010* (UN Doc S/2010/115) 4 March 2010.

[445] SC Res 1923 of 25 May 2010.

[446] ibid, paras 6 and 7.

[447] ibid, para 9.

[448] ibid, para 10.

[449] An Amnesty International report describes the Chadian government's record of ensuring security and protecting human rights in Eastern Chad as 'dismal' (Amnesty International, *Chad: 'We Too Deserve Protection' – Human Rights Challenges as UN Mission Withdraws* (AI Index: AFR 20/009/2010), July 2010, 18).

[450] Patrick Worsnip, 'UN Wants to Keep Chad Peacekeepers, Gov't Says No', *Reuters*, 17 February 2010.

7.2 Evaluation

7.2.1 Adherence to the 'Fundamental Principles'

MINURCAT's authorisation to use force beyond self-defence was extremely limited in scope (in Chad, civilian protection, protection of UN personnel and protection of delivery of humanitarian aid; in CAR, to contribute to security, to execute operations to extract civilians and humanitarian workers and to protect UN personnel) and duration (from 15 May 2009 to May 2010).

The Security Council considered host state consent to be an important factor both when it established the mission under Resolution 1778[451] and when it strengthened its mandate under Resolution 1861. The fact that the strengthened operation's authorisations to use force were different in the CAR and Chad suggests that a considerable amount of negotiation may have taken place in order to gain each state's consent. Finally, it appears clear that the reduction in the forcefulness of the mandate from May 2010 was linked to the Security Council's desire to obtain the consent of the government of Chad.[452] So too was its premature departure. UN Under-Secretary-General for Peacekeeping Operations, Alain Le Roy, was quoted as saying that the Security Council was 'very much interested in maintaining MINURCAT on the spot', but noting that 'of course we have to take into account the views of the authorities of Chad'.[453] Elsewhere he reportedly observed: '[W]e cannot stay without the consent of the host country[;] that is very clear.'[454]

The issue of the impartiality of the strengthened MINURCAT caused some controversy. The Secretary-General took the view that the impartiality of the strengthened force would be 'fundamental to its success. The force's impartiality would be exercised through liaison with all armed elements in the subregion, including the armed forces of Chad and any other armed elements with influence in the area of responsibility.'[455] The government of Chad, however, stressed its understanding that MINURCAT was 'not a conventional peacekeeping [operation] implying some kind

[451] The Security Council, in the resolution establishing MINURCAT, stressed that it was acting 'in consultation with the authorities of Chad and the Central African Republic' (SC Res 1778 of 25 September 2007, para 1).

[452] Erin Weir, 'Greater Expectations: UN Peacekeeping and Civilian Protection', *Refugees International*, July 2009, 14.

[453] Worsnip (n 450).

[454] Scott Stearns, 'Chad Seeks Withdrawal of UN Peacekeepers Protecting Food Distribution', *VOA News*, 23 March 2010, www.voanews.com/english/news/africa/Chad-Wants-Withdrawal-of-UN-Peacekeepers-Protecting-Food-Distribution-88911452.html (accessed 1 April 2011).

[455] United Nations, *Report of the Secretary-General on the United Nations Mission in the Central African Republic and Chad* (UN Doc S/2008/601), 12 September 2008, para 66.

of "neutrality", "impartiality" or "good offices" within the framework of any type of peace agreement'.[456] Instead, it noted that it was established 'to respond to the hopes for security placed in it by the humanitarian organizations that were at the origin of the appeal for this operation and by the affected populations in eastern Chad, refugees, displaced persons and host civilian populations'.[457]

7.2.2 Constitutional Basis

From early 2009, when MINURCAT's mandate was strengthened,[458] until May 2010, when its mandate was modified such that it was no longer authorised under Chapter VII to use 'all necessary means', it had its constitutional basis in part in Chapter VII. That is to say, the new tasks set out at paragraph 7 of Resolution 1861 were Chapter VII functions; the other functions were based on host state consent. Given that it was authorised to use 'all necessary means', it would appear that its Chapter VII tasks had their basis in Article 42. However, the very limited use of force actually engaged in by MINURCAT may lend support to an argument that it may find its constitutional basis in Article 41 or 40. The better view, however is that regardless of how limited the force actually used was, the fact that MINURCAT was authorised to take 'all necessary measures', means that those tasks are incompatible with both Article 40 and 41.

The other tasks in MINURCAT's mandate were not assigned by means of a mandatory invocation of Chapter VII. As such, consent of the host state is required and they most likely find their constitutional basis in Chapter VI or, arguably, in a non-mandatory article in Chapter VII, such as Article 39 or 40.

7.2.3 Conclusion and Assessment of Success

While the operation was militarised for a brief period only, the problems associated with MINURCAT's ability to carry out the militarised aspects of its mandate are by now familiar. Secretary-General Ban Ki-moon was to learn that a suggestion to the Security Council that MINURCAT should not become operational until the required troops and equipment were assembled was just that, a suggestion, and would be ignored if it was inconvenient. The approach of establishing the operation first and then hoping for the best resource-wise once again prevailed – perhaps due in part to

[456] United Nations, *Letter Dated 28 October 2008 from the Permanent Representative of Chad to the United Nations Addressed to the President of the Security Council* (UN Doc S/2008/679), 30 October 2008, 1.

[457] ibid.

[458] Resolution 1861 was passed on 14 January 2009 and the strengthened mandate was to be effective upon the withdrawal of EUFOR Chad/CAR on 15 March 2009.

the fact that the permanent Security Council Member State, France, took a particular interest in the operation.[459] Once again, the force was very slow to deploy and had significant problems obtaining sufficient equipment, including helicopters,[460] factors that doubtless contributed the initial criticisms of the force's effectiveness with regard to civilian protection.

[459] France is said to have provided the bulk of the military forces, as well as 'the necessary political pressure to deploy' (Weir (n 453) 14).
[460] ibid.

Chapter 7

Conclusions

> The demands on UN peacekeeping are greater today than ever before. UN peacekeeping is not only stretched in terms of the size of the deployments, but also in terms of the challenges posed by complex mandates and difficult logistical and security environments . . . A number of our missions face risks that are so significant that I cannot discount the potential for mission failure, with all the consequences that would entail for the United Nations.
>
> Alain Le Roy, Under-Secretary-General for Peacekeeping Operations[1]

1. INTRODUCTION

THIS FINAL CHAPTER will summarise the various problems that have emerged from the UN's militarised peacekeeping practice. It will then offer conclusions as to how that practice has informed our understanding of the legal bases of militarised peacekeeping. Finally, it will argue that the time has come for the UN to abandon militarised peacekeeping and revert to the more traditional type of peacekeeping that it successfully engaged in for over 60 years.

2. OVERVIEW OF THE PROBLEMS

The preceding chapters have revealed a UN which is fundamentally ill-suited to conducting militarised peacekeeping operations. Although some problems certainly manifest themselves in peacekeeping operations where force is limited to self-defence, where peacekeeping operations are militarised the existing problems are generally exacerbated and new problems emerge. The problems encountered by militarised peacekeeping operations are attributable to a wide variety of factors, which I will examine under the following four headings:[2] (1) difficulties of establishment; (2) management

[1] United Nations, *Remarks of the Under Secretary-General for Peacekeeping Operations, Mr Alain Le Roy, to the Special Committee on Peacekeeping Operations*, 23 February 2009, www.un.org/en/peacekeeping/articles/article230209.htm (accessed 1 April 2011).

[2] Of course the categories overlap to an extent and many of the problems discussed may fall within more than one.

difficulties; (3) problems relating to the need for host state consent or cooperation; and (4) problems relating to expectations.

2.1 Difficulties of Establishment

Unlike a state, which will (ideally, at any rate) have a well-trained, well-equipped professional army on standby – and the authority to conscript additional troops from its broader population where necessary – the UN is entirely dependent on donated troops. Former Secretary-General Kofi Annan likened the UN establishing a peacekeeping operation to a fire brigade that must acquire a fire engine before it can attempt to put out a fire that is already burning.[3] As we have seen, the particular set of circumstances relating to a crisis can impact on whether or not there will be the political will among members of the Security Council to establish a peacekeeping force. The enthusiasm of Security Council Member States – and in particular the influential permanent members – may be affected by a wide variety of political considerations, including whether the state in which a peacekeeping operation is being contemplated has a particular connection with a permanent member of the Security Council – for example, the state may be a former colony of a permanent Member State – and the level of media attention in relation to human suffering in the state. This can lead to perceptions of selectivity or unfairness.

Even where the political will exists to establish an operation, there will be various factors at play which influence whether Member States are willing to donate troops and equipment. With operations authorised to use force beyond self-defence, the political costs are greater and states are less likely to volunteer. For example, Brazil, which took a lead role in MINUSTAH, was criticised internationally for not acting forcefully enough; at the same time the Brazilian government risked criticism domestically for risking the lives of participating nationals in a situation in which Brazil had little or no national interest.[4] It may be due to a fear of such domestic criticism that those Member States with the most highly skilled militaries tend to be the least interested in volunteering troops for militarised peacekeeping operations. It is much safer politically to stay outside the fray. Moreover, the UN is reliant on donations from Member States in order to equip operations and to provide them with intelligence. Member States have displalyed variable levels of generosity in this regard.

Despite the fact that it is the Security Council that establishes militarised operations, the Member States comprising it – and in particular the

[3] See his comments at www.un.org/apps/sg/offthecuff.asp?nid=785 (accessed 1 April 2011). See also unattributed, 'Peacekeeping: Call the Blue Helmets', *The Economist*, 6 January 2007.

[4] See chapter 6, section 4.

permanent members – have generally been parsimonious about contributing troops. There would appear to be little correlation between the enthusiasm of a Security Council Member State for the establishment of a militarised peacekeeping operation and its willingness to contribute troops. Because of the relatively few forces contributed by the Security Council's permanent Member States, there is a risk that those states will be willing to see a militarised peacekeeping force go ahead in circumstances in which they would not allow a national force of a similar nature to go ahead.[5] *The Economist* described a 'two-tiered structure' to peacekeeping:

> [P]owerful countries decide the missions (and pay for them) while poor countries such as India, Pakistan, Bangladesh, Nepal and Jordan supply the soldiers. They receive a payment for doing so; this becomes for some a subsidy for their own armed forces, while the deployment also provides their troops with training.[6]

As illustrated by the role of the UK in Sierra Leone, France in Côte d'Ivoire and, latterly, Australia in East Timor, a practice has developed whereby states with more sophisticated militaries have opted to serve alongside a militarised peacekeeping operation rather than under UN command. Many decision-makers in the US have long maintained that it would be inappropriate to allow its forces to serve under UN command; indeed, the US Congress considered legislation in 1996 to prohibit the expenditure of any funds on US armed forces that served under UN operational and tactical command.[7] This unwillingness undermines the authority of peacekeeping forces and sends a signal that the leadership of militarised peacekeeping operations is of dubious quality. In addition, when a national force works alongside a UN force, the perception may develop that only the (generally better equipped and more highly trained) national force poses a genuine threat to spoilers. The UN militarised force may be viewed as a paper tiger.[8]

Moreover, the presence of a national force in parallel with a peacekeeping operation can lead to disagreements between the two forces, or to them working at cross purposes. The US force in Somalia in 1993 did not consult with UNOSOM II; when a US mission failed and US personnel were captured, a UN peacekeeper was killed and many others were wounded coming to the aid of the US force. In addition, when a national force works alongside a militarised peacekeeping operation but not under

[5] For example, in February 2000 the Security Council authorised a force of some 5,500 troops for MONUC in the DRC; 'eight months earlier, when Serbian forces had withdrawn from Kosovo, the council had authorized a NATO force eight times as large to secure a region about one-sixtieth the size of the DRC'. James Traub, *The Best Intentions: Kofi Annan and the UN in the Era of American World Power* (London, Bloomsbury, 2006) 340.

[6] *The Economist* (n 3).

[7] John Yoo, 'UN Wars, US War Powers' (2000) 1 *Chicago Journal of International Law* 355, 366 n 39.

[8] As discussed in chapter 6, section 3, this was reportedly the case with the French forces in Côte d'Ivoire.

its command, the priorities of the parallel force will inevitably be different from those of the peacekeeping force. As a result, the interests of the peacekeeping force may not be well served.[9] The DPKO's *Lessons Learned* report on Sierra Leone put it this way:

> The UN must be able to provide adequate security for the safety of UN personnel, property and equipment in a conflict area, particularly if the national authorities have no capacity to provide such protection. The provision of such security should be under UN authority and should not be dependent on external forces that may not be willing or able to provide it, particularly during times of crisis.[10]

An additional difficulty that results from the ad hoc nature of peacekeeping is that the Secretary-General is put in a difficult position when advising the Security Council regarding the number of troops and level of equipment required. Should the Secretary-General estimate too generously, the operation might be a non-starter; should his estimate be too low, the peacekeeping operation will be unable to carry out its mandate, perhaps becoming a target itself. As was noted in the *Lessons Learned* report on UNOSOM II, there is a risk that the planning of a militarised peacekeeping operation will be undertaken on a most-favourable-case basis rather than on a basis that reflects the 'realities on the ground'.[11] While this problem exists to some extent with all peacekeeping operations, it is compounded when the operation might involve the significant use of force and, therefore, a significant risk of casualties to peacekeepers.

Moreover, the Secretary-General may be subject to political pressure from the Security Council (or individual members with particular interests in a situation) not to recommend too great a number of troops. Of course, when the Secretary-General does recommend a force which is sufficiently large and well-equipped to deal with the realities on the ground, it is entirely possible that his recommendation will be ignored by the Security Council. As we have seen, such advice regarding the necessary number of troops has, at times, been ignored, as has advice regarding the functions that a force might effectively undertake. The Security Council may add tasks that the Secretary-General thinks are inappropriate or disallow tasks that the Secretary-General considers to be important.[12]

[9] Examples here include UNOCI's reliance on the French forces in Côte d'Ivoire (chapter 6, section 3) and UNAMSIL's reliance on British forces in Sierra Leone (chapter 5, section 2).

[10] United Nations Best Practices Unit (DPKO), *Lessons Learned from the United Nations Peacekeeping Experiences in Sierra Leone*, September 2003, http://pbpu.unlb.org/pbpu/library/SL-LL%20Report.pdf (accessed 1 April 2011), 33.

[11] United Nations Best Practices Unit (DPKO), *The Comprehensive Report on Lessons Learned from United Nations Operation in Somalia (UNOSOM): April 1992–March 1995*, March 1995, www.peacekeepingbestpractices.unlb.org/PBPS/Pages/PUBLIC/ViewDocument.aspx?docid=509&cat=8&scat=18&menukey=_5_3_30 (accessed 1 April 2011), para 13.

[12] With UNAMSIL (chapter 5, section 2) and MONUC (chapter 5, section 4) the Security Council augmented the mandates for the forces recommended by the Secretary-General by adding civilian protection duties.

2.2 Management Difficulties

In view of the fact that peacekeeping operations are composed of troops of different nationalities, management difficulties will inevitably be greater than those likely to occur with a force that is nationally homogenous. These problems are compounded when the force is charged with using force. Difficulties can manifest themselves in a variety of ways, including language and cultural issues and problems acclimatising to new surroundings. For example, according to an International Crisis Group Report:

> Differences of language, culture and approach have made it hard for the [Jordanian troops contributing to MINUSTAH] to handle the urban complexities, particularly when they have been the target of sniper and other attacks. As a result, they have been criticised for using excessive firepower in densely populated areas, particularly following the killing of two of their members.[13]

Moreover, troops from different states are likely to have different levels of training, standards of professionalism and military traditions. Where troops come from developing countries, there is a greater chance that they will not have had the benefit of comprehensive military training or be in possession of ultramodern weaponry. At the same time, forces from certain states may take an approach that is more focused on engaging with spoilers or hostile civilians in a constructive way – winning 'hearts and minds' – and less confrontational than the approach of other states.[14] Where there is a disparity in training or a difference in approach among troops from the various contributing states, command problems may result.[15]

Such problems are further complicated by the tendency on the part of some governments to overrule decisions of the force commander, in particular decisions relating to the use of force that may lead to casualties among peacekeepers. Governments may advise their national commanders working for a militarised peacekeeping operation to disregard certain

[13] International Crisis Group, *Haiti After the Elections: Challenges for Préval's First 100 Days*, Crisis Group, Latin America/Caribbean Briefing No 10, 11 May 2006, http://merln.ndu.edu/archive/icg/Haiti11May06.pdf (accessed 1 April 2011), 8.

[14] Allard contended that the presumably well-trained US troops in Somalia interpreted the rules of engagement such that they stressed aggressive enforcement (Trevor Findlay, *The Use of Force in UN Peace Operations* (Oxford, Oxford University Press for the Stockholm International Peace Research Institute (SIPRI), 2002) 215, relying on K Allard, *Somalia Operations: Lessons Learned* (Washington, DC, National Defence University, Institute for National Strategic Studies, 1995)). For consideration of Canada's use of force in that operation, and its tragic consequences, see Katia Boustany, 'Brocklebank: A Questionable Decision of the Court Martial Appeal Court of Canada' (1998) 1 *Yearbook of International Humanitarian Law* 371. See also Robert M Young and Maria Molina, 'Sharing Canada's Lessons Learned from Somalia' (1998) 1 *Yearbook of International Humanitarian Law* 362.

[15] As discussed, at times, in the context of UNAMSIL (chapter 5, section 2) and MONUC (chapter 5, section 4), orders from a commander from one nation were ignored by troops of another.

orders and to order their co-nationals to do the same, a practice known as 'playing the red card'. This is said to have occurred with MONUC, where a Uruguayan commander reportedly telephoned government authorities in Montevideo and was told to ignore orders given to him by the UN commander that might jeopardise the Uruguayan troops' safety.[16] Alternatively, a state may simply decide that the risks are too high and withdraw its troops from a peacekeeping operation. This was the basis of Belgium's decision to withdraw its forces from UNAMIR at the start of the genocide in Rwanda.[17] It also led to the shrinking and gradual withdrawal of UNOSOM II from Somalia.[18] It may be in part because of an awareness of this possibility on the part of force commanders that militarised peacekeeping operations only occasionally employ force beyond self-defence. In nearly all of the situations considered, the peacekeeping operations used relatively little force – at least until pressed into doing so in self-defence or in response to a particularly egregious attack on civilians.

An additional management difficulty relating to the use of force in militarised peacekeeping operations is that, because troops are generally governed by their national laws, peacekeepers from different states may be authorised to use force in different circumstances. Troops from different states may have different rules of engagement as well as different penalties for violating such rules. Where there are violations of international humanitarian law – as was alleged to have occurred with Bangladeshi troops from MONUC and UNOCI[19] – these may be due to both a lack of discipline on the part of the troops and the shortcomings of the UN command structure.

Finally, unlike those states that have Departments or Ministries of Defence capable of engaging in coordination and oversight of the military, the UN Secretariat does not possess the capability to supervise large and complicated forceful operations. This point was made by former Secretary-General Boutros-Ghali in 1992 when advising the Security Council on the way forward in the face of the security crisis in Somalia in late 1992: 'The Secretariat, already overstretched in managing greatly enlarged peacekeeping commitments, does not at present have the capability to command and control an enforcement operation of the size and urgency required by the present crisis in Somalia.'[20] Based on this book's analysis of militarised

[16] See chapter 5, section 4.

[17] United Nations, *Letter Dated 15 December 1999 from the Secretary-General Addressed to the President of the Security Council [Enclosing the Report of the Independent Inquiry into Actions of the United nations During 1994 in Rwanda, 15 December1999]* (UN Doc S/1999/1257 16 December 1999) 19.

[18] See chapter 4, section 4.1.2.

[19] See chapter 5, section 4 and chapter 6, section 3, respectively.

[20] United Nations, *Letter Dated 29 November 1992 from the Secretary-General addressed to the President of the Security Council* (UN Doc S/24868), 30 November 1992.

peacekeeping operations in the twenty-first century, it is clear that little has changed in this regard.

2.3 Problems Relating to the Need for Host State Consent or Cooperation

As discussed, where a peacekeeping operation has not been established by the Security Council in exercise of its enforcement powers under Article 41 or 42 or as a mandatory measure under Article 40, the Security Council is legally obliged to obtain the consent of the host state. And, where host state consent *is* legally required, the host state, arguably, may revoke it and call for the operation to leave.[21] We have seen that even where host state consent is *not* legally required, the Security Council tends to obtain it as a means to encourage cooperation. As a result, militarised peacekeeping operations may find themselves in a very precarious position. If they are to use force against all parties who are causing harm to civilians or impeding security, this will frequently need to include the host state. However, if force is used against the host state, it may cease cooperation; if not, the peacekeeping force may rightly be perceived as partial. This perception of partiality will be even greater where the militarised peacekeeping force works alongside the host state's military forces in operations where force is used against certain rebel groups, as was the case with MONUC in the Congo.

Moreover, we have seen that a reluctant host state may attempt to undermine a militarised peacekeeping operation. For example, one reason why ONUB in Burundi was not in a position to prevent the Gatumba massacre in August 2004 (nor was it even aware of its occurrence until some 10 hours after the attack)[22] was that the host state had put in place a curfew on ONUB and 'consistently refused ONUB permission to patrol after curfew hours'.[23] Similarly, the government of Sudan has worked tirelessly to obstruct UNAMID. So brazen is its contempt for UNAMID that it appointed Ahmad Harun to a national monitoring group overseeing UNAMID after Harun had been indicted by the ICC for crimes against humanity and war crimes.[24]

[21] As discussed in chapter 3, section 5.3.2, some commentators take the position that when a state consents to a peacekeeping operation, it enters into an implied agreement not to withdraw that consent until the known mandate is fulfilled.

[22] Stephen Jackson, *The United Nations Operation in Burundi (ONUB) – Political and Strategic Lessons Learned [Independent External Study]*, July 2006, www.peacekeepingbestpractices.unlb.org/pbpu/library/ONUB%20Lessons%20Learned.pdf (accessed 1 April 2011), 17.

[23] ibid.

[24] United Nations (Department of Public Information), *International Criminal Court Prosecutor Tells Security Council Sudan's Government 'Not Cooperating' in Darfur Investigation, Massive Crimes Continue* (UN Doc SC/9186), 5 December 2007.

The dependence of a peacekeeping operation on the goodwill of the host state is compounded by the wording of civilian protection mandates – typically authorising force 'without prejudice to' the government of the host state. This wording suggests that the peacekeeping operation's role in relation to civilian protection is subordinate to the will of the host state, which retains primary responsibility. The wording also appears to envision a collaborative relationship between the host state – in practice, its police or military forces – and the peacekeeping operation. Such a relationship may, if based on good faith, be feasible. However, in some of the situations examined in this book, the national forces or police were among the worst offenders as regards civilian harm.[25] This may mean that the peacekeeping operation is unable to effectively carry out its civilian protection task.

We have also seen that some peacekeeping operations have considered it necessary or desirable to work hand-in-hand with the national police or armed forces. Examples include the alliance between MONUC and the FARDC in the DRC and between MINUSTAH and the HNP in Haiti. In the case of MONUC, its alliance with the FARDC led to reprisal attacks against MONUC. It also led to MONUC finding itself in the unsavoury position of having to downplay the extent of the damage caused to civilians by the actions of the FARDC – an organisation described in most unflattering terms by the Secretary-General – presumably in order to sustain good relations with the government.[26] Similarly, the fact that MINUSTAH undertook many of its security activities in collaboration with the HNP has risked bringing that peacekeeping force into disrepute, given the HNP's reputation as a frequent violator of human rights.[27]

2.4 Problems Relating to Expectations

The civilian status of peacekeepers under international humanitarian law is lost (at least temporarily) when the troops become combatants.[28] While the circumstances in which militarised peacekeepers might be considered combatants in international law are strictly limited, the perceptions of non-governmental factions in a civil conflict may be another matter.[29]

[25] See, for example, discussion of the operations in Burundi (chapter 6, section 5), Côte d'Ivoire (chapter 6, section 3) and Sudan (chapter 6, section 6).

[26] See chapter 5, section 4.

[27] See chapter 6, section 4.

[28] See chapter 3, section 1.

[29] An argument was made in the RUF case before the Special Court for Sierra Leone that UNAMSIL peacekeepers there were combatants – and therefore offensive force could be used against them; this argument was rejected by the Court. It held that, in the circumstances, the RUF knew or had reason to know of the peacekeepers' civilian status (*Prosecutor v Issa Hassan Sesay, Morrison Kallon and Augustine Gbao* (Case No SCSL-04-15-T: Special Court for Sierra Leone, Trial Chamber I, 2 March 2009, paras 1938–43).

Where they perceive the militarised peacekeeping force to be aligned with the government – and against them – they are likely to take the view that they are warranted in using force against the peacekeepers. In February 2005, nine MONUC peacekeepers were killed in the Ituri region in what was characterised as a retaliatory attack.[30]

Worse still, a perception on the part of rebels that a militarised peacekeeping force is targeting it and/or is aligned to the government, is likely to affect their perception of the entire force – whether the peacekeepers are military troops or unarmed civilians. As we saw in Sierra Leone, once the RUF came to consider UNAMSIL an enemy, it made no distinction between armed troops attached to the force and civilian peacekeepers.

The impartiality of a peacekeeping operation (or the perception thereof) is likely to be imperilled where a militarised peacekeeping operation operates at the same time as a quasi-enforcement operation. As we saw in the former Yugoslavia in the early 1990s, when the NATO-led quasi-enforcement force and UNPROFOR operated hand-in-hand, it was not always clear to which entity the use of force could be attributed, leading to a perception that the use of force by NATO was that of the UN mission.

When a peacekeeping operation is militarised and it is vested with duties such as civilian protection or the maintenance of security, the metrics of success change. While it will generally be unfair to expect a peacekeeping operation – especially one subject to the panoply of problems discussed in this book – to improve longstanding security problems overnight, or indeed at all, the above discussion shows that, time and time again, politicians, NGOs, citizens, media and others expect nothing less. When such expectations are not met, these actors tend to turn to the peacekeeping operation as the object of their criticism. Many will point to the continued existence of security problems, civilian killings and unrest *despite* the fact that a militarised peacekeeping operation is present, as evidence of failure. This impacts negatively not just on a particular mission, but on peacekeeping as an endeavour and on the UN more generally.[31]

Regrettably, once a militarised peacekeeping operation has been established, these critics rarely go behind the scenes to ask the necessary questions: Have Member States – in particular states on the Security Council – pledged the necessary troops or equipment? And, importantly, why, if the Security Council decided that an operation using force beyond self-defence was required, did it not establish a quasi-enforcement operation?

[30] Marc Lacey, 'Militia Fighters Kill 9 UN Peacekeepers in Congo as Instability Continues', *New York Times*, 26 February 2005.

[31] As we have seen, MINUSTAH's reluctance to use force led many Haitians to describe them as being in the country 'on vacation'. Similarly, MONUC forces were labelled by some as 'tourists' or '"butterflies" – pretty to look at, but otherwise useless'. These criticisms echo the criticisms of UN militarised peacekeeping in the former Yugoslavia (Christine Gray, *International Law and the Use of Force*, 3rd edn (Oxford, Oxford University Press, 2008) 285–86).

As such, militarised peacekeeping operations may serve as an 'alibi' – to use the word of former Secretary-General Annan – or, put another way, a whipping-boy, for the Security Council. The Security Council can point to the creation of a militarised peacekeeping operation, even one that is hopelessly underfunded or ill-suited to the enormity of the task with which it has been charged, as evidence that it has taken action. If the peacekeeping operation is unable to prevent civilian harm or if its commander, in his or her discretion, decides that it lacks the capacity to protect civilians or to engage in preemptive action, then the Security Council – and to an extent the Secretariat – has scope to argue that the force commander's decision was ill-advised or not what was intended. The former Force Commander of UNAMIR, Lieutenant-General Roméo Dallaire, in an open letter to the new UNAMID Force Commander designate, General Martin Agwai, made the following observation, which was reproduced in the epigraph to chapter 6 above but which bears repeating:

> You can anticipate being let down by everyone on whom you depend for support, be that troops, funding, logistics or political engagement. Only by shining a spotlight on those failures in every possible way can you mobilise the attention necessary to get the action you need. Bear in mind that whoever fails you will, in the end, be the most active in blaming you for whatever goes wrong.[32]

3. LEGAL CONCLUSIONS

Throughout this book, conclusions have been posited as to the constitutional bases of the militarised peacekeeping operations discussed herein. The powers of the Security Council vary depending on the Chapter of the UN Charter and the particular article under which an operation is wholly or partially authorised.

The Security Council is empowered to impose measures on states without their consent only when it is acting under Chapter VII. One factor common to all militarised peacekeeping operations is that Chapter VII was invoked in relation to the establishment or modification of the mandate or in relation to certain aspects thereof. With the exception of ONUC, the Security Council invoked Chapter VII explicitly; as regards ONUC, the Security Council's invocation of Articles 25 and 49 in Resolution 146 of 9 August 1960 and the nature of the force authorised make it clear that the Security Council was acting under Chapter VII. Where the Security Council characterises the situation as a threat to international peace and security and states that it is '*Acting* under Chapter VII of the Charter of the United Nations' in the preamble to a resolution establishing or modifying a militarised peacekeeping operation, it is clear that the whole of the

[32] www.guardian.co.uk/commentisfree/2007/sep/17/adauntingmandate (accessed 1 April 2011).

operation falls under Chapter VII and host state consent is not required. However, since the turn of the century, the Security Council has, at times, invoked Chapter VII in relation to certain tasks only. Of the 15 militarised peacekeeping operations considered in chapters 3, 4 and 5,[33] nine were adopted under Chapter VII[34] and six were given Chapter VII authorisations in relation part of their mandates.[35] With a selective invocation of Chapter VII, it would appear that the tasks that are *not* given a Chapter VII basis fall outside that Chapter. After all, while it is not the practice of the Security Council to *explicitly* exclude the application of Chapter VII to the other tasks, it is reasonable to presume that by specifically stating that it is acting under Chapter VII as regards certain provisions, it is signalling that it is not acting under Chapter VII as regards the other provisions.[36] As such, militarised peacekeeping operations may be entirely authorised as an exercise of the Security Council's mandatory powers under Chapter VII or a mix of measures which are partly consent-based and partly mandatory.

For the Security Council to establish a peacekeeping operation (or some of its tasks) as a mandatory measure under Chapter VII, it must rely on its powers in Article 40, 41 or 42, each of which has its own restrictions.[37] There are two impediments to a militarised peacekeeping operation (or certain of its tasks) being established as a mandatory measure pursuant to the Security Council's Article 40 powers: such an operation must not engage in the use of force beyond self-defence and it must be impartial. The only significant impediment to the Security Council establishing a militarised peacekeeping operation as an exercise of its Article 41 powers is that a measure authorised thereunder must not 'involv[e] the use of armed force'. Finally, a peacekeeping operation established by means of an exercise of the Security Council's Article 42 powers must involve the use of armed force.

[33] This number is arrived at by counting the two operations in East Timor (UNTAET and UNAMSIL), the two operations in the Sudan (UNMIS and UNAMID), and the two 21st century operations in the Congo (MONUC and MONUSCO) separately.

[34] These were ONUC (even though the invocation of Chapter VII was not explicit with ONUC, it is clear that the Security Council did not intend to treat certain of that operation's tasks as having a different constitutional basis from others), UNPROFOR (after February 1993), UNOSOM II, UNTAET, MONUC (after July 2003), MONUSCO, UNMIL, UNOCI (after February 2004) and ONUB.

[35] These were UNAMSIL, UNMISET, MINUSTAH, UNMIS, UNAMID and MINURCAT. Despite the fact that the Security Council only invoked Chapter VII in relation to one paragraph of the resolution establishing UNMISET, it invoked Chapter VII for the whole mandate.

[36] On the other hand, it might be argued that because, even where the Security Council invokes Chapter VII in relation to certain tasks only, its practice is to find a 'threat to international peace and security' in relation to the *whole* of the resolution, it is nonetheless acting under Chapter VII, but doing so in the form of non-binding measures under Article 39 or 40.

[37] As noted, the Security Council may act under Chapter VII in a non-mandatory way; however, its practice indicates that an invocation of Chapter VII carries with it the implication that it is acting mandatorily.

While there is scope for argument that an authorisation to use a limited amount of force beyond self-defence may fit within the restrictions associated with Articles 40 and 41, this does not appear to comport with the overall structure of Chapter VII, which only provides that the Security Council may authorise force in Article 42 and implies that it may only do so as a last resort. Moreover, in the case of Article 41, such an argument goes against the wording of the article. Even if the argument that Article 40 or 41 can support the use of limited force beyond self-defence were accepted, neither article could form the basis of a Security Council authorisation for a militarised peacekeeping force to take 'the necessary action' or wording to a similar effect.[38] As discussed, an authorisation to take 'the necessary action' is similar in wording to the power vested in the Security Council in Article 42 to 'take such action . . . as may be necessary'.[39]

With UNMIL and MINUSTAH, the Security Council indicated an intention to authorise force beyond self-defence without authorising those Chapter VII operations to take 'the necessary action' (or words of a similar nature). Here, if one accepts that limited force beyond self-defence may be based in Article 40 or 41, an argument may be made that the level of force beyond self-defence intended by the Security Council was sufficiently limited to fall within the parameters of either article. A similar argument might be advanced where the Security Council has indicated that it is authorising 'the necessary action' in relation to certain paragraphs only,[40] if one were to conclude that even in those paragraphs where it has not authorised 'the necessary action', it intends that the operation will have a limited authorisation to use force beyond self-defence. However, any measures where the Security Council is relying on its Article 40 powers must comport with that article's requirement that the operation be

[38] In addition to authorising militarised peacekeeping operations to 'take the necessary action', the Security Council has authorised them to use or take 'all necessary means', 'the necessary measures', 'the necessary steps' and 'all necessary measures' generally or in relation to certain of the tasks assigned to them. While a definite pattern is difficult to discern, it could be argued that the phrase 'necessary steps' or 'necessary action' authorises a lesser use of force than the phrase 'all necessary means'. With UNOCI in Côte D'Ivoire, as the government became less collaborative with the Security Council, the language changed from 'take the necessary steps' to '[use] all necessary means' and the circumstances in which force was authorised were increased. With regard to the operation in Darfur, the wording 'all necessary means' was modified to 'the necessary action' (and the circumstances in which force could be used were reduced), after the Security Council was unable to obtain the host state's consent to a version of a mandate featuring the former phrase.

[39] Where the phrase 'all necessary means' or 'to take the necessary measures' is used in a resolution establishing a Chapter VII peacekeeping operation, it is 'beyond all doubt' that the Security Council had made use of its powers under Chapter VII of the Charter to authorise armed force beyond self-defence. (United Nations, 'Note to the Under-Secretary-General of the Department of Peacekeeping Operations, United Nations' [2003] *United Nations Juridical Yearbook*, 13 October, Part Two, Chapter VI, 538–40 (UN Sales No E.07.V.1) 539).

[40] See eg ONUB, UNMIS, UNAMID and MINURCAT.

impartial, in the sense that it must not be designed to bring about a permanent change in the rights of the parties being relied upon.[41]

In short, Article 42 is the only article in the Charter that squarely provides a constitutional basis for militarised peacekeeping operations or those tasks where the use of force beyond self-defence is authorised explicitly or implicitly. As such, militarised peacekeeping operations have become similar in many ways to quasi-enforcement operations, such as UNITAF or *Opération Turquoise*, also established under Article 42. Indeed, as noted in chapter 2, many commentators group the two types of operation together, collectively labelling them peace-enforcement. As we have also seen in relation to both Article 42 militarised peacekeeping and quasi-enforcement, although the Security Council's tendency is to obtain host state consent, it is not legally required where it is acting mandatorily under Chapter VII. The most obvious difference between the two types of operation is that militarised peacekeeping operations are UN-led instead of being led by a state or a coalition of the willing. And this has been one of the main weaknesses of militarised peacekeeping.

4. FINAL REMARKS: THE WAY FORWARD

The operation in the Congo in the 1960s was *sui generis*. The period in the early 1990s when militarised peacekeeping operations were relied upon was short-lived; the Security Council, the Secretary-General and the international community favoured a return to a concept of peacekeeping that did not feature enforcement-type activities. In each case, the move away from militarised peacekeeping was attributable to the lack of success of the operations.

What, then, of the UN's current reliance on militarised peacekeeping, which has become more firmly entrenched than ever before? It is clear that there are powerful arguments for maintaining the status quo.[42] However, the merits of militarised peacekeeping operations need urgently to be reconsidered. Based upon their performance to date, we see that such operations are under-funded, ill-equipped and poorly managed. And there is little to indicate that this is likely to change. We also see that the

[41] The fact that the Security Council will sometimes stipulate that a militarised peacekeeping operation's authorisation to take 'the necessary action' for civilian and UN protection tasks is to be 'without prejudice to the responsibility' of the government of the host state, recalls the requirement in Art 40 that measures taken thereunder 'shall be without prejudice to the rights, claims, or positions or the parties concerned'. However, an argument that this wording signals that such an authorisation is based in the Security Council's powers under Art 40 is refuted by the level of force beyond self-defence authorised by the words 'the necessary action'.

[42] As noted in chapter 1, some of these arguments are motivated by a genuine desire to protect civilians and others may have less worthy motives, such as allowing the UN to *appear to be* taking effective measures, whether it is or not.

raised expectations associated with such operations are almost inevitably dashed, at considerable cost to the reputation of peacekeeping generally and the UN as a whole.

The return to more a traditional kind of peacekeeping must not be seen as an abandonment of civilians. In fact, a move away from militarised peacekeeping should lead to an improvement in the treatment of civilians, as militarised peacekeeping operations will no longer impede the establishment of quasi-enforcement operations or, where established, provide contributing states with an excuse to withdraw the quasi-enforcement operation before the security situation is well and truly restored. It must be recognised that quasi-enforcement forces are the only effective way to stop harm to civilians or restore security – something apparently understood by those states that either refuse to participate in militarised peacekeeping operations or which will only assist by participating alongside such operations rather than under their command.

To militarise a peacekeeping operation is to ask too much of it.

Index

Introductory Note

References such as '178–9' indicate (not necessarily continuous) discussion of a topic across a range of pages. Wherever possible in the case of topics with many references, these have either been divided into sub-topics or only the most significant discussions of the topic are listed. Because the entire work is about 'peacekeeping' the use of this term (and certain others which occur constantly throughout the book) as an entry point has been minimised. Information will be found under the corresponding detailed topics.

www.ingramcontent.com/pod-product-compliance
Ingram Content Group UK Ltd.
Pitfield, Milton Keynes, MK11 3LW, UK
UKHW021910150926
475560UK00003B/286